ISBN 978-1-334-71633-1
PIBN 10702420

THE ECONOMIC WRITINGS OF SIR WILLIAM PETTY

London: C. J. CLAY AND SONS,
CAMBRIDGE UNIVERSITY PRESS WAREHOUSE,
AVE MARIA LANE.
Glasgow: 263, ARGYLE STREET.

Leipzig: F. A. BROCKHAUS.
New York: THE MACMILLAN COMPANY.
Bombay: E. SEYMOUR HALE.

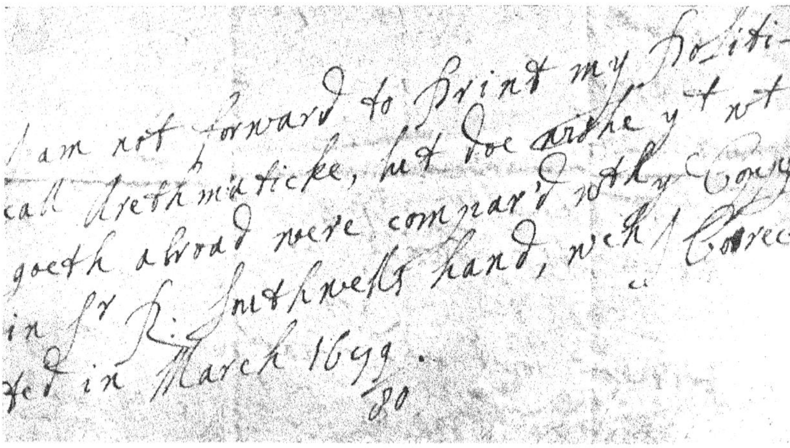
I am not forward to Print my Politi-
call Arethmaticke, but doe wishe yt wt
goeth abroad were compar'd wth ye Copy
in Sr R: Southwells hand, wch I Correc-
ted in March 1679/80.

Petty to Aubrey, 12 July, 1681 (Aubrey MS. 11, fol. 101[a], Bodleian Library), referring to his corrections of the Southwell MS. of the *Political Arithmetick*. Cf. pp. 236—238.

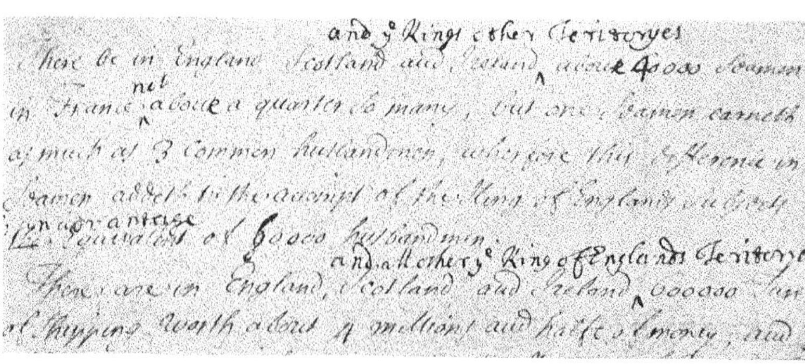
There be in England Scotland and Ireland and ye Kings other Territoryes about 40000 Seamen
in France not above a quarter so many, but one Seaman earneth
as much as 3 common husbandmen, wherefore this difference in
Seamen addeth to the accompt of the King of Englands advantage
the Equivalent of 80000 husbandmen.
There are in England, Scotland and Ireland and all other ye King of Englands Territoryes 000000 Tun
of Shipping worth about 4 millions and halfe of money, and

One of Petty's corrections of the Southwell MS. of the *Political Arithmetick* (now Addl. MS. 21,128, British Museum, fol. 26[a]). Cf. pp. 292—293.

To face Title Vol. I.

THE

ECONOMIC WRITINGS

OF

SIR WILLIAM PETTY

TOGETHER WITH THE

OBSERVATIONS UPON THE BILLS OF MORTALITY

MORE PROBABLY BY

CAPTAIN JOHN GRAUNT

EDITED BY

CHARLES HENRY HULL, PH.D.

CORNELL UNIVERSITY

VOL. I

CAMBRIDGE

AT THE UNIVERSITY PRESS

1899

Cambridge:
PRINTED BY J. AND C. F. CLAY,
AT THE UNIVERSITY PRESS.

TO

M. J. H.

b

PREFACE.

THE writings of Sir William Petty may be roughly divided into three classes. The first relates to his activities as surveyor of forfeited lands in Ireland under the Protectorate; its present interest is chiefly biographical. The second includes his papers on medicine and on certain mathematical, physical and mechanical subjects. These are now forgotten. The third class comprises his economic and statistical writings. The merit of these has been freely recognized. No writer on the history of political economy who touches the seventeenth century at all has failed to praise them; but the scarcity of the scattered pamphlets in which they were published has prevented them from becoming as generally known as they deserve to be. The present edition of Petty's Economic Writings is designed to meet this difficulty. It has not been undertaken without warrant. Critics as diverse as McCulloch, Roscher and Ingram have noted the need of a collected edition of Petty's economic pamphlets, and it appears that his descendants have twice considered its publication. But the project of the Earl of Kerry was interrupted by his untimely death[1],

[1] 21 August, 1836. See Thomas More's *Memoirs*, VII. 152, 167.

and Lord Edmond Fitzmaurice, who had contemplated supplementing his "Life of Petty" by an edition of Petty's works, generously surrendered his intention upon learning that a similar undertaking was already under way.

The editor has endeavoured to include all of Petty's published writings which bear upon economic or statistical subjects. The "Observations upon the Bills of Mortality of London," though they probably were not written by Petty, are also reprinted—not less on account of their intrinsic merits than because of their close connection with his acknowledged works. The text selected for reproduction is, in each case, that of the best published edition, and the original paging is indicated in the margin. By good fortune authentic manuscripts of several of the works are still preserved, and their readings, given in the foot-notes, make a number of passages clear which, as heretofore printed, were confusing or absurd. One considerable tract, the "Treatise of Ireland," and a few fragments, are added from manuscripts hitherto unpublished.

The notes are confined, for the most part, to the economic or biographical aspects of the passages commented upon, and no attempt has been made to elucidate purely historical questions. Thus when Petty asserts that in the Irish Court of Claims after the Restoration all claimants were fully heard, the editor does not enter upon a discussion upon that disputed point. In the introductory sections, likewise, he has not used the opportunity to sketch the general history of political economy apropos of Petty and Graunt, but has confined himself to such remarks as are thought to bear directly upon them and their writings. On the other hand the history of the London bills of mortality has been entered into at some length, as no place seemed more appropriate to that purpose than a reprint of the writings which first indicated the importance of the bills.

In preparing this book, the editor has received help from a number of persons, to all of whom he would express his appreciation of their kindnesses. It gives him especial pleasure to acknowledge the gracious permission of the Marquis of Lansdowne to consult the Petty papers at Bowood—though it became impossible for him to make use of that privilege—and to thank Lord Edmond Fitzmaurice for repeated suggestions. He has received valued assistance from J. Eliot Hodgkin, Esq., of Richmond-on-Thames, from the Rev. Dr William Cunningham of Trinity College, Cambridge, from Professor F. York Powell of Oxford, from Professor V. John of Innsbruck, from his colleagues H. Morse Stephens and Walter F. Willcox of Cornell, and from his sister. None of these however should be held responsible for such errors as may be found in the book.

Various officials of the British Museum, the Record Office, the Royal Society, the Bodleian Library, the libraries of Cambridge University and of Brasenose College, Oxford, of the Royal Irish Academy, the King's-Inns, and Trinity College, Dublin, of the Institute of France, the Universities of Leipzig and of Pennsylvania, and of Harvard and Cornell Universities have allowed the editor the use of sundry books and manuscripts. For privileges of this character he is under especial obligation to Professor Michael Foster, Secretary of the Royal Society, and to the Rev. Llewellyn J. M. Bebb, Librarian of Petty's college. He cannot omit to mention, likewise, the services of the proof-readers who have made comparisons with manuscripts and original editions to which he has no present access.

Last but by no means least, he wishes to acknowledge both the generosity of the Syndics of the University Press in providing for the publication of a book whose editor might have looked in vain for assistance at home, and the untiring patience of their Secretary, Mr Richard T. Wright, who must have been sorely tried by its slow passage through the press.

C. H. H.

CORNELL UNIVERSITY.
24 *April*, 1899.

CONTENTS OF VOLUME I.

INTRODUCTION.

PETTY'S LIFE.

WILLIAM PETTY[1] was born on Monday, 26 May, 1623, at the house of his father, a poor clothier of Romsey in Hampshire.

According to the detailed account of his childhood which he gave to Aubrey, his chief amusement consisted in "looking on the artificers, e.g. smyths, the watchmaker, carpenters, joiners, etc.[2]" until he "could have worked at any of their trades." "At twelve years of age he had acquired a competent smattering of Latin," and before his sixteenth year he was well advanced in Greek, mathematics and navigation. It was, perhaps, in his fourteenth year that Petty

[1] The earliest printed notice of Petty's life is in Wood's *Athenæ Oxonienses* (1691). It is based upon memoranda by Petty procured for Wood by John Aubrey (cf. post, p. xl), and upon Petty's published writings. His autobiographical will was first published in the *Tracts relating chiefly to Ireland* (1769; see Bibliography, no. 27) and various letters by and about him were printed in Boyle's *Works* (1744) and in the *Capel Correspondence* (1770). In 1813 Aubrey's *Lives* were included in the "Bodleian Letters" edited by Walker and Bliss, and soon thereafter the printing of Evelyn's and of Pepys's diaries brought further facts to light. In 1851 Petty's *History of the Down Survey* was edited for the Irish Archæological Society. Finally, in 1895, appeared Lord Edmond Fitzmaurice's *Life of Sir William Petty, chiefly from Private Documents hitherto unpublished* (London: John Murray), a record of Petty's acts and thoughts which leaves little to be desired in point of completeness and authenticity. Of the private documents used by Lord E. Fitzmaurice, the most important appear to be the letters exchanged between Petty and Sir Robert Southwell (pp. lvi—lvii). In preparing the above account of Petty, which is confined to those phases of his life that may have suggested, or may serve to explain parts of his writings, I have drawn upon the *Life* without reserve, and have cited other authorities, in general, only in case the citation given is not to be found in the *Life*.

[2] Aubrey, *Brief Lives, ed. by A. Clark* (Oxford, 1898), II. 140. This is far preferable to the 1813 ed.

was overtaken by an accident which gave him opportunity to turn his precocity to good account. After some ten months' service as cabin boy on an English merchantman, he had the misfortune to break his leg. Hereupon the crew set him ashore on the French coast, not far from Caen. The unhappy lad, thus left to shift for himself, recounted his misfortunes in Latin so excellent that the Jesuit fathers of that city not only cared for him but straightway admitted him a pupil of their college[1]. Here he prosecuted his former studies and incidentally learned the French language as well. Meanwhile he supported himself in part by teaching navigation to a French officer and English to a gentleman who desired to visit England—Latin serving, apparently, as the medium of communication in both cases—and in part by traffic in "pittiful brass things with cool'd glasse in them instead of diamonds and rubies." Upon his return to England he appears to have spent some months in the Royal Navy, but in 1643, "when the civil war betwixt the King and Parliament grew hot," he joined the army of English refugees in the Netherlands and "vigorously followed his studies, especially that of medicine," at Utrecht, Leyden[2] and Amsterdam. By November, 1645, he had made his way to Paris where he continued his anatomical studies, reading Vesalius with Hobbes and forming many acquaintances in the group of scholars that gathered around Father Mersen and the Marquis of Newcastle. In the following year he returned to Romsey, and appears to have taken up for a time the business formerly carried on by his father[3]. At Romsey he busied himself also with an instrument for double writing, which he had so far completed by March, 1647, that a patent upon it was then granted him for a term of seventeen years. In November, if not earlier, he went to London with the intention of selling this device[4]. His expectations were not realized, and it may be inferred from his subsequent remarks upon patent monopolies[5] that his career as an inventor proved far from gainful. In London Petty was "admitted

[1] Some printed versions of Petty's will read "University of Oxon," instead of "University of Caen."

[2] At the University of Leyden he was matriculated as a student of medicine the 26th May, 1644, his twenty-first birthday. *Album studiosorum Acad. Lugd. Bat.*, 350.

[3] Anthony Petty, the father, was buried 14 July, 1644. Latham's transcript of the Romsey parish register, Addl. MS. 26,775, f°. 10b, British Museum.

[4] Cf. his prospectuses, Bibliography, 1, 2.

[5] Pp. 74—75.

into several clubbs of the virtuosi," and secured the friendship, among others, of Milton's friend, Samuel Hartlib, to whom he addressed the "Advice of W. P. for the Advancement of some Particular Parts of Learning[1]." It was upon Hartlib's encouragement, also, that he began his abortive "History of Trades[2]."

In 1648 Petty removed from London to Oxford, where the University had been recently reorganized by the parliamentary party. He was soon made deputy to Clayton, the professor of anatomy, and succeeded him in January, 1650, "Dr Clayton resigning his interest" in the professorship "purposely to serve him." Meanwhile he had become a doctor of medicine and a fellow of Brasenose College[3], and, in December, 1650, had added to his reputation by participating in the reanimation of one Ann Green, a wench hanged at Oxford for the supposed murder of her child[4]. At about the same time he was chosen vice-principal of Brasenose and professor of music in Gresham College. The vice-principalship he retained until 9 August, 1659, the Gresham professorship until 8 March, 1660[5]. In April, 1651, the visitors to the University had granted him the unusual favour of two years' leave of absence, with an allowance of £30 per annum[6]. The occasion of this grant and the nature of his occupation during the next few months are unknown; Lord Edmond Fitzmaurice conjectures that he travelled. However that may be, there soon came to him an appointment which exercised a determining influence upon the entire course of his subsequent life;

[1] Bibliography, no. 3.

[2] Hartlib to Boyle, 16 Nov., 1647, Boyle's *Works*, VI. 76; Petty's *Reflections*, 164. Cf. note on p. 118, and supplement to the Bibliography.

[3] On Petty's connection with the Royal College of Physicians, which began about this time, see the note on p. 27.

[4] An account of this exploit, embellished with verse in English and in Latin, is contained in the pamphlet, *News from the Dead*, which was published at Oxford by Robinson in 1650 and again in 1651. The second edition is carelessly reprinted in Morgan's *Phœnix Britannicus*, 233—248. The authorship of the pamphlet has not been ascertained. Wood ascribes it to Richard Watkins Clark, *Life and Times of Wood*, I. 155. But Derham, who wrote in 1707, had been informed that the writer was Dr Ralph Bathurst, one of the participating physicians. Derham's *Psycho and Astro-theology*, I. 236, note. I see no sufficient reason for thinking that Petty wrote it. The mention of Hester Ann Green among his "works" (Suppl. to Bibliography) may refer to the experiment of resuscitation, and not to the account of it.

[5] Ward, *Lives of the Professors of Gresham College*, 228.

[6] Burroughs, *Register*, 335.

he was made physician to the army in Ireland and to the family and person of the Lieutenant-General. Thenceforward his chief interests, both material and intellectual, were intimately connected with affairs beyond St George's Channel.

As physician to the army Petty resided in Ireland nearly seven years, returning to England in 1659[1] as the bearer of Henry Cromwell's letter of acquiescence in the government set up by the Rump. It was during this first period of his Irish residence that he made the "Down Survey" of Ireland[2], a work which laid the foundation of his fortune and constituted his earliest title to fame. After the suppression of the Irish rebellion of 1641 the government prepared to distribute the forfeited lands of the rebels, one moiety among the soldiers of the victorious army, the other among the adventurers who, under the provisions of 17 Car. I., c. 34, had advanced money for the army's support. As a preliminary to the proposed distribution, it was necessary that the situation and area of the forfeited holdings be determined. When Petty first reached Ireland he found a survey for this purpose already in progress. He soon concluded that this survey was being "most insufficiently and absurdly managed" by its director, one Benjamin Worsley, and he promptly proposed to make a more satisfactory survey himself[3]. This he promised to complete, duly set down in maps

[1] He appears to have left Ireland 16 June, 1659 (*History of the Down Survey*, 301) and to have reached London within a week. *Mercurius Politicus*, 23 June, 1659. H. Cromwell's letters commending Petty are printed in Ward's *Lives*, 220.

[2] The chief authorities on the seventeenth century surveys of Ireland are W. H. Hardinge's papers in the publications of the Royal Irish Academy (*Transactions*, XXIV. Antiquities, pp. 3—118, 265—316, 379—420, *Proceedings*, VIII. pp. 39—55) and General Sir T. A. Larcom's edition of Petty's *History of the Down Survey*, published for the Irish Archæological Society. See also Prendergast's *Cromwellian Settlement* and chapter two of Fitzmaurice's *Life of Petty*.

[3] The contest between Petty and Worsley, who belonged to the extreme wing of the English in Ireland, was complicated with the differences between Fleetwood and Henry Cromwell in ways which it is not now possible to trace. Cromwell, who became Petty's steadfast friend, took up his residence at Dublin as Major-General of the Forces and virtual Deputy in July, 1655, while the Down Survey was still in progress; Fleetwood returned to England in the following September. Concerning both the dispute with Worsley and that with Sanchey, which followed the completion of the survey, it should be borne in mind that we have Petty's story only. General Larcom apparently had a high opinion of Worsley's abilities. See his note to Petty's *History*, 320—321.

and books, within a year and a month. After much discussion his proposals were accepted, 11 December, 1654, but the time for the completion of the survey was afterwards extended to thirteen months from February, 1655. Petty thus agreed to measure and record, on a scale of forty perches to an inch, all forfeited lands, profitable and unprofitable, set aside for the satisfaction of the officers and soldiers, —the so-called "army lands"—down to the smallest recognized civil denominations. He also undertook to survey and map, for general use and upon a smaller scale, the bounds of all baronies, whether forfeited or not, in all counties which contained forfeited lands. By March, 1656, the survey of the army lands was virtually completed, and he applied to the Council for payment and for release from his bond. His work was referred to a committee representing the army and was by them pronounced satisfactory. Worsley, on the contrary, pointed out a number of minor errors. These were such, in Petty's view, as should "bee not charged uppon" him "as faults; but rather such accidents and disasters as ever attend vast and variable undertakings[1]." Nevertheless he attempted a detailed answer to Worsley's objections. General Larcom, a judge eminently competent, declares that he met the charges "satisfactorily, indeed triumphantly: for whatever shortcomings or blemishes might be detected in so great a work, performed with such extraordinary rapidity, over so great an extent of country at the same time, there can be no doubt that, on the whole, it exceeded the articles of agreement, and that the delay which will be seen to have taken place in the payment, was vexatious and unjust." Nevertheless Petty was obliged to wage a prolonged contest for his rights, the final order for his payment being postponed until March, 1657, while his bond was not released until December of the same year. The publication of the results of the general survey, on the other hand, appears to have been delayed for several years[2].

The completion of the Down Survey of the army lands by no means concluded Petty's "services and sufferings" in Ireland. On the 7th July, 1656, he was named a member of the commission to distribute among the officers and soldiers the forfeited lands which he had surveyed. Vincent Gookin, one of his associates on the commission, presently departed for England to attend Parliament, and fear of offending military friends deterred the other member,

[1] *History*, 119. [2] See note on p. 6, cf. Bibliography.

Major Miles Symner, from taking an active part in its labours[1]. Petty was therefore, obliged, "to manage the executive part of that vast and intricate work, as if it were alone, Few other Commissioners (for fear of falling into some Error) adventuring to do business without" him, "Whereby all displeasures real or imaginary, were accounted not onely" his "Permission but Commission: Not onely" his "simple Act, but design, contrivance and revenge[2]." Working thus single-handed, he set out their lands to the army with such dispatch that the distribution was completed in February, 1657. Meanwhile he had begun, in conjunction with Worsley, a survey of the adventurers' moiety of the forfeited lands. Distribution based upon this survey was delayed by disagreements among the adventurers at London until finally, in May, 1658, the patience of the Lord Deputy was exhausted by their indecision and he sent Petty to treat with them for the appointment of a commission which should adjust their claims out of hand. Upon his arrival in London, Petty found the adventurers already in receipt of an anonymous communication from Dublin, alleging that he intended if possible to cheat them as, it was charged, he had cheated the army. In the face of this charge he won the entire confidence of the adventurers' committee, and was provided by them with a petition to the Council at Dublin requesting "that, instead of all the said Commissioners, Dr Petty alone may bee authorized and approved by your Lordshipps, to act as well in behalfe of your Lordshipps as the adventurers, as a person best able to give the business a dispatch[3]." The news of his triumph at London stirred up Petty's enemies at Dublin to prepare a second letter—Petty called it a libel[4]—directed ostensibly to the adventurers and assuring them that his dishonesty in surveying and setting out the army lands had gone unpunished only because of his position as a clerk of the Council and prime favourite of the Lord Deputy. By prearrangement this letter was intercepted on its way to London and was brought to the attention of Henry Cromwell. Cromwell, whose confidence in Petty never wavered, at once referred the charges to a committee of seven officers. "Whilst these things were doeing in Ireland, the doctor rides night and day from London, in the end of December [1658], and through many hazards comes to

[1] *History*, 208. After a time, but not until its work was nearly completed, a fourth member was added to the commission.

[2] *Reflections*, 116—117.

[3] *History*, 248.

[4] *History*, 258—262.

Dublyn, God having kept him safe in the greatest storme that ever was knowne, as he thankfully construed it, to preserve him for his vindication." At Petty's request the officers' committee already appointed was increased by the addition of "the Receiver-General, Auditors-General, and one Mr Jeoffryes, a person well reputed for his integrity and skill in accompts, that, having given a satisfactory accompt unto these able and proper ministers of the State, he might all under one bee discharged both from the State and armyes further question or suspicion." A majority of the committee as thus constituted declared the charges to be without foundation. Three of the officers, a minority of the original committee, for a time dissented from this finding, but eventually, affecting to believe that in a new attack brought against Petty from an unexpected quarter "his Excellency himselfe was strucke att," they declined to "muddle or make further in the business."

The scruples of the officers in Ireland were by no means groundless. The death of the Lord Protector had reanimated the purely parliamentarian party of the army in England to an activity that boded no good to his sons. Petty was, throughout his life, a firm supporter of the family of Cromwell, and it was as Henry Cromwell's friend that he had been elected member for West Looe in Richard's parliament. It is not surprising, therefore, that the charges of bribery and breach of trust now preferred against him in the House of Commons by Sir Jerome Sanchey[1] should have appeared to the officers at Dublin as a blow struck at the Lord Deputy himself. A letter from speaker Bampfield[2] brought Sanchey's[3] charges to Petty's

[1] *H. C. Journals*, VII. 612.

[2] *History*, 289.

[3] Sanchey, or Zankey, a son of a clergyman of Salop, was a member of Clare Hall, Cambridge, and received his B.A. in 1641. More given to manly exercises than to logic and philosophy, a boisterous fellow at cudgelling and foot-ball (Wood, *Fasti Oxon.* II. 69), he exchanged his gown for a trooper's jacket and soon rose to be a colonel in the parliamentary army. Whitelocke, *Memorials*, 302. In March, 1649, the parliamentary visitors to Oxford called him from the army to become sub-warden of All Souls. In this capacity he received Oliver Cromwell, upon his visit to the University, and presented him for his degree. Burrows, *Register*, 227. By the end of the year he was once more in command of a troop of cavalry and met with much military success in Ireland. He was repeatedly chosen a member of the Irish parliament and was knighted by Henry Cromwell. Cromwell's *Letters and Speeches*, II. 254, 302. In August, 1659, he brought his regiment to England to join Lambert, and was prominent in the disputes between the army and the Rump. Ludlow, *Memoirs*, (Firth's ed.), II. 110, 118, 130, 135, 151, 162; Whitelocke, 436, 445, 509, 530, 678, 682,

attention. On the day set for his reply he appeared in the House and defended himself with great moderation. The charges were vague and there was no proof. In so extensive and difficult a work as the distribution of the army's lands it was inevitable that he should make many enemies, while he had the opportunity to make scarce any friends. He had nothing to conceal. He had often endeavoured to bring himself to a trial, but his adversaries had now done more for him than he was ever able to do for himself: they had brought him to the very fountain of justice and he willingly threw himself into it to be washed of all that was foul and superfluous. The manner of his trial and vindication he committed to the wisdom and justice of the House, asking only that instead of Sanchey's heaps of calumnies and reproach, he might receive a more distinct and particular charge, whereby he might be put in a way to vindicate himself effectually. Sanchey replied in a speech which, as reported by Petty, is remarkable for its violence and incoherence[1]. The House lost all patience with him and he was ordered to bring in his charges in writing. The next day, 22 April, Richard Cromwell dissolved Parliament and Petty was once more defrauded of his desired vindication.

Upon the dissolution of Parliament Petty hastened to Ireland, but soon returned to England again, being sent by Henry Cromwell to Fleetwood as one whom he could best trust now his nearest concernments were at stake[2]. Sanchey, now a person of importance in the republican reaction, took advantage of Petty's presence in London to present to the Rump Parliament, 12 July, no less than eleven "new Articles of high misdemeanours, frauds, breach of trusts and several other crimes" chargeable against him. The Rump promptly referred them to the Commissioners for Ireland, before whom they never came to trial. The possibility of an official vindication being thus precluded, Petty resolved to carry his case before the bar of public opinion. With this end in view he published a succinct

685. In Dec., 1660, he was arrested (Rugge's MS. Diary, quoted by Taylor, *England under Charles II.* 40) on suspicion of taking part in an alleged plot against kingly power, and his name appears as one of the thirty republicans whom the House of Commons proposed, 24 May, 1661, to exempt from pardon and confirmation of estates. Carte, *Ormond*, II. 226 n, 228. After that he disappears from public view, but it is known that he died in Ireland about 1685.

[1] *History*, 299, 301; *Reflections*, 70—75.

[2] H. Cromwell to Fleetwood, June, 1659, Thurloe, VII. 684.

account of the dispute with Sanchey down to 13 July, 1659[1], and the succeeding year he followed it up with a volume of nearly two hundred pages[2] describing the work of survey and distribution, answering the charges brought against him, and explaining how they arose "from the envy and hatred of several parties promiscuously" and "from particular designing persons and parties" in Ireland. About October, 1659, he also prepared for the press, at great length, a History of the Down Survey[3], containing what he regarded as a complete vindication of his conduct, and two further works, now probably lost, upon the same subject[4].

Among the clubs of the virtuosi to which, as Petty's will relates, it was his privilege to be admitted[5] soon after he came to London[6], none is more memorable than that company of "capacious and searching spirits inquisitive into natural philosophy and other parts of human knowledge," whose habit it was to meet for discussion either at Dr Goddard's lodgings in Wood Street or at the Bull's Head Tavern in Cheapside[7]. There is no evidence that Petty was an original member of this company. But it appears probable that he was early invited to join their Invisible College[8], and it is certain that when parliamentary reorganization of the more visible colleges at Oxford brought Goddard, Wallis, Wilkins, and other followers of

[1] *A Brief of Proceedings between Sr Hierome Sankey and Dr William Petty*, 1659. See Bibliography, no. 4.

[2] *Reflections upon some Persons and Things in Ireland*, 1660. See Bibliography, no. 5.

[3] It was not published until 1851, see Bibliography, no. 31 and cf. pp. xiii, xiv. Mr Hardinge declares that "the accuracy of the facts adduced" by Petty "in his defence have [sic] been fully borne out by the researches I have made amongst the yet surviving documents of the period." *Trans. R. I. Acad.* XXIV. Antiquities, p. 21.

[4] They are known only by his account of them in the *Reflections* (pp. 60—61): "I have also written a profest Answer to Sir Hieromes Eleven last and greatest Articles, containing the proofs of what is herein but barely alledged, which I may not publish till after my tryal....There is another piece of quite a contrary nature, being indeed a Satyre; which though it contain little of seriousness, yet doth it allow nothing of untruth: 'Tis a Gallery wherein you will see the Pictures of my chief Adversaries hang'd up in their proper colours; 'tis intended for the honest recreation of my ingenious friends."

[5] P. 23, note.

[6] Ante, p. xiv.

[7] Dr John Wallis's *Account of some passages in his own Life*, in Hearne's ed. of Langtoft's *Chronicle* (1725), vol. I. p. clxiv. This with Sprat's History of *the Royal Society*, gives nearly all that is known of Petty's connection with the inchoate Society.

[8] Masson, *Life of Milton*, III. 665; Fitzmaurice, 15.

the new philosophy to the venerable home of the old, they there found in Petty an enthusiastic colleague. Their Oxford meetings were held first in his lodgings at the apothecary's because of the convenience of examining drugs and the like when there was an occasion, "and after his removal to Ireland (though not so constantly) at the lodgings of Dr Wilkins[1]." Those of the company who remained in London meanwhile continued their inquiries in a somewhat desultory manner until the Restoration brought back to the city the more prominent members of the Oxford branch, when it became necessary to change their place of meeting from the Bull's Head to the halls of Gresham College. Here the reunited company was in the habit of assembling for the discussion of questions in natural philosophy. They met regularly on Wednesdays and Thursdays, after the astronomy lectures of Christopher Wren and the geometry lectures of Lawrence Rooke[2], and on Wednesday, the 28th of November, 1660, after Wren's lecture, the conversation chancing to turn upon foreign institutions for promoting physico-mathematical experimental learning, the company then present, of whom Petty was one, resolved to improve this meeting to a more regular way of debating things and that they might do something answerable and according to the manner in other countryes for the promoting of experimental philosophy[3]. Among those who, in pursuance of this plan, were invited to read papers before the association thus informally organized, Petty's name appears repeatedly[4], and when, with fitting circumstance, the association was incorporated (15 July, 1662) as the Royal Society for Improving of Natural Knowledge, he was named a charter member of its council.

Petty's famous plan for a "double bottomed" vessel, a sort of catamaran, which should excel in swiftness, weatherliness and stability any "single body" afloat, was probably set forth in one of his papers[5] before the Society. To demonstrate the correctness of

[1] Wallis, *loc. cit.*

[2] Ward, *Lives of the Professors of Gresham College*, 91, 96.

[3] Birch, *History of the Royal Society*, I. 14.

[4] Birch, I. 7, 12, 13, 15, 19, 55—65, 83, 124 etc.; cf. Bibliography, no. 7.

[5] Anthony à-Wood's suggestion that the "Thoughts on the Philosophy of Shipping" which Petty presented to the Society in 1662, may be the same as the *Treatise of Naval Philosophy* printed over his name in Hale's *Account of Several New Inventions* in 1691 (Bibliography, no. 25) cannot be reconciled with the extraordinary value which the members of the Society appear to have set upon Petty's "thoughts." But if we recall the extravagant expectations of his "sluice

his views he built at least three such "sluice boats.' The first was laid down at Dublin in 1662. She distinguished herself by beating all the boats in the harbour, and subsequently outsailed the Holyhead packet, the swiftest vessel that the King had there. Hereupon Petty brought her to England[1], where, probably through the intervention of his friend Pepys, the attention of the Duke of York, then Lord High Admiral, and eventually the notice of the King himself was turned to the novel craft. Charles II. appears to have combined wonder at Petty's energy with quizzical amusement at his numerous projects. He at first chaffed the naviarchal Doctor without mercy[2], but relented sufficiently to attend the launching of a new Double Bottom which he dubbed "The Experiment[3]." She also proved herself a swift sailor, but was presently lost in the Irish Channel. This disaster, followed by the burning of several of his London houses in the great fire and by the adverse decisions of some of his Irish law suits[4], restrained Petty from further shipbuilding experiments for nearly a score of years; but in 1682, while he was considering the establishment at Dublin of a philosophical society similar to that of London, the fit of the Double Bottom, as he tells us, did return very fiercely upon him. His new vessel, however, performed as abominably, as if built on purpose to disappoint in the highest degree every particular that was expected of her and caused him to stagger in much that he had formerly said. But so much did he prefer truth before vanity and imposture that he resolved to spend his life in examining the greatest and noblest of all machines, a ship, and if he found just cause for it to write a book against himself[5].

The Restoration brought Petty no misfortune. A royal letter dated 2 Jan., 1660[6], secured to him all lands that he had held on

boat" which he himself cherished, it is easy to see why Lord Brouncker, as president of the Society, might declare with alarm that a paper describing it was "too great an arcanum of state to be commonly perused," and accordingly forbid its printing. Cf. Aubrey, *Brief Lives*, II. 147. Pepys appears to have had a copy of Petty's paper in 1682. Pepys to Wood, 16 June, 1682, Rawlinson MS. A 194, f°. 279, Bodleian Library.

[1] Or perhaps another boat built upon similar lines.

[2] Pepys, *Diary*, 1 Feb., 1664. [3] Evelyn, *Diary*, 22 Mch., 1675.

[4] See pp. xxiv, xxv.

[5] To Southwell, 18 Oct., 1682, Fitzmaurice, 256—257. I cannot find that he ever wrote the book.

[6] Officially confirmed Feb., 1661, Carte Papers, XLII. 492, Bodleian Library. On the 25 March, 1661, certain unprofitable lands in Kerry were settled on Petty

the 7th May, 1659, and the Acts of Settlement and of Explanation confirmed them to him by name. Like other owners of forfeited lands in Ireland, he suffered by the operation of the Court of Innocents in 1662, and was never able to convince himself that all who claimed innocency were in fact innocent[1]. But in spite of his losses, he retained large Irish estates, and, in evidence of the King's approval, he was knighted[2] and appears to have been appointed Surveyor-General of Ireland[3]. The duties of this office at the time cannot have been more than nominal, for Petty continued to reside in London. During the Plague he withdrew to Durdens in Surrey where Evelyn found him, with Dr Wilkins and Mr Hooke, busied in contriving mechanical inventions[4].

In the spring of 1666 Petty was once more called to Ireland by the operations of the Court of Claims, and took up his residence in Dublin. During the ensuing period of his second prolonged stay in Ireland, he thoroughly identified himself with the material interests of that kingdom. As an army physician and surveyor of forfeitures, he had felt himself at most but a sojourner. As a Kerry landholder, able from Mount Mangerton in that country to behold 50,000 acres of his own land[5], he found abundant occupation, first in defending his titles during the sessions of the Court of Claims, and subsequently in managing his property. The uncertainty of titles in Ireland was great. "The Truth is," said Essex, "ye Lands of Ireland have bin a meer scramble[6]." Flaws and defects of various sorts, based on allegations of illegal forfeiture, or of unpaid

"in consideration of his early endeavours for the King's Restoration, the good affection he bears his Majesty, and his abilities to serve him." *Fourteenth Rept. Hist. MSS., Com.* pt. 7, p. 70.

[1] See pp. 199, 601. It was during a brief residence in Ireland, undertaken with a view to defending his interests against the Innocents, that Petty built the first Double Bottom and began his enquiries into the Dublin bills of mortality. See p. 398, note.

[2] 11 April, 1661, Le Neve, *Pedigrees of the Knights*, 133; Birch, I. 41.

[3] Fitzmaurice, 107; *Cabinet Portrait Gallery*, VIII. 37. Hardinge, however, says that John Pettie, apparently Sir William's cousin, "was Surveyor-General from the Restoration in 1660 to the 13th of February, 1667, when Sir James Sheen succeeded Pettie." *Trans. R. I. Acad.* XXIV. Antiquities, p. 18.

[4] *Diary*, 4 Aug., 1665. Petty appears to have given up his medical practice some years before the Plague of 1665. His plan for lessening the plagues of London (p. 109, note) contains no medical suggestion whatsoever.

[5] Aubrey, *Brief Lives*, II. 142.

[6] To Harbord, 28 March, 1674, *Essex Papers*, I. 201.

quit rents, were being continually found out, and it had become "A principal trade in Ireland to...prevail with persons conversant with the Higher Powers to give grants of these Discoveries, and thereupon, right or wrong, to vex the Possessors into such a Composition as may be of Profit to the Prosecutors[1]." Petty by no means escaped such attacks. He refused to compromise, and in consequence his time was so fully occupied with defending himself that in 1667 he grimly entered "Lawsuits" as his only work accomplished[2].

Upon his escape from "the fire of this legal purgatory" Petty at once set about the improvement of what remained. His household was established at Dublin[3], but his most extensive possessions were at Kenmare in Kerry, and there he gradually built up an "industrial colony" of protestants. To this enterprise he gave the closest attention, making the difficult overland journey to that "obscure corner of the world twice a year through thick and thin[4]." The prospect was not encouraging. His Irish neighbours were hostile, and of Kenmare itself a well informed contemporary reported that while the harbours were very good for ships to load at, the place was so rocky and bare that it would hardly maintain people enough to keep a brogue-maker employed[5]. But there were compensating advantages. The remote bay abounded with salmon. Abundance of wood made charcoal cheap and therefore he established iron and copper works, hoping vainly to discover Irish ores for their supply. The protestant colonists prospered in trade, as he had

[1] *Polit. Anat.* ch. XI. post, p. 195.

[2] Collection of his "several works" in supplement to Bibliography. At a later date Petty seems to have attempted the "trade" which he so strongly reprehended. In 1673 he joined Sir Henry Ingoldsby in a proposal to make Charles II. an annual money payment for a patent of certain "concealed lands" in Ireland. Essex declared that "nothing can be more illegall & oppressing to ye subject than such a Patent, whereby opportunity & warr^t^ will be given to these Projectors to raveell into ye Settlement of all men's Estates whatever, who, tho' they had never so just & clear Titles, will rather come to a composition than endure ye charges and vexations that these men will put them to." To Shaftesbury 4 May, 1673, *Essex Papers*, I. 82.

[3] He married 7 June, 1667, Elizabeth, daughter of his friend, Sir Hardress Waller.

[4] Petty to Graunt, 24 Dec., 1672, Fitzmaurice, 234.

[5] Peter Bronsdon to the Navy Commissioners, 17 March, 1671, *C.S.P. Dom.* 1671, pp. 135, 184. Bronsdon had examined much of Ireland in search of timber for the Navy (*ib.* p. xxxiv.) and found none so well suited for the purpose as that growing on Petty's Kerry estates. *Ib.* p. 77, 136, 183, 207, 521.

observed the heterodox everywhere to do[1], and Kenmare clearly demonstrated what thrift, backed by sufficient capital and directed by conspicuous shrewdness, could do for the real settlement of Ireland even under Charles II. After the accession of James II. the colonists fell victims to the jealousy of the surrounding Irish, whose violence was encouraged by Tyrconnel's policy, and thus the most successful of Petty's numerous experiments finally came to naught[2].

As Petty's stake in the prosperity of Ireland grew larger, his interest in the affairs of the kingdom likewise increased. He had been a member of the Irish parliament of the Restoration[3], and one of the commissioners appointed to execute the Act of Settlement, he had taken a prominent part in opposing the bill which prohibited the importation of Irish cattle into England[4], and he had even attempted, though apparently quite ignorant of the law, to fill the position of a judge of admiralty; but the incidental discharge of these public duties had little or no effect upon the subsequent course of his life. His concern with the public revenues of Ireland was far more significant. As early as 1662 he had "frequently applied to present state and affairs of Ireland" certain of the conclusions reached in his "Treatise of Taxes." To the mere theoretical interest in the subject thus evinced, the events of later years added an interest of a very practical character. In 1668 charges of mismanagement of the Irish revenues were brought against Ormond, the Lord Lieutenant, and Anglesey, the Lord Treasurer[5], by certain persons who desired to farm the revenues themselves. Their intrigue was successful, and the King agreed with them for seven years from Christmas, 1668, for £219,500 per annum[6]. The management of the new farm was both unsatisfactory to the exchequer and oppressive to the

[1] *Political Arithmetick*, p. 263.

[2] A spirited account of Kenmare, based on Smith's *Ancient and Present State of Kerry*, is given by Macaulay, *History of England*, Vol. III., ch. XII., pp. 108—110.

[3] He served with Sir William Temple on the Commons' Committee upon the means of advancing the trade of Ireland. Mountmorres, *History of the Irish Parliament*, 96. Cf. post, pp. 225—231.

[4] See note on pp. 161, 162.

[5] Carte, II. 368; *Cal. S. P. Dom.*, 1667—68, pp. 532, 543, 557, 564; 1668, 90.

[6] Howard, *Revenue and Exchequer of Ireland*, I. 57.

subject[1]. Especially did the energy of the farmers in collecting alleged arrears of quit-rents stir the landowners thus charged to active resistance. Among them was Petty. He promptly took up a "legal fight with the farmers," an account of which occupies for several years a large space in his correspondence with Southwell. His tone makes it evident that a considerable spice of personal animosity was thus added to his previous disgust with the inequalities of Irish taxation and in part explains his subsequent conduct. As the time drew near for the farm of 1668 to expire, he resolved to carry the war into the enemy's camp. Accordingly in the latter part of 1673 he made his way to London and became a bidder, on what he considered a reformed basis, for the new farm beginning Christmas Day, 1675. It appears that an agreement with him was actually made[2] but Ranelagh's influence with Buckingham was sufficient to procure its abrogation and the substitution of the scandalous contract under which Ranelagh, Lord Kingston, and Sir James Shaen continued to mismanage the finances of Ireland until Ormond finally exposed them[3]. Meanwhile Petty remained more than two years in London, renewing his old acquaintances and becoming once more a member of the Council of the Royal Society[4].

In the summer[5] of 1676 Petty once more took up his residence in Ireland, where, save for visits to London in the spring of 1680, he remained almost five years[6]. It was during this period that he wrote the "Political Anatomy of Ireland," the "Political Arithmetick," and the "Observations on the Dublin Bills[7]." He also fell into a new quarrel with the farmers, the result of which for a time overclouded even his invincible cheerfulness. His chief adversary, Ranelagh, being Chancellor of the Exchequer as well as farmer of

[1] On the 30 Sept., 1670, the deficit for the half year was £72,953 and the debt was £245,510. *Cal. S. P. Dom.*, 1671, p. 54.

[2] Essex to the Lords Justices, 28 Sept., 1675, *Capel Correspondence*, 403—404.

[3] Carte, *Ormond*, II. 451—464.

[4] Birch III. 112. In December, 1673, he was elected Vice-President of the Society (*ib.* 123) and in the following November he read before it his *Discourse of Duplicate Proportion* (see pp. 622—624, also Bibliography, no. 8), the only printed production of this visit to London. Cf. Aubrey, *Brief Lives*, II. 144.

[5] On 1 July, 1676, Dr Ent wrote that Petty was about to go to Ireland. Ballard MS. 33, f°. 4, Bodleian Library.

[6] He reached Chester on his way to London, 5 June, 1682. Fitzmaurice, 250.

[7] Cf. pp. 122, 235, 236, 480.

the taxes, was able to procure his imprisonment for contempt of court[1]. Thus vexed by the wicked works of man, he refreshed himself by pondering the wonderful works of God. The result was a Latin metrical translation of the 104th psalm, copies of which he sent with long complaints to Southwell and to Pepys. But his native whimsicality soon reasserted itself. "Lord," he exclaims, "that a man fifty-four years old should, after thirty-six years discontinuance, return to the making of verses which boys of fifteen years old can correct: and then trouble Clerks of the Council and Secretaries of the Admiralty with them[2]."

The reappointment of Ormond in 1677 to the Lord Lieutenancy of Ireland, in the room of Essex, whose opinion of Petty was not high[3], brought about a lull in his dispute with the farmers, and after his recovery from the illness which had alarmed him in November of that year, there remained nothing to mar his pleasure in the prosperity of his affairs. He even began to think seriously of the possibility of exercising greater influence in public matters. About the time of his marriage he had been approached concerning a peerage. The condition then suggested was the payment of such a sum as, in view of his recent losses, Petty did not care to spend "in the market of ambition," and he thanked the royal emissary with scant courtesy[4]. In 1679, when Temple was planning to remodel the Irish Privy Council upon the same lines that he had followed in England and the protestant party at court had marked Petty for appointment to the reconstituted body[5], the offer of a peerage was again made to him. He seems in the mean time to have changed his opinion of "people who make use of titles and tools" and accordingly he made a journey to London, apparently with the intention of securing both the title and the seat at the

[1] See, in addition to Fitzmaurice, pp. 169—173, the extracts from Petty's letters in Thorpe's *Cat. lib. MSS. bibl. Southwellianæ*, no. 710; cf. Petty's opinion of the Chancellor and Sir Richard Cox's comment on it, p. 205, post.

[2] To Southwell, 3 April, 1677, Fitzmaurice, 172. Not all Petty's friends thought so meanly of his verses as he himself professed to do. In the privacy of his diary Evelyn wrote of Petty (22 March, 1675) "there is no better Latin poet living when he gives himself that diversion." See Bibliography, no. 9.

[3] "I am confident in all his Majestie's 3 Kingdomes, there lives not a more grating man than Sir William Petty" wrote Essex to Shaftesbury, 4 May, 1673. *Essex Papers*, I. 83.

[4] His letter is given by Fitzmaurice, p. 155. [5] Carte, *Ormond*, II. 494, 495.

Council table[1]. But Charles II. answered the protestants that by their good leave he would chose his own council for Ireland, and Petty fearing that "a bare title without some trust might seem to the world a body without soul or spirit[2]," declined the peerage for a second time. Perhaps he consoled himself, as on the previous occasion, by reflecting that he "had rather be a copper farthing of intrinsic value than a brass half-crown, how gaudily soever it be stamped and guilded."

Upon his return to Ireland, 22 March, 1680, his old controversy with the farmers broke out again, and the vigour of his attack upon their abuses[3] attracted such attention that he was summoned to London in June, 1682, to take part in the discussion then going on before the Privy Council, as to the reorganization of the Irish revenues. He proposed the abolition of the farm, which was finally accomplished, and the imposition of a heavy ale license. Apparently he was not adverse to undertaking the direct collection of the taxes himself, but "by good luck" he "never solicited anybody in the case." His old rival, Sir James Shaen, now offered to increase the King's revenue nearly £80,000 a year upon a new farm—"a farm indeed, as it was drawn up" says Temple, "not of the revenue but of the crown of Ireland[4]." But the powerful influence of Essex, whom Temple charges with intriguing for a reappointment to the Lord Lieutenancy, was thrown in Shaen's favour, Petty was represented by some to be a conjurer and by some to be notional and fanciful near up to madness[5], the needs of the Exchequer were urgent, and the plan that promised ready cash was adopted. Deeply disappointed, Petty returned to Ireland in the summer of 1683 and

[1] Ossory to Ormond, 5 June, 1680, from Windsor: "Sir William Petty has desired mee to gett him to be made a Councellor....Without your permission I shall not move in this matter." *Seventh Rept. Hist. MSS. Com.*, 739 b.

[2] Lady Petty to Edmund Waller, 8 March, 1680, Fitzmaurice, 245.

[3] The farmers were also far behind in their payments to the Exchequer. On the 18 Feby., 1679, Danby wrote to Ormond that if some speedy care be not taken the present farm of the revenue of Ireland must break in the hands of those which now manage it. *Fourteenth Rept. Hist. MSS. Com.*, pt. 7, p. 50.

[4] *Works*, II. 526. Ranelagh predicted that Shaen would prove unable to execute his proposals. Ranelagh to Ormond, 12 July, 1681, *Fourteenth Rept. Hist. MSS. Com.*, pt. 7, p. 53.

[5] Ormond's report to Petty, 16 Sept., 1682, Fitzmaurice 252. In Ackerman's *Monies received and paid for Secret Services of Charles II. and James II.*, p. 58, is an entry, dated 9 Dec., 1682, of £2 "for copies of l'res concerning Sr Wm Petty and others."

solaced himself with a journey into Kerry, and presently with a renewal of the experiments that had occupied his mind some twenty years before[1]. He built a new double bottom and was active in the establishment of the Dublin Philosophical Society[2], for which he wrote several papers[3].

News of the accession of James II. caused Petty to return to London in the early summer of 1685. The new occupant of the royal office had been not less gracious to him than was his predecessor, and Petty fancied the time now ripe to secure for Ireland the adminstrative reforms on which his heart was set. His plans for the revision of the farm and for the establishment, under his own supervision, of an Irish statistical office[4] seemed for a time to be going well, and he attributed undue importance to the interviews which the King granted him[5] upon this and other Irish matters. It was not until later that he appreciated the extent to which, under the new regime, his own personal interests were being drawn to his disadvantage into the larger currents of public affairs. Among the policies which, from time to time, were indistinctly indicated by the vacillations of James II., that looking towards independence of Louis XIV. and the resumption by England of a leading place in the affairs of Europe appealed to Petty with peculiar force. Ten years before, in the "Political Arithmetick," he had argued England's material fitness for such a place, and had proved, to his own satisfaction at least, that in wealth and strength she was potentially, if not actually, as considerable as France. He now reverted to the same theme, writing a series of essays, in order, by the methods of his political arithmetick, to demonstrate to the satisfaction of the King that London was the greatest city in the world. These efforts excited some attention among the curious, both at home and abroad[6], but they produced no traceable effect upon the policy of James II.

Petty appears to have realized that independence of France demanded harmony at home, and to have welcomed James's

[1] See p. xxiii above.

[2] Molyneaux Correspondence, in *Dublin University Magazine*, XVIII. 489; Birch, IV. 341; Wilde, in *Proc. R. I. Acad.*, III. 160—176. On Petty's previous connection with the College of Physicians at Dublin, cf. p. 165 n.

[3] Bibliography, 14—16. There were also papers on concentric circles and other subjects which have not been printed, Wilde, *op. cit.*, 164, 171, 172.

[4] See pp. 480, 485, 486, cf. 396.

[5] See p. 546.

[6] See pp. 452, 502, 503, 522, 524.

Declarations of Indulgence as wise measures for the unification of national sentiment. Knowing as he did the immense material preponderance of the protestant interest both in England[1] and especially in Ireland[2]—a preponderance of which he did his best to convince the King by written and by oral argument[3]—he was unable to believe that the Declarations, whose sentiments quite accorded with his own views[4], were really issued in the sole interest of the Roman Catholics, and he continued to regard the boastings of Tyrconnel and the extreme Irish faction as without foundation in the intentions of the king[5]. But at length tidings of the alarm prevalent among the English protestants in Ireland, and especially the news that McCarthy had been appointed governor of the province of Kerry, brought home to him the danger with which he himself, as well as the other protestants in Ireland, were threatened.

It is not certain whether Petty lived to know that Kenmare was destroyed. For some months he had been unwell. In spite of a "great lameness" he attended the annual dinner of the Royal

[1] Cf. his *Telling of Noses*, p. 461 note [where read 11870 for 11878 and $178\frac{10}{13}$ for $178\frac{10}{10}$]. Regarding "the Bishops late numbering of the Communicants," upon which Petty's calculations for England were based, Mr W. C. Abbott kindly writes me that "in 1676 the Earl of Danby, then Lord High Treasurer and Chief Minister to Charles II., ordered a census of religious bodies in England by dioceses and committed the task of making it to the Anglican clergy. Among the Leeds papers (*Hist. MSS. Com.*, vol. XI. pt. 7, pp. 14 seq.), in consequence, we find several documents dealing with the matter. The first is a letter from Danby to Bishop Morley regarding this inquiry, which was set on foot to demonstrate to the King by actual figures the vast superiority in numbers of the Anglican Church over all other religious bodies in England. This, as the Bishop says, will probably break down the king's objection to the rigid suppression of conventicles, and he assumes that it is for that purpose. Rather, one would say from a political point of view, it was to demonstrate to Charles the absolute futility of his religious policy."

[2] The figures from the *Political Anatomy*, pp. 156, 138—144, are familiar from the use made of them by Macaulay and Lecky. Those in the *Treatise of Ireland*, pp. 561, 590—596, now first published, are not less striking.

[3] Fitzmaurice, 280.

[4] Cf. pp. 70—73, 262—264, post; Fitzmaurice, pp. 234—243, 270. In Rawlinson MS. A 171, ff. 274—275, is a dialogue on Liberty of Conscience endorsed "S[r] W[m] Petty's Paper written at my desire & given me by himselfe a little before his Death. S[amuel] P[epys]." The only theological suggestion contained in "Twelve articles of a good catholique and good patriot's creed" found in Petty's pocket after his death (Fitzmaurice, 310) is "that Liberty of Religion and Naturalization be secured."

[5] Cf. pp. 577, 591.

Society on St Andrew's day. He went home ill. His foot gangrened and on December 16 he died at his house in Piccadilly.

On Trinity Sunday, June 2, 1667, Petty had married Elizabeth, daughter of his old friend Sir Hardress Waller, and widow of Sir Maurice Fenton. Though Lady Petty, "a very beautifull and ingeniose lady, browne, with glorious eies[1]," was much younger than her husband and of a taste as magnificent as his was simple[2], their married life was most happy. Nowhere does Petty appear to greater advantage than in his letters to his wife, and her letters to him fully bear out Evelyn's judgment, "she was an extraordinary wit as well as beauty and a prudent woman."

Three of Petty's contemporaries, men of different temperaments and attainments, have put on record their impressions of him. John Aubrey says that he was a proper handsome man, measured six-foot high, with a good head of brown hair moderately turning up. His eyes were a kind of goose-grey, very short sighted and as to aspect beautiful; they promised sweetness of nature and they did not deceive, for he was a marvellous good natured person. His eye-brows were thick, dark and straight, his head very large. Evelyn declared him so exceeding nice in sifting and examining all possible contingencies that he ventured at nothing which is not demonstration. There was not in the whole world his equal for a superintendent of manufactures and improvement of trade, or to govern a plantation. "If I were a prince, I should make him my second counsellor at least. There is nothing difficult to him... Sir William was, with all this, facetious and of easy conversation, friendly and courteous, and had such a faculty of imitating others that he would take a text and preach, now like a grave orthodox divine, then falling into the Presbyterian way, then to the fanatical, the Quaker, the monk and friar, the Popish priest, with such admirable action and alteration of voice and tone, as it was not possible to abstain from wonder, and one would swear to hear several persons, or forbear to think he was not in good earnest an enthusiast and almost beside himself; then,

[1] Aubrey, II. 142.

[2] "When I who knew him in mean circumstances, have been in his splendid palace, he would himself be in admiration how he arrived at it; nor was it his value and inclination for splendid furniture or the curiosities of the age; but his elegant lady could endure nothing mean, or that was not magnificent. He was very negligent himself, and rather so of his own person, and of a philosophic temper. What a to do is here he would say, I can lie in straw with as much satisfaction." Evelyn, *Diary*, 22 March, 1675.

he would fall out of it into a serious discourse; but it was very rarely he would be prevailed on to oblige the company with this faculty, and that only amongst most intimate friends. My Lord Duke of Ormond once obtained it of him, and was almost ravished with admiration; but bye and bye, he fell upon a serious reprimand of the faults and miscarriages of some Princes and Governors, which, though he named none, did so sensibly touch the Duke, who was then Lieutenant of Ireland, that he began to be very uneasy, and wished the spirit laid which he had raised, for he was neither able to endure such truths, nor could he but be delighted. At last, he melted his discourse to a ridiculous subject, and came down from the joint stool on which he had stood; but my lord would not have him preach any more. He never could get favour at Court, because he outwitted all the projectors who came near him. Having never known such another genius, I cannot but mention these particulars, among a multitude of others that I could produce." And Pepys, who had heard everybody, found Petty "the most rational man that ever he heard speak with a tongue."

GRAUNT'S LIFE.

John Graunt, the author of the "Natural and Political Observations upon the Bills of Mortality" was the son of Henry Graunt, a Hampshire man[1] but a citizen of London[2], who carried on the business of a draper at the sign of the Seven Stars in Birchin Lane. Of the eight children born to Henry Graunt and Mary, his wife, John, who first saw the light between seven and eight in the morning of April 24th, 1620, was probably the eldest[3]. While a boy he had been educated in English learning and he afterwards acquired Latin and French by studying mornings before shop-time. There is also some indication that he was not lacking in artistic tastes. He was apparently not only the friend of Samuel Cooper, the miniaturist[4], and of the portrait painter John Hayls[5], but he was also a collector himself. Pepys found his prints "indeed the best collection of anything almost that ever I saw, there being the prints of most of the greatest houses, churches and antiquitys in Italy and France, and brave cutts[6]." Graunt was bound apprentice to a haberdasher of small wares, and he mostly followed that trade, though free of the Drapers' Company. That he became a person of standing in his world we have ample assurance. He went through all the offices of the City as far as common council-man, bearing that office two years. He was known as a great peace-maker and was often chosen an arbitrator between disputing merchants. He had, before the completion of his thirtieth year, sufficient influence to secure for his friend Petty the professorship of

[1] Aubrey, *Brief Lives*, I. 271—274.

[2] *Register of St Michael, Cornhill* (*Harleian Society*), 33.

[3] His is the earliest recorded christening among the children of Henry Graunt. *Register*, 114; cf. pp. 114, 116, 117, 119, 121, 122, 239.

[4] Pepys's *Diary*, 2 Jan, 1662.

[5] Pepys, 26 April, 1668.

[6] Pepys, 20 April, 1663. "I had not time," he characteristically adds, "to look them over as I ought."

music at Gresham College[1], and at the time of the Fire he had become "an opulent merchant of London, of great weight and consideration in the city[2]." So much, in large part but inference, it is still possible to collect concerning the earlier career of John Graunt, citizen and draper. It is, however, to his "Observations upon the Bills of Mortality," first published in 1662, that Graunt owes whatever posthumous reputation he has attained, and the merit of that book is great enough to entitle him to wider fame than he has achieved.

Why Graunt began his examination of the London Bills, or when, we can but conjecture. He himself speaks of his studies with a certain lightness. Having engaged his thoughts, he knew not by what accident, upon the bills of mortality, he happened to make observations, for he designed them not, which have fallen out to be both political and natural[3]. Thus does Graunt insist, somewhat over-elaborately, upon the casualness of studies which must, in fact, have demanded both time and patience. In the appendix to the third edition, however, after the recognized success of the "Observations" had established their author's position in the scientific world, he speaks with more assurance of his "long and serious perusal of all the bills of mortality which this great city hath afforded for almost four score years[4]." This is certainly in strong contrast not only to the apologetic air of the original dedication, but also to the care with which, in the preface to the first edition, the tradesman-author excused himself, as it were, to the philosophers of Gresham College, for his presumption in invading the field of scientific investigation. He had observed that the weekly bills were put by those who took them in to little use other than to furnish a text to talk upon in the next company[5]; and he "thought that the Wisdom of our City had certainly designed the laudable practice of taking and distributing these Accompts for other and greater uses... or at least that some other uses might be made of them." It is probably to the latter suggestion, supplied perhaps by his friend Petty, and perhaps by Graunt's own "excellent working head," rather than to his belief in the prescience of the corporation of London that we owe the writing of the "Observations."

[1] Aubrey, II. 141; Ward, *Lives of the Professors of Gresham College*, 217.

[2] Fitzmaurice, 233.

[3] Graunt's Epistles dedicatory, pp. 320, 322.

[4] P. 398. [5] P. 333.

The preface to the first edition of the "Observations" is dated 25 January, 166½. They met apparently a favourable reception. Before they had been in print two months, Pepys, ever alert to hear some new thing, was buying a copy at Westminster Hall[1]. To others, as to him, they must have "appeared at first sight to be very pretty," for a new edition was called for within the year[2]. The greatest compliment however, which Graunt received on account of his book, and doubtless the compliment which he most appreciated, was his election into the Royal Society. The 5th February, 1662, fifty copies of the "Observations" were presented by Dr Whistler on behalf of the author to the "Society of Philosophers meeting at Gresham Colledg." The epistle dedicatory to their president, Sir Robert Moray, was at once read, whereupon thanks were ordered to be returned to Graunt, and he was proposed a candidate[3]. Bishop Sprat says that Graunt was recommended to the Royal Society—for as such the Society of Philosophers were presently incorporated—by no one less than the King himself, and that "in his election it was so far from being a prejudice that he was a shopkeeper of London, that His Majesty gave this particular charge to His Society, that if they found any more such tradesmen, they should be sure to admit them all, without any more ado[4]." The Society, however, seems to have had, even thus early in its history, a fitting sense of its own dignity. At any rate it took adequate precautions that Graunt be not admitted until his fitness for membership had been established beyond question. On the 12th February a formidable committee, composed of Sir William Petty, Dr Needham, Dr Wilkins, Dr Goddard, Dr Whistler, and Dr Ent, was appointed to examine the book. Their report is not preserved by Birch, but it must have been favourable, for 26th February Graunt was elected a fellow of the Society. In spite of his assertion, in the epistle dedicatory to Sir Robert Moray, that he was none of their number nor had the least ambition to be so[5], Graunt promptly accepted the election and subscribed his name at the next meeting of the Society[6]. His connection with the Royal Society appears to have been, on the whole, rather formal than vital. He was, indeed, for some five years after his election a frequent attendant at its meetings, he proposed

[1] *Diary*, 24 March, 1662.

[2] Cf. Bibliography.

[3] Birch, *History of the Society*, I. 75.

[4] Sprat, *History of the Royal Society*, 67.

[5] P. 324, post.

[6] Birch, I. 76—77.

one candidate, Sir John Portman, for election as a member, he served on several committees, and he was even a member of the Council of the Society from 30 Nov., 1664 to 11 April, 1666. He took, however, but small part in the scientific proceedings. Only once did he make a communication in any way similar to his "Observations," and in that communication[1], although he spoke of the rapid increase of carp by generation, what obviously interested him was not, as we might have expected, the increase of the fish in numbers, but rather their growth in size.

The disappearance of Graunt's name from the minutes of the Royal Society's meetings after 1666 must be accounted one of the results of his large losses by the Fire of London. Even with the substantial assistance of his devoted friend Petty[2], Graunt could not recover from the business reverses he then sustained. His conversion from protestantism to the Roman Catholic Church[3] seems also to have worked to his disadvantage in worldly matters, and his affairs went from bad to worse until his death, 18 April, 1674. He was buried in St Dunstan's church, Fleet Street. "A great number of ingeniose persons attended him to his grave. Among others, with teares, was that great ingeniose virtuoso, Sir William Petty."

Of the esteem in which John Graunt was held by his contemporaries we have sufficient evidence. His old acquaintance Richard Smith, the famous book-collector, esteemed him "an understanding man of quick witt and a pretty schollar[4]." Pepys, who also knew him well, considered his "most excellent discourses" well worth hearing[5]." Aubrey, who had found him "a pleasant facetious companion and very hospitable," declares that "his death was lamented

[1] Printed on p. 432.

[2] Fitzmaurice, 232—236. Cf. in the MS. called "Dr Petty's Register" in the Public Records Office at Dublin (1 C. 8c. 131, ff. 63—64), the articles, dated 10 Jan., 166 6/7, whereby Petty and Graunt jointly undertook to rebuild, at a cost of £12,000, nine burned houses on Petty's land in Lothbury. An indication of their earlier business relations is afforded by Petty's power of attorney, 6 March, 1660, to "my trusty friend, John Graunt," etc., among the Rawlinson MSS. (A. 174, ff. 319—325) at the Bodleian Library. It was perhaps upon Petty's recommendation that Ormond employed Graunt, in 1667, to collect Walloon weavers about Canterbury and remove them into Ireland. Carte, *Ormond*, II. 342.

[3] Aubrey, *loc. cit.* Graunt's conversion apparently antedated the Fire, though he may have been one of those whose change of faith was caused by it. Cf. p. xlv.

[4] Smith's *Obituary, ed. by Sir H. Ellis*, 102.

[5] *Diary*, 23 Jan., 1663, 11 Jan., 1664, 26 April, 1668.

by all good men that had the happinesse to knowe him[1]." And Anthony à-Wood, professing to give only "an exact history of all the bishops and writers who have had their education in the most antient and famous University of Oxford," goes out of his way to append to a sketch of Edward Grant, the classicist, an account of this man who owed his education to no university. The account begins with these enthusiastic words, "Now that I am got into the name of Grant I cannot without the guilt of concealment but let you know some things of the most ingenious person, considering his education and employment, that his time hath produced. ....The said John Graunt was an ingenious and studious person, generally beloved, was a faithful friend, a great peace-maker, and one that had often been chosen for his prudence and justness an arbitrator. But above all his excellent working head was much commended, and rather for this reason, that it was for the public good of learning, which is very rare in a trader or mechanic."

[1] *Brief Lives*, I. 273.

THE AUTHORSHIP OF THE NATURAL AND POLITICAL OBSERVATIONS UPON THE BILLS OF MORTALITY[1].

Concerning the authorship of the "Natural and Political Observations upon the Bills of Mortality" there seems at first to be no possibility of raising a question. Their title-page bears the name of Captain John Graunt, and the preface gives a plausible account of the manner in which he came to write them. At the time of their publication he was commonly reputed their author. Because of this repute he was elected a member of the Royal Society, and he accepted the membership. Such conduct by such a man would seem to leave no room for doubt that he was the author of the book issued under his name. There are, nevertheless, certain grounds for thinking that the book was in fact written not by Graunt, but by Sir William Petty. Persons who knew one or both of them have asserted that Petty was the author, and later writers[2] have added certain lines of argument to the same effect, based on internal evidence and on corroborative probabilities.

The first of Petty's friends to assert his authorship of the London Observations was John Evelyn.

In his diary, under date of March 22, 1675, Evelyn wrote:

Supp'd at S[r] William Petty's with the Bp of Salisbury and divers honorable persons. We had a noble entertainment in a house gloriously furnish'd; the master and mistress of it were extraordinary persons.... He is the author of the ingenious deductions from the bills of mortality, which go under the name of Mr Graunt; also of that useful discourse of

[1] By permission of the editors of the *Political Science Quarterly* I have here used in revised form a large part of an article upon the above-named subject, which was originally printed in Vol. XI. pp. 105—132 of that journal.

[2] Mr W. B. Hodge writing in the *Assurance Magazine*, VIII. 94, 234—237, (1859) and Dr W. L. Bevan in his *Sir William Petty, a study* (1894), have elaborated the arguments in favour of Petty. On the other hand Dr John Campbell (*Biographia Britannica*, IV. 2262—2263, note), McCulloch (*Literature of Political Economy*, 271), Roscher (*Zur Gesch. d. engl. Volkswirthschaftslehre im* 16 *und* 17 *Jahrh.*, 73, note), De Morgan (*Assurance Magazine*, VIII. 166, 167; *Budget of Paradoxes*, 68, 69), John (*Geschichte der Statistik*, 170), and Cunningham (*Growth of English Industry, Modern Times*, 247) have all decided for Graunt. But none of these writers has discussed the question thoroughly.

the manufacture of wool[1], and several others in the register of the Royal Society. He was also author of that paraphrase on the 104th Psalm in Latin verse[2], which goes about in MS. and is inimitable. In a word, there is nothing impenetrable to him.

The next witness for Petty—and also against him—is his intimate friend, John Aubrey, the antiquary. Aubrey assisted Anthony à-Wood in the compilation of his "Athenæ Oxonienses" by furnishing him a number of "minutes of lives[3]." From his letters to Wood concerning them[4], it appears that Aubrey began his sketch of Petty in February, 1680, and that shortly before March 27, "Sir W. P. perused my copie all over & would have all stand." The chaotic condition of Aubrey's notes[5] renders it impossible to say how much of the manuscript now in the Bodleian Library was approved by Petty; but it seems not improbable that Aubrey showed him folios 13 and 14, bringing the narrative down to Petty's departure for Ireland, 22 March, 1680. If so, we have Petty's approval of the statement (on folio 14) that he was elected professor in Gresham College by the interest of "his friend captaine John Graunt (who wrote the Observations on the Bills of Mortality)[6]." In June, 1680, Aubrey sent this manuscript to Wood[7], but he appears to have recalled it, about ten years later, for the purpose of making additions and corrections. To this later period at least a portion of the memoranda on folio 15 must be assigned, for one of them speaks of certain matters subsequent to Petty's death (1687) which have already escaped Aubrey's memory, It is not so clear that the very incomplete catalogue of Petty's writings on folio 15 was likewise added after the return of the manuscript to Aubrey, since there stand opposite two of the titles mentioned in it notes by Wood telling where copies of the books may be found. Still it is at least probable that this, like what immediately follows it on the same folio, was added by Aubrey after Petty had perused his copy all over. And the probability is heightened by the presence on folio 15 of an assertion directly contradictory to what Petty had approved in 1680. Near the end of the list of Petty's writings Aubrey writes, "Observations on the Bills of Mortality were really his."

The third witness for Petty is Edmund Halley. Halley was the most famous of English students of the Bills of Mortality, and the

[1] Bibliography, no. 28.
[2] Bibliography, no. 9, cf. p. xxviii.
[3] Cf. p. xiii.
[4] Ballard MS. XIV. ff. 126—132, Bodleian Library.
[5] See Mr Clark's description, *Brief Lives*, I. 4.
[6] *Brief Lives*, II. 141.
[7] *Ibid.*, I. 10—12.

vast results that have flowed from his "Estimate of the Degrees of Mortality of Mankind" predispose us to regard as authoritative anything that he may have said as to the work of his predecessors. It should be remembered, however, that Halley was a much younger man than Petty and did not become a member of the Royal Society until five years after Graunt's death. His famous memoir[1] begins with these words:

> The contemplation of the mortality of mankind has, besides the moral, its physical and political uses, both which have some time since been most judiciously considered by the curious Sir William Petty, in his moral and political Observations upon the Bills of Mortality of London, owned by Captain John Graunt. And since in a like treatise on the Bills of Mortality of Dublin....But the deductions from those bills of mortality seemed even to their authors [*sic*] to be defective.

Bishop Burnet, the fourth of Petty's contemporaries to assert his authorship of the Observations, had no such interest in them as did Halley; indeed his allusion to the subject is merely casual. In the first volume of his "History of his own Time," published in 1723, but probably written before 1705, he makes the charge[2] that Graunt, being a member of the New River Company, stopped the pipes at Islington the night before the London fire, September 2, 1666. Burnet's account of this alleged occurrence begins: "There was one Graunt, a papist, under whose name Sir William Petty published his observations on the bills of mortality."

Such is the direct testimony for Petty. The direct testimony in favour of Graunt comes from five sources. First, from the work whose authorship is in issue. Four editions of the "Observations" published during his lifetime and one published by Petty after Graunt's death, all bear on their title-pages Graunt's name as author. Second, Petty's own testimony in his books and in his private correspondence. In his acknowledged writings he mentions the Observations at least seventeen times[3]. In nine of these instances Graunt's name is mentioned, in seven he is not named, and in the remaining case, the "Political Arithmetick," as printed in 1690, makes Petty speak of "the observators upon the bills of mortality."

[1] *Philosophical Transactions*, no. 196 (1693), p. 596.

[2] Vol. I. p. 231. The charge against Graunt was thoroughly disproved by Bevil Higgons in his *Historical and Critical Remarks on Bishop Burnet's History of his own Time*, 149, and by Maitland, *History of London*, I. 435.

[3] Pp. 27, 45, 303, 458, 461, 481, 483, 485, 526, 527, 534, 535 (twice), 536, 541, 608, and in the *Discourse of Duplicate Proportion*, which justifies its double dedication by the example of "Graunt's" observations.

Since the "Political Arithmetick" was written in 1676, *i.e.*, before Petty's own "Observations upon the Dublin Bills," this expression might be construed as a claim by Petty to a share in the authorship of the "Observations" of 1662. But reference to the Southwell and the Rawlinson manuscripts of the "Political Arithmetick" in the Bodleian Library, bearing Petty's autograph corrections, shows conclusively that he here intended to set up no such claim[1]. Moreover, in a private letter, to his most intimate friend and relative, Sir Robert Southwell (August 20, 1681), Petty twice speaks of "Graunt's" and once of "our friend Graunt's" book[2].

In contrast with Petty's direct testimony to Graunt's authorship of the London "Observations" stands the title-page of his statistical firstling, the Dublin "Observations" (1683), which reads "By the Observator on the London Bills of Mortality[3]." This might be construed as claiming the London Observations for Petty, but an explanation at least equally plausible would make it a mere bookseller's trick of Mark Pardoe[4], the publisher, to commend the Dublin "Observations" to a public that had recently greeted a fifth edition of the London "Observations" with favour. The device, if such it were, appears to have failed, for Pardoe had sheets of the Dublin "Observations" still on hand in 1686, and when he reissued them, with additions, as a "Further Observation on the Dublin Bills," Petty's name appeared[5] on the title-page, without any mention of the London "Observations." Nor did the change occur here alone. In the first (1683) edition of "Another Essay in Political Arithmetick. By Sir William Petty," the original Dublin "Observations" are advertised as "by the Observator on the London Bills of Mortality." In the second edition of the Essay, published in 1686, but before the "Further Observation," the advertisement of the original Dublin "Observations" reads: "By Sir William Petty[6]."

Contemporary testimony in favour of Graunt comes, thirdly, from the Royal Society and from various members of it. The circumstances of his election have been recounted in the preceding section[7]. The opinion of the Society and of its historian as there

[1] See pp. 303, 236, 237.

[2] Rawlinson MS., A. 178, ff. 71—72, Bodleian Library. See also Petty's letter of 4 Feby., 1663, to Lord Brouncker printed on page 398.

[3] See facsimile, p. 479. [4] P. 480. [5] See p. 493.

[6] These advertisements were not included in the present reprint of *Another Essay*, pp. 451—478, post.

[7] P. xxxvi.

expressed was later confirmed by its Secretary. During the Plague[1] Oldenburg wrote from London:

Though we had some abatement in our last week's bill, yet we are much afraid it will run as high this week as ever. Mr Graunt, in his appendix to his Observations upon those bills (now reprinted) takes notice, that forasmuch as the people of London have, from Anno 1625 to this time, increased from eight to thirteen, so the mortality shall not exceed that of 1625, except the burials should exceed 8400 per week[2].

The case for Graunt is further strengthened by the testimony of John Bell, clerk of the Company of Parish Clerks[3]. The author of the "Observations" asserts[4] that he visited the hall of the Parish Clerks, and used their records in the preparation of his book. Bell, therefore, who was in charge of the Clerks' register, could scarcely have been deceived as to his identity. Now in *London's Remembrancer*, after explaining and defending the manner in which the bills of mortality were prepared by the Company of Parish Clerks, Bell proceeds:

I think I need not trouble myself herein [*i.e.*, in describing the form of the bills], since that worthy and ingenious Gentleman, Captain John Graunt, in his Book of Natural and Political Observations on the Bills of Mortality, hath already so well described them.

The last of the witnesses in the case is Sir Peter Pett. Born, probably, in 1627, a member of Oxford University while Petty was there, a charter fellow of the Royal Society, Pett was a life-long friend of Sir William[5], and it is probable that he knew Graunt also[6]. In 1688 Pett published a folio volume designed to vindicate the Earl of Anglesey from the charge of being a Roman Catholic[7]. This gigantic pamphlet discusses many matters not germane to the charge

[1] About the same time the Society reaffirmed its judgment by ordering the reprinting of "the Observations upon the Bills of Mortality by Mr John Graunt." See p. 314.

[2] Oldenburg to Boyle, 18 Sept., 1665, Boyle's *Works*, VI. 194.

[3] Concerning Bell, see p. lxxx.

[4] P. 333.

[5] Fitzmaurice, 248—250.

[6] Carte, *Ormond*, II. 342, cf. p. xxxvii. In mentioning the employment of Graunt to collect weavers in England and remove them thence to Ireland with a view to establishing there the manufacture of Norwich stuffs, as recommended in a memorial which Sir Peter Pett had presented to Ormond, Carte describes Graunt as "a man well known by his observations on the bills of mortality." Carte wrote about 1735.

[7] *The Happy Future State of England*, London: 1688. *Anon.*

against Anglesey, and among them England's growth in population. In the course of the discussion Pett alludes four times to the London "Observations," but without mentioning the name of either Petty or Graunt:

If any of our monkish historians . . . had given the world rational estimates of the numbers of . . . the males then between the years of 16 and 60 [from the military returns] . . . we might now easily by the help we have from the Observator on the Bills of Mortality conclude, what the entire number of the people then was. [Page 91.]

'T is very remarkable that in the Code Louys which he [Louis XIV.] published in April, 1667, he made some ordinances with great care for the registring the christenings and marriages and burials, in each Parish . . . having perhaps been informed by his ministers that many political inferences, as to the knowing the number of people and their encrease in any state, are to be made from the bills of mortality, on the occasion of some such published about 3 years before by the Observator on the Bills of Mortality in England. [Pages 248—249.]

It must be acknowledged that the thanks of the age are due to the Observator on the Bills of Mortality, for those solid and rational calculations he hath brought to light, relating to the numbers of our people: but such is the modesty of that excellent author that I have often heard him wish that a thing of so great publick importance to be certainly known, might be so by an actual numbering of them. . . . Mr James Howel . . . saith, that in the year 1636 . . . the Lord Mayor of London . . . took occasion to make a cense of all the people and that there were of men, women and children, above 7 hundred thousand that lived within the barrs of his jurisdiction alone . . . and . . . more now . . . But I am to suspect that there was no such return in the year 1636 . . . and do suppose that Mr Howel did in that point mistake . . . partly because I find it mentioned by the curious Observator on the Bills of Mortality, p. 113 and 114 [of the 1676 ed.] that anno 1631, ann. 7 Caroli I. the number of men, women and children in the several wards of London and liberties . . . came in all to but 130178, and finally because the said curious Observator (for that name I give that author after My Lord Chief Justice Hales [*sic*] hath given or adjudged it to him in his Origination of Mankind) having by rational calculations proved that there dyes within the Bills of Mortality a thirtieth part, or one in thirty yearly, and that there dies there 22000 per annum. . . . If there were there according to Howel a million and a half people, it would follow that there must dye but 1 out of 70 per annum. [Pages 112–113.]

We are told by the Observator on the Bills of Mortality, that anxiety of mind hinders Breeding, and from sharp anxieties of divers kinds hath the Protestant Religion rescued English minds. [Page 119.]

In these passages from Pett two peculiarities need to be explained. The first is the omission of Petty's name. If Pett regarded Petty as the author of the "Observations," why should he consistently omit to mention him here as "Sir W. P."—a form of reference which he repeatedly uses when speaking elsewhere of Petty's other works[1]? The second fact to be explained is Pett's manifest desire to avoid mentioning by name "that excellent author," "the most curious Observator." It certainly is not by chance that Pett, whose laborious book is a medley of duly credited extracts from almost all English and classical literature, instead of mentioning the author of the "Observations," here carefully took refuge behind a quotation—or rather a misquotation[2]—from Sir Matthew Hale. I believe that Pett's peculiar course at this point can be best explained on the assumption that he considered Graunt the author of the work. He was attempting, at a time when Oates' absurd stories of the popish plot were still heartily believed[3], to vindicate Anglesey from the charge of leaning towards Roman Catholicism. He was therefore careful not to betray any sympathy with the Romanists. Now according to Wood, when Graunt had been a major two or three years, he

> then laid down his trade and all public employments upon account of religion. For though he was puritanically bred, and had several years taken sermon-notes by his most dextrous and incomparable faculty in short-writings and afterwards did profess himself for some time a Socinian, yet in his later days he turned Roman Catholic, in which persuasion he zealously lived for some time and died.

May not this explain Pett's obvious unwillingness to praise the author of the "Observations," Graunt, by name? Pett does not afford demonstration, but he furnishes corroboration.

The second line of argument includes all appeals to internal evidence, whether advanced by supporters of Graunt or of Petty. Here again the supporters of Petty shall speak first. Between parts of the "Observations" and portions of his acknowledged writings

[1] Pp. 92, 106, 122, 192, 193, 245, and pp. 1 and 27 of the preface.

[2] Hale's *Primitive Origination of Mankind*, published in 1677, the year after his death, was probably written before 1670. The passages (pp. 205, 206, 213, 237) which allude, with warm praise, to the London *Observations*, do not, so far as I can see, give or adjudge the name of Observator to the author at all. Hale quotes the title of "this little book," but makes no mention of its author.

[3] He began to write in 1680 though his book was not published until 1688. Cf. pp. 1, 2 and 5 of *The Future Happy State*.

they find numerous similarities so striking as to constitute, in the opinion of Dr Bevan, an effective way of testing the question of authorship[1]. An examination of these parallel passages reveals their very unequal significance for the present discussion. For example, the remark in both the London "Observations" and the "Treatise of Taxes" concerning the causes of the westward growth of London cannot be used to establish their common authorship, John Evelyn having set the idea afloat in the preceding year[2]. In like manner the talk about equalizing the parishes was a current commonplace of the Restoration[3]. On the other hand the remaining parallels, especially that between Graunt's Conclusion (pp. 395—397, post) and various passages in Petty's writings, are doubtless important.

In addition to these parallel passages, other bits of internal evidence have been adduced by the supporters of Petty. "The most notable thing in the first few pages of the 'Bills,'" says Dr Bevan, "is the amount of space devoted to a description of different diseases. They are described with a familiarity and precision which only a physician could be expected to have[4]." Upon a layman the discussions in chapters two and three of the similarities between rickets and liver-growth, and between the green sickness, stopping of the stomach, mother, and rising of the lights, undoubtedly make a learned impression. Whether they were in fact the discussions of a learned or of an ignorant man, a specialist

[1] Bevan, *Petty*, 44. The similar passages discovered in previous discussions of this subject, together with a few others upon which I had chanced, were printed in parallel columns in my article in the *Political Science Quarterly*, XI. 118—122. The passages in question may be found in this edition by comparing the following pages and lines:

in the London "Observations"	in Petty's Writings.
p. 321, l. 6, 7, p. 380, l. 30—33, p. 381, l. 8, 13—15.	p. 41, l. 22—31.
p. 353, l. 1—23.	p. 29, l. 24—29, p. 30, l. 9—10, p. 31, l. 8—14, p. 83, l. 12—17, p. 118, l. 1—6.
p. 377, l. 14—17, 35—38.	p. 25, l. 15—18, p. 68, l. 22—26.
p. 382, l. 20—22.	p. 23, l. 23, p. 24, l. 36.
p. 395, l. 30—p. 397, l. 9.	p. 49, l. 28—p. 50, l. 9, p. 49, l. 6—10, p. 52, l. 33—p. 53, l. 4, p. 34, l. 26—28, p. 26, l. 33—p. 27, l. 4, p. 270, l. 14—21.

[2] See his *Fumifugium* (1661), p. 16, and cf. pp. 41, 380, 381, post.

[3] Cf. p. 5, note.

[4] Bevan, *Petty*, 46; cf. pp. post, 346—363.

in the history of English medicine before Sydenham could probably say. But one need not be a medical antiquarian to see that, in the most elaborate of these discussions, the one concerning rickets and liver growth, and indeed, throughout all the discussions of this sort, the method of the writer of the "Observations" is distinctly statistical, is marked, indeed, by considerable statistical acuteness, and is scarcely at all diagnostic or pathological, as a physician's method, nowadays at any rate, would probably be. He enquires whether the same disease has been returned in different years under different rubrics; and he finds his answer by investigating the fluctuations from year to year in the number of deaths from each. Moreover, it is in the midst of these discussions of diseases that the variations in the number of those who died of rickets from year to year provokes this curious passage:

> Now, such back-startings seem to be universal in all things; for we do not only see in the progressive motion of wheels of *Watches*, and in the rowing of *Boats*, that there is a little starting or jerking backwards between every step forwards, but also (if I am not much deceived) there appeared the like in the motion of the *Moon*, which in the long *Telescopes* at *Gresham College* one may sensibly discern. [Page 358 post.]

De Morgan points out[1] the improbability that "that excellent machinist, Sir William Petty, who passed his day among the astronomers," should attribute to the motion of the moon in her orbit all the tremors which she gets from a shaky telescope[2].

Other peculiarities of the "Observations" which are held by Dr Bevan to indicate Petty's authorship are the "references to Ireland derived apparently from personal observation," and the fact that "Hampshire, Petty's native county, is the only English county mentioned." The latter inference might have been made much stronger for Petty. The author of the "Observations" bases many of his most interesting conclusions upon a comparison between the tables of London mortality and the "Table of a Country Parish," and this country table is unquestionably derived from the parish register of the Abbey of St Mary and St Ethelfleda, at Romsey, the

[1] *Budget of Paradoxes*, 68; *Assurance Magazine*, VIII. 167.

[2] Mr Hodge replies: "The paragraph objected to stands unaltered in the fifth edition, edited by Petty, and the question naturally arises, how came he to publish as an editor that which, it is asserted, he must have known to be so grossly absurd that it is impossible he could have published it as a writer?" *Assurance Magazine*, VIII. 235, 236. This is ingenious, but fallacious. The fifth edition is a mere reprint and in no sense a revision.

church in which Petty's baptism is recorded and in which he lies buried[1]. But the fact by no means implies Petty's authorship of the "Observations." It is not less reasonable to suppose that Graunt, when studying the London bills, applied to Petty for such comparative material as he afterwards sought from four other friends in various parts of England[2]. As for the allusions to Ireland, they indicate rather that the author had not been in that kingdom at all than that he had made personal observations there. One of them is a casual remark in connection with his belief that deaths in child-bed are abnormally frequent "in these countries where women hinder the facility of their child-bearing by affected straitening of their bodies... What I have heard of the Irish women confirms me herein[3]." In the other passage the author says "I have heard,...I have also heard" this and that about Ireland[4].

Those who have agreed that Graunt was the author of the "Observations," need not leave to their opponents the exclusive use of internal evidence. They, for their part, may first point out that there are considerable differences of language between Petty's works and Graunt's[5]. Every one at all familiar with seventeenth-century English pamphlets has sympathized with Sir Thomas Browne's solicitude lest "if elegancy still proceedeth, and English pens maintain that stream, which we have of late observed to flow from many, we shall within few years be fain to learn Latin to understand English." Petty's "Reflections" and his "Treatise of Taxes and Contributions" are of about the same size as the "Observations." I have run through all three and counted the Latin words, phrases and quotations, excluding those which, like *anno*, *per annum*, *per centum*, are virtually English. The "Reflections," in the 154 pages which are indisputably by Petty[6], contain at least twenty-four Latin phrases, the "Treatise" at least forty-two. The "Observations" show, aside from the sentiment on the title-page, but six Latin phrases; and of the six, three are within as many pages of the "Conclusion" (pages 395—397, post) in precisely the passage which exhibits the

1 See pp. 412, note, 388, 400.
2 See p. 399.
3 P. 361, 362.
4 P. 396.
5 Dr Bevan (p. 44) would dissent: "It is difficult to discover any great diversity in style, language, or in any other point between the 'Bills' and Petty's authentic writings."
6 The letters ostensibly addressed to Petty were probably written by him, but, to be on the safe side, I excluded them. Cf. Fitzmaurice, 92.

most conspicuous of all the parallels between the "Observations" and the "Treatise[1]."

The supporters of Graunt may properly claim, in the second place—and upon this they may insist, since heretofore it has not received adequate emphasis—that the statistical method of the "Observations" is greatly superior to the method of Petty's acknowledged writings upon similar subjects. Graunt exhibits a patience in investigation, a care in checking his results in every possible way, a reserve in making inferences, and a caution about mistaking calculation for enumeration, which do not characterize Petty's work to a like degree. This difference cannot escape any person of statistical training who may read carefully first the "Observations" and then Petty's "Essays."

In the third place, it deserves to be noted that the chief parallels to Petty's writings do not occur in parts of the "Observations" which are vital or organic. In his patient investigations of the movement of London's population, imperfect and frequently erroneous though they were, and, for lack of data, necessarily must have been, the author of the "Observations" displays admirable traits for which Petty's writings, however meritorious otherwise, may still be searched in vain. The passages in which the parallels occur are, as it were, the embroideries with which Graunt's solid work is decorated—possibly by Petty's hand. For example, the passage concerning beggars and charity in Holland[2] is appended to the contention that, since "of the 229,250, which have died, we find not above fifty-one to have been starved, except helpless infants at nurse," therefore there can be no "want of food in the country, or of means to get it." The argument is statistical; the appended passage about beggars is not. It has no real connection, and if it were omitted, the argument proper would lose nothing of its cogency. The longest and closest parallel between the "Observations" and the "Treatise" is of like character. It occurs in and indeed pervades "The Conclusion." And this conclusion, instead of offering, as one might expect, a sober summary in the style of the book itself[3],

[1] Mr Higgs has pointed out also (*Economic Journal*, v. 72) that Graunt feared London was "too big," whereas Petty wished it still bigger. Cf. pp. 320, 470—476, post.

[2] P. 353.

[3] The similarity in style of the conclusion to Petty's writings, and its dissimilarity to the earlier parts of the *Observations* is noted by Mr Hodge, *Assurance Magazine*, VIII. 235.

is an obvious and, one must own, a not altogether unsuccessful attempt "to write wittily about these matters[1]."

The third group of arguments—those based upon the probabilities of the case—should be considered as corroborative, rather than as of independent weight. In advancing them the partisans of each writer must seek to strengthen a case already built up by direct testimony and internal evidence rather than to establish their contentions *ab initio*[1]. In general, the probabilities strongly favour Graunt. In the first place, he was a citizen and a native of London. He thus had opportunity to collect the bills and incentive to study them; and the author's account of the way in which he came to make the study tallies in every particular with the known facts of Graunt's life. Petty, on the other hand, was of provincial birth, and had been a resident of London but a short time when the "Observations" were published. In the second place, the "Observations" are not the product of a few leisure hours, or even of a few hurried weeks. Their laborious compilation demanded time—how much, those will best appreciate who have attempted similar tasks. Graunt may well have had the necessary leisure, whereas Petty, in defending his Irish survey, in writing for the Royal Society, and in working for political self-advancement at the Restoration, must have been otherwise well occupied during the years 1660 and 1661[3]. In the third place, the assumption that a man of Graunt's standing in the city would consent to be a screen for Petty's book, has never been put upon a sound basis, or indeed upon any basis at all. Finally it may be noted that the "Observations" contained nothing offensive[4]; they were not only novel, but popular, and it was by no means Petty's nature to refuse credit for a good thing which he had done[5]. Nevertheless the "Observations" had been out almost fifteen years, had passed through four editions, and had received unusual honours at the hands of the Royal Society, and apparently of the king also, before there was a whisper of Petty's authorship.

Opposed to these probabilities in favour of Graunt stand two analogous arguments for Petty. One argument Dr Bevan advances:

[1] P. 397.

[2] McCulloch and Roscher take the contrary course.

[3] Cf. pp. xx—xxiv.

[4] Cf. Shelburne's dedication of the 1690 edition of the *Political Arithmetick*, p. 240.

[5] His *Treatise* was indeed published anonymously, but when it succeeded, its authorship soon became known.

"We are not able to assign a reason for Petty's wish to conceal his authorship under the name of a friend, but we do know that several of his works were published anonymously during his lifetime." It need scarcely be said that publishing a book anonymously is a different thing from publishing it under the name of somebody else—and that somebody a well-known man. The other argument is put by Mr Hodge in these words:

> If I were disposed to argue the matter upon probabilities, I might ask what other proof Graunt gave of his capacity for writing such a work. . . . It is certainly strange, if Graunt were the man, that he should have stopped short after having made such a remarkable step. Of Petty's abilities for dealing with the subject it is unnecessary to speak[1].

The argument that Graunt cannot have written one book because he did not write a second[2], is scarcely of a cogency sufficient to prevail against the favourable opinion of those who knew him. Aubrey had a very high opinion of his abilities, and Pepys, who seems also to have known him well, accepted his authorship without the slightest hesitation.

To sum up the whole discussion: The "Observations" were published over Graunt's name. Everything about them, as well as everything known of his life, was consistent with the assumption that he wrote them; he had the incentive, the opportunity, the time, and in the opinion of his contemporaries the ability. The book was at once accepted by intelligent people as his, and unusual honours were bestowed upon him. Until after his death (1673) he was generally esteemed the author of the work. Between 1675 and 1705, however, four persons attributed the book to Petty; and later writers have pointed out striking resemblances between passages in the "Observations" and passages in Petty's avowed writings. It is substantially upon the testimony of Evelyn and of Aubrey and upon these similarities, that the whole case for Petty rests. Before we can admit Petty's authorship we must be convinced that Graunt and Petty, aided and abetted by Bell, were parties to a singularly purposeless[3] conspiracy whereby, with remarkable shrewdness in

[1] *Assurance Magazine*, VIII. 236.

[2] In fact he did write "Observations on the Advance of the Excise," but they were never printed. Aubrey, I. 273.

[3] Mr Hodge says: "It is not necessary for us to determine what could have been Petty's object in making such an arrangement,—whether it was for some

covering their tracks and giving to their fraud the appearance of truth, they deceived not only the general public but also their intimates in the Royal Society. Does the evidence adduced for Petty so far outweigh the evidence for Graunt as to convince us that they were guilty of this contemptible conduct? If not, can the direct testimony for Petty, and the similarities noted, be explained without conceding the authorship of the "Observations" to him? I believe that they can be so explained.

In view of Evelyn, Aubrey's second statement and the parallel passages on one hand, and of the strong evidence for Graunt on the other, it seems almost certain that neither Graunt nor Petty was the exclusive author of all parts of the "Observations," as we have them. There is, moreover, competent authority for this view. Anthony à-Wood, speaking of Petty's "Observations on the Dublin Bills," published in 1683, says: "He also long before assisted or put into a way John Graunt in the writing of his Nat. and Pol. Observations on the Bills of Mortality of London." And in his sketch of Graunt, Aubrey says: "He wrote *Observations on the bills of Mortality* very ingeniosely (but I believe, and partly know, that he had his hint from his intimate and familiar friend Sir William Petty)." That is to say, Graunt and Petty collaborated. But the character of their collaboration was rather complementary than coöperative. They were not, properly speaking, joint authors. The essential and valuable part of the "Observations" seems to be Graunt's. Petty perhaps suggested the subject of the inquiry, he probably assisted Graunt with comments upon medical and other questions here and there; he procured the figures from Romsey for the "Table of the Country Parish;" and he may have revised, or even written, the Conclusion, and possibly, also, the curious "epistle dedicatory to Sir Robert Moray," commending the book and its author to the Royal Society. Such assistance constituted authorship neither in Petty's mind nor in the mind of any one else. But after he had perhaps assisted in the enlargement of the third edition, and had prepared for the press a fifth edition, again enlarged, of the ever-popular "Observations," he for the time being persuaded himself that he was their virtual author. After a few years he thought better of it, and assigned the honour to Graunt, to whom it rightfully

personal convenience or advantage to himself or to gain a reputation for Graunt." (*Assurance Magazine*, Vol. VIII. p. 235.) To be sure it is not necessary; but does not absence of motive justify doubt as to the fact?

belonged. All this seems, I am aware, an elaborate edifice of shaky conjecture. I hope so to shore it up with chronological props that it may present at least the appearance of stability.

The fifth edition of the "Observations" is dated "London, 1676." Now Evelyn gave the earliest intimation of a Pettian authorship after supping at Petty's house in 1675. In 1680 Aubrey, in an account perused by Petty, assigned the "Observations" to Graunt, and in his life of Graunt asserted that they were done by him upon a hint from Petty. In or about 1682 Petty himself included "Observations on the Bills of Mortality of London, 1660" in a chronological list of his several works since 1636[1]. Subsequently Aubrey also asserted that they were "really" Petty's. These are, strictly speaking, the only direct testimonies for Petty's authorship of the London "Observations." As already noted, Halley and Burnet were less intimate with Petty, and what they say is of little independent weight. Meanwhile Petty, if indeed he had ever publicly held himself out as the author of the London "Observations," appears to have repented. The title-page and advertisement of 1683, indirectly attributing that book to him, were altered at the first opportunity to a form consistent with what seem to be the facts, and when he has occasion, in his later works, to mention the "Observations," he repeatedly speaks of them as Graunt's, although he specifically cites the fifth edition, in which his share was larger than in either of the others. In short, the "Observations upon the Bills of Mortality of London" are essentially Graunt's work, and he deserves the credit for them. Petty probably made contributions to the book which may have helped to bring it to popular, and even to scientific notice, but he added little, if anything, to its real merits. He edited it in 1676 with further additions, and for a while perhaps caused or allowed it to be supposed that he was the author. Subsequently he corrected the error.

The general conclusion thus reached makes Graunt in every proper sense the author of the "Observations." This conclusion is by no means new. But those who have held it have not hitherto explained the countervailing testimony for Petty; nor can it be explained save by a chronological examination of the evidence. Consequently one party has accepted Evelyn and Aubrey's second statement, while the other party has ignored them. The attempt here made to explain the testimony for Petty without forgetting the

[1] Fitzmaurice, 317; reprinted in supplement to Bibliography, post.

stronger testimony for Graunt seeks to correlate the facts and to harmonize the probabilities more completely than has heretofore seemed possible. The opinion that Graunt, and not Petty, was really the author of the "Observations," I hope thus to have raised in the minds even of readers who do not forget Evelyn and Aubrey, to the grade of probability, if not to that of demonstration[1].

[1] A large part of this section was originally printed in the *Political Science Quarterly*, XI. 105—132, and is here used, in revised form, by permission of the editors of that journal.

PETTY'S LETTERS AND OTHER MANUSCRIPTS.

By long-continued activity Petty had accumulated, as he discovered with chagrin when preparing for final departure from Ireland, no less than fifty-three chests[1] of papers of one sort and another. To be sure many of the papers relating to the Down Survey, which must have stuffed a goodly row of chests, were rather prepared under his direction than written by his pen, and it is probable that further chests relating to his estates, and to the Irish revenues were among the fifty-three. But enough is known of his habits in writing to warrant the inference that a number of the chests were likewise filled with manuscripts of his own production. While he was still a young man it had become his habit, when entering upon any weighty undertaking, "to meditate and fill a quire with all that could in nature be objected and to write down his answer to each. So that when any new thing started, he was prepared, as it were extempore, to shoot them dead." During the busy days of the surveys in Ireland, "his way was to retire early to his lodgings where his supper was only a handful of raisins and a piece of bread. He would bid one of his clerks, who wrote a fair hand, go to sleep, and while he eat his raisins and walked about he would dictate to the other, who was a ready man at shorthand. When this was fitted to his mind the other was roused and set to work, and he went to bed, so that next morning all was ready[2]." By no means all the manuscripts which Petty must have prepared are now in existence. Many of those relating to the Irish Surveys were destroyed by the fire at the Council office in Essex Street in 1711[3], and others have been lost in ways not so easy to trace. But a considerable fraction

[1] Fitzmaurice, 292.

[2] Addl. MS. 21,128, f°. 441.

[3] See p. 178, note. It was formerly supposed that all had been lost, but the diligence of Mr W. H. Hardinge has brought a number of maps and papers to light.

remains, comprising both letters and manuscripts that have proved of value in preparing this edition of Petty's economic writings.

Of Petty's letters several hundred are extant and parts of some six score are in print. They range in date from his nineteenth year to the month of his death and touch upon a great variety of subjects. The earliest are addressed to Dr John Pell[1] and are concerned with Petty's pursuits as a student on the continent. Later he corresponded with Boyle[2] and Hartlib as to his plans for education and for a history of trades, and after the Restoration he sent a number of letters to the Royal Society concerning his double-bottomed ship and other topics[3]. His interest in shipping led also to a prolonged correspondence with Pepys, and among others to whom letters by him are known there may be mentioned Henry Cromwell, Ormond, Anglesey, Sir Peter Pett and John Aubrey[4]. It was, however with his wife's kinsman, Sir Robert Southwell[5], that Petty carried on his

[1] Pell was born at Southwick in Sussex, 11 March, 1611. He graduated B.A. at Cambridge in 1628 and in 1643 he succeeded Hortensius in the chair of mathematics at Amsterdam, where Petty made his acquaintance. The letters to him, dated 14 Aug., 1644, 8 Sept., 1644, and 8 Oct., 1645, are in the British Museum (Lansdowne MS. 4279) and are printed in Halliwell's *Collection of Letters illustrative of the Progress of Science in England*, pp. 81, 90.

[2] Brit. Mus. Addl. MS. 6193, f. 70—72, printed in Boyle's *Works*, VI. 136—140.

[3] These letters are dated 1662 or 1663 and are addressed either to Brouncker, the president, or to Sir Robert Moray, the secretary of the Royal Society; or to Graunt: Royal Society's Letter book, P. 1. f. 11—33, cf. Halliwell's *Catalogue of MS. Letters in the possession of the R. S.*, 143, also p. 398 note, post.

[4] Some of the later letters to Pepys, dated 1683—1687, are in the Bodleian Library, Rawlinson MSS. A. 189, f. 17—19, A. 190, f. 21, cf. pp. 546, 547, post; others are in the possession of J. Eliot Hodgkin, Esq., of Richmond on the Thames. *Fifteenth Report, Hist. MSS. Comm.*, pt. 2, p. 181. To Cromwell, in the British Museum, Lansdowne MS. 823; to Ormond at Kilkenny Castle (*3rd Rept. Hist. MSS. Comm.*, 429, *4th Rept.*, 551, *7th Rept.*, 742); to Anglesey in the Bodleian Library (Rawlinson MS. A. 185, f. 219—a copy, the original is probably at Longleat, cf. *3rd Rept.*, 199); to Pett at Bowood (Fitzmaurice, 249); to Aubrey in the Bodleian (Aubrey MS. II. f. 100—104).

[5] Southwell was born 31 Dec., 1635, at Battin Warwick on the river Bandon, near Kinsale, where his father was collector of customs. After graduating B.A. at Oxford University, reading for a time in Lincoln's Inn and travelling for two years on the continent, he returned to London in 1661. In Sept., 1664, he was named a clerk of the Privy Council and displayed much method and diligence in that office. Between November, 1665 and August 1669, he was twice envoy to Portugal where he negotiated the Treaty of Lisbon. The following ten years, save the brief period of his mission to Brussels, he passed in London. In

most active correspondence. His business affairs, his domestic afflictions, his political aspirations, every act and thought of his last twenty years found a reflection in the hundreds of letters which he showered upon his faithful cousin. It was the life-long habit of that much-enduring man to preserve every scrap of writing that came into his possession, and though he did not hesitate to reprove Petty's aggressive self-confidence[1], he had nevertheless an unusually high regard for all that his outspoken kinsman said or did. Soon after the completion of the "Political Arithmetick," of which Petty gave him a copy in MS.[2], Southwell wrote of "an ebony cabinet wherein I keep as in an archive all the effects of your pen; for I look on them as materials fit for those I would take most care of and hope they will hand them over with like estimation[3]." During Petty's contest for the farm of the Irish revenues[4] Southwell asked for the papers he had delivered in, "for I shrine up all and premise that in after times I shall be resorted to for your works as Mr Hedges[5] is for the true Opobalsamum[6]." Four years later he renewed the assurance of his care: "as to your fifty years' adventures I have them and keep them more preciously than Cæsar's commentaries[7]"; and within a fortnight after Petty's death he set out to secure such MSS. of his friend as were not already in his possession, writing to Pepys the 23rd December, 1687, for a paper which Petty had lately

December, 1679, he resigned his clerkship of the reorganized Privy Council and soon retired to his seat at King's Weston, near Bristol, where he really congratulated himself upon proving no favourite of his neighbours, as he much preferred philosophy before drinking. Letter to Petty, 28 Nov., 1681, Thorpe's Catalogue (1834), no. 710. In spite of this sentiment Smith's *Life, Journals and Correspondence of Pepys*, I. 282, makes Southwell declare that his health was worn out by long sitting at the sack bottle! What the poor man wrote was "inck bottle." Cf. Macray, *Annals of the Bodleian*, 2nd ed., 236. After the Revolution he was for a time Secretary of State for Ireland. He died at King's Weston, 11 September, 1702. The condition of Southwell's papers now in the British Museum, as well as the orderly letter-books of the Royal Society during the period of his presidency (1690—1695) give sufficient evidence of his methodical habits.

[1] Fitzmaurice, 175, 283—284.

[2] Pp. 237—238 post.

[3] Southwell to Petty, Aug. or Sept., 1677, Thorpe, *loc. cit.*

[4] Cf. pp. xxix, and 438, post.

[5] Perhaps Dr Nathaniel Hodges (1629—1688) the physician who remained in London during the great plague.

[6] Same to Same, 11 Sept., 1682, Thorpe, *loc. cit.*, cf. Fitzmaurice, 292.

[7] Same to Same, Nov., 1686, Fitzmaurice, 292.

lent him[1]. Sir Robert's collection of letters and papers, including those from Petty for which he had promised such pious care, remained in his family and was apparently kept intact until 1834 when, upon the death of his descendant Lord De Clifford they were all sent to the auction block[2]. Of the letters by Petty thus brought to light, the greater part were bid in by Thomas Thorpe[3], who subsequently sold them to the third Marquis of Lansdowne to be added to the collection at Bowood. The amount of light which Petty's letters, especially those to Southwell, are capable of throwing upon his writing as well as upon the circumstances of his life, may be inferred from the use made of them by Lord Edmond Fitzmaurice. By his kind intervention, I received from the Marquis of Lansdowne generous permission to consult the Petty correspondence at Bowood; but the necessity of returning to the United States unfortunately prevented my making use of the privilege. The letters, however, are printed with much fulness in the "Life of Petty" by Lord Edmond Fitzmaurice, and he assured me that they contain nothing bearing upon his economic writings beyond what has already been given to the public.

The preservation of excellent manuscript copies of Petty's most important economic works is likewise due to Southwell. Inasmuch as some of the pamphlets were printed in London while Petty himself was in Ireland[4], and others, including the "Political Anatomy" and the authorized version of the "Political Arithmetick," were first issued after his death, a number of gross errors which he doubtless would have removed, were allowed to stand in the published versions[5]. The printer of the "Reflections upon some

[1] *Fifteenth Rept. Hist. MSS. Comm.*, pt. II. p. 181.

[2] *Catalogue of a very Important and Highly interesting Collection of MSS., State Papers and Autograph Letters, received by Sir Robert Southwell while Clerk of the Privy Council* [*etc.*], *the Property of Lord De Clifford deceased.* Sold by Messrs Christie, Feby. 11, 1834. The principal papers by Petty are entered as lots 261, 290—304, 597—600.

[3] *State Papers: Catalogus Librorum MSS. Bibliothecæ Southwellianæ now on sale by Thomas Thorpe*, 1834, pp. 399—409. A few of Petty's letters were bought by the British Museum, and 32 of them, dated from January to September, 1686, fell to a Mr Cockran of London. At the sale of Mr Austin Cooper's library at Dublin in 1831, the same Mr Cockran, apparently, bought a number of Petty's papers relating to the Down Survey. *Notes and Queries*, 2nd series, viii. 130. I have not been able to find any further trace of these papers.

[4] Cf. pp. 4, 238.

[5] *E.g.* on pp. 103, 136—138, 142, 188, 259, 273, 277, etc.

Persons and Things in Ireland"[1] frankly confesses that, not being acquainted with the island wherein the copy of that discourse was written, he was forced to guess at many interlined and imperfectly obliterated words and sentences, as also at the true places of many of them. Wherefore he desires the reader to excuse the literal errata, and as for others to enquire of Dr Petty himself for his own sense and direction concerning them[2]. The printers of his other works were less frank but hardly more accurate, and to enquire of Dr Petty himself is no longer an available solvent of perplexity. Under such circumstances the beautiful manuscripts of the "Political Anatomy," the "Political Arithmetick," and the hitherto unpublished "Treatise of Ireland," which passed (indirectly) from Southwell to the British Museum[3], assume a high degree of importance. They all bear Petty's autograph corrections and by their use it has been possible to make his economic writings plain in several passages which heretofore were hopelessly obscure. Authentic manuscripts of the "Verbum Sapienti[4]" and of the "Report from the Council of Trade[5]" have also been used, but no good manuscript was found of the "Treatise of Taxes," the "Quantulumcunque" or the various Essays.

Of these manuscripts none but that of the "Treatise of Ireland" has been exactly followed in preparing the present edition of Petty's Economic Writings. The pamphlets previously published are all reprinted from the first editions except Graunt's "Observations," and the variations of the manuscripts are mentioned in foot notes in every case where it seemed possible that the manuscript reading could modify the sense of the printed version.

[1] Bibliography, no. 5. [2] *Op. cit.* end of the contents.

[3] Their history is traced in detail on pp. 123—124, 236—237, 547—548.

[4] Cf. p. 100. [5] Cf. p. 212.

PETTY'S ECONOMIC WRITINGS.

Those who hitherto have discussed Petty as a writer on economic subjects have confined themselves pretty closely to summary and criticism of his theories. The writings are now before the reader, who may summarize and criticize as his purpose demands or his taste suggests. It remains for the editor to account, if he can, for the writings as they are.

A man of force makes his way in this world through no impalpable ether. The medium through which he moves is dense, and deflects his course now this way, now that, according to the form and temper of the surface that he presents to the buffeting of affairs. His intellectual orbit cannot be precisely calculated even with a knowledge of the initial direction and velocity of his mind and of the attraction which draws its flight towards a fixed centre. But every man not wholly erratic is at once impelled by his circumstances and restrained by his training. Postulate these, and you may discover in his actual course some trace of the mean orbit which calculation would predict.

The inspiration of Petty's writings is not far to seek. Written before the days of formal treatises on political economy, they are neither the systematized abstractions of a metaphysician condescending to every-day affairs, nor the less systematic but no less abstract arguments of a man of affairs with an undisciplined bent toward speculative thinking. Least of all are they the eclectic treatise of a professional economist laborously dovetailing the ideas of his predecessors one into another. Indeed it is doubtful whether Petty had any acquaintance worth mentioning with such economic writings as existed in his day. In his earlier years, to be sure, he had been a man of the library as well as of the laboratory; but experience taught him to value the education of life above that of books, and in his writings he uses authorities seldom and not well. To Aubrey he declared that he had read little since his twenty-fifth year, and was of Hobbes's mind, that had he read much, as some men have, he had not known as much as he did[1]. His writings then are not conscious elaborations of some economic system, more or less clearly conceived. Each of them, on the contrary, was prompted by some circumstance of the times, and addresses itself, in fact if not in form, to some question of the day. The "Treatise of Taxes" the most systematic of them all, grows out of the changes in the revenue which the Restoration occasioned. The "Verbum Sapienti" is due to the costliness of the first Dutch war, the "Quantulumcunque" is the recoinage projects of Halifax. The moral of the "Political Arithmetick," implicit but clearly implied, is that Charles II. may, if he will, make himself independent of the bribes of Louis XIV. "The doctrines of this essay offended France[2]." The "Essays in Political Arithmetick" instruct James, wavering on the verge of an independent policy, that London is more considerable than the two best cities of the French monarchy[3]. The unedited "Treatise of Ireland" plainly avows its political purpose. Even the "Political Anatomy" though suggested by Chamberlayne's enclyclopaedic "State of England[4]" is seen, upon briefest examination, to be crowded with such discussions of current questions as nowhere occur in its prototype. Nevertheless they are all marked, in part because of his method of investigation, by certain common and characteristic features.

The form of Petty's discussions is as directly traceable to his training as is the contents of them to his circumstances. Such a title as "Political Anatomy" is reminiscent of his early studies, but the education which vitally affected his writing was rather that of converse with his scientific friends than that afforded by the instruction of his formal teachers. I shall try, therefore, to account in part for Petty's economic writings by taking up first the intellectual influences which gave them their characteristic form, and afterwards the circumstances, within the limits prescribed by that form, which suggested their content.

Petty has been represented, not without reason, as the disciple of Hobbes[5]. We have seen that he studied with Hobbes at Paris,

[1] Aubrey, II. 144.
[2] Cf. pp. 240, 237—238.
[3] Pp. 503, 524.
[4] See Pp. 122—123.
[5] Dr Bevan supports this view with energy, *Petty*, 87—92, and it is also held by Lord Edmond Fitzmaurice, *Life of Petty*, 16, 186, 188, 236.

and we know that all through Hobbes's quarrels their friendship remained unbroken[1]. Petty's high opinion of the author of the treatise "De Cive" is indicated by the inclusion of that work in the list of books which he wished his sons to read,—and the list is not a long one[2]. In his economic writings too there are traces of Hobbes's influence, but it is—if the distinction be admissible—upon Petty as a politician rather than upon Petty as an economist that his influence was chiefly exerted. It appears most strikingly in the assumption that the government is justified in doing anything by which the national wealth can be increased. Again and again Petty advocates sweeping public measures which take no account whatever of the rights and sensibilities of the citizen. He is quite ready to suggest that the majority of the Irish and Scotch be transplanted to England whether they consent or not[3]. In this general sense he is certainly of the political school of Hobbes rather than of Harrington[4].

The attempt to trace Hobbes's influence in Petty's attitude towards the relation of church and state does not seem altogether successful. In harmony with his general views, Petty agrees with Hobbes that the state may suppress dissent. Beyond this initial proposition they part company. The political theory of "The Leviathan" tolerates no division of sovereignty. Dissenters from the church by law established are political offenders who must be reduced to conformity because their dissent impairs the sovereignty of the government. Petty's reason why dissent may be suppressed is quite different from this. He thinks that "the Magistrate may punish false Believers, if he believes he shall offend God in forbearing it,...for the same reasons that men give for Liberty of Conscience and universal tolleration[5]." In other words a man vested with magisterial powers is morally justified in using them as his conscience dictates. But Petty himself is far from thinking it either necessary or expedient to use such powers to secure uniformity of worship. On the contrary he warmly commends the heterodox, though with curious reservations lest by going too far he give offence[6], and he

1 Aubrey, I. 365—368.

2 Fitzmaurice, 302—304. The *De Cive* is not, as Dr Bevan asserts "the only English book mentioned." The instructions for Henry, the younger son, direct him to read "The English Chronicle" and "Bacon's Collections."

3 Pp. 285—290, 302, 563 ff. 4 Cf. p. 23, note. 5 P. 70.

6 Pp. 71, 72, 262, 263. On the other hand his attitude towards clerics of all sorts is uniformly contemptuous, pp. 72, 73, 79, 158, 199, 218, 223, 263, etc.

regards dissent as not only harmless but inevitable. Thus upon a calculation of the number of sermons annually preached in England, he remarks that "It were a Miracle, if a Million of Sermons Composed by so many Men, and of so many Minds and Methods, should produce Uniformity upon the discomposed understandings of about 8 Millions of Hearers[1]," and suggests that misbelievers, provided they keep the public peace[2], may wisely be indulged by the magistrate, upon payment of "well proportioned, tolerable pecuniary mulcts, such as every conscientious Nonconformist would gladly pay, and Hypocrites by refusing, discover themselves to be such[3]." For "no man can believe what himself pleases and to force men to say they believe what they do not, is vain, absurd, and without honour to God." Besides "where most indeavours have been used to help Uniformity, there Heterodoxy hath most abounded[4]." The best policy therefore is for the government to pluck with moderation the geese who persist in their unauthorized beliefs[5].

Upon Petty as an economist the influence of Hobbes was far outweighed by that of Bacon. There was of course no personal connection here. When the founder of the New Philosophy was dying at Highgate, the future political arithmetician was a weaver's brat in Hampshire. But the youth became, as he grew to manhood, an eager member of that group of experimental investigators, working in the spirit of the "Novum Organum," who began the systematic pursuit of scientific knowledge in England[6]. At the close of a century distinguished above its predecessors not so much by the spirit of research as by the passion for accuracy in the determination

[1] Pp. 472—473. [2] P. 70.
[3] P. 22. [4] P. 263.

[5] For his own part, Petty regarded the non-essentials of religion with indifference. But there is a note of sincerity very characteristic of the man in the confession of faith with which he closed his will: "As for religion, I dye in the profession of that faith, and in the practice of such worship, as I find established by the Law of my country, not being able to believe what I myself please, nor to worship God better than by doing as I would be done unto, and observing the Laws of my country, and expressing my love and honour to Almighty God by such signes and tokens as are understood to be such by the people with whom I live, God knowing my heart even without any at all."

[6] On Petty's connection with the Royal Society, see pp. xxi—xxiii. For evidence, if any be required, that the founding of the Society was due to the impulse given by Bacon to the study of experimental science, and that the more eminent men among its earliest members were deeply imbued with the spirit of his teachings, see *Novum Organum*, edited by Fowler, 111—116.

of results, it is easy to find food for indulgent merriment in their crude apparatus. Not less amusing are their experiments with "a toad set in the middle of a circle of powder made with unicorne's horne," whose supposed charm it refused to recognize, incontinently hopping out of the circle again and again; or Sir Kenelm Digby's recommendation of "calcined powder of todes reverbrated applyed in bagges upon the stomach of a pestiferate body"—a pungent treatment of pestiferous bodies, whose obsolescence with the gradual mollification of social usages some will be found to regret. But the mere willingness to put the conduct of the toad to the test and to abide by the result argues confidence in the usefulness of experiment, and by implication in the uniformity of nature. It points the way to that precise knowledge of the world which alone can afford a firm foundation for invention and thus lead to the rule of man. It exhibits the Baconian rather than the Spinozistic sense of the maxim Knowledge is Power. It explains why the "Novum Organum" treats "De interpretatione naturæ *sive* de regno hominis." With the spirit of this philosophy Petty was strongly imbued[1]. In a session of the Royal Society when some one chanced to use the words "considerably bigger," "Sir William Petty cautioned, that no word might be used but what marks either number, weight, or measure[2]." The caution may serve to indicate the nature of Bacon's influence over him. It was an influence exerted primarily upon Petty's method, and only indirectly, through his method, upon the substance of his economic speculations.

In the field of his peculiar interests Petty sought the same quantitative precision which he demanded of his scientific colleagues. Now in economic investigation, as writers on the method of political economy never weary of iterating, the experimental method is in general precluded by the nature of the materials. The far seeing minister of an autocratic Czar may sometimes make industrial experiments on a gigantic scale and even isolate them from the disturbing influences of parliaments and newspapers, but he is not at all likely to utilize them for purposes of economic speculation. A favoured

[1] In his writings Petty twice invokes Bacon's authority, once in the *Political Anatomy*, 129, post, and once in the *Advice to Hartlib*, *Harl. Misc.* VI. 14, where he refers to the *Advancement of Learning* to justify his proposed *History of Trades*. If we consider him the author of the epistles dedictory of Graunt's *Observations*, as seems not unreasonable, he is to be credited with a third appeal to Bacon, p. 322, post.

[2] Birch, IV. 193.

economist like Von Thünen—with whose aims Petty's thought exhibits much affinity though he lacks Von Thünen's conspicuous patience—may make similar experiments upon a small scale. Most of us, however, must get on as best we may without any economic laboratory whatever. In this respect Petty was no exception. Experiment being impossible, he substituted what he called Political Arithmetick, a beginning of what is now called statistics. It was by no happy chance that he turned to this new device. He had a perfectly clear conception of the end which he desired to reach and of the means by which he proposed to reach it. "The Method I take," he says, "is not yet very usual; for instead of using only comparative and superlative Words, and intellectual Arguments, I have taken the course (as a Specimen of the Political Arithmetick I have longed aimed at) to express my self in terms of *Number*, *Weight*, or *Measure*; to use only Arguments of Sense, and to consider only such Causes, as have visible Foundations in Nature; leaving those that depend upon the mutable Minds, Opinions, Appetites, and Passions of particular Men, to the Consideration of others: Really professing my self as unable to speak satisfactorily upon those Grounds (if they may be call'd Grounds), as to foretel the cast of a Dye; to play well at Tennis, Billiards or Bowles, (without long practice,) by virtue of the most elaborate Conceptions that ever have been written *De Projectilibus & Missilibus*, or of the Angles of Incidence and Reflection[1]."

He even anticipated the modern conclusion that statistical investigation, applied to wisely selected circumstances, affords perhaps the best substitute for experimentation that is open to an economist. In this sense he says, in the preface to the "Political Anatomy of Ireland," "As Students in Medicine, practice their inquiries upon cheap and common Animals, and such whose actions they are best acquainted with, and where there is the least confusion and perplexure of Parts; I have chosen Ireland as such a Political Animal, who is scarce Twenty years old; where the Intrigue of State is not very complicate, and with which I have been conversant from an Embrion; and in which, if I have done amiss, the fault may be easily mended by another[2]." The obvious meaning is, not that

[1] P. 244. Cf. ch. II. of the *Treatise of Ireland*, pp. 558—560, and Petty's praise of Graunt's *Observations* on p. 481. The question of their respective contributions to the developement of statistics is discussed on pp. lxvi, lxxv.

[2] P. 129.

he literally experimented upon Ireland himself, but that he examined by the best available means, the effects of such experiments as had been made there. The means turns out to be the use of political arithmetick, and that he considers the best means because it gives precise results. As we shall see, Petty's results were, at times, less accurate than precise, for his statistical materials were frequently inadequate and his employment of such as he had was sometimes injudicious. But the root of the matter was in him. The application of an appropriate method "not yet very usual" to a field of knowledge in which it was altogether new, justifies him in associating himself with the most eminent followers of the new philosophy, and even distinguishes him among his colleagues. It was by no misapprehension of his true significance that Narcissus Luttrell wrote in his diary simply, "Sir William Petty of the Royal Society is dead[1]."

The data of statistics do not now, nor did they ever present themselves spontaneously for scientific elaboration. In order therefore that legal provision should be made, and that money should be forthcoming, for their ascertainment, it was first necessary that the value of possible statistical deductions from accurate data should be demonstrated by the intelligent use of those sparse materials which lay ready to the student's hand. It is in this sense that we must judge the essays of Graunt and Petty, which pioneered the way of modern statistics, and so judged they will be found worthy of high praise. Graunt's book has the advantage of priority[2] and the greater advantage of dealing with a body of statistical data sufficiently extended and complete to warrant some confidence in deductions properly made from it. Petty's materials, on the other hand, were highly defective. A few scattering bills from Paris and Dublin, haphazard returns from various tax offices, a guess here or there as to the area of a city[3]—the list is soon exhausted. Petty realized the incompleteness of his data, and repeatedly urged the institution of regular statistical returns[4]. He drew up a pattern for an improved bill of mortality for Dublin[5]. He even tried to secure the establishment of an Irish statistical office under his own management[6]. But it is not clear that anything of importance resulted from his efforts

[1] *Brief Relation*, I. 485.

[2] On Petty's probable share in it, see p. lii.

[3] Cf. pp. 451, 485, 490, 532.

[4] *E.g.* on pp. 49, 51, 53, 104, 115, 129, 170, 180, 245, 270, 476, 485. Cf. also pp. 396, 397 in Graunt's *Observations*.

[5] Pp. 485—491.

[6] Fitzmaurice, 283.

in this direction. Meanwhile he made shift with such tools as came to hand—"a commin Knife and a Clout," as he says "instead of the many more helps which such a Work requires[1]." When he could not ascertain directly the number, weight or measure of some phenomenon in which he was interested, he reckoned out what he desired to know upon the basis of what he already knew. In other words he pursued the method of political arithmetic as distinguished from statistics. Statistics demands enumeration. The validity of its inferences depends upon the theory of probabilities as expressed in the Law of Large Numbers. Therefore it adds, it does not multiply. Political arithmetic, as exemplified by Petty, multiplies freely; and the value of its results varies according to the nature of the terms multiplied. For example, in the absence of a census Petty had to calculate the population of London, of England, and of Ireland. His calculations for London[2] are based upon the number of burials and upon the number of houses, facts which at least bear some relation to the number of people. The burials he multiplies by thirty, an arbitrary figure for which he pleads Graunt's authority[3]; the houses he multiplies, now by six[4], and now by eight[5], as suits his purpose. The sources of probable error are obvious. The population of England, he further estimates at eleven times that of London because London pays one eleventh of the assessment. The chance of error is thus raised to the second degree. Nevertheless the calculation is not altogether unreasonable, and Petty asserts that the results "do pretty well agree" with the accounts of the hearth money, the poll money, and the bishops' numbering of the communicants[6]—figures which he neglects to give. To see from what refractory materials he can extract a result when hard pushed, we must turn to his discussion of the Irish rebellion of 1641. He finds that above one-third more "superfluous oxen and sheep, butter and beef" was exported from that kingdom in 1664 than before the rebellion, "which shows there were $\frac{1}{3}$ more people in 1641 than in 1664[7]." Unfortunately the use of rash calculations grew upon

[1] P. 130. [2] Pp. 459—460, 528.

[3] Cf. pp. 332, 393. Graunt's solution of the same problem for London is on pp. 383—386. [4] Pp. 527, 534. [5] P. 459.

[6] Cf. p. 461, note, where it appears that the agreement between Petty's estimate and the bishops' survey is not strikingly close.

[7] P. 149. Cf. the more elaborate calculation of the same problem on pp. 608, 609. Other striking examples may be found on pp. 175, 311, 462—469, 566—567.

Petty, and, as was to be expected, he gives widely varying estimates of the same things[1]. It must be added that he is frequently inaccurate in his use of authorities[2] and careless in his calculations[3] and upon at least one occasion he is open to suspicion of sophisticating his figures[4].

Petty's economic writings thus exhibit both the strength and the weakness of his characteristic method. When his terms of number, weight and measure result from an actual enumeration they are generally of value, for he has a considerable capacity of segregating the really significant factors of an economic problem. But the difficulties in the way of enumeration were great, and in his eagerness for results he often resorted to calculations which were nothing more than guesses. When he stopped to think, he was well enough aware of their conjectural character. "I hope," he writes to Aubrey, "that no man takes what I say about the living and dyeing of men for a mathematical demonstration[5]." But in the ardour of argument he was himself more than once mislead into fancying that his conclusions were accurate because their form was definite. His mistake is not without its modern analogies. Mathematical presentations of industrial facts, both symbolic and graphic, have by their definiteness, encouraged many an investigator in the false conceit that he now knew what he sought, whereas he had at most but a neat name for what he sought to know. Nevertheless the substitution of symbols for Petty's "terms of number" is an improvement in this, that calculations made in symbols must be consciously translated into the terms of actual life before any practical use—or misuse—can be made of them, whereas calculations in figures of number, weight and measure are already concrete and appear to tell something intelligible even to a common man. Had Petty calculated the advantages of his "perpetual settlement of Ireland with a natural improvement of England and Ireland by transplanting a million of people out of Ireland into England" in the form of curves and triangles, that astounding proposition might have passed for something highly scientific.

[1] Cf. p. 454, note.

[2] Pp. 45, 145, 253, 308, 457, 459, 463, 483, 517, 518, 526, 533, 535, 536.

[3] Pp. 136, 137, 146, 147, 459, 484, 536, 585, 588, 608.

[4] Cf. pp. 528 and 533 with 506.

[5] Aubrey MS. in Bodleian, quoted by Bevan, p. 51.

It would be quite possible to take up the various economic topics discussed by Petty according to modern conceptions of them, and to do so would afford a ready-made standard for judging his economic notions. But it would also involve the risk of asking what he thought about problems concerning which it never occurred to him to think at all. No possible answer to such a question can be correct, for the question itself is irrational. Accordingly I leave to those who have a taste for mosaic work and are not yet satisfied with the amount on hand, the task of determining in what details Petty anticipated Smith or Ricardo or Böhm-Bawerk. It will be enough for the present purpose to indicate a few of the chief economic questions which engaged his attention and to attempt to understand why he attacked them and how he solved them.

The economic method which Petty chiefly pursued, taken in combination with the limited extent of his materials, of necessity confined him to the discussion of a few out of the many questions that must have thronged upon his active mind. In no other field of economic interest were so many figures available as in that of taxation, and the fiscal changes of the Restoration, chancing to come just at the time when he first had leisure to return to his studies, gave to his economic inquiries a direction from which he never wholly departed. The only topic neither an outgrowth of his fiscal discussions nor otherwise dictated by his arithmetical method upon which he wrote at length was that of coinage. And it is noteworthy that his little excursions into this relatively foreign field are marked by as great perspicuity and good sense as distinguish his more arithmetical writings. The "Quantulumcunque," indeed, shows Petty very nearly at his best.

As an economic writer then, Petty is essentially a cameralist rather than a mercantilist. Unlike Robinson and Mun and Child, he had little connection with foreign trade[1]; nevertheless he was too much infected by prevalent mercantile views to see the advantages of unrestricted commerce as clearly as North was able to do. Accordingly while he leans, on the whole, towards a policy of commercial freedom, and is quite clear and consistent in opposing all restraints upon the export of coin or bullion, he seems at times to evade the discussion of the free trade problem—*e.g.* he does not mention the Act of Navigation—and his utterances on the

[1] Unless, that is, Ireland be considered foreign to England in commercial matters. Cf. pp. 159—160.

preferability of treasure to other forms of wealth, on the balance of trade, and on the policy of restriction generally are contradictory, not to say vacillating. On almost all questions of public revenue and public expenditure, on the contrary, his opinions are well developed, clear and consistent. The great changes in the fiscal system which were made by the Convention Parliament gave rise to no other discussion at all comparable with his "Treatise of Taxes and Contributions[1];" and it is scarcely too much to say that English economic literature before Hume can show no tract of such range and force, characterized by such wealth of suggestion and such power of analysis, as is Petty's masterpiece. It contains the germ of nearly every theory which he afterwards elaborated. Even his method of political arithmetic is exemplified in the calculations of its second chapter[2]. The calculations are, to be sure, both slight and unsatisfactory; but rather from lack of trustworthy data than from any failure on Petty's part to appreciate the importance of such devices. On the contrary he demands for economic purposes a thorough survey of lands and their produce[3], and of money, wages and population, for "until this be done trade will be too conjectural a work for any man to employ his thoughts about[4]." Before the publication of the "Treatise" he was indeed acquainted with Graunt's "Observations[5]," but the suggestions of that book had not had as yet sufficient time to exert their full influence upon him. Consequently the number of the people, which becomes in the "Verbum Sapienti" (1664) a key to the national wealth, and thus affords a basis for the distribution of taxation much more satisfactory than expenditure[6], is used in the "Treatise" but incidentally to a minor question of retrenchment[7].

To the problem of national wealth Petty never tires of applying the methods of his political arithmetic. The "Verbum Sapienti" shows both the reason that led him to attack the problem and the method which he employed for its solution. The introduction explains that taxation is unequal, "which disproportion is the true and proper grievance of taxes[8]." To the end that the public charge be laid proportionally it is necessary that the total effects of the

[1] The application of the *Treatise of Taxes* to the condition and affairs of Ireland is an obvious afterthought, intended to relieve the author from all imputation of criticising domestic matters.

[2] Pp. 23—28. [3] P. 49. [4] P. 53.

[5] Pp. 27, 45. [6] Cf. p. 91. [7] P. 23.

[8] P. 104.

nation be ascertained. In the first chapter, accordingly, Petty estimates separately the value of the lands, the houses, the shipping, the cattle, the money and the miscellaneous goods of the country, unblushingly confirming one guess by showing its satisfying conformity to another. Now-a-days more abundant and more accurate figures are available upon which to base guesses, but the methods of modern calculations of national wealth are, so far, not essentially different from his[1]. The second chapter, however, adds to the calculation of the first an element of national wealth which seldom figures in modern tables headed *£ s. d.* This element is "the value of the people," which it was his consistent practice to include in all his estimates. Fewness of people he thought was real poverty[2]. Hands were the father as lands were the mother of wealth[3], and neither of the pair might be omitted from a stock-taking of the public household. The suggestion that people are wealth was probably much older than Petty[4], and his originality would consist rather in the application to it of his political arithmetic than in the invention of the notion. Now in order to add hands to lands he must reduce them to a common denominator. The necessity and the difficulty of thus making "a par and equation between lands and labour" must have been brought home to him by his experience as surveyor and commissioner of allotments, charged with rewarding soldiers on the one hand and loaners of money on the other by proper assignment of the forfeited lands in Ireland[5], and it is not merely for theoretical purposes that he regards this task as "the most important consideration in political oeconomies[6]." The common denominator chosen being money, it is necessary to determine the money value of the people. But the people in question are neither bought nor sold[7], and so he resorts to a calculation. Assuming the expenditure of the people of England to be forty million pounds per annum, he finds that their income from property is sufficient to meet only fifteen millions of it. The source of the remaining twenty-five millions of income is worth as much as the fee of land that would rent for that sum, "for although the individiums of mankind be

[1] Cf. Giffen, *Growth of Capital*, I. 74—91. [2] P. 34.
[3] P. 68. [4] Pp. 377—378, note. [5] See pp. xvi—xix.
[6] P. 181, cf. pp. 44—45. This expression, by the way, is very near to being "Political Economy;" and on p. 60 Petty speaks of "politics and oeconomicks" in quite the modern way.
[7] Petty once avails himself (p. 512, where read *Algier* for *Argier*) of the price of slaves, but only to support a result arrived at by other means.

reckoned at about eight years purchase, the species of them is worth as many as land, being in its nature as perpetual for ought we know[1]." The figures to which Petty applies this formula are conjectural, even capricious, but the formula itself is essentially sound, and the ingenious calculation shows that he had a firm grasp upon the problem of capitalization. The various components of the national wealth being thus ascertained, Petty proceeds to use them as a basis for distributing taxation. He holds that, the *ratio formalis* of riches lying rather in proportion than in quantity, men would be no poorer than now they are should each lose half his estate[2]. Accordingly he proposes various taxes[3] intended to place upon the possessors of each source of income such a proportion of the aggregate burden as the capitalized amounts of their respective incomes may bear to the national wealth which he has calculated.

Petty's interest in the amount of the national wealth thus sprang from his discussion of taxation, and it is clear that traces of its origin hang about it to the end. But he soon came to employ the notion for another purpose also; that is, as a means of comparing England with her commercial rivals, Holland and France. In 1664, Petty had made a "Collection of the Frugalities of Holland[4]," and he repeatedly commended various Dutch practices for adoption in England[5]. Nevertheless, he seems to have considered the current estimate of the Dutch somewhat exaggerated[6], and the conviction apparently grew upon him that it was rather with France than Holland that Englishmen must reckon[7]. In the "Treatise of Taxes" (1662), the Dutch system is held up as a model for English imitation, while no French taxes are mentioned except the gabelle[8], of which he disapproves. In the "Political Arithmetick" (1676) Holland still occupies the first place, but it serves merely as a stalking-horse to disguise the main argument regarding the potential superiority of England to France. In the "Five Essays" (1687) the Netherlands are openly relegated to second place. In making these international comparisons Petty realizes that national wealth is something different from the revenue of the exchequer[9], and is of independent importance to the commonweal. Nevertheless he is unable to divest himself entirely of the cameralistic notions out of which his discussion

[1] P. 108. [2] P. 26. [3] Pp. 111—112.
[4] See Bibliography. It was lost at sea. [5] *E.g.*, pp. 26, 95, 261—267.
[6] P. 258. [7] Cf. Temple's *Works*, I. 58—60, 210—222.
[8] Pp. 74, 83. [9] *E.g.*, p. 299.

arose, and always lays especial weight upon the distinctively fiscal importance of lands and goods and people.

Income[1] being with Petty the starting point for estimating wealth, he feels the necessity of explaining those sorts of income—rent and interest—which do not result evidently from current labour. Now the fundamental question arising alike in a theory of rent and in a theory of interest is this: why does the right to receive a definite annual payment throughout an infinite succession of years command in the market only a finite sum? As applied to rent, this is the question of the number of "years purchase," and Petty, who frequently employs that common phrase, also discusses the problem[2]. But this was aside from his main purpose, and he neither dwelt on the suggestion nor applied it to money. He recognized that the value of the fee depended[3] upon the rent which the land would yield, and was therefore interested rather in ascertaining as a factor in his studies of national wealth and its growth, why a specific piece of land bears a certain rent and neither more nor less, than in determining the capital value of that rent. The answer is given in a remarkable passage in the "Treatise of Taxes[4]," and is elaborated in the "Political Anatomy of Ireland[5]." The corn rent of agricultural lands, he says, is determined by the excess of their produce over the expenses of their cultivation, paid in corn, and the money value of this excess will be measured by the amount of silver which a miner, working for the same time as the cultivator of the corn land, will have left, after meeting his expenses with a part of the silver which he secures. The labour theory of value thus adopted was probably suggested by Hobbes[6]. But to the question why there should be any surplus of value above costs either in corn-farming or mining he has an answer of his own. This answer differs from that now become familiar. The notion of diminishing returns, forcing recourse to fields of inferior natural and indestructible powers in order to supply the market and thus giving rise to a differential rent, did not occur to him. On the contrary he probably thought that with proper cultivation, the profitable fertility of

[1] Measured by expenditure, to which he assumes income at least equal.

[2] P. 45.

[3] Though in varying proportion, according as some special honour, pleasure or privilege attaches to the possession of certain lands intrinsically like others, p. 46. Cf. p. 286.

[4] Pp. 42—45 and 48—49.

[5] Pp. 181—182.

[6] *De Cive*, ch. XXIV. *Opera omnia*, III. 185. It was certainly adopted, without credit, by Benjamin Franklin, whose cast of mind generally was curiously like Petty's. Cf. Franklin's *Works*, I. 371.

land could be indefinitely increased[1]. But he suggested in the "Treatise[2]," and asserted in the "Political Arithmetick[3]" that the amount of rent per acre is determined by the density of the population dependent for food upon the land, and varies inversely as the said density. In other words the rent of land is attributed to its situation[4] rather than to its technical fertility. The formula has a similar arithmetical neatness to that of the formula commonly called Ricardian, and it comes, on the whole, perhaps quite as near to measuring the commercial facts[5]. This praise, if praise it be, is not deemed unduly high.

In interest Petty recognizes two elements, a compensation for risk[6], and a payment for the inconvenience which a man admits against himself in giving out his money so that he may not demand it back until a certain time, whatever his own necessities shall be in the mean time[7]. The amount of this last payment, upon any specific sum—in modern language the rate of interest per cent.—cannot be less than the rent of so much land as that sum would buy[8]. Exchange he explains as "local usury" meaning, apparently, a compensation for the costs of moving money, of which costs risk is the largest.

A theory of wages was not demanded by Petty's method of calculating national wealth. For that purpose he could take them as a given fact, or rather as a fact inferable from the labourer's expenditures, and as he had no conception of the problem of distribution in the modern sense and was interested rather in the aggregate number of labourers than in their individual differences, he contents himself with a passing suggestion that wages generally are the result of, and equal to, the increase which a man can effect by his labour in the spontaneous productivity of the soil[9]. The only other distributive suggestion regarding wages is the remark, wholly incidental, that when wages of husbandmen rise rents of land must consequently fall[10].

[1] Cf. p. 249. [2] Pp. 48—49. [3] Pp. 286—287.

[4] Cf. Commons, *Distribution of Wealth*, 27—29.

[5] Cf. R. Jones, *Essay on the Distribution of Wealth*, 260—268. Petty is not mentioned by Jones.

[6] Pp. 48, 304. [7] P. 47.

[8] P. 48. This is similar to a remark of Turgot's, whom Böhm-Bawerk pronounces "the first who tried to give a scientific explanation of natural interest on capital." Petty is, of course, open to the same criticism of reasoning in a circle which Böhm-Bawerk passes on Turgot. *Capital and Interest*, 61—66.

[9] P. 181. [10] P. 267.

GRAUNT AND THE SCIENCE OF STATISTICS.

As statistical writing Graunt's "Observations upon the Bills of Mortality" are superior to any of Petty's works. Indeed they alone can claim to be "statistics"; Petty's "Essays" are so different in character that his own name of "political arithmetick" is still their most accurate description. The difference, as has been pointed out[1], arises in part rather from Graunt's sparing use of calculation than from any especial merit in such calculations as he does make. His estimate of London's population[2] is superior to Petty's in no way unless it be by reason of priority; and his table of mortality is as pure guess work as anything that Petty ever wrote[3]. But the difference between them cannot be wholly explained by the circumstance that Graunt's temptation to reckon was less than Petty's because his data were more complete. The spirit of their work is often different when no question of calculation enters. Petty sometimes appears to be seeking figures that will support a conclusion which he has already reached: Graunt uses his numerical data as a basis for conclusions, declining to go beyond them[4]. He is thus a more careful statistician than Petty, but he is not an economist at all.

Some of the most important facts which the study of vital statistics has yet discovered were first brought to light by Graunt. Though they may be read at length in his "Observations" here reprinted, it is essential to an adequate appreciation of his merits that the more pregnant of his discoveries be brought together by way of summary. Four are particularly noteworthy. In the first place, the regularity of certain social phenomena which appear to

[1] P. lxvi. [2] Pp. 384—386.

[3] On p. 387. I have there suggested a reason for suspecting that Petty may have concocted the table.

[4] Cf. pp. 355 § 12, 357 § 21.

be, in their individual occurrence, the sport of chance, was first made evident by Graunt's studies. One of his earliest observations is, "That among the several *Casualties* some bear a constant proportion unto the whole number of *Burials*; such are *Chronical* Diseases, and the Diseases whereunto the City is most subject; as for Example, *Consumptions*, *Dropsies*, *Jaundice*, *Gout*, *Stone*, *Palsie*, *Scurvy*, *Rising of the Lights* or *Mother*, *Rickets*, *Aged*, *Agues*, *Fevers*, *Bloody Flux* and *Scowring*: nay, some Accidents, as *Grief*, *Drowning*, *Men's making away themselves*, and being *Kill'd by several Accidents*, *&c.* do the like[1]." From the regularity of these phenomena, however, for example of suicide, Graunt deduces no such moral implications as Quetelet and Buckle, not to mention living writers, have sought to place upon it. In the second place Graunt first noted the excess of male over female births and the approximate numerical equality of the sexes, and upon it he bases some remarks about Divine approval of monogamy[2]. His suggestion had great vogue and is often repeated. The third among the important facts which Graunt discovered is the high rate of mortality during the earlier years of life; the fourth is the excess of the urban over the rural death rate. In establishing the first two of these four facts Graunt called attention to truths previously unrecognized. It is not improbable, on the other hand, that the facts regarding mortality had been conjectured before his time. But he was the first to verify conjecture by observations so extended that they resulted in demonstration. Proof, indeed, is the characteristic feature of his book. The fulness of his proof and the care with which he elaborates it raise his "Observations" to a higher plane than is reached by any similar investigation of social phenomena during the century that lies between Graunt and Süssmilch.

It cannot be contended that Graunt was completely master of the method of investigation to which he made noteworthy contributions. His imperfect apprehension of the so-called law of large numbers appears clearly in his discussion of the country bills. "The proportion," he says[3] "Between the greatest and the least mortalities in the Country is far greater than at London...as in London in no Decad the burials of one year are double to those

[1] P. 352. "Die Lehre von der sogenannten Gesetzmässigkeit der scheinbar freiwilligen Handlungen ist schon von Condorcet [!] ausgesprochen." Meitzen, *Geschichte, Theorie und Tecknik der Statistik*, 118.

[2] Pp. 374—378.

[3] Pp. 391—392.

of another, so in the Country they are seldom not more than so... which shows that the opener and freer Airs are most subject to the good and bad Impressions." This is an attempt to explain by physical conditions the wide range in the observed country death rate which is really due to the narrowness of the field—a single market town—under investigation. It is, perhaps, the gravest statistical mistake that can be charged against Graunt. And when we remember that he was a statistical pioneer, blazing his way through a trackless forest, we must confess surprise that his faults are so few and his merits so many. He had not enjoyed the academic training of most of his associates in the Royal Society, but he was permeated with the spirit of that new philosophy which bade curiosity turn for satisfaction rather to observation than to speculation. His book, with all its faults, deserves a place among the penetrating and fearless treatises which, marred though they were by much now known to be absurd, still contributed to render even the early years of the Royal Society illustrious.

Graunt's influence upon later statistical writers can be traced with remarkable distinctness. Petty is the first to acknowledge as he was the first to feel it; but his obligation is of that vital sort which no series of quotations can sufficiently express. How largely his best work depends upon Graunt can be appreciated only by reading in connection with Graunt's "Observations" the second volume of Petty's Economic Writings. Upon Halley's "Estimate of the Degrees of Mortality of Mankind" (1693) Graunt's influence is not quite so obvious. But anyone who has read, as to some extent I have, the scattered letters of Petty, Southwell, Williamson, Pett, and Justel, all members of the Royal Society and friends of Petty, and all but Justel acquainted with Graunt, cannot fail to see how, as a result of Graunt's and Petty's efforts, the air surrounding Halley was full of political arithmetic. He turned his great abilities as it were casually and but for a few days to that subject; but he seized at once upon Graunt's most striking discovery, the regularity of death, and utilized it for the first suggestion of life insurance. Of Gregory King and Charles Davenant it is not necessary to speak. They belong rather to Petty's school than to Graunt's. The next link in the chain of Graunt's influence is the Rev. William Derham (1657–1735). As Boyle lecturer in 1711–12 Derham, having the honour to be a member of the Royal Society as well as a divine, was minded to try what he could do toward the improvement of philosophical matters to theological uses. While writing his lectures[1] with this in view, he happened upon Graunt's book, which caused him to see that the constant proportion of marriages to births and of births to burials constitutes "a wise means to keep the balance of mankind even;" and he concludes his discussion by asking "upon the whole matter, what is all this but admirable plan and management? What can the maintaining, throughout all ages and places, of these proportions of mankind, and all other creatures; this harmony in the generations of man be but the work of One that ruleth the world?[2]" Of themselves Derham's remarks, which are but incidental to a comprehensive argument from design, would be of small significance in the history of statistics. But they chanced, because they were in a theological book, to fall into the hands of a Prussian tutor and military chaplain, who made them matter for investigation.

Johann Peter Süssmilch (1707–1767) was not, as Roscher asserts[3], the first to make the growth of population a subject of independent investigation on its own account[4]: Graunt certainly anticipated him in that. But he was perhaps the first who clearly grasped the fact, which escaped Graunt, that when and only when sufficiently large numbers are taken into account, order and not accident appear. It is not my intention to describe Süssmilch's book, the great ability of which is now everywhere recognized. But since many of his countrymen have represented him as the founder of statistics in the modern sense, or of vital statistics, it is worth while to point out that Süssmilch himself considers Graunt his master. "Die göttliche Ordnung" was first suggested, he tells us, by

[1] *Physico-theology; or a Demonstration of the Being and Attributes of God from his Works of Creation.* 1713. I cite the "new edition" of 1798.

[2] *Ibid.*, I., 267.

[3] *Geschichte der Nationalökonomik in Deutschland*, 421.

[4] The title of Süssmilch's book shows plainly that, like Derham, he was interested primarily in the theological implications of vital statistics. It runs: Die göttliche Ordnung in den Veränderungen des menschlichen Geschlechts aus der Geburt, dem Tode und der Fortpflanzung desselben erwiesen...worin die Regeln der Ordnung bewiesen werden, welche Gottes Weisheit und Güte in dem Lauf der Natur zur Erhaltung, Vermehrung und Verdopplung des menschlichen Geschlechts festgesetzt hat,...Berlin, J. C. Spener, 1741. I cite the pirated ed. published at Berlin by Gahls in 1742. See W. F. Willcox and F. S. Crum, *A trial bibliography of the writings of Süssmilch*, *Publ. Amer. Statistical Assn*, V. 310—314.

the observations collected by Derham[1]. Becoming interested in the subject, he sent to England for the writings of Graunt and Petty[2], and was thus induced to publish his book partly because the observations already made were known to very few people, partly because the lists which he had collected in Germany enabled him to go further in some respects than Graunt and Petty had done[3]. But to Graunt, as he acknowledges[4], the first and most distinguished praise belongs. Graunt first sought to utilize the bills for the discovery of the new truths. Parish registers had been kept for centuries, but who before Graunt used them to lay bare "Die göttliche Ordnung?" The discovery was as possible as that of America, all that was wanting was a Columbus who should go further than others in his survey of old and well known truths and reports. That Columbus was Graunt[5].

The influence of Süssmilch upon Malthus has never been traced. The first suggestion of the "Essay on the Principle of Population" owes nothing to "Die göttliche Ordnung," but in every edition after the first Süssmilch is cited between forty and fifty times. It was doubtless to one of the later editions that the author of "The Origin of Species" acknowledges his indebtedness for what is perhaps the central idea of his work.

"The Observations upon the London Bills of Mortality," wrote Petty at the outset of the statistical work which first engaged his own attention[6], "have been a new Light to the World; and the like Observation upon those of Dublin may serve as Snuffers to make the same candle burn clearer." It is improbable that even Petty, in spite of the openness of his mind and the vigour of his imagination, appreciated to the full the significance of Graunt's discoveries; but it may perhaps be noted that he wrote of another great work of his day, "Poor Mr Newton...I have not met with one man that putt an extraordinary value on his book. I would give 500*l.* to have been the author of it; and 200*l.* that Charles understood it[7]."

[1] Süssmilch, 13. [2] *Ibid.*, 16. [3] *Ibid.*, 27.
[4] *Ibid.*, 17. [5] *Ibid.*, 18. [6] P. 398, note.
[7] To Southwell, 9 July, 1687, Fitzmaurice, 306, 307. Charles was Petty's eldest son.

ON THE BILLS OF MORTALITY.

Almost all of Graunt's "Observations" and a large portion of Petty's "Essays" are based on the London bills of mortality. Some knowledge of the history and character of the bills is therefore necessary to an appreciation of those writings. Accordingly the gradual elaboration of the Parish Clerk's bills from crude weekly returns of the progress of the plague, through a long series of changes, to the form finally superseded by the Registrar-General's bills in 1840, is here traced as far as the year 1686, the last year of whose bills Petty made use, and an attempt is made to estimate the accuracy of the seventeenth century bills in several particulars.

So far as is known, no set of the London bills of mortality before 1658 escaped the great fire of September, 1666[1], and there is, in consequence, some doubt as to the time at which they originated. Graunt's assertion[2] that the bills first began in the year 1592 accords with the official statement put forth, after the Plague of 1665 and before the Fire, by John Bell, clerk to the Company of Parish Clerks, to rectify "the many and gross mistakes which have been imposed upon the World, by divers Ignorant Scriblers[3] about the weekly Accompts of former Visitations[4]." Bell says that he could find in the Parish Clerks' Hall no record of more antiquity than 21 December, 1592; the bills, therefore, must have begun at that date. In 1595, he continues, the plague ceased, and on the 18th December of that year the bills were accordingly discontinued

[1] Creighton, *History of Epidemics*, I. 532.

[2] P. 335.

[3] See p. 426.

[4] *London's Remembrancer: or A true Accompt of every particular Weeks christnings and mortality In all the Years of pestilence Within the Cognizance of the Bills of Mortality. London: Printed and are to be sold by E. Cotes, Printer to the Company of Parish Clerks*, 1665. 4to. unpaged.

and were laid aside as useless until 21 December, 1603, "at which time they were again resumed and continued unto this day." On this point Bell is particularly emphatic. "I deny not," he says, "that there might be, and I believe was, a very grievous Pestilence which raged here in some part of the Year 1603....You may ask me why then I do not give a better account of that Pestilential Year? I answer, That in that Year the Parish Clerks gave not any accompt thereof; and although I think it not impossible, yet it is very improbable, that any particular man should give a just accompt thereof."

In regard to the date at which the bills began, both Bell and Graunt are mistaken. There may have been bills even as early as 1517[1], and original weekly bills assigned, with much probability, to 1532[2] and to 1535[3], are still preserved. These bills doubtless owe their existence to the known timidity of Henry VIII. in the face of the plague, and it is probable that they were not long continued after the disease ceased. Indeed, the French ambassador, though he was very certain that fear of infection could not be, as was given out, the true reason why Anne of Cleves went to Richmond in the summer of 1540, was still unable to find any better ground for his scepticism than the mere assertion that "there is no talk at present of the plague" in London[4]. Throughout the period from 1550 to 1563 there was, probably, little or no plague in the city and consequently less occasion to continue the weekly reports[5]. But the new outbreak of the epidemic in the last named year apparently caused them to be resumed, and we know of weekly figures for 1563–1566[6], for 1574[7], for 1578–1583[8], for 1592–1595[9],

[1] *Hist. MSS. Com.*, x. pt. 4, p. 447; Creighton, I. 290, 294, note.

[2] Brit. Mus. Egerton MSS. 2603, fol. 4; transcribed by Creighton, I. 295—296.

[3] Record Office, State Papers, Henry VIII., 4633.

[4] Marrilac to Montmorency, 6 July, 1540, *Letters and Papers, Foreign and Domestic*, XV. 419. The inference seems to be confirmed by J. G. Nichols's note to Machyn's *Diary*, 319, and by Caius's *Councill against the Sweat* (1552), as reprinted by Hecker, *Epidemics of the Middle Ages*, third ed., p. 330.

[5] Creighton, I. 304. It seems, however, that reports were made for a few weeks during the sweat of 1551. *Ibid.*, 261.

[6] Stow's memoranda in *Three Fifteenth Century Chronicles*, edited by Gairdner (Camden Soc., n. p. 28) 123—125, 144—147.

[7] Holinshed's *Chronicle*, IV. 325.

[8] Creighton, I. 341—343; the original figures are at Hatfield House.

[9] Graunt, p. 335, post. Bell above.

and for 1597–1600[1]. Inasmuch as a large portion of these returns, those preserved by Stow from 14 July, 1564, to 26 July, 1566 and all the Bodleian figures, 1597–1600, cover periods almost free from infection, it may perhaps be inferred that after 1563 the weekly returns continued to be made out with considerable regularity during the rest of the century. In any event it is clear that they antedate 1592 and were not discontinued from 1595 to 1603. We might perhaps save Bell's reputation for accuracy in the matter by assuming that the sixteenth century bills were compiled by some one else than the Company of Parish Clerks. We know, indeed, that the deaths in 1535 were certified by the Lord Mayor[2], and we do not know how he ascertained the facts; but it is probable that he employed the Parish Clerks even then to collect the information, and it is almost certain that in and after 1563 the bills were made out by that company[3].

Graunt professes to give[4] the deaths from the plague and from other causes in each week of 1603 from 17 March to the end of December. Apparently he had also the figures, at least of the christenings, from December, 1602 to March, 1603[5]. In other words he claims information for a whole year of which Bell asserts that the Parish Clerks gave no account until December twenty-first. And Graunt's figures are confirmed in part, while Bell's assertion is completely refuted, by an original printed bill for the week 13—20 October, 1603, preserved in the Guildhall Library[6]. Concerning the figures for 1592, also, there is a disagreement between Bell and Graunt. Graunt gives figures of the total deaths and of the plague deaths from 17 March, 1592, to the 22nd December[7], whereas Bell believes that the 21st December of that year marks the beginning of the bills. Noting that "the Weekly and General Bills in the year 1593 did bare date from Thursday to Thursday......and that they continued that course until the year 1629," Bell goes on to observe that "all the Papers that make mention of the Great Plague

[1] Bodleian Library, Ashmole MS., 824, ff. 196—199; printed pp. 433—435, post.

[2] *Letters and Papers, Foreign and Domestic*, IX. no. 151, 279, 341, 451.

[3] Christie, *Some Account of the Parish Clerks*, 133—135. The bills of 1603, concerning which Graunt and Bell disagree, are admitted to be the Clerks' work.

[4] In the table at p. 426.

[5] See p. 366.

[6] In "Political Tracts, 1680, PP." There are also other reasons for believing Graunt correct, see pp. 426—428, post.

[7] In the table at p. 426.

in the years 1592, 1593, 1603 and 1625 bear date the 17th of March in all the said years...making that day Epidemical as well as the year Pestilential." "But I think it very strange," says he, "nor do I believe that the 17th March in all the said years did fall out to be on a Thursday: but I conceive that what is contained in them, was gleaned from some false scattered papers, printed in some of those years." In this opinion Bell is right, so far as Graunt's figures for 1592 are concerned[1]; but in his inference that no bills existed in 1592 he is plainly mistaken.

The manner in which the bills were first published is not altogether clear. In Graunt's time they were regularly printed, and the weekly bills were supplied to subscribers at four shillings a year. The editor of the "Collection of the yearly Bills of Mortality" says[2] that "In 1625, the bills of mortality having now acquired a general reputation, the company of parish clerks obtained a decree or act, under the seal of the High-commission-court, or Star-chamber, for the keeping of a printing press in their hall, in order to the printing of the weekly and general bills within the city of London and liberties thereof; for which purpose a printer was assigned by the Archbishop of Canterbury. And on the 18th of July that year, a printing press was accordingly set up, and an order then made[3], that from henceforth the weekly reports of the burials, within the limits aforesaid, should be printed, with the number of burials against every parish; which till that time had not been done." This Dr Ogle interprets[4] to mean that the bills were first printed in 1625. But it is certain that in one instance, at least, a weekly bill was printed as early as 1603 "by John Windet, printer to the Honourable City of London," and in 1610 the printing of a blank form for the weekly bills appears to have been the custom[5]. Still it is not improbable that the Parish Clerks possessed no press of their own until 1625, and that may be all that the editor of the "Collection" intends to assert.

If the method by which the bills were made public during the earlier part of the seventeenth century is uncertain, the manner of their publication in the sixteenth century is involved in still greater

[1] Cf. p. 426—427.

[2] P. 9.

[3] Confirmed on 24 February, 1636, *State Papers, Dom., Charles I., Docquet.*

[4] *Inquiry into the Trustworthiness of the old Bills of Mortality*, in *Jour. Stat. Soc.*, LV. 437—460

[5] See p. 336, note also p. 426.

obscurity. Graunt implies[1] that for the figures before 1629 he was forced to have recourse to the unpublished records in the Parish Clerks' Hall, and Dr Ogle suggests[2] that the earlier figures preserved by Stow may have been obtained by that antiquary in a similar way. On the other hand letters of the sixteenth century, preserved at the State Paper Office, show that in times of infection the weekly figures were known to many persons. Perhaps the facts were regularly ascertained after 1563 but were made public during the pestilence only.

Whatever may have been the first year of the bills, and however early their first publication, they were regularly made out by the Parish Clerks for more than two centuries after 1603. In 1849 they ceased, being practically superseded by the new bills issued, since 1840, under the authority of the Registrar-General.

With the growth of London the number of parishes included within the bills of mortality steadily increased. The MS. bill of 16—23 November, 1532, enumerates thirty-seven parishes in which persons died of the plague, and adds "there is this weke clere iii^{xx} and iii paryshes." In the bill of 1535, likewise, one hundred parishes are included, but in 1563 the number has risen to one hundred and eight in the city and liberties[3]. In 1595 the bills gave returns, it is said[4], for one hundred and nine parishes arranged alphabetically without distinction of locality[5]. In 1604 the included area was enlarged to 120 parishes and these were divided, for the purpose of the bills, into three groups. The first group comprised the ninety-six parishes within the walls. This group was subsequently increased by the addition, after 1622, of St James, Duke Place[6], completing the group of "97 parishes within the walls" as enumerated by Graunt on pages 338—340. During the period discussed by Graunt and by Petty (1604—1686) no further change

[1] P. 335. [2] *Inquiry*, 439.

[3] Ogle, *Inquiry*, 437 n., citing Stow's *Annals* (ed. 1631), 657.

[4] Maitland, II. 737.

[5] The number 109 is confirmed by the abstracts of weekly bills for 1597—1600 in the Bodleian Library, Ashmole MS., 824, f. 196. See pp. 433—436.

[6] This church was consecrated 2 January, 1622, and in the first year of Charles I. it was, after a dispute with St Katharine Creechurch, judicially declared a parish church. Seymour, *Survey*, I. 313. Bell says the parish was not included in the bills until 1626. It appears, however, in the weekly bill of 4—11 August, 1625 (Brit. Mus. 1298 m. II.).

of importance was made in the area or in the composition of this group of parishes, save that the weekly bills from September, 1666, to May, 1669 have, instead of ninety-seven parishes, "the 16 parishes (now standing) within the walls."

The second of the three groups formed in 1604 included the parishes without the walls, but partly within the liberties of the city. Thirteen of these were within the bills in 1597. In 1604 there were added St Bartholomew the Great, Bridewell Precinct, and Trinity in the Minories, making up the "sixteen parishes without the walls, standing part within the Liberties and part without, in Middlesex and Surrey." This group, enumerated by Graunt on pages 340—341, remained unaltered until 1673, when its area was diminished by the transfer of part of St Saviour's parish, under the name of Christ Church, Surrey, to the group of twelve out-parishes then existing[1].

The third of the groups of parishes instituted in 1604 has a more varied history. Consisting originally of the eight "out parishes" first brought within the bills in 1604, it was enlarged, in 1606, by the addition of St Mary, Savoy, making the "Nine out Parishes in Middlesex and Surrey" which Graunt names on page 341. In 1647 the number of parishes but not the area of this group was further increased by the introduction into the bills of St Paul, Covent Garden[2], taken, Graunt says[3], out of St Giles and St Martin.

In addition to these three groups—the parishes within the walls, the parishes without the walls but at least partly within the liberties, and the parishes in Middlesex and Surrey, situated without the liberties but adjacent to London—the bills also included, after 1626, the city of Westminster, which was, for this purpose, reckoned as St Margaret parish. During the plague of 1636 there were added[4] the six circumjacent parishes of Islington, Hackney, Stepney, Rotherhithe, Newington, and Lambeth, thus raising the total number of parishes within the bills to one hundred and twenty-nine or, after 1647, to one hundred and thirty. This is the classification of parishes which Graunt has in view in his discussion of the growth of the city[5].

[1] See below p. lxxxvi.

[2] The Act erecting this parish passed the House of Commons 7 January, 1645. *Commons' Journal*, IV. 398.

[3] P. 380.

[4] In the weekly bill of 14—21 April, see p. 344—345 and table at p. 426.

[5] Chapter IX. pp. 378—381 post.

The year 1660 saw a regrouping of the parishes which established the classification still in force when Petty wrote[1]. The two groups of parishes within the liberties remained, with the exception of Christ Church, Southwark, above noted, as they had been before 1660. But the third group, "the Out-parishes, now called ten, formerly nine, and before that eight[2]," was divided. Four parishes of this group[3] were classified with St Margaret as "the five parishes within the city and liberties of Westminster," while the remaining six parishes were joined with the six parishes added in 1636 to make the "twelve parishes lying in Middlesex and Surrey[4]." After 1660 there were, therefore, four groups of parishes within the bills, *viz.* the ninety-seven parishes within the walls, the sixteen parishes without the walls, the five parishes in Westminster, and the twelve out-parishes in Middlesex and Surrey. To these one hundred and thirty parishes there were added, between 1660 and 1686, four others. St Paul, Shadwell[5], which first appeared in the weekly bill of 4—11 April, 1671, was reckoned the thirteenth out-parish, and a fourteenth out-parish, Christ Church, Surrey[6], was added in the bill of 16—23 December, 1673. Since Christ Church had been formerly a part of St Saviour, Southwark, this change made no alteration in the total area within the bills. It simply transferred to the group of out-parishes an area which, since 1604, had been reckoned to the parishes within the liberties. This transfer is without significance for Petty's arguments. The two remaining additions are St James, Westminster[7] and St Anne, Westminster[8], raising the Westminster group of parishes to six, and afterwards to seven[9]. Since both of these parishes were taken out of St Martin-in-the-Fields, which already belonged to the Westminster group, no change of area or of distribution was effected[10].

[1] In 1683—86, p. 457.

[2] Graunt, p. 380.

[3] St Clement Danes, St Paul, Covent Garden, St Martin-in-the-Fields, and St Mary, Savoy.

[4] P. 345.

[5] Erected by Private Act of 22 Charles II. 27. Taken out of Stepney.

[6] Erected by Private Act 22, 23 Charles II. 12, an Act for making the Manor of Paris Garden a Parish. Seymour, *Survey*, II. 816.

[7] In the weekly bill 14—21 July 1685. The Act, 1 James II. is the last in the table of statutes printed for 1685.

[8] In the weekly bill 30 March—6 April, 1686. Private Act, 30 Charles II. 7.

[9] See p. 457 note.

[10] Ogle's *Inquiry* has an appendix on "Successive Changes in the Area covered by the Bills." *Jour. Stat. Soc.*, IV. 453—455.

The form and contents of the bills of mortality have varied greatly since their beginning. In 1532 and 1535 the weekly bills gave the total number of burials and the number of plague burials by parishes, adding a summation of parishes clear and parishes infected. As early as 1578, if not before, the bills gave also the number of christenings[1]. In 1603, if not earlier, the figures of the weekly bills are summed up in December, by a "general or yearly bill[2]." According to Graunt[3], the yearly bill did not particularize the several parishes until the year 1625, and his assertion is implicitly confirmed by Bell, who thus excuses himself from describing the form of bills: "I think I need not trouble myself herein, since that worthy and ingenious gentleman, Captain John Graunt, in his Book of Natural and Political Observations on the Bills of Mortality, hath already so well described them." In the absence of definite evidence to the contrary it may be assumed, therefore, that Graunt is right and that the yearly bills did not enumerate the several parishes until much later than the weekly bills.

The gradual extension of the bills to include territory not originally comprised within their limits, has been already traced. It remains to describe their enlargement by the addition of matter new to them. The first additional matter of importance was the specification of those casualties and diseases, other than the plague, which resulted in death. According to Graunt the causes of non-plague burials were ascertained and entered in the Hallbooks "in the very first year[4]." Bell likewise says that the parishes within the walls, "ever since the year 1604, brought to the Company of Parish Clerks Hall, not only the number of all the christenings and burials, but also an accompt of all the diseases and casualties, although no such accompt was published to the world until the Year 1629." The correctness of Bell's assertion turns upon the interpretation of the word "published," for it is certain that the weekly bills of 5—12 November, 1607, and 10—17 August, 1609, were endorsed in MS. with various causes of death[5]. I have found,

[1] Creighton, I. 341, citing the MS. at Hatfield House.

[2] Maitland says he saw a general bill for 1563 in the library of Sir Hans Sloane. *Hist. of London*, II. 736. Sloane's library has passed to the British Museum, but the general bill for 1563 appears not to be there.

[3] P. 337.

[4] P. 346.

[5] It seems probable that the causes of death other than the plague were made public before 1629. Thus Dr Mead, writing to Sutteville, gives the weekly

however, no early weekly bills upon which the causes of death were printed[1]. The next additional matter introduced into the bills was a distinction of the burials and christenings according to sex. This distinction, introduced for the returns from London and its liberties, in 1629[2] was extended, in 1660, to Westminster and the out-parishes[3]. Important features not appearing in the bills before 1686 are the number of marriages, the omission of which Graunt notes[4], and the age at death, which he makes an attempt to supply by an estimate[5]. Both of these details Petty desired to see introduced into the Dublin bills[6], and they were actually included in the London bills of a later date.

The general trustworthiness of the bills, and consequently the validity of all conclusions based upon them, is conditioned by the accuracy and the completeness with which the Parish Clerks knew the facts that they professed to report. It is therefore important to enquire how they obtained their knowledge of the number of christenings, marriages, and burials and of the causes of death within their respective parishes. The earliest indication of the method pursued is found in the plague orders of the Lord Mayor, issued in 1581. He directed the aldermen:

"To appoynt two honest and discreete matrons within euery parish who shall bee sworne truely to search the body of euery such person as shall happen to dye within the same parish, to the ende that they make true reporte to the clerke of the parish church of all such as shall dye of the plague, that the same clerke may make the like reporte and certificate to the wardens of the parish clerkes thereof according to the order in that behalfe heretofore provided.

If the viewers through favour or corruption shall giue wrong certificate, or shall refuse to serue being thereto appointed, then to punish

deaths of smallpox in May and June, 1628. [Birch's] *Court and Times of Charles I.* Vol. I. p. 359, cited by Creighton, II. 435.

[1] Much interest appears to have been taken in the form of bills by Lord Mayor Chamberlain (1607) and his successors, and several changes were made, particulars of which cannot now be recovered. Christie, 138—140; cf. note, p. 336, post. So considerable were the disagreements, especially with some of the out-parishes, that in 1611 the Company of Parish Clerks were reincorporated and their powers more precisely defined. *State Papers, Dom., James I.* Vol. XLVII. *Docquet*, 31 December, 1611.

[2] Graunt, p. 342.

[3] Bell (unpaged).

[4] P. 347.

[5] Pp. 386—387.

[6] Pp. 488—489.

them by imprisonment in such sorte as may serue for the terror of others[1]."

The manner in which all the searches proceeded in a case of death is thus described by Graunt:

> When any one dies, then, either by tolling, or ringing of a Bell, or by bespeaking of a grave of the Sexton, the same is known to the Searchers, corresponding with the said Sexton. The Searchers hereupon (who are ancient Matrons, sworn to their Office) repair to the place where the dead Corps lies, and by view of the same, and by other Enquiries, they examine by what Disease or Casualty the Corps died. Hereupon they make their report to the Parish Clerk[2].

Graunt, who clearly understood how difficult it sometimes is to determine the cause of death, discusses at considerable length the question whether such ancient matrons, "perhaps ignorant and careless," could make correct returns even if they would[3], and he hints pretty strongly that inaccuracies due to their ignorance may be increased in some cases by their veniality[4]. He is therefore inclined to distrust their reports in the more difficult cases[5]. Petty, with characteristic practical shrewdness, proposed to meet this difficulty by the enumeration, in his model Dublin bills, of but twenty-four casualties, "being such as may be discerned by common sense and without Art, conceiving that more will perplex and imbroil the account[6]." His suggestion remained without effect. Indeed it seems that the very lame defence of the searchers put forth by Bell in reply to Graunt's strictures, must have been considered quite adequate[7], for in spite of the sharp but just criticism passed by

[1] *State Papers, Elizabeth*, Vol. XLVIII. no. 70, printed by Creighton, I. 319. The date of the order "heretofore provided" regarding searches cannot be determined, but they are mentioned at Shrewsbury as early as 1539. *Ibid.*, I. 320.

[2] P. 346. [3] P. 347. [4] Pp. 356, 357.

[5] Pp. 347—361.

[6] P. 491; the London bills in Graunt's day distinguished no less than 81 causes of death. Cf. the table facing page 406.

[7] Bell says, "Searchers are generally ancient women, and I think are therefore most fit for their office. But sure I am they are chosen by some of the eminentest men of the Parish to which they stand related; and if any of their Choosers should speak against their abilities they would much disparage their own judgements. And after such choice they are examined touching their sufficiency, and sworn to that office by the Dean of Arches, or some Justice of the Peace, as the cause shall require." This seventeenth century English demonstration of official competence, which, mutatis mutandis, sounds strangely familiar to nineteenth century American

Maitland[1] in 1756 and by the editor[2] of the "Collection of the Yearly Bills" in 1759, no material amendment was effected in the administration of the London Vital Statistics until they came under the supervision of the Registrar-General[3].

To determine the mere number of persons who died, or were born or married, is much less difficult than to determine the causes of their death; but even in the former respects the seventeenth century bills leave much to be desired. Graunt himself pointed out "that there hath been a neglect in the Accompt of the Christenings[4]," and explains that this "hath been neglected more than that of Burials" because religious scruples played a larger part in the former case[5]. But even the record of burials included, as a rule, only those buried according to the service of the Church of England. Roman Catholics and non-conformists interred in their own burying grounds were entirely omitted from the bills. Now as late as 1676 Petty calculated on the basis of the Bishop's Survey, that these omitted classes were nearly five per cent of the population of England[6], and it is generally admitted that in the twenty-five years after the Restoration the proportion of non-conformists had considerably decreased. Besides this, it seems that even conformists buried elsewhere than in the parish churches or cemeteries, *e.g.* in St Paul's, the Charter House, or the hospitals, were omitted from the bills[7]. Further than this Dr Ogle has shown by comparison of the printed or manuscript registers of many parish churches with the number of burials returned from those parishes by the bills, that the Parish Clerks were often careless in making the returns even of members of the Established Church buried in their own parish cemeteries, and that the number in the bills is more frequently an understatement than an exaggeration. It seems, however, that

ears, Bell clinches by adding "I presume there cannot be a stricter obligation than an oath to bind any person." *London's Remembrancer* (not paged).

1 *History of London*, II. 740, seq.

2 Probably Dr Heberden. See Bibliography, no. 17.

3 *Penny Cyclopædia* (1835), Vol. IV. pp. 407, 408, s.v. Bills of Mortality.

4 Pp. 361—362. 5 P. 361. 6 P. 461.

7 Maitland, *Hist. of London*, II. 740—743; Ogle, *loc. cit.* 446; Short, *New Observations*, p. x. Petty says (p. 511) that in 1685 there were buried from St Bartholomew's and St Thomas's alone 451 persons, which is over two per cent. of the 23,222 burials returned in the annual bill for that year (p. 517 note). In 1729, when the bills returned 29,722 deaths, Maitland finds that 3038 were omitted.

when a sufficient series of years is taken, the discrepancy arising from this source during the seventeenth century is not large[1]. And, finally, the number of persons who died in London but were buried in the country far exceeded the number dying in the country but buried in London. How great the error due to this fact may have been in the seventeenth century, we have no means of knowing. In the middle of the eighteenth it was very plausibly calculated at one sixth of the whole number[2]. Taking all these facts into account, it is not too much to assume that we must add a correction of at least fifteen per cent. to the figures of burials in the pre-Restoration bills, and not less than ten per cent. to the later figures which Petty uses, in order to obtain an approximately correct estimate of the actual mortality of London at the dates in question. Inasmuch as both Graunt and Petty base their estimates of London's population upon the burials reported in the bills, the numbers which they deduce must be pronounced too small, even upon the assumption of a death rate that justified them in multiplying by only thirty. But their other important deductions from the bills, such as the determination of the approximate numerical equality between the sexes, the discovery that the most healthy years are also the most fruitful, and even their calculations of the growth of the city, are far less affected by the incompleteness of the original returns. In fact if the cases omitted were, as seems not improbable, similar or proportional to those included, the effect of the omissions upon the validity of most of their conclusions would be almost negligibly small.

So far as the "country bills" used by Graunt are concerned, it is probable that the parish registers from which they were derived were kept more carefully after Cromwell's registration Act of 1653 than before it. If so we can account not only for the increase of the weddings, which Graunt explains in another way[3], but also for the contemporaneous increase of the births and the burials.

[1] Ogle, 443—445.

[2] *Collection of Yearly Bills*, 5; Maitland, II. 742; Ogle, 447—448.

[3] P. 400.

A

TREATISE

OF

Taxes & Contributions.

Shewing the Nature and Measures of

Crown-Lands.	Penalties.
Assessements.	Monopolies.
Customs.	Offices.
Poll-Moneys.	Tythes.
Lotteries.	Raising of Coins.
Benevolence.	Harth-Money.
	Excize, &c.

With several interesperst Discourses and Digressions concerning

Warres.	Beggars.
The Church.	Ensurance.
Universities.	Exportation of { Money. Wool.
Rents & Purchases.	Free-Ports.
Usury & Exchange.	Coins.
Banks & Lombards.	Housing.
Registries for Conveyances.	Liberty of Conscience, &c.

The same being frequently applied to the present State and Affairs of

IRELAND.

London, Printed for *N. Brooke*, at the Angel in *Cornhill*. 1662.

NOTE ON THE "TREATISE OF TAXES."

THE Treatise of Taxes and Contributions is the earliest of Petty's economic writings. Since it mentions[1] Graunt's Observations, published in January, 1662, as "lately made," and inasmuch as Petty was in Ireland before the end of October[2], the Treatise was probably composed in the early months of 1662. About this time Petty, relieved from his political anxieties, returned with vigour to his scientific pursuits[3]. He experimented with the Double Bottom, and wrote, in addition to the Treatise, his Discourse concerning the Making of Cloth, his Apparatus to the History of Dying, and a paper on shipping[4].

The precise date of the publication of the Treatise is not known. If we take the phrase[5] "a parliament most affectionate to his [Ormond's] person" as an allusion to the gift of £30,000 voted to Ormond by the Irish House of Commons 4 March, 1662[6] and acknowledged by him in a letter from Whitehall 19 April, we may well believe White Kennett's assertion[7] that the Treatise first appeared in May, 1662. If, on the other hand, we note Petty's statement that its birth "happened to be about the time of the Duke of Ormond's going Lord Lieutenant into Ireland," we shall place the publication nearly two months later. It appears, however, that Ormond's departure, postponed by the King's marriage until the beginning of July, was originally planned to take place in April[8].

[1] P. 27.

[2] Letter to Sir Robert Moray, Roy. Soc. MS. Letter Book, P, I, p. 11.

[3] Fitzmaurice, 104—107.

[4] Birch, *History of the Royal Society*, I, 65, also Bibliography, 7, 28.

[5] P. 9.

[6] *Polit. Anat.*, ch. IX.

[7] Kennett, *Register and Chronicle*, 703.

[8] Carte, *Ormond*, II, 257.

We can, therefore, bring the two passages into harmony by assuming that Petty wrote his preface, above quoted, in April, when he expected Ormond to go to Ireland at once, and that the Treatise was published in May, 1662.

Four editions of the Treatise were issued during Petty's lifetime[1]. Of these it is probable that the first alone was authorized by him. The second (1667) was printed at London during his absence in Ireland, and the edition of 1679 seems to have been issued against his expressed wishes. On the 29th May, 1678, he wrote to Aubrey, "As for the Reprinting the Booke of Taxes I will not meddle with it. I never had thanks for any publick good I ever did, nor doe I owne any such booke[2]." And on the 5th October following, in a letter to Sir Robert Southwell, he again expressed his unwillingness to have the Treatise reprinted[3]. The edition of 1685, being but a re-issue, with a new title-page, of the sheets printed in 1679, is of no independent authority. The first edition, here reprinted[4], must, therefore, be esteemed the most authentic of the four, and although no MS. has been found, the language of the preface gives assurance that it was not set forth without the author's approval. The edition is anonymous. The first public recognition of its authorship which I have noted occurs in the "Suppliment" to Brief Considerations concerning Trade and the Interest of Money. By J[osiah] C[hild]. London, Elizabeth Calvert, 1668[5].

[1] See Bibliography, 6.

[2] Fitzmaurice, 258. The original letter is in the Bodleian Library, Aubrey MS. 11, f. 110; Lord E. Fitzmaurice used the copy in the British Museum, Egerton MS. 2231, f. 90.

[3] Thorpe's *Catalogus lib. MSS. bibl. Southwellianæ* (1834), p. 403.

[4] The edition of 1662 is carelessly printed. Obvious misspellings, such as "enrease" for "encrease" (original, p. 4), "statseman" for "Statesman" (p. 41), "Beeer" for "Beer" (p. 74), have been corrected in this reprint. In all other cases the original has been scrupulously followed, but mistakes noted in the "errata" are indicated in footnotes. The "errata" are also reprinted on pages 96 and 97.

[5] Reprinted in Child's *New Discourse of Trade* (1693), p. 26.

The Preface.

YOung and vain persons, though perhaps they marry not primarily and onely on purpose to get Children, much less to get such as may be fit for some one particular vocation; yet having Children, they dispose of them as well as they can according to their respective inclinations: Even so, although I wrote these sheets but to rid my head of so many troublesome conceits, and not to apply them to the use of any one particular People or Concernment; yet now they are born, and that their Birth happened to be about the time of the *Duke of Ormond's* going Lord Lieutenant into *Ireland*, I thought they might be as proper for the consideration of that place, as of any other, though perhaps of effect little enough in any.

Ireland is a place which must have so great an Army kept up in it, as may make the Irish desist from doing themselves or the English harm by their future Rebellions. And this great Army || must occasion great and heavy Leavies upon a poor people and wasted Countrey; it is therefore not amiss that *Ireland* should understand the nature and measure of Taxes and Contributions.

2. The Parishes of *Ireland* do much want Regulation, by uniting and dividing them[1]; so as to make them fit Enclosures

[1] In 1662 the Parliament of Ireland passed an Act for the real union and division of parishes—14 & 15 Charles II., c. 10. It is not clear that Petty had any connection with this Act, but the preamble seems to reflect his ideas: "Whereas parishes are in some parts of this Kingdom so little that five or six lie together within a mile or two, whereby subjects are likely to be much burdened with the unnecessary charge of building and repairing so many churches,

wherein to plant the Gospel: wherefore what I have said as to the danger of supernumerary Ministers, may also be seasonable there, when the new Geograpy we expect of that Island[1] shall have afforded means for the Regulation abovementioned.

3. The great plenty of *Ireland* will but undo it, unless a way be found for advantageous Exportations, the which will depend upon the due measure of Custom and Excize here treated on.

4. Since *Ireland* is under-peopled in the whole, and since the Government there can never be safe without chargeable Armies, until the major part of the Inhabitants be English, whether by carrying over these, or withdrawing the other[2];

and the means also are made so small that many of them will not serve for the sustention of one incumbent: and on the other side in some places parishes are so vast, or extended in length, that it is difficult for the parishioners to repair to their parish churches, and return home the same day, and many times so inconveniently divided that the parishioners of one parish may with much more convenience repair to another parochial church than their own," etc., therefore from Michaelmas, 1662, the chief governor, with the consent of all concerned, may unite or divide parishes.

[1] Probably an allusion to Petty's engraved maps of Ireland, based upon the original maps of the Down Survey, which had indicated the boundaries of parishes. Petty's *Hist. of the Down Survey, ed. by* Larcom, 49. In 1665 Petty petitioned the King for "assistance to finish the Map of Ireland" and the petition was granted. *Ib.*, 400—401, 323. It seems doubtful, however, whether he actually received assistance sufficient to complete his scheme, since in 1672 he asserted that he had, at his own charge, caused distinct maps to be made of every barony or hundred, as also of every county, graven on copper, and the like of every province, and of the whole kingdom. *Polit. Anat.*, ch. IX. The county maps, at least, were subsequently published, without date, under the title *Hiberniae Delineatio*. See Bibliography. Copies of this undated edition are in the British Museum and in the Bodleian Library. The Library of Trinity College, Dublin, has three copies. All of these, except the first mentioned, contain a portrait of Petty ("Edwin Sandys sculp."), dated 1683. The British Museum *Catalogue of Printed Maps*, likewise, assigns to the collection the conjectural date of 1685. But the "General Map of Ireland" ("Sutton Nicholls sculp."), which is mentioned in the title of the *Delineatio*, bears an engraved advertisement of Cox's *History of Ireland*, the first volume of which was issued in 1689. The copy in the National Library of Ireland is a reissue dedicated to Petty's son Henry as Earl of Shelburne. It must have been published, therefore, after 1719, the date at which the earldom of Shelburne was created, and before 1751, when Shelburne died.

[2] The settlement of the Irish question by the fusion of Irish and English

I think there can be no better encouragement to draw English thither, then to let them know, that the Kings Revenue being above $\frac{1}{10}$ part of the whole Wealth, Rent, and Proceed of the Nation; that the Publick Charge || in the next Age will be no more felt there then that of Tythes is here; and that as the Kings Revenue encreases, so the causes of his Expence will decrease proportionably, which is a double advantage.

6. The employing the Beggars in *England* about mending the High-wayes, and making Rivers Navigable will make the Wool and Cattle of *Ireland* vend the better.

7. The full understanding of the nature of Money, the effects of the various *species* of Coins, and of their uncertain values, as also of raising or embasing them, is a learning most proper for *Ireland*, which hath been lately much and often abused for the want of it[1].

8. Since Lands are worth but six or seven years purchase, and yet twenty years just cross the Channel, 'twere good the people of *Ireland* knew the reasons of it at a time when there is means of help.

Lastly, if any man hath any Notions which probably may be good for *Ireland*, he may with most advantage expose them to publick examination now, when the Duke of *Ormond*[2] is Chief Governour: for,

was a favourite notion of Petty's from 1655, when, in collaboration with Vincent Gookin, he is said to have opposed the segregation of the Irish by transplantation into Connaught, to the year of his death. Fitzmaurice, 31, 32, also Petty's *Treatise of Ireland*.

[1] During the Commonwealth the issue of private token money had been much abused in Ireland, and shortly before Petty went thither certain Londoners had been executed for introducing counterfeit and clipped English money and base Peru pieces into the island. Simon, *Essay on the Irish Coins*, 48—49. Nevertheless the abuse continued, *Ib.*, 49—52, 118—122. The 29th January, 1660—1, a proclamation (*Ib.*, 123—124) was issued fixing rates for gold and silver coin, and the 17th August, 1661, a proclamation was issued against tokens. Ruding, *Annals of the Coinage*, II. 4. Cf. Fleetwood to Thurloe, 16 Feb., 1653, *State Papers*, II, 94.

[2] It is as unnecessary as it is impossible to give an adequate notice of Ormond in a foot-note. James Butler, twelfth Earl and first Duke of Ormond, thrice Lord Lieutenant of Ireland (born 1610), had been a loyal supporter of the royal cause, and his devotion as well as his ability had received appropriate recognition at the Restoration. In November, 1661, he was for the second time appointed Lord

1. His Grace knows that Countrey perfectly || well, as well in times and matters of Peace as War, and understands the Interests as well of particular persons, as of all and every factions and parties struggling with each other in that Kingdom; understanding withall the state of *England*, and also of several Forreign Nations, with reference to *Ireland*.

2. His Grace hath given fresh demonstration of his care of an English Interest in *Ireland*, and of his wisdom in reconciling the several cross concernments there so far as the same is possible.

3. His Graces Estate in Lands there is the greatest that ever was in *Ireland*, and consequently he is out of the danger incident to those *Proreges* against whom *Cambden* sayes, *Hibernia est semper querula*; there being no reason for ones getting more Land, who hath already the most of any.

4. Whereas some chief Governours who have gone into *Ireland*, chiefly to repair or raise fortunes, have withdrawn themselves again when their work hath been done, not abiding the clamours and complaints of the people afterwards: But his Grace hath given Hostages to that Nation for his good Government, and yet hath taken away aforehand all fears of the contrary.

5. His Grace dares do whatever he understands || to be fitting, even to the doing of a single Subject Justice against a Confederate multitude; being above the sinister interpretations of the jealous and querulous; for his known Liberality and Magnificence shall ever keep him free from the clamor of the people, and his through-tried fidelity shall frustrate the

Lieutenant, and his administration of that office justified the high estimation in which he was held. His recall, in 1669, appears to have been the result of unworthy intrigue and not of loss of the royal confidence, which he had done much to deserve. Again appointed Lord Lieutenant in 1677, he was recalled to England in 1685 and died 21 July, 1688. The warm admiration which Petty entertained for Ormond finds frequent expression in his letters, and it appears that Ormond, also, was well disposed towards Petty. See Aubrey to Anthony à Wood, St John Evangelist's Day, 1681, Ballard MS. 14, f. 135, in the Bodleian Library, also Fitzmaurice, 104, 138—139, 151, 173—174. See however, Ormond to Ossory, 15 Aug., 1668, in Carte's *Ormond*, Appendix, lxxxii, p. 63.

force of any subdolous whisperings in the Ears of His Majesty.

6. His good acceptance of all ingenious endeavours, shall make the wise men of this Eastern *England* be led by his Star into *Ireland*, and there present him with their choicest advices, who can most judiciously select and apply them.

Lastly, this great Person takes the great Settlement in hand, when *Ireland* is as a white paper, when there sits a Parliament most affectionate to his Person, and capable of his Counsel, under a King curious as well as careful of Reformation; and when there is opportunity, to pass into Positive Laws whatsoever is right reason and the Law of Nature.

Wherefore by applying those Notions unto *Ireland*, I think I have harped upon the right string, and have struck whilest the Iron is hot; by publishing them now, when, if ever at all, they be useful. I would now advertise the || world, that I do not think I can mend it, and that I hold it best for every mans particular quiet, to let it *vadere sicut vult*; I know well, that *res nolunt male administrari*[1], and that (say I what I will or can) things will have their course, nor will nature be couzened: Wherefore what I have written, (as I said before) was done but to ease and deliver my self, my head having been impregnated with these things by the daily talk I hear about advancing and regulating Trade, and by the murmurs about Taxes, &c. Now whether what I have said be contemned or cavilled at, I care not, being of the same minde about this, as some thriving men are concerning the profuseness of their Children; for as they take pleasure to

[1] This is a favourite quotation with Petty. It occurs in his *Discourse of Duplicate Proportion* (1674, see note to Dedication of *Polit. Arith.*), and in his letter to Southwell, 2 June, 1686, Fitzmaurice, 274. In the modified form "Ingenia solent res nolunt male administrari," it is the motto of his *Speculum Hiberniae*. Brit. Mus. Addl. MS. 21,128, f. 38. Sir Josiah Child (*loc. cit.*) apparently considered Petty the author of it. But Sir Peter Pett, who declares it a sentence of late (1680) much in vogue and one which he had heard some men living falsely vouched for the author of, traces it to Bede's *Axiomata Philosophica* [Migne, XC. 1023] and to Aristotle's *Metaphysica*, [XII. 10, ed. Schwegler (1847), I. 258]. Pett, *Happy future State of England*, 250.

get even what they believe will be afterwards pissed against the wall, so do I to write, what I suspect will signifie nothing: Wherefore the race being not to the swift, &c. but time and chance happening to all men, I leave the Judgement of the whole to the Candid, of whose correction I shall never be impatient. ||

The Index.

CHAP. I.

Of the several sorts of Publick Charges.

THe Publick Charges of a State, are, *That of its Defence* by Land and Sea, of its Peace at home and abroad, as also of its honourable vindication from the injuries of other States; all which we may call the Charge of the Militia, which commonly is in ordinary as great as any other Branch of the whole; but extraordinary, (that is, in time of War, or fear of War) is much the greatest.

2. Another branch of the Publick Charge is, the Maintenance of the Governours, Chief and Subordinate; I mean, such not onely as spend their whole time in the Execution of their respective Offices, but also who †spent much in fitting themselves as well with abilities to that end, as in begetting an opinion in their Superiours of such their ability and trustworthiness.

3. Which Maintenance of the Governours is to be in such a degree of plenty and splendour, as private Endeavours and Callings seldom reach unto: To the end, that such Governours may have the natural as well as the artificial Causes of Power to act with.

4. For if a great multitude of men should call one of their number King, unless this instituted Prince, appear in greater visible splendour then others, can reward those that obey and please him, and do the contrary to others; his
2 Insti||tution signifies little, even although he chance to have greater corporal or mental faculties, than any other of the number.

† between [*who* and *spent*] interline [*have*]

5. There be Offices which are but *πάρεργα*, as Sheriffs, Justices of the Peace, Constables, Churchwardens, &c. which men may attend without much prejudice to their ordinary wayes of livelihood, and for which the honour of being trusted, and the pleasure of being feared, hath been thought a competent Reward.

6. Unto this head, the Charge of the administring justice may be referred, as well between man and man, as between the whole State or Commonalty and particular members of it; as well that of righting and punishing past injuries and crimes, as of preventing the same in time to come.

7. A third branch of the Publick Charge is, that of the *Pastorage of mens Souls*, and the guidance of their Consciences; which, one would think (because it respects another world, and but the particular interest of each man there) should not be a publick Charge in this: Nevertheless, if we consider how easie it is to elude the Laws of man, to commit unproveable crimes, to corrupt and divert Testimonies, to wrest the sense and meaning of the Laws, &c. there follows a necessity of contributing towards a publick Charge, wherewith to have men instructed in the Laws of God, that take notice of evil thoughts and designs, and much more of secret deeds, and that punisheth eternally in another world, what man can but slightly chastise in this.

8. Now those who labour in this publick Service, must also be maintained in a proportionable splendour; and must withall have the means to allure men with some kinde of reward, even in this life; forasmuch, as many heretofore followed even Christ himself, but for the Loaves he gave them.

9. Another branch is, the Charge of Schools and Universities, especially for so much as they teach above *Reading, Writing, and Arithmetick*; these being of particular use to every man, as being helps and substitutes of Memory and Reason, Reckoning being of the latter, as Writing and Reading are of the former; for whether Divinity, &c. ought || to be 3
made a private Trade, is to me a question.

10. 'Tis true, that Schools and Colledges are now for the

most part but the Donations of particular men, or places where particular men spend their money and time upon their own private accounts; but no doubt it were not amiss, if the end of them were to furnish all imaginable helps unto the highest and finest Natural Wits, towards the discovery of Nature in all its operations; in which sense they ought to be a publick Charge: The which Wits should not be selected for that work, according to the fond conceits of their own Parents and Friends, (Crows that think their own Birds ever fairest) but rather by the approbation of others more impartial; such as they are, who pick from out of the Christians Children the ablest Instruments and Support of the Turkish Government. Of which Selections more hereafter.

11. Another branch is, that of the *Maintenance of Orphans, found and exposed Children*, which also are Orphans; as also of Impotents of all sorts, and moreover such as want employment.

12. For the permitting of any to beg is a more chargeable way of maintaining them whom the law of Nature will not suffer to starve, where food may possibly be had: Besides, it is unjust to let any starve, when we think it just to limit the wages of the poor, so as they can lay up nothing against the time of their impotency and want of work.

13. A last Branch may be, the Charge of High-wayes, Navigable Rivers, Aquæducts, Bridges, Havens, and other things of universal good and concernment.

14. Other Branches may be thought on, which let other men either refer unto these, or adde over and above. For it suffices for my purpose to have for the present set down these the chief and most obvious of all the rest. ||

CHAP. II.

Of the Causes which encrease and aggravate the several sorts of Publick Charges.

HAving thus spoken of the several sorts of Publick Charges, we shall next consider the Causes which encrease them both in general and in particular.

Among the general Causes is, First, the unwillingness of the people to pay them; arising from an opinion, that by delay and reluctancy they may wholly avoid them, with a suspition that what is imposed is too much, or that what is collected is embezelled or ill expended, or that it is unequally leavied and assessed. All these resolving into an unnecessary Charge to collect them, and of forcing their Prince to hardships towards the people.

2. Another Cause which aggravates Taxes is, the force of paying them in money at a certain time, and not in commodities, at the most convenient seasons.

3. Thirdly, Obscurities and doubts concerning the right of imposing.

4. Fourthly, Scarcity of Money, and Confusion of Coins.

5. Fifthly, Fewness of people, especially of Labourers and Artificers.

6. Sixthly, Ignorance of the numbers, Wealth and Trade of the people, causing a needless repetition of the charge and trouble of new additional Levies, in order to amend mistakes.

7. As to particulars. The Causes of encreasing the Military Charge are the same with those that encrease Wars, or fear of Wars, which are Forreign or Civil.

8. An Offensive Forreign War is caused by many, and those very various, secret, personal distastes coloured—with publick pretences; of which we can say nothing, but that the common encouragement unto them particularly here in *Eng-||land* is a false opinion, that our Countrey is full peopled, 5
or that if we wanted more Territory, we could take it with

less charge from our neighbours, then purchase it from the *Americans*; and a mistake, that the greatness and glory of a Prince lyeth rather in the extent of his Territory, then in the number, art, and industry of his people, well united and governed. And moreover, that it is more glorious to take from others by fraud or rapine, then to gain ones self out of the bowels of the Earth and Sea.

9. Now those States are free from Forreign Offensive Wars (arising as abovesaid out of Personal and Private Causes) where the chief Governours Revenue is but small, and not sufficient to carry on such Wars, the which if they happen to be begun, and so far carryed on, as to want † more Contributions, then those who have the power to impose them, do commonly enquire what private persons and Ends occasioned the War, and so fall upon the Authors, rather then contribute to the Effect; otherwise then to quench it.

10. Defensive Wars are caused from unpreparedness of the offended State for War, as when defective Stores are served into the Magazines by corrupt Officers at the rate of good; when Armies are falsly Mustered; when Souldiers are either Tenants or Servants to their Commanders, or else persons, who for their Crimes or Debts, want protection from Justice; when the Officers are ignorant of their business, and absent from their Commands; and withal afraid to punish, because unwilling to pay. Wherefore, to be alwayes in a posture of War at home, is the cheapest way to keep off War from abroad.

11. The causes of Civil Wars here in *Europe* proceed very much from Religion, *viz.* the punishing of Believers heterodox from the Authorized way, in publike and open places, before great multitudes of ignorant people, with loss of life, liberty, and limbs, rather then by well proportioned tolerable pecuniary mulcts, such as every conscientious Non-Conformist would gladly pay, and Hypocrites by refusing, discover themselves to be such.||

12. Civil Wars are likewise caused by peoples fansying, that their own uneasie condition may be best remedied by an

† after [*want*] read [*general*] instead of [*more*]

universal confusion; although indeed upon the upshot of such disorders they shall probably be in a worse, even although they survive and succeed, but more probably perish in the contest.

13. Moreover, the peoples believing that Forms of Government shall in a few years produce any considerable alteration as to the wealth of the Subject; that the Form which is most ancient and present is not the best for the place; that any established family or person is not better then any new pretender, or even then the best Election that can be made; that Sovereignty is invisible, and that it is not certainly annexed unto some certain person or persons[1].

14. Causes of Civil War are also, that the Wealth of the Nation is in too few mens hands, and that no certain means are provided to keep all men from a necessity either to beg, or steal, or be Souldiers.

Moreover, the allowing Luxury in some, whilst others †starve.

The dispensing of benefits upon casual and uncertain Motives; the giving vaste Emoluments to persons and parties of no certain visible merit. These are the things which cause animosities among the totter-headed multitude, who are the tinder that the sparks of a few Designers may easily inflame.

15. The ‡Cause of Publick Charge in matters of Religion, are †† the not having changed the limits of Parishes and Cures with the Change of Religion from Popery, and with the Changes in Plantation and Trade. For now when the Ministers of the Gospel preach unto multitudes assembled in one place, may not Parishes be bigger? that is, may not Flocks be more numerous, then when every particular sheep was, as heretofore, drest and shorn three or four times *per annum* by Shrift. If there be in *England* and *Wales* but about five millions of people, what needs more than 5000.

[1] Probably an allusion to the discussions in Harrington's Rota Club, and to his theories of election and of sovereignty. "Dr William Petty was a Rota man," says Wood, "and would sometimes trouble Harrington in his club"—whether on account of real divergence of opinion or purely from love of an argument may be questioned.

† befoie [*starve*] interline [*needlesly*]
‡ before [*cause*] read [*one*] instead of [*the*]
†† read [*is*] instead of [*are*]

Parishes? that is 1000. Sheep under every Shepheard. Whereas in the middling Parishes of *London* there are about 5000. souls in each. Upon which account there needs be in *England* and *Wales* but a 1000. Parishes, whereas there are near 10000.

16. Now the saving of half the Parishes, would (reckoning the Benefices one with another, but at 100 l. *per Annum* a piece) save 500000 l. Besides, when the number of Parochial Parsons were halved, then there would need but half the present number of Byshops, Deans and Chapters, Colledges and Cathedralls, which perhaps would amount to two or three hundred thousand pounds more: And yet the Church of God would be more regularly served then now, and that without prejudice to that sacred, ancient Order of Episcopacy, and the way of their Maintenance by Tythes; and all this in a method of greater Reformation and suitableness thereunto.

18[1]. But suppose it be said, that in some wild Countreys, a thousand people do not live in a less scope of ground then of eight miles square. To which I answer, that there are few or no such places, the largest Parishes I know, being not more capacious then of three or four miles square, in which is no difficulty, for the people to meet once a week at some central place within that scope.

19. Moreover I say, that a Curate of small Learning, if of good life, and duly Ordained, may officiate in four Chappels of Ease every Sunday; and the Preacher, who indeed should be a person of Learning and Eloquence, may preach every other Sunday in every of the said Chappels, by preaching in two of them one day, and in the other two, the other day: And this with Catechizing, and Extra-Lectures upon the Week-dayes, would perform as much as now is performed, and as much as by the blessing of God is necessary to salvation; for the yoak of Christ is easie, and his burthen light.

20. But to put an end to this doubt; I affirm, that if England and Wales were cut out in parcels of three miles square, there would be found few above four thousand such, of which to make Parishes.

[1] In the 1662 edition paragraphs 17 to 20 are erroneously numbered 18 to 21.

21. Now if it be said, that the Alienation of these Tythes is Sacriledge; I answer, that if the same be employed to defend the Church of God against the Turke and Pope, and the Nations who adhere to them, it is not at all; or less, then
to || give $\frac{3}{4}$. of the same to the Wives and Children of the 8
Priests which were not in being when those allowances were set forth?

21. If I had not an abhorrence from propounding the lessening of the Church Means, I could say, that the retrenching part of each remaining Parsons Tythes and Emoluments, and leaving him† for part, to the free Contributions of his‡ Flocks, were a way to promote the Gospel, and to give less offence to such as think that their whole maintenance should be made in that manner.

22. I might also say, that forasmuch as there be more Males then Females in *England*[1], (the said disproportion *pro tanto* hindering procreation) that it were good for the Ministers to return to their Cælibat; or that none should be Ministers, whilst they were married, it being easie among five millions of people to finde out 5000. that could and would live single, that is one in a thousand: And then our unmarried Parson might live as well with half, as now with the whole of his Benefice.

23. Alwayes provided, that though the number of Parishes, and the measure of Benefices were lessened, yet that the same ought to be done without dammage to the present Incumbents.

24. As for lessening the Charge of Offices relating to the Government and the Law, the same will consist in abolishing the superfluous, supernumerary, and antiquated; and withall, in retrenching the Fees of others, to what the labour, art, and trust of their respective employments do require. For there be many Offices wholly executed by Deputies for small wages, whereas the Masters of them have ten times as much, although they know nothing either of what is done, or ought to be done in the business.

25. Now such Surplusages as these should be either

[1] See Graunt, ch. VIII.

† read [*them*] for [*him*]

‡ read [*their*] for [*his*]

restored unto the people who gave them unto the King, at a time when those Fees made up but a just reward for the Officer; or else the King keeping them still might take them for so much toward the Publick Charge, but not
9 give them away to stop || the importunate suits of any particular person, in whom and in all his dependants, such benefits do but cause a laziness as to the true original gain of the Nation, and themselves in particular, together with a total negligence and ignorance of the publick good.

26. Many are the particulars that might be instanced of this kinde; but my aim not being to prejudice any man in particular, I descend no lower, wishing onely that there might be an universal Reformation of what length of time hath warped awry, in which case no particular men are to be troubled; for if all suffer, none suffers, and all men would be no poorer then now they are if they should lose half their Estates; nor would they be a whit the richer if the same were doubled, the *Ratio formalis* of Riches lying rather in proportion then quantity.

27. To lessen the charge of Universities, unto which I adde the Inns of Court, which is not much, were to lessen the number of the Students in Divinity, Law and Medicine, by lessening the use of those Professions.

Now having spoken already of Divinity, I come next to the Law, and say; that if Registers were kept of all mens Estates in Lands, and of all the Conveyances of, and Engagements upon them; and withal if publick Loan-Banks, Lombards, or Banks of Credit upon deposited money, Plate, Jewels, Cloth, Wooll, Silke, Leather, Linnen, Mettals, and other durable Commodities, were erected[1], I cannot apprehend how there could be above one tenth part of the Law-suits and Writings, as now there are.

28. And moreover, if by accompt of the people, of their

[1] The demand for the introduction into England of the Dutch registers and of Lombards is common to all the "imitators of Holland." Roscher, *Gesch. der engl. Volkswirthschaftslehre*, 63; also Child, *Brief Observations* (1668), repr. in *New Discourse*, 5, 7; Temple, *Observations upon the United Provinces* (1673), 83—85, 200.

Land and other wealth, the number of Lawyers and Scriveners were adjusted, I cannot conceive how their should remain above one hundredth part of what now are; forasmuch as I have heard some affirm, that there be now ten times as many as are even now necessary; and that there are now ten times as many Law-suits, as upon the abovementioned Reformation, there would be. It follows therefore, that upon the whole there would not need one in a hundred of the present || number of Retainers to the Law, and Offices of Justice; the occasions as well of crimes as injuries being so much retrenched.

29. As for Physicians, it is not hard by the help of the observations which have been lately made upon the Bills of Mortality, to know how many are sick in *London* by the number of them that dye, and by the proportions of the City to finde out the same of the Countrey; and by both, by the advice of the learned Colledge of that Faculty to calculate how many Physicians were requisite for the whole Nation[1]; and consequently, how many Students in that art to permit and encourage; and lastly, having calculated these numbers, to adoptate a proportion of Chyrurgeons, Apothecaries, and Nurses to them, and so by the whole to cut off and extinguish that infinite swarm of vain pretenders unto, and abusers of that God-like Faculty, which of all Secular Employments our Saviour himself after he began to preach engaged himself upon.

30. Moreover, if it were agreed, what number of Divines, Physicians and Civilians (that is, of men bred in Universities) were requisite to the publick service? As suppose 13000. in the present way, and perhaps not above 6000. in that way of

[1] Petty had been admitted a candidate of the College of Physicians 25 June, 1650. The 14th of July, 1655, he was elected fellow of the College, but, being then in Ireland, he was not admitted to his new rank until 25 June, 1658. Munk, *Roll*, 2nd ed., I. 271. He was also one of the forty fellows named in the charter granted 26 March, 1664. Goodall, *The Royal College of Physicians* (1684), p. 70. His suggestion is not wholly out of keeping with the purpose of a corporation established "with a view to the improvement and more orderly practice of the art of physic, and the repression of irregular, unlearned, and incompetent practicioners of that faculty."

Retrenchment which we propound; then supposing that but one in forty dyes *per annum*, it follows that less than 350. might suffice to be sent yearly out of the Universities: Where supposing they stay five years one with another, it followeth also that about 1800. is the number of Students fit to be allowed in the Universities at a time; I mean, of such as intend to make Learning their Trade and way of Livelihood.

31. I might intimate, that if 1800. Students were enough, and that if there were 40000. Parish Children and Foundlings in *England*, it were probable that one in twenty of them might be of excellent wit and towardness.

Now since the Publick may dispose of these Children as they please, and since there is Maintenance in both Universities for above 1800. what if our Professors of Art were in this manner selected and educated? But of this but *in transitu.* ||

11 32. Hereunto may be added, that by reason of Loan Banks aforementioned, whereby the Credits and Estates of all Dealers may be known, and all the mysterious dangers of money prevented, and that by good Accompts of our growth, Manufacture, Consumption, and Importation, it might be known how many Merchants were able to mannage the Exchange of our superfluous Commodities with the same of other Countreys: And also how many Retailers are needful to make the subdistributions into every Village of this Nation, and to receive back their superfluities. Upon these grounds I presume a large proportion of these also might be retrenched, who properly and originally earn nothing from the Publick, being onely a kinde of Gamesters, that play with one another for the labours of the poor; yielding of themselves no fruit at all, otherwise then as veins and arteries, to distribute forth and back the blood and nutritive juyces of the Body Politick, namely, the product of Husbandry and Manufacture.

33. Now if the numerous Offices and Fees relating to the Government, Law, and Church; and if the number of Divines, Lawyers, Physicians, Merchants, and Retailers were also lessened, all which do receive great wages for little work done to the Publick, with how much greater ease would

common expences be defrayed? and with how much more equality would the same be assessed?

34. We enumerated six Branches of the Publick Charge, and have slightly spoken how four of them might be lessened; we come next to the other two Branches, whereof we shall rather recommend the augmentation.

The first of these two Branches I call, generally speaking, Care of the Poor, consisting of Receptacles for the aged, blinde, lame, &c. in health; Hospitals for noysome, chronical, curable and uncurable, inward and outward Diseases. With others for acute and contagious. Others for Orphans, found and exposed Children; of which latter sort none should be refused, let the number be never so great, provided their names, families, and relations were well concealed: The choice of which Children being made at their being about eight || or ten years old, might afford the King the fittest 12
Instruments for all kinde of his Affairs, and be as firmly obliged to be his faithful servants as his own natural Children.

35. This is no new nor rare thing, onely the neglect of it in these Countreys, is rather to be esteemed a rare and new project: Nor is it unknown what excellent fruits there have been of this Institution, of which we shall say much more, upon another occasion hereafter.

36. When all helpless and impotent Persons were thus provided for, and the lazy and thievish restrained and punished by the Minister of Justice, it follows now, that we finde out certain constant Employments for all other indigent people, who labouring according to the Rules upon them, may require a sufficiency of food and raiment. Their Children also (if small and impotent) as aforesaid, being provided for elsewhere.

37. But what shall these Employments be? I answer, such as were reckoned as the sixth Branch of the Publick Expence, *viz.* making all High-wayes so broad, firm, and eaven, as whereby the charge and tedium of travelling and Carriages may be greatly lessened. The cutting and scowring of Rivers into Navigable; the planting of usefull Trees for timber, delight, and fruit in convenient places.

The making of Bridges and Cawseys.

The working in Mines, Quarries, and Colleries.

The Manufactures of Iron, &c.

38. I pitch upon all these particulars, first, as works wanting in this Nation; secondly, as works of much labour, and little art; and thirdly, as introductive of new Trades into *England*, to supply that of Cloth, which we have almost totally lost[1].

In the next place it will be asked, who shall pay these men? I answer, every body; for if there be 1000. men in a Territory, and if 100. of these can raise necessary food and raiment for the whole 1000. If 200. more make as much commodities, as other Nations will give either their commodities or money for, and if 400. more be employed in the ornaments, pleasure, and magnificence of the whole; if
13 there || be 200. Governours, Divines, Lawyers, Physicians, Merchants, and Retailers, making in all 900. the question is, since there is food enough for this supernumerary 100. also, how they should come by it? whether by begging, or by stealing; or whether they shall suffer themselves to starve, finding no fruit of their begging, or being taken in their stealing be put to death another way? Or whether they shall be given away to another Nation that will take them? I think 'tis plain, they ought neither to be starved, nor hanged, nor given away; now if they beg, they may pine for hunger to day, and be gorged and glutted to morrow, which will occasion Diseases and evil habits, the same may be said of stealing; moreover, perhaps they may get either by begging or stealing more then will suffice them, which will for ever after indispose them to labour, even upon the greatest occasion which may suddenly and unexpectedly happen.

[1] The opinion was common about 1662 that England's trade in cloth had declined. *The golden Fleece*, by W. S. (1656), p. 11; Answer of the Hamburg Company to the Exeter "Interlopers" (1662), quoted in Smith's *Memoirs of Wool*, I. 206—207; Fortrey, *England's Interest* (1663), 16; Mun, *England's Treasure* (written ca. 1630, publ. 1664), p. 11 of Ashley's ed. Cf. the well-known statutes for the encouragement of the clothing trade, 12 Charles II., c. 32; 14 Charles II., c. 18; 18 & 19 Charles II., c. 4.

39. For all these Reasons, it will be certainly the safer way to afford them the superfluity which would otherwise be lost and wasted, or wantonly spent: Or in case there be no overplus, then 'tis fit to retrench a little from the delicacy of others feeding in quantity or quality; few men spending less then double of what might suffice them as to the bare necessities of nature.

40. Now as to the work of these supernumeraries, let it be without expence of Foreign Commodities, and then 'tis no matter if it be employed to build a useless Pyramid upon *Salisbury Plain*, bring the Stones at *Stonehenge* to *Tower-Hill*, or the like; for at worst this would keep their mindes to discipline and obedience, and their bodies to a patience of more profitable labours when need shall require it.

41. In the next place, as an instance of the usefulness of what hath been propounded, I ask what benefit will the mending of High-wayes, the building of Bridges and Cawseys, with making of Rivers navigable produce, besides the pleasure and beauty of them? To which I also answer, as an instance of the premises, that the same, together with the numerous missions of Cattle and Sheep out of *Ireland*, shall pro-||duce a vaste superfluity of English Horses, 14
the which because they have the many excellent qualities of beauty, strength, courage, swiftness, and patience concentrated in them, beyond the Horses of other places, would be a very vendible Commodity all over *Europe*; and such as depending upon the intrinsick nature of the English Soyle could not be counterfeited, nor taken away by others. Moreover, an Horse is such a Commodity as will carry both himself and his Merchant to the Market, be the same never so distant.

CHAP. III.

How the Causes of the unquiet bearing of Taxes may be lessened.

WE have slightly gone through all the six Branches of the Publick Charge, and have (though imperfectly and in haste) shewn what would encrease, and what would abate them.

We come next to take away some of the general Causes of the unquiet bearing of Taxes, and yielding to Contributions, *viz.*

2. 1. That the people think, the Sovereign askes more then he needs. To which we answer, 1. That if the Sovereign were sure to have what he wanted in due time, it were his own great dammage to draw away the money out of his Subjects hands, who by trade increase it, and to hoard it up in his own Coffers, where 'tis of no use even to himself, but lyable to be begged or vainly expended.

3. 2. Let the Tax be never so great, if it be proportionable unto all, then no man suffers the loss of any Riches by it. For men (as we said but now) if the Estates of them all were either halfed or doubled, would in both cases remain equally rich. For they would each man have his former state, dignity and degree; and moreover, the Money leavied not going out of the Nation, the same also would remain as rich in comparison of any other Nation; onely the Riches of the Prince and People would differ for a little while, namely, until the money leavied from some, were again refunded upon the same, or other persons that paid it: In which case every man also should have his chance and opportunity to be made the better or worse by the new distribution; or if he lost by one, yet to gain by another.

4. 3. Now that which angers men most, is to be taxed above their Neighbours. To which I answer, that many times these surmizes are mistakes, many times they are chances,

which in the next Tax may run more favourable; and if they be by design, yet it cannot be imagined, that it was by design of the Sovereign, but of some temporary Assessor, whose turn it may be to receive the *Talio* upon the next occasion from the very man he has wronged.

5. 4. Men repine much, if they think the money leavyed will be expended on Entertainments, magnificent Shews, triumphal Arches, &c. To which I answer, that the same is a refunding the said moneys to the Tradesmen who work upon those things; which Trades though they seem vain and onely of ornament, yet they refund presently to the most useful; namely, to Brewers, Bakers, Taylours, Shoemakers, &c. Moreover, the Prince hath no more pleasure in these Shews and Entertainments then 100000. others of his meanest Subjects have, whom, for all their grumbling, we see to travel many miles to be spectators of these mistaken and distasted vanities.

6. 5. The people often complain, that the King bestows the money he raises from the people upon his Favourites: To which we answer; that what is given to Favourites, may at the next step or transmigration, come into our own hands, or theirs unto whom we wish well, and think do deserve it.

7. Secondly, as this man is a Favourite to day, so another, or our selves, may be hereafter; favour being of a very slippery and moveable nature, and not such a thing as we need much
to envy; for the same way that———[1] leads up an hill, || leads 16
also down the same. Besides, there is nothing in the Lawes or Customes of *England*, which excludes any the meanest mans Childe, from arriving to the highest Offices in this Kingdom, much less debars him from the Personall kindness of his Prince.

8. All these imaginations (whereunto the vulgar heads are subject) do cause a backwardness to pay, and that necessitates the Prince to severity. Now this lighting upon some poor, though stubborn, stiffnecked Refuser, charged with Wife and Children, gives the credulous great occasion to

[1] The dash occurs in all editions.

complain of Oppression, and breeds ill blood as to all other matters; feeding the ill humours already in being.

9. 6. Ignorance of the Number, Trade, and Wealth of the people, is often the reason why the said people are needlesly troubled, *viz.* with the double charge and vexation of two, or many Levies, when one might have served: Examples whereof have been seen in late Poll-moneys; in which (by reason of not knowing the state of the people, *viz.* how many there were of each Taxable sort, and the want of sensible markes whereby to rate men, and the confounding of Estates with Titles and Offices) great mistakes were committed.

10. Besides, for not knowing the Wealth of the people, the Prince knows not what they can bear; and for not knowing the Trade, he can make no Judgment of the proper season when to demand his Exhibitions.

11. 7. Obscurities and doubts, about the right of imposing, hath been the cause of great and ugly Reluctancies in the people, and of Involuntary Severities in the Prince; an eminent Example whereof was the Ship-money, no small cause of twenty years calamity to the whole Kingdom.

12. 8. Fewness of people, is real poverty; and a Nation wherein are Eight Millions of people, are more then twice as rich as the same scope of Land wherein are but Four; For the same Governours which are the great charge, may serve near as well, for the greater, as the lesser number.

13. Secondly, If the people be so few, as that they can live, *Ex sponte Creatis*, or with little labour, such as is Grazing, &c. they become wholly without Art; No man that will not exercise his hands, being able to endure the tortures of the mind, which much thoughtfulness doth occasion.

14. 9. Scarcity of money, is another cause of the bad payment of Taxes; for if we consider, that of all the wealth of this Nation, *viz.* Lands, Housing, Shipping, Commodities, Furniture, Plate, and Money, that scarce one part of an hundred is Coin; and that perhaps there is scarce six millions of Pounds now in *England*[1], that is but twenty shillings a

[1] In the *Polit. Arith.*, ch. IX., Petty repeats this guess and supports it by calculation.

head for every head in the Nation. We may easily judge, how difficult it is for men of competent estates, to pay a Summe of money on a sudden; which if they cannot compass, Severities, and Charges ensue; and that with reason, though unluckie enough, it being more tolerable to undoe one particular Member, then to endanger the whole, notwithstanding indeed it be more tolerable for one particular Member to be undone with the whole, then alone.

15. 10. It seems somewhat hard, that all Taxes should be paid in money, that is†, (when the King hath occasion to Victual his Ships at *Portsmouth*) that Fat Oxen, and Corn should not be received in kind, but that Farmers must first carry their Corn perhaps ten Miles to sell, and turn into money; which being paid to the King, is again reconverted into Corn, fetcht many miles further.

16. Moreover, the Farmer for haste is forced to under-sell his Corn, and the King for haste likewise, is forced to over-buy his provisions. Whereas the paying in kinde, *Pro Hic & Nunc*, would lessen a considerable grievance to the poor people.

17. The next consideration shall be of the consequences, and effects of too great a Tax, not in respect of particular men, of which we have spoken before, but to the whole people in general: To which I say, that there is a certain measure, and proportion of money requisite to drive the trade of a Nation, more or less then which would prejudice the same. Just as there is a certain proportion of Farthings necessary in a small retail Trade, to change silver money, and || to even 18
such reckonings, as cannot be adjusted with the smallest silver pieces. For money, (made of Gold and silver) is to the τὰ χρήσα‡ (that is to the matter of our Food and Covering) but as Farthings, and other local extrinsick money, is to the Gold and Silver species.

18. Now as the proportion of the number of Farthings requisite in comerse is to be taken from the number of people, the frequency of their exchanges; as also, and principally from the value of the smallest silver pieces of money; so in

† read [*viz.*] for [*that is*]

‡ read [τὰ χρῆςα] instead of [τὰ χρήσα]

like maner, the proportion of money requisite to our Trade, is to be likewise taken from the frequency of commutations, and from the bigness of the payments, that are by Law or Custome usually made otherwise. From whence it follows, that where there are Registers of Lands. whereby the just value of each mans interest in them, may be well known; and where there are Depositories of the τὰ χρήσα, as of Metals, Cloth, Linnen, Leather, and other Usefuls; and where there are Banks of money also, there less money is necessary to drive the Trade. For if all the greatest payments be made in Lands, and the other perhaps down to ten pound, or twenty pound be made by credit in Lombars or Money-Banks: It follows, that there needs onely money to pay sums less than those aforementioned; just as fewer Farthings are requisite for change, where there be plenty of silver two Pences, then where the least silver piece is six Pence.

19. To apply all this, I say, that if there be too much money in a Nation, it were good for the Commonalty, as well as the King, and no harm even to particular men, if the King had in his Coffers, all that is superfluous, no more then if men were permitted to pay their Taxes in any thing they could best spare.

20. On the other side, if the largeness of a publick Exhibition should leave less money then is necessary to drive the Nations Trade, then the mischief thereof would be the doing of less work, which is the same as lessening the people, or their Art and Industry; for a hundred pound passing a hundred hands for Wages, causes a 10000 l.[1] worth
19 of Commodities to || be produced, which hands would have been idle and useless, had there not been this continual motive to their employment.

21. Taxes if they be presently expended upon our own Domestick Commodities, seem to me, to do little harm to the whole Body of the people, onely they work a change in the Riches and Fortunes of particular men; and particularly by transferring the same from the Landed and Lazy, to the Crafty and Industrious. As for example, if a Gentleman

[1] The edition of 1679 has "one thousand pounds."

have let his Lands to Farm for a hundred pound *per annum*, for several years or lives, and he be taxed twenty pound *per annum*, to maintain a Navy; then the effect hereof will be, that this Gentlemans twenty pound *per annum*, will be distributed amongst Seamen, Ship-Carpenters, and other Trades relating to Naval matters; but if the Gentleman had his Land in his own hands, then being taxed a Fifth part, he would raise his Rents near the same proportion upon his under Tenants, or would sell his Cattle, Corn, and Wooll a Fifth part dearer; the like also would all other subdependents on him do; and thereby recover in some measure, what he paid. Lastly, but if all the money levied were thrown into the Sea, then the ultimate effect would onely be, that every man must work a fifth part the harder, or retrench a fifth part of his consumption's, *viz.* the former, if forreign Trade be improveable, and the latter, if it be not.

22. This, I conceive, were the worst of Taxes in a well policyed State; but in other States, where is not a certain prevention of Beggary and Theevery, that is a sure livelihood for men wanting imployment; there, I confess, an excessive Taxe, causes excessive and insuperable want, even of natural necessities, and that on a sudden, so as ignorant particular persons, cannot finde out what way to subsist by; and this, by the law of Nature, must cause sudden effects to relieve it self, that is, Rapines, Frauds; and this again must bring Death, Mutilations, and Imprisonments, according to the present Laws which are Mischiefs, and Punishments, as well unto the State, as to the particular sufferers of them. ‖

CHAP. IV.

Of the several wayes of Taxe, and first, of setting a part, a proportion of the whole Territory for Publick uses, in the nature of Crown Lands; and secondly, by way of Assessement, or Land-taxe.

BUt supposing, that the several causes of Publick Charge are lessened as much as may be, and that the people be well satisfied, and contented to pay their just shares of what is needfull for their Government and Protection, as also for the Honour of their Prince and Countrey: It follows now to propose the several wayes, and expedients, how the same may be most easily, speedily, and insensibly collected. The which I shall do, by exposing the conveniencies and inconveniences of some of the principal wayes of Levyings, used of later years within the several States of *Europe*: unto which others of smaller and more rare use may be referred.

2. Imagine then, a number of people, planted in a Territory, who had upon Computation concluded, that two Millions of pounds *per annum*, is necessary to the publick charges. Or rather, who going more wisely to work, had computed a twenty fifth part of the proceed of all their Lands and Labours, were to be the *Excisium*†, or the part to be cut out, and laid aside for publick uses. Which proportions perhaps are fit enough to the affairs of *England*, but of that hereafter.

3. Now the question is, how the one or the other shall be raised. The first way we propose, is, to Excize the very Land it self in kinde; that is, to cut out of the whole twenty five Millions, which are said to be in *England* and *Wales*, as much Land *in specie*, as whereof the Rack-rent would be two Millions, *viz.* about four Millions of Acres, which is about a sixth part of the whole; making the said four Millions to
21 be || Crown Lands, and as the four Counties[1] intended to be

[1] The counties of Dublin, Kildare, Carlow, and Cork.

† read [*Excisum*] not [*Excisium*]

reserved in *Ireland* upon the forfeitures were. Or else to excize a sixth part of the rent of the whole, which is about the proportion, that the Adventurers and Souldiers in *Ireland* retribute to the King, as Quit Rents. Of which two wayes, the latter is manifestly the better, the King having more security, and more obliges†; provided the trouble and charge of this universal Collection, exceed not that of the other advantage considerably.

4. This way in a new State would be good, being agreed upon, as it was in *Ireland*, before men had even the possession of any Land at all; wherefore whosoever buyes Land in *Ireland* hereafter, is no more concerned with the Quit Rents wherewith they are charged, then if the Acres were so much the fewer; or then men are, who buy Land, out of which they know Tythes are to be paid. And truly that Countrey is happy, in which by Original Accord, such a Rent is reserved, as whereby the Publick charge may be born, without contingent, sudden, superadditions, in which lies the very *Ratio* of the burthen of all Contributions and Exactions. For in such cases, as was said before, it is not onely the Landlord payes, but every man who eats but an Egg, or an Onion of the growth of his Lands; or who useth the help of any Artisan, which feedeth on the same.

5. But if the same were propounded in *England*, *viz.* if an aliquot part of every Landlords Rent were excinded or retrenched, then those whose Rents were settled, and determined for long times to come, would chiefly bear the burthen of such an Imposition, and others have a benefit thereby. For suppose *A.* and *B.* have each of them a parcel of Land, of equal goodness and value; suppose also that *A.* hath let his parcel for twenty one years at twenty pound *per annum*, but that *B.* is free; now there comes out a Taxe of a fifth part; hereupon *B.* will not let under 25 l. that his remainder may be twenty, whereas *A.* must be contented with sixteen neat; nevertheless the Tenants of *A.* will sell the proceed of their bargain at the same rate, that the Tenants of *B.* shall do. || The effect of all this is; First, that the Kings fifth 22

† read [*obligees*] not [*obliges*]

part of *B.* his Farm shall be greater then before. Secondly, that the Farmer to *B.* shall gain more then before the Taxe. Thirdly, that the Tenant or Farmer of *A.* shall gain as much as the King and Tenant to *B.* both. Fourthly, the Tax doth ultimately light upon the Landlord *A.* and the Consumptioners. From whence it follows, that a Land-taxe resolves into an irregular Excize upon consumptions, that those bear it most, who least complain. And lastly, that some Landlords may gain, and onely such whose Rents are predetermined shall loose; and that doubly, *viz.* one way by the raising[1] of their revenues, and the other by exhausting† the prices of provisions upon them.

6. Another way is an *Excisium* out of the Rent of Houseing, which is much more uncertain then that of Land. For an House is of a double nature, *viz.* one, wherein it is a way and means of expence; the other, as 'tis an Instrument and Tool of gain: for a Shop in *London* of less capacity and less charge in building then a fair Dining-Room in the same House unto which both do belong, shall nevertheless be of the greater value; so also shall a Dungeon, Sellar, then a pleasant Chamber; because the one is expence, the other profit. Now the way‡ Land-taxe rates housing, as of the latter nature, but the Excize, as of the former.

7. We might sometimes†† adde hereunto, that housing is sometimes disproportionately taxed to discourage Building[2], especially upon new Foundations, thereby to prevent the growth of a City[3]; suppose *London*, such excessive and overgrown Cities being dangerous to Monarchy, though the more secure when the supremacy is in Citizens of such places themselves, as in *Venice*.

8. But we say, that such checking of new Buildings

[1] Perhaps "by the not raising" was intended.

[2] Act of 1656, c. 24, Scobell, II. 484; An Act for preventing the Multiplicity of Buildings in and about the suburbs of London. Cunningham, *Engl. Industry*, II. 174.

[3] A more intelligible punctuation would be: "of a City, suppose London; such excessive and overgrown cities."

† read [*enhansing*] not [*exhausting*]

‡ between [*way* and *Land-Tax*] interline [*of a*]

†† deleatur [*sometimes*]

signifies nothing to this purpose; forasmuch as Buildings do not encrease, until the People already have increased: but the remedy of the above mentioned dangers is to be sought in the causes of the encrease of People, the which if they can be nipt, the other work will necessarily be done. ||

But what then is the true effect of forbidding to build 23
upon new foundations? I answer to keep and fasten the City to its old seat and ground-plot, the which encouragement for new Buildings will remove, as it comes to pass almost in all great Cities, though insensibly, and not under many years progression.

9. The reason whereof is, because men are unwilling to build new houses at the charge of pulling down their old, where both the old house it self, and the ground it stands upon do make a much dearer ground-plot for a new house, and yet far less free and convenient; wherefore men build upon new free foundations, and cobble up old houses, until they become fundamentally irreparable, at which time they become either the dwelling of the Rascality, or in process of time return to waste and Gardens again, examples whereof are many even about *London.*

Now if great Cities are naturally apt to remove their Seats, I ask which way? I say, in the case of *London,* it must be Westward, because the Windes blowing near $\frac{3}{4}$. of the year from the West[1], the dwellings of the West end are so much the more free from the fumes, steams, and stinks of the whole Easterly Pyle; which where Seacoal is burnt is a great matter. Now if it follow from hence, that the Pallaces of the greatest men will remove Westward, it will also naturally follow, that the dwellings of others who depend upon them will creep after them. This we see in *London,* where the Noblemens ancient houses are now become Halls for Companies, or turned into Tenements, and all the Pallaces

[1] Evelyn had proposed that all works using sea-coal be removed by Act of Parliament to a point on the Thames five or six miles below London, because at any less interval they would not only prodigiously infect his Majesty's royal seat but during our nine months Etesians (for so we may justly name our tedious Western-winds) utterly darken and confound one of the most princely and magnificent prospects that the world has to show. *Fumifugium* (1661), 16.

are gotten Westward; Insomuch, as I do not doubt but that five hundred years hence, the King's Pallace will be near *Chelsey*, and the old building of *Whitehall* converted to uses more answerable to their quality. For to build a new Royal Pallace upon the same ground will be too great a confinement, in respect of Gardens and other magnificencies, and withall a disaccommodation in the time of the work; but it rather seems to me, that the next Palace will be built from the whole present contignation of houses at such a distance
24 as the old Pallace[1] of *Westminster* || was from the City of *London*, when the Archers began to bend their bowes just without *Ludgate*, and when all the space between the *Thames*, *Fleet-street*, and *Holborn* was as *Finsbury-Fields* are now.

10. This digression I confess to be both impertinent to the business of Taxes, and in it self almost needless; for why should we trouble our selves what shall be five hundred years hence, not knowing what a day may bring forth; and since 'tis not unlikely, but that before that time we may be all transplanted from hence into *America*, these Countreys being overrun with Turks, and made waste, as the Seats of the famous Eastern Empires at this day are.

11. Onely I think 'tis certain, that while ever there are people in *England*, the greatest cohabitation of them will be about the place which is now *London*, the *Thames* being the most commodious River of this Island, and the seat of *London* the most commodious part of the *Thames*; so much doth the means of facilitating Carriage greaten a City, which may put us in minde of employing our idle hands about mending the High-wayes, making Bridges, Cawseys, and Rivers navigable: Which considerations brings me back round into my way of Taxes, from whence I digress.

12. But before we talk too much of Rents†, we should endeavour to explain the mysterious nature of them, with reference as well to Money, the rent of which we call usury; as to that of Lands and Houses, afore-mentioned.

[1] 1679 ed., "whole Pallace."

† between [*Rents* and *we*] interline [*in order to Taxes*]

13. Suppose a man could with his own hands plant a certain scope of Land with Corn, that is, could Digg, or Plough, Harrow, Weed, Reap, Carry home, Thresh, and Winnow so much as the Husbandry of this Land requires; and had withal Seed wherewith to sowe the same. I say, that when this man hath subducted his seed out of the proceed of his Harvest, and also, what himself hath both eaten and given to others in exchange for Clothes, and other Natural necessaries; that the remainder of Corn is the natural and true Rent of the Land for that year; and the *medium* of seven years, or rather of so many years as makes up the Cycle, within which || Dearths and Plenties make their 25
revolution, doth give the ordinary Rent of the Land in Corn.

14. But a further, though collaterall question may be, how much English money this Corn or Rent is worth? I answer, so much as the money, which another single man can save, within the same time, over and above his expence, if he imployed himself wholly to produce and make it; *viz.* Let another man go travel into a Countrey where is Silver, there Dig it, Refine it, bring it to the same place where the other man planted his Corn; Coyne it, &c. the same person, all the while of his working for Silver, gathering also food for his necessary livelihood, and procuring himself covering, &c. I say, the Silver of the one, must be esteemed of equal value with the Corn of the other: the one being perhaps twenty Ounces and the other twenty Bushels. From whence it follows, that the price of a Bushel of this Corn to be an Ounce of Silver.

15. And forasmuch as possibly there may be more Art and Hazzard in working about the Silver, then about the Corn, yet all comes to the same pass; for let a hundred men work ten years upon Corn, and the same number of men, the same time, upon Silver; I say, that the neat proceed of the Silver is the price of the whole neat proceed of the Corn, and like parts of the one, the price of like parts of the other. Although not so many of those who wrought in Silver, learned the Art of refining and coining, or out-lived the dangers and diseases of working in the Mines. And this also is the way

of pitching the true proportion, between the values of Gold and Silver, which many times is set but by popular errour, sometimes more, sometimes less, diffused in the world; which errour (by the way) is the cause of our having been pestred with too much Gold heretofore, and wanting it now[1].

16. This, I say, to be the foundation of equallizing and ballancing of values; yet in the superstructures and practices hereupon, I confess there is much variety, and intricacy; of which hereafter.

17. The world measures things by Gold and Silver, but
26 principally the latter; for there may not be two measures, || and consequently the better of many must be the onely of all; that is, by fine silver of a certain weight: but now if it be hard to measure the weight and fineness of silver, as by the different reports of the ablest Saymasters I have known it to be; and if silver granted to be of the same fineness and weight, rise and fall in its price, and be more worth at one place then another, not onely for being farther from the Mines, but for other accidents, and may be more worth at present, then a moneth or other small time hence; and if it differ in its proportion unto the several things valued by it, in several ages upon the increase and diminution thereof, we shall endeavour to examine some other natural Standards and Measures, without derogating from the excellent use of these.

18. Our Silver and Gold we call by severall names, as in *England* by pounds, shillings, and pence, all which may be called and understood by either of the three. But that which I would say upon this matter is, that all things ought to be valued by two natural Denominations, which is Land and Labour; that is, we ought to say, a Ship or garment is worth such a measure of Land, with such another measure of Labour; forasmuch as both Ships and Garments were the creatures of Lands and mens Labours thereupon: This being true, we should be glad to finde out a natural Par between

[1] In 1661, the exportation of gold continuing in spite of the proclamation of 10th June directed against it, the King and council took expert advice and raised the value of gold coin. 20 Nov., 1661, a further remedy was attempted by a proclamation forbidding the gilding of coaches. Ruding, *Annals*, II. 4.

Land and Labour, so as we might express the value by either of them alone as well or better then by both, and reduce one into the other as easily and certainly as we reduce pence into pounds. Wherefore we would be glad to finde the natural values of the Fee simple of Land, though but no better then we have done that of the *usus fructus* above-mentioned, which we attempt as followeth.

19. Having found the Rent or value of the *usus fructus per annum*, the question is, how many years purchase (as we usually say) is the Fee simple naturally worth? If we say an infinite number, then an Acre of Land would be equal in value to a thousand Acres of the same Land; which is absurd, an infinity of unites being equal to an infinity of thousands. Wherefore we must pitch upon some limited number, and that I ap-||prehend to be the number of years, which I conceive 27
one man of fifty years old, another of twenty eight, and another of seven years old, all being alive together may be thought to live[1]; that is to say, of a Grandfather, Father, and Childe; few men having reason to take care of more remote Posterity: for if a man be a great Grandfather, he himself is so much the nearer his end, so as there are but three in a continual line of descent usually co-existing together; and as some are Grandfathers at forty years, yet as many are not till above sixty, and *sic de cæteris*.

20. Wherefore I pitch the number of years purchase, that any Land is naturally worth, to be the ordinary extent of three such persons their lives. Now in *England* we esteem three lives equal to one and twenty years, and consequently the value of Land, to be about the same number of years purchase. Possibly if they thought themselves mistaken in the one, (as the observator on the Bills of Mortality thinks they are[2]) they would alter in the other, unless the consideration of the force of popular errour and dependance of things already concatenated, did hinder them.

21. This I esteem to be the number of years purchase where Titles are good, and where there is a moral certainty of

[1] Cf. Wieser, *Natural Value*, 159—160.

[2] Graunt does not discuss the point directly, *Observations*, ch. XI.

enjoying the purchase. But in other Countreys Lands are worth nearer thirty years purchase, by reason of the better Titles, more people, and perhaps truer opinion of the value and duration of three lives.

22. And in some places, Lands are worth yet more years purchase by reason of some special honour, pleasures, priviledge or jurisdiction annexed unto them.

23. On the other hand, Lands are worth fewer years purchase (as in *Ireland*) for the following reasons, which I have here set down, as unto the like whereof the cause of the like cheapness in any other place may be imputed.

First, In *Ireland*, by reason of the frequent Rebellions, (in which if you are conquered, all is lost ; or if you conquer, yet you are subject to swarms of thieves and robbers) and the envy
28 which precedent missions of English have against the || subsequent, perpetuity it self is but forty years long, as within which time some ugly disturbance hath hitherto happened almost ever since the first coming of the English thither.

24. 2. The Claims upon Claims which each hath to the others Estates, and the facility of making good any pretence whatsoever by the favour of some one or other of the many Governours and Ministers which within forty years shall be in power there; as also by the frequency of false testimonies, and abuse of solemn Oaths.

25. 3. The paucity of Inhabitants, there being not above the $\frac{1}{8}$.th part so many as the Territory would maintain, and of those but a small part do work at all, and yet a smaller work so much as in other Countreys.

26. 4. That a great part of the Estates, both real and personal in *Ireland*, are owned by Absentees, and such as draw over the profits raised out of *Ireland* refunding nothing; so as *Ireland* exporting more then it imports doth yet grow poorer to a paradox.

27. 5. The difficulty of executing justice, so many of those in power being themselves protected by Offices, and protecting others. Moreover, the number of criminous and indebted persons being great, they favour their like in Juries, Offices, and wheresoever they can : Besides, the Countrey

is seldom † enough to give due encouragement to profound Judges and Lawyers, which makes judgements very casual; ignorant men being more bold to be apt and arbitrary, then such as understand the dangers of it. But all this with ‡ a little care in due season might remedy, so as to bring *Ireland* in a few years to the same level of values with other places; but of this also elsewhere more at large, for in the next place we shall come to Usury. ||

CHAP. V. 29

Of Usury.

WHat reason there is for taking or giving Interest or Usury for any thing which we may certainly have again whensoever we call for it, I see not; nor why Usury should be scrupled, where money or other necessaries valued by it, is lent to be paid at such a time and place as the Borrower chuseth, so as the Lender cannot have his money paid him back where and when himself pleaseth, I also see not. Wherefore when a man giveth out his money upon condition that he may not demand it back until a certain time to come, whatsoever his own necessities shall be in the mean time, he certainly may take a compensation for this inconvenience which he admits against himself: And this allowance is that we commonly call Usury.

2. And when one man furnisheth another with money at some distant place, and engages under great Penalties to pay him there, and at a certain day besides; the consideration for this, is that we call Exchange or local Usury[1].

As for example, if a man wanting money at *Carlisle* in the heat of the late Civil Wars, when the way was full of Souldiers and Robbers, and the passage by Sea very long, troublesome,

[1] The attempted analogy between usury and exchange is hardly established. In case of usury he who is to receive gets the consideration, in case of exchange he who is to pay. Cf. *Quantulumcunque*, qu. 28—32.

† between [*seldom* and *enough*] interline [*rich*]

‡ deleatur [*with*]

and dangerous, and seldom passed; why might not another take much more then an 100 l. at *London* for warranting the like Summe to be paid at *Carlisle* on a certain day?

3. Now the Questions arising hence are; what are the natural Standards of Usury and Exchange? As for Usury, the least that can be, is the Rent of so much Land as the money lent will buy, where the security is undoubted; but where the security is casual, then a kinde of ensurance must be enterwoven with the simple natural Interest, which may advance the Usury very conscionably unto any height below the Principal it self. Now if things are so in *England*, that
30 really there is || no such security as abovementioned, but that all are more or less hazardous, troublesome, or chargeable to make, I see no reason for endeavoring to limit Usury upon time, any more then that upon place, which the practice of the world doth not, unless it be that those who make such Laws were rather Borrowers then Lenders: But of the vanity and fruitlessness of making Civil Positive Laws against the Laws of Nature, I have spoken elsewhere, and instanced in several particulars.

4. As for the natural measures of Exchange, I say, that in times of Peace, the greatest Exchange can be but the labour of carrying the money *in specie*, but where are hazards† emergent uses for money more in one place then another, &c. or opinions of these true or false, the Exchange will begoverned by them.

5. Parallel unto this, is something which we omit‡ concerning the price of Land; for as great need of money heightens Exchange, so doth great need of Corn raise the price of that likewise, and consequently of the Rent of the Land that bears Corn, and lastly of the Land it self; as for example, if the Corn which feedeth *London*, or an Army, be brought forty miles thither[1], then the Corn growing within a mile of *London*, or the quarters of such Army, shall have added unto its natural price, so much as the charge of bringing it thirty nine miles doth amount unto: And unto perishable Commodities, as fresh fish, fruits, &c. the ensurance

[1] The 1679 ed., "forty miles together."

† after [*hazards*] interline [*and*]

‡ read [*omitted*]

upon the hazard of corrupting, &c. shall be added also; and finally, unto him that eats these things there (suppose in Taverns) shall be added the charge of all the circumstancial appurtenances† of House-rent, Furniture, Attendance, and the Cooks skill as well as his labour to accompany the same.

6. Hence it comes to pass, that Lands intrinsically alike near populous places, such as where the perimeter of the Area that feeds them is great, will not onely yield more Rent for these Reasons, but also more years purchase then in remote places, by reason of the pleasure and honour extraordinary of having Lands there; for

——*Omne tulit punctum qui miscuit utile dulci*[1]. ||

7. Having finished our digression upon the measures of 31
the Rents and Values of Lands and Moneys, we now return to our second way of leavying Publick Charges, which was the taking of a proportion of the Rent (commonly called Assessment) it follows next to speak of the way of computing the said Rents, otherwise then according to the bargains which a few men make one with another, through ignorance, haste, false suggestion, or else in their passion or drink: Although I acknowledge, that the medium or common result of all the bargains made within three years (or other such Cycle of time, as within which all contingencies of Land revolve) may be very sufficient to this purpose, being but the summe synthetically computed by casual opinions, as I would endeavour to cast up analytically by a distinct particularizing of the Causes.

8. 1. Therefore I propound a Survey of the Figures, Quantities, and Scituations of all the Lands both according to the civil bounds of Parishes, Farms, &c. and the natural distinctions thereof by the Sea, Rivers, ridges of Rocks, or Mountains, &c.

9. 2. I propound that the quality of each denomination were described by the Commodities it had usually born, in some Land, some sort of Timber, Grain, pulse or root growing more happily then in others: Also by the encrease of things

[1] Horace, *de arte poetica*, 343.

† read [*apparatus*] instead of [*appurtenances*]

sown or planted, which it hath yielded *communibus annis*; and withall, the comparative goodness of the said Commodities not unto the common Standard money, but to one another. As for example; if there be ten acres of Land, I would have it judged whether they be better for Hay or Corn; if for Hay, whether the said ten Acres will bear more or less of Hay then ten other Acres; and whether an hundred weight of the said Hay will feed or fatten more or less, then the same weight of other Hay, and not as yet comparing it to money, in which the value of the said Hay will be more or less, according to the plenty of money, which hath changed strangely since the discovery of the *West Indies*, and according to the multitudes of people living near this Land,
32 together || with the luxurious or frugal living of them; and besides all, according to the Civil, Natural, and Religious Opinions of the said people: As for example, Eggs in the fore-part of Lent (because their goodness and delicacy decayes before Lent be done) being worth little in some Popish Countreys; nor Swines flesh among the Jews, nor Hedgehogs, Frogs, Snails, Mushrooms, &c. to those that fear to eat them, as poisonous or unwholesome; nor Currans and Spanish Wines, if they were all to be destroyed as the great thieves of this Nations, by an Edict of the State[1].

10. This I call a Survey or Inquisition into the† intrinsick Values of Land,‡ that of extrinsick or accidentall follows[2]. We said, that the change of the store of money would change the rates of commodities according to our reckoning in names and words, (pounds, shillings, and pence being nothing else) as for example:

If a man can bring to *London* an ounce of Silver out of the Earth in *Peru*, in the same time that he can produce a bushel of Corn, then one is the natural price of the other;

[1] See 12 Charles II., c. 18, § 8.

[2] Conjectural emendation: This former I call a Survey or Inquisition into the intrinsick Values of Land, the latter of extrinsick or accidentall follows. Cf. Graunt, "Conclusion."

† after [*the*] interline [*former*]

‡ after [*Land*] read [*this latter*] instead [*of the*]

now if by reason of new and more easie Mines a man can get two ounces of Silver as easily as formerly he did one, then Corn will be as cheap at ten shillings the bushel, as it was before at five shillings *cæteris paribus*.

11. It behoves us therefore to have a way, whereby to tell the money of our Countrey (which I think I have, and that in a short time, and without cost, and (which is more) without looking into particular mens pockets; of which hereafter.) Now if we know what Gold and Silver we had in *England* two hundred years ago, and could tell it again now; and though we also knew the difference of our denominations then, when thirty seven shillings were made out the same quantity of Silver as sixty two are now[1]; also that of the alloy, labour in Coinage, remedies for weight and fineness, and duties to the King; nay, if we also knew the Labourers wages then and now, yet all this would not shew the difference of the Riches of our Nation even in money alone.

12. Wherefore we must adde to the premises, the know-||
ledge of the difference of the numbers of the people, and 33
conclude, that if all the money in the Nation were equally divided amongst all the people both then and now, that that time wherein each Devisee had wherewith to hire most labourers, was the richer. So that we want the knowledge of the People and Bullion which is now in this Land, and which was heretofore; all which I think may be found out even for the time past, but more probably for the time present and to come.

13. But to proceed; suppose we had them, then we would pitch the accidental values upon our Lands about *London*; as thus; *viz.* We would first at hazzard compute the materials for food and covering, which the Shires of *Essex*, *Kent*, *Surrey*, *Middlesex* and *Hertford*, next circumjacent

[1] In 49 Henry VI. (1460) one pound of silver old standard (viz. 11 oz. 2 ʒ fine silver and 18 ʒ alloy) were coined into 37*s.* 6*d.* by tale instead of the 30*s.* previously coined. Pursuant to the indenture between the King and Sir Ralph Freeman, (12 Charles II. 1661), the same weight of bullion was thenceforward coined into £3. 2*s.* Lowndes, *Report*, 39, 40, 54, 55.

to *London*, did *communibus annis* produce; and would withal compute the Consumptioners of them living in the said five Shires, and *London*. The which if I found to be more then were the Consumptioners living upon the like scope of other Land, or rather upon as much other Land as bore the like quantity of Provisions. Then I say, that Provisions must be dearer in the said five Shires then in the other; and within the said Shires cheaper or dearer, as the way to *London* was more or less long, or rather more or less chargeable.

14. For if the said five Shires did already produce as much Commodity, as by all endeavour was possible; then what is wanting must be brought from a far, and that which is near, advanced in price accordingly; or if by† the said Shires by greater labour then now is used, (as by digging instead of Ploughing, setting instead of sowing, picking of choice feed instead of taking it promiscuously, steeping it instead of using it wholly unprepared, and manuring the ground with salt instead of rotten straw, &c.)‡ then will the Rent be as much more advanced, as the excess of encrease exceeds that of the labour.

15. Now the price of labour must be certain, (as we see it made by the Statutes which limit the day wages of several work men;) the non-observance of which Laws[1], and the not adapting them to the change of times, is by the way very ||
34 dangerous, and confusive to all endeavours of bettering the Trade of the Nation.

16. Moreover, the touchstone to try whether it be better to use those improvements or not, is to examine whether the labour of fetching these things even from the places where they grow wilde, or with less Culture, be not less then that of the said improvements.

17. Against all this will be objected, that these computations are very hard if not impossible to make; to which I answer onely this, that they are so, especially if none will

[1] Cunningham, *English Industry*, II., 199—200.

† deleatur [*by*]

‡ between [*&c* and *then*] interline [*could be fertilized*]

trouble their hands or heads to make them, or give authority for so doing: But withall, I say, that until this be done, Trade will be too conjectural a work for any man to employ his thoughts about; for it will be the same wisdom in order to win with fair Dice, to spend much time in considering how to hold them, how much to shake them, and how hard to throw them, and on what angles they should hit the side of the Tables, as to consider how to advance the Trade of this Nation; where at present particular men get from their neighbours (not from the earth and sea) rather by hit then wit, and by the false opinions of others, rather then their own judgements; Credit every where, but chiefly in *London*, being become a meer conceit, that a man is responsible or not, without any certain knowledge of his Wealth or true Estate. Whereas I think the nature of credit should be limited onely to an opinion of a mans faculties to get by his art and industry. The way of knowing his Estate being to be made certain, and the way of making him pay what he owes to the utmost of his ability, being to be expected from the good execution of our Laws.

18. I should here enlarge upon a Paradox, to prove that if every mans Estate could be alwayes read in his forehead, our Trade would much be advanced thereby, although the poorer ambitious man be commonly the more industrious. But of this elsewhere.

19. The next objection against this so exact computation of the Rents and works[†] of lands, &c. is, that the Sovereign would know too exactly every mans Estate; to which I an-||swer, that if the Charge of the Nation be brought as low 35
as it may be, (which depends much upon the people in Parliament to do) and if the people be willing and ready to pay, and if care be taken, that although they have not ready money, the credit of their Lands and Goods shall be as good; and lastly, that it would be a great discommodity to the Prince to take more then he needs, as was proved before; where is the evil of this so exact knowledge? And as for the proportion of every Contributor, why should any man hope or accept[1] to

[1] The 1679 ed., "expect."

† read [*worth*] not [*work*]

ease himself by his craft and interest in a confusion? or why should he not fear, though he may be advantaged this time, to suffer in the next.

CHAP. VI.

Of Customs and Free Ports.

CUstom is a Contribution of[1] Excisium out of Goods sent out or imported into the Princes Dominions: In these Countreys of a twentieth part not according to the Prices currant among Merchants of each respective Commodity, but according to other standing Rates set by the State, though advised for the most part by concerned Persons.

2. I cannot well imagine what should be the natural Reasons, why a Prince should be paid this duty inward and outward both; there seems indeed to be some, why he should be paid for indulging the Exportation of some such things as other Countreys do really want.

3. Wherefore I think, that Customs at the first were a *præmium* allowed the Prince for protecting the Carriage of Goods both inward and outward from the Pyrats; and this I should verily believe, if the Prince were bound to make good losses of that kinde. And I thought that the proportion of five pound *per cent.* was pitched upon computation, that the
36 Mer-||chants before the said undertaking and composition, had usually lost more by Pyracy: And finally, that the Customs had been an ensurance upon losses by enemies, as the ensurance now usual, is of the casualities of sea, winde, weather, and Vessel, or altogether; or like the ensurance in some Countreys of Houses from Fires for a certain small part of their yearly Rent. But be it what it will, it is anciently established by Law, and ought to be paid until it shall be abolished. Onely I take leave as an idle Philosopher to discourse upon the Nature and Measures of it.

[1] The 1679 ed., "or."

4. The Measures of Customs outwards may be such, as after reasonable profit to the Exporter will leave such of our own Commodities as are necessary to Forreigners somewhat cheaper unto them then they can be had from elsewhere.

As for example, Tin is a Native Commodity, which governs the Market†, that is, there is none so good and so easie to be had and exported.

Now suppose Tin might be made in *Cornwall* for four pence the pound, and that the same would yield twelve pence at the nearest part in *France*, I say, that this extraordinary profit ought to be esteemed as a Mine Royal, or *Tresor Trouvè*, and the Sovereign ought to have his share in it: Which he will have, by imposing so great a duty upon Tin Exported, as on one side may leave a subsistence to the Workmen, (and no more) with a competent profit to the owners of the ground; and on the other side, may leave the price abroad less then that for which Tin may be had from any other place.

5. The same Imposition might also be made on the Tin spent at home, unless it be as impossible so to do, as for the King of *France* to impose the Gabel upon Salt in the very places where it is made.

6. But it is observed, that such high duties make men endeavour not to enter any such Goods at all, or pay for them, provided the charge of smuckling and bribing, with the hazzard of being seized do not *communibus vicibus* exceed the Duty.

7. Wherefore the Measures of this Nature are, that it be ||
more easie, safe and profitable for men to keep the Law, then 37
to break it, unless it be in such cases, where the Magistrate can with certainty execute the Law. As for example, it would be hard to save the Duties upon Horses shipped at a small Port, without adjacent Creeks, and that but some certain two hours every Tide, forasmuch as Horses cannot be disguised, put up in bags or cask, or shipped without noise and the help of many hands.

8. The Measures of Customs upon imported Commodities are; 1. That all things ready and ripe for Consumption may

† after [*market*] interline [*abroad*]

be made somewhat dearer then the same things grown or made at home, if the same be feasible *cæteris talibus*†.

2. That all Superfluities tending to Luxury and sin, might be loaded with so much Impost, as to serve instead of a sumptuary Law to restrain the use of them. But here also care is to be had that it be not better to smuckle then to pay.

9. On the contrary, all things not fully wrought and Manufactured, as raw Hides, Wool, Beaver, Raw-silk, Cotton; as also all Tools and Materials for Manufacture, as also Dying-stuff, &c. ought to be gently dealt with.

10. If to leavy the payment of these Duties could be most exactly performed, Princes might strangely practice one upon another; wherefore since they cannot, the people pay no more then they cannot with greater safety upon the whole matter save, nor observe any more of these Laws, then they cannot elude.

11. The Inconveniences of the way of Customs, are, *viz.*

1. That Duties are laid upon things not yet ripe for use, upon Commodities in *fieri*, and but in the way of their full improvements, which seems the same ill-husbandry, as to make fuel of young Saplings, instead of Dotards and Pollards.

2. The great number of Officers requisite to Collect the said Duties, especially in a Countrey where the Harbours are many, and the Tides convenient for shipping of Goods at any time.

3. The great facility of smuckling by Briberies, Collusi-||
38 ons, hiding and disguising of Commodities, &c. and all this notwithstanding Oaths and Penalties, and withall by the several wayes of mitigating and taking off the said Penalties even after discovery.

4. The Customs or Duties upon the few Commodities of the growth of *England* exchanged with Forreigners, make too small a part of the whole Expence of the people of this Kingdom, which (perhaps is not less then fifty millions of pounds *per annum*) out of which to bear the common Charges thereof, so as some other way of Leavy must be practised together with it; whereas by some one way, if the best, the

† read [*paribus*] not [*talibus*]

whole work may be absolved : wherefore 'tis an inconvenience in the way of Customs, that it necessitates other wayes then it self.

12. Now as a small attempt of a Remedy or Expedient herein, I offer rather, that instead of the Customs upon Goods shipped, every Ship that goes in or out, may pay a Tonnage, the same being collectible by a very few hands, as a matter visible to all the world ; and that the said Duty be but such a part of the Fraight, as the like whereof being excinded out of the whole Consumption, would defray all the Publique Charge ; which part perhaps is 4. *per Cent.* or thereabouts, *viz.* two millions *per annum* out of fifty.

13. The other is, that the Customs be reduced into the nature of an Ensurance-*præmium*, and that the same be augmented and fitted, as whereby the King may afford to ensure the goods as well against the Sea as Enemies ; by which means the whole Nation would be concerned in all such losses, and then the Merchant for his own sake would more willingly enter and pay for whatsoever he would have ensured.

14. But it will be here objected, that although the duty of Customs be abrogated, yet that there must be almost[1] the same number of Officers maintained as now to prevent the bringing in and carrying out of prohibited Commodities. Wherefore we shall here state the nature of such Prohibitions by two or three grand instances.

15. To prohibit the Exportation of Money, in that it is
a || thing almost impracticable, it is almost nugatory and 39
vain ; And the danger of it resolves either into a kinde of Ensurance answerable to the danger of being seized, or unto a Surcharge of a Composition by bribing the Searchers. As for example, If but one in fifty Exportations are seized, or if twenty shillings be usually taken for coining† at fifty pounds, then the Commodities bought with this Money must be sold two at least *per cent.* the dearer to the Consumptioner. Now if the Trade will not bear this Surcharge, then Money will not be exported with discretion. Now the use of this Prohibition,

[1] The 1679 ed., "always."

† read [*conniving*] not [*coyning*]

supposing it practicable, is to serve as a sumptuary Law, and to binde the Nation in general not to spend more then they get; for if we could export no Commodity of our own growth or manufacture then by prohibiting the going out of Money, it is also *ipso facto* commanded that nothing forreign should be brought in. Again supposing, that ordinarily we export enough to furnish us with all Forreign Commodities, but upon some extraordinary decay of our Land or hands, we are able to export but half as much as would procure our ordinary proportion of Forreign Goods, then the Prohibition of Money performs indeed the part of a sumptuary Law, in hindring us to bring in any more then half as much Forreign Commodities as we formerly used, onely it leaves it to the discretion of the Merchant, to chose which he will neglect or forbear to bring in, and which not; whereas in sumptuary Laws the State taketh this care upon themselves. As for example, If we wanted Exportations to ballance our Importations by forty thousand pounds, and suppose for examples sake, that the Importation of forty thousand pounds worth of Coffee-Berries, or the like of Spanish Wine must be retrenched; in this case, the said Prohibition of Money will do one, or some of† one, and some of the other as much harm‡ as the Merchant himself pleases: But the sumptuary Law determines, whether we shall encourage and keep fair with the Nation that sends us wine rather then that which sends us Coffee,†† whether the Expence of Wine or Coffee be most prejudicial to our people, &c.||

16. The benefits alledged for the free Exportation of Money is merrily‡‡ this, *viz.* that if a Ship carrying out of *England* forty thousand pounds worth of Cloth, might also carry with it forty thousand pounds in Money, then could the Merchant stand the stiffer upon his terms, and in fine would buy cheaper, and sell dearer; but by the way, the Merchant buyes this power with the Intrest and [1] of the Money he carries, which if it amount to five pound *per Cent.* then he had better sold his Goods at four pound *per Cent.* under rate,

[1] The 1679 ed. supplies "advantage." "Exchange" is another possible reading.

† between [*of* and *one*] interline [*the*]

‡ deleatur [*as much harm*]

†† after [*Coffee*] inter [*and*]

‡‡ read [*meerly*] for [*merrily*]

then to have fortified himself with Money as aforesaid. But of this more may be said, we hasten to the great point of Wool.

17. The Hollanders having gotten away our Manufacture of Cloth, by becoming able to work with more art, to labour and fare harder, to take less fraight, Duties and Ensurance, hath so madded us here in *England*, that we have been apt to think of such exorbitantly fierce wayes of prohibiting Wool and Earth to be exported[1], as perhaps would do us twice as much harm as the losse of our said Trade. Wherefore to return to our Wits and Trade again, before we can tell what to do in this case, we must consider;

1. That we are often forced to buy Corn from abroad, and as often complain that we are pestered with abundance of idle hands at home, and withall that we cannot vend the Woollen Manufactures even which our few working hands do produce. In this case were it not better to lessen our sheep-trade, and convert our hands to more Tillage? Because 1. Flesh becoming dearer, there would be encouragement for Fish, which will never be till then. 2. Our Money would not run so fast away for Corn. 3. We should have no such Gluts of Wool upon our hands. 4. Our idle hands would be employed in Tillage and Fishing, one man by the way of grazing, tilling as it were many thousand Acres of Land by himself and his Dog.

2. Suppose we wanted no Corn; nor had any idle hands, and yet that we abounded with more Wool then we can work up; in this† certainly Wool might be exported, because 'tis || supposed, that the hands which work, are already 41
employed upon a better Trade.

3. Suppose the Hollander outdo us by more art, were it

[1] The 15th August, 1660, the House of Commons had desired the king to issue a proclamation forbidding the exportation of wool, woolfells, yarn, and fullers' earth, and had directed that a bill for the same purpose be brought in. The bill was passed, and became 12 Charles II., c. 32. At the next session of Parliament a similar but more stringent bill was introduced, 4 March, 1662. As this did not become a statute—14 Charles II., c. 18—until the following May it was probably pending at the time when Petty wrote. *H. C. Jour.*, VIII. 120, 236, 378, 414, 432.

† before [*certainly*] interline [*case*]

not better to draw over a number of their choice Workmen, or send our most ingenious men thither to learn; which if they succeed; it is most manifest that this were the more natural way, then to keep that infinite clutter about resisting of Nature, stopping up the windes and seas, &c.

4. If we can make Victual much cheaper here then in *Holland*, take away burthensome, frivolous, and antiquated Impositions and Offices.

I conceive even this were better then to perswade Water to rise out† of it self above its natural Spring.

5. We must consider in general, that as wiser Physicians tamper not excessively with their Patients, rather observing and complying with the motions of nature, then contradicting it with vehement Administrations of their own; so in Politicks and Oconomicks the same must be used; for

Naturam expellas furcâ licet usque recurrit[1].

18. Nevertheless, if the Hollanders advantages in making Cloth be but small and few in comparison of ours, that is, if they have but a little the better of us, then I conceive that Prohibitions to export Wool may sufficiently turn the scales. But whether this be use‡, I leave to others, being my self neither Merchant nor Statesman.

19. As for Prohibition of Importations, I say that it needs not be, until they much exceed our Exportations. For if we should think it hard to give good necessary Cloth for debauching Wines, yet if we cannot dispose of our Cloth to others, 'twere better to give it for Wine or worse, then to cease making it; nay, better to burn a thousand mens labours for a time, then to let those thousand men by non-employment lose their faculty of labouring. In brief, what may be further said hereupon, resolves into the Doctrine and *Ingenium* of making sumptuary Laws, and judicious use of them *pro hic & nunc*.

20. Unto this Discourse of Customs appertains that of ||
42 Free Ports, which (in a Nation that onely trades for it self, *viz.* vents its own superfluities, and imports onely Necessaries for it self) are of no use, but rather harm; for suppose Wines be

[1] Horace, *Epist.*, I. x. 24.

† dele [*out*] ‡ read [*so or not*] instead of [*use*]

brought into a Free Port, be there housed and privately sold, but the Cask filled up with stained water, and put on ship-board again to be staved as soon as the ship is out at sea: In this case, the Duties of those Wines are defrauded, as it also may be many other wayes[1].

21. Now if it be said, that although we should trade but for ourselves, yet that our Ports (being more commodious then those of other Nations) would be the more frequented; for being free, and consequently the more enriched, by the expence of Sea-men and Passengers, hire of Labourers, and Warehouses, &c. even without any Custom at all upon the Goods. Nevertheless 'tis reason that a small duty should be paid upon the ship as aforesaid for such use of our Ports, and that *eo nomine*; not expecting all our Benefit from the said hire of Cellaridge, Porters, and Carmen, which also might be had over and above for their proper reasons.

22. But if we could attain to be the Merchants between other Nations, there is then no reason for exacting Duties (as was said before[2]) upon things *in fieri*, and which are but in the way of their improvement: And as for the fraud that may be committed, as in the case of Wines abovementioned, I affirm that our Excize upon the Consumption, would overcome and elude them.

CHAP. VII.

Of Poll-money.

POll-money is a Tax upon the Persons of men, either upon
all simply and indifferently, or else according to some
known Title or mark of distinction upon each; and that
either of bare honour, or else of some Office sought or im-
posed, || or of some Faculty and Calling without respect to 43
Riches or Poverty, Incomes or Expence, Gain or Loss accrew-
ing by the said Title, Office or Faculty.

[1] Arguments such as Petty attempts to refute are contained in *Free Ports, the Nature and Necessitie of them stated.* [Signed: B. W.] London, printed by William Du Gard. 1652, f°.

[2] See p. 56.

2. The Poll-moneys which have been leavied of late have been wonderfully confused; as taxing some rich single persons at the lowest rate; some Knights, though wanting necessaries, at twenty pounds, encouraging some vain fellows to pay as Esquires, on purpose to have themselves written Esquires in the Receipts; making some pay ten pounds as Doctours of Physick or Law, who get nothing by the Faculty, nor minde the practice; making some poor Tradesmen forced to be of the Liveries of their Companies to pay beyond their strength; and lastly, some to pay according to their Estates, the same to be valued by those that know them not; thereby also giving opportunity to some Bankrupts to make the world credit them as men of such Estates, at which the Assessors did rate them by Collusion[1].

3. So as by this Confusion, Arbitraries, Irregularities, and hotch-pot of Qualifications, no estimate could be made of the fitness of this Plaister to the Sore, nor no Checque or way to examine whether the respective Receipts were duly accompted for, &c.

4. Wherefore wholly rejecting the said complicated way of Tax, I shall speak of Poll-money more distinctly, and first of the simple Poll-money upon every head of all mankinde alike; the Parish paying for those that receive alms, Parents for their Children under age, and Masters for their Apprentices, and others who receive no wages.

5. The evil of this way is, that it is very unequal; men of unequal abilities, all paying alike, and those who have greatest charges of Children paying most; that is, that by how much the poorer they are, by so much the harder are they taxed.

[1] A poll tax according to a complicated scale such as Petty complains of was imposed by 12 Charles II., c. 9, in September, 1660. It was payable within twelve days and was expected to produce £400,000 for the speedy disbanding of the army. By the 24th November it had produced but £252,167. 1*s*. 4*d*., *H. C. Jour.*, VIII. 196. Two supplementary bills for remedying the defects of the tax were introduced in the same year, but they appear to have failed of passage on account of the dissolution of Parliament, 29 December. The Parliamentary career of these bills was complicated. See *H. C. Jour.*, VIII. 38 to 234 *passim*, and, for an instance of evasion, Pepys' *Diary*, 10 December, 1660, vol. I., p. 283.

6. The Conveniencies are; first, that it may be suddenly collected, and with small charge: Secondly, that the number of the people being alwayes known, it may be sufficiently computed what the same will amount unto. Thirdly, It seems to be a spur unto all men, to set their Children to some || profitable employment upon their very first capacity, out of 44
the proceed whereof, to pay each childe his own Poll money.

7. The next Poll-money is upon every head, but distinguished by Titles of meer Honour, without any kinde of Office or Faculty; as, Dukes, Marquesses, Earls, Viscounts, Barons, Baronets, Knights, and Esquires, *viz*, the eldest Sons of Knights *in perpetuum*, and Gentlemen if they write themselves so. This way is much more equal then the other; forasmuch as those who are Titled, are for the most part rich proportionably; or if they were not, yet men so dignified shall command a preheminence and place, even although they do not or cannot buy it of the vulgar by their Expence: my meaning hereby is, that a Title may possibly save a man as much as his Poll-money may exceed the Plebeian Level by reason of such title.

8. Moreover, good and multiform Accompts being kept of the People, this Tax may be also easily speedily and inexpensively collected; and also being capable of being computed aforehand, may be fitted and seized according to the needs of the Prince.

9. As for Offices, they are indeed Dignities for the most part, but paid for by the trouble of administring them; as for example, to be an Alderman suppose of *London*, is indeed an honour, yet many pay five hundred pounds to be excused from receiving it.

Nevertheless it may not be improper to tax Offices sought, or such as are accepted, although they might be refused: And on the other side no *Titulado*[1] should be forced to pay

[1] In the Irish census of 1659 "in addition to mere numbers, the returns supply the names of the principal or distinguished occupiers of townlands and streets under the Anglo-Spanish compound designation of Tituladoes." Hardinge, *Earliest known MS. Census Returns of the People of Ireland*, in *Trans. R. I. Academy*, vol. XXIV., Antiquities, p. 319. See also Gilbert, *Calendar of the ancient Records of Dublin*, vol. IV., p. xiii.

Poll-money according to his Title[1], if he be contented to lay it down, and never resume it more.

10. The Titles of Faculties and Callings ought to be no Qualification in a Poll-money, because they do not necessarily nor probably inferr ability to pay, but carry with them vaste inequalities. But therefore if a man by his Licence to practise get much, it may be presumed he will spend accordingly; in which net the way of Excize will certainly take him, as it will the Officers aforementioned. ||

45 11. Harth-money seems to be a Poll-money, but is not, being rather a way of Accumulative Excize; of which hereafter.

CHAP. VIII.

Of Lotteries.

MEn that accept Titles may foresee, that they may be taxed by them as aforesaid, (although it be unlikely (one House of Parliament being all Tituladoes, and the greatest part of the other being such also) that any such way of Leavy should pass) and therefore they do as it were *à priori* consent unto the Tax in their own Individuals.

2. Now in the way of Lottery men do also tax themselves in the general, though out of hopes of Advantage in particular: A Lottery therefore is properly a Tax upon unfortunate self-conceited fools; men that have good opinion of their own luckiness, or that have believed some Fortune-teller or Astrologer, who had promised them great success about the time and place of the Lottery, lying Southwest perhaps from the place where the destiny was read.

3. Now because the world abounds with this kinde of fools, it is not fit that every man that will, may cheat every man that would be cheated; but it is rather ordained, that the Sovereign should have the Guardianship of these fools, or

[1] 1679, "this title."

that some Favourite should beg the Sovereigns right of taking advantage of such mens folly, even as in the case of Lunaticks and Idiots.

4. Wherefore a Lottery is not tollerated without authority, assigning the proportion in which the people shall pay for their errours, and taking care that they be not so much and so often cousened, as they themselves would be.

5. This way of Lottery is used but for small Leavies, and rather upon privato-publick accompts, (then for maintaining ||
Armies or Equipping Fleets,) such as are Aque-Ducts, Bridges, 46
and perhaps Highwayes, &c. Wherefore we shall say no more of it upon this occasion.

CHAP. IX.

Of Benevolence.

THe raising of Money by Benevolence, seems to be no force upon any man, nor to take from any man but what himself knows he can spare, nevertheless there is more in it; for to be but brow-beaten by a Prince or Grandee, proves often as heavy as to be distrained upon for an Assessment or Subsidy; and the danger of being misrepresented by linsy pick-thanks and Informers as disaffected to the Cause for which the Leavy is made, is more frequent then the payment of any summe in a due proportion with all other men (which I have said is no impoverishment) can possibly be hurtful.

The benefits of this way are these, *viz.* That forasmuch as it sometimes falls out (as in the late Differences with the Scots, *annis* 1638. and 1639. when the Church Dignitaries were most concerned) that the cause of the Expence concerns some men more then others, that then an Imposition should not pass upon all for the sakes of a part; Sometimes it happens, that one sort of men have received greater and fresher favours then another; as upon the late Restoration of his Majesty *Anno* 1660.[1] those who needed an Act of Indempnity did: And sometimes it is visible, that some men have had better times of gain and advantages then others, as the Clergy most eminently have had since his Majesties said Restoration. In all these Cases, the proposal of a Benevolence may be offered, although in no cases it be without its inconveniencies; the which are principally these.

1. The abovementioned Brow-beating and distaste given, ||
47 if a man have not contributed as largely as envious observers think he should have done.

2. A Benevolence in many cases may divide a whole Nation into parties, or at least make the strength of Parties too well known to such as need not know it: and withall it may (on the contrary and upon design) disguize the same, and elude the measures which the Governours thought to have taken by such an exploratory artifice.

3. Some men may have particular reasons to contribute large, *viz.* complacency with, and hopes of being repaired by the favour of some Grandee, who favours the business, and the very same may make to the prejudice of others.

4. Men of sinking Estates, (who nevertheless love to live high, and appear splendid, and such who make themselves friends, (by their hospitality paid for, in effect by others) enough to be protected, even from Justice) do often upon this occasion of Benevolence set extravagant Examples unto others, who have laboured hardly for what they have; those not caring what they pay, because it encreaseth their credit, to borrow the more, so as at length the whole burthen of such Bankrupts Benevolence, lights upon the frugal Patriots, by whom the Publique Weal subsists.

[1] See 13 Charles II., Stat. 1. c. 4 (1661), An Act for a free and voluntary present to his Majesty.

CHAP. X.

Of Penalties.

THe usual Penalties are Death, Mutilations, Imprisonment, Publick disgrace, Corporal transient pains, and great Tortures, besides the Pecuniary Mulcts. Of† which last we shall most insist, speaking of the others but in order to examine whether they may not be commuted for these.

2. There be some certain Crimes, for which the Law of God appoints death; and these must be punished with it, unless we say that those were but the Civil Laws of the Jewish ‖ Commonwealth, although given by God himself; of 48
which opinion certainly most modern States are, in as much as they punish not Adulteries, &c. with death, as among the Jewes, and yet punish small Thefts with Death instead of multiple reparation.

3. Upon this supposition we shall venture to offer; whether the reason of simple Death be not to punish incorrigible Committers of great faults?

4. Of publick Death with Torments, to affright men from Treasons, which cause the deaths and miseries of many thousand innocent and useful people?

5. Of Death secretly executed, to punish secret and unknown Crimes, such as Publick Executions would teach to the World? Or else to suffocate betimes some dangerous Novelties in Religion, which the patient suffering of the worst man would much spread and encourage.

6. Mutilations suppose of Ears, Nose, &c. are used for perpetual disgrace, as standing in the Pillory is for temporary and transient; which and such other punishments have (by the way) made some corrigible offenders, to become desperate and incurable.

7. Mutilations of parts as of Fingers, are proper to disable such as have abused their dextrous use of them, by Pocket-picking, Counterfeiting of Seals and Writings, &c.

† read [*on*] for [*of*]

Mutilations of other parts, may serve to punish and prevent Adulteries, Rapes, Incests, &c. And the smaller Corporal pains, serve to punish those, who can pay no pecuniary mulcts.

8. Imprisonment seems rather to be the punishments of suspected then guilty persons, and such as by their carriage give the Magistrate occasion to think, either they have done some smaller particular Crime, as Thefts, &c. or that they would commit greater; as Treasons and Seditions. But where Imprisonment is not a securing men untill their Trialls, but a sentence after Triall, it seems to me proper onely to seclude such men from conversation, whose Discourses are bewitching, and Practices infectious, and in whom neverthelesse
49 remains some hopes of their future Amendments, || or usefulnesse for some service not yet appearing.

9. As for perpetual Imprisonment by sentence, it seems but the same with death it self, to be executed by nature it self, quickened with such Diseases, as close living, sadness, solitude, and reflections upon a past and better condition, doth commonly beget: Nor do men sentenced hereunto live longer, though they be longer in dying.

10. Here we are to remember in consequence of our opinion, [That Labour is the Father and active principle of Wealth, as Lands are the Mother] that the State by killing, mutilating, or imprisoning their members, do withall punish themselves; wherefore such punishments ought (as much as possible) to be avoided and commuted for pecuniary mulcts, which will encrease labour and publick wealth.

11. Upon which account, why should not a man of Estate, found guilty of man-slaughter, rather pay a certain proportion of his whole Estate, then be burnt in the hand?

12. Why should not insolvent Thieves be rather punished with slavery then death? so as being slaves they may be forced to as much labour, and as cheap fare, as nature will endure, and thereby become as two men added to the Commonwealth, and not as one taken away from it; for if *England* be under-peopled, (suppose by half) I say that next to the bringing in of as many more as now are, is the making

these that are, to do double the work which now they do; that is, to make some slaves; but of this elsewhere.

13. And why should not the solvent Thieves and Cheats be rather punished with multiple Restitutions then Death, Pillory, Whipping? &c. But it will be asked, with how manifold Restitutions should picking a pocket (for example) be punished? I say, 'twere good in order to the solution hereof, to enquire of some candid Artists in that Trade, how often they are taken one time with another practising in this work? If but once in ten times, then to restore even but seven-fold, would be a fair profit; and to restore but ten-fold, were but an even lay; wherefore to restore twenty-fold, that is, double to the hazard, is rather the true *ratio* and measure of punishment by double reparation.

14. And surely the restoring two, three, four, and seven-fold mentioned in *Moses* Law must be thus understood, or else a man might make thieving a very fair and lawful profession.

15. The next question is, in such multiple Restitutions how many parts should be given to the sufferer. To which I answer, never above one, and scarce that, to oblige him to more care, and self-preservation, with three parts to discoverers, and the rest to publick uses.

16. Thirdly, In the case of Fornications, most of the punishments not made by pecuniary mulcts and commuted, are but shame, and that too but towards some few persons, which shame for ever after obdurates the Offender, what ever it work upon such whose fames are yet intire: Of all which men take little consideration, standing upon the brink of such precipices as makes them giddy; and when they are in danger of such faults as are rather madnesses, distempers, and alienations of the minde and reason, as also insurrections of the passions, then deliberate acts of the understanding.

17. Moreover, according to that Axiom of, *In quo quis peccat, in eodem puniatur;* if the *Ratio formalis* of the sin of *Concubitus Vagi*, be the hindering of procreation, let those who by their miscarriages of this kinde are guilty thereof, repair unto the State the misse of another pair of hands with

the double labour of their own, or which is all one, by a pecuniary mulct; and this is the practice of some wise States in punishing what they will never be able to prevent: Nor doth the Gospel specifie any punishment in this world, onely declaring they shall not be received into the joyes of the next.

18. I could instance in more particulars, but if what I have already said be reasonable, this little is enough; if not, then all the rest would be too little also: wherefore I shall adde but one instance more, as most suitable to our present times and occasions, which is the way of punishing Heterdox Professors of Religion.

19. That the Magistrate may punish false Believers, if he believe he shall offend God in forbearing it, is true; for the same reasons that men give for Liberty of Conscience,
51 and || universal tolleration; and on the other side, that he may permit false Worships, seems clearly at least by the practice of all States, who allow Ambassadours their freedom (be the† Worship never so abominable) even when they come to negociate but upon temporal and small matters.

20. Wherefore, since the Magistrate may allow or connive at such Worships as himself thinks fit, and yet may also punish; and since by Death, Mutilations, and imprisonments of the Subjects, the State not onely punisheth it self, but spreadeth the Pseudodoxies; it follows, that pecuniary Mulcts are the fittest wayes of checking the wantonness of men in this particular: forasmuch as that course savours of no bitterness at all, but rather argues a desire to indulge, provided such indulgence may consist with the indempnity of the State; for no Heterodox‡ will desire to be tollerated longer then he keeps the Publick Peace; the which if he means to do, he cannot take it ill of the Magistrate, to keep him steddy unto that his duty, nor grudge to contribute towards so much charge for that purpose as himself occasions.

21. Moreover, as there seems a reason for indulging some conscientious misbelievers, so there is as much for being severe

† read [*their*] for [*the*]
‡ after [*Heterodox*] interline [*Believer*]

towards Hypocrites, especially such as abuse holy Religion to cloak and vizzard worldly ends: Now what more easie and yet effectual way is there to discern between these two, then well proportioned pecuniary mulćts? for who desiring to serve God without fear, and labouring ten hours *per diem* at his Calling, would not labour one hour more for such a freedom? even as religious men spend an hour *per diem* more then the looser sort do at their Devotions; or who weaving† Cloth of one and twenty shillings the yard, would not be contented with that of twenty shillings, for the same advantage of his liberty in Worship? Those that kick at this, being unwilling either to do or suffer for God, for whose sake they pretend so much.

22. It may be here objećted, that although some bad Religions might be tollerated, yet that all may not, *viz.* such as consist not with the Civil Peace. To which I answer. ||

First, that there is no Schisme or Separation, be it never so 52
small, consistent with that unity and peace as could be wisht; nor none so perfectly conscientious, but may also be civilly most pernicious: For that *Venner*[1] and his Complices ańted upon internal motives, the most free exposing of themselves to death may evince; and yet their holding the King to be an Usurper upon the Throne and Right of Jesus Christ was a Civil mischief neither to be pardoned or parallel'd.

23. And yet on the other hand there is no Pseudodoxy so great, but may be muzzled from doing much harm in the State, without either Death, Imprisonment, or Mutilation: To make short, no opinion can be more dangerous, then to disbelieve the immortality of the Soul, as rendring man a beast, and without conscience, or fear of committing any evil, if he can but elude the penaltie of humane Laws made against it, and letting men loose to all evil thoughts and designs

[1] Thomas Venner, the London wine-cooper, who led the revolt of the Fifth Monarchy Men, 6 January, 1661. See *A relation of the Arraignment and Trial of those who made the late Rebellious Insurrection in London*, 1661, in Somers' *Tracts* (1812), VII. 469—472; Howell, *State Trials*, VI. 105—120, 67—70 n.; Burnet, *Own Time*, I. 160—161.

† read [*wearing*] for [*weaving*]

whereof man can take no notice: Now I say, that even this Misbeliever may be adæquately punished if he be kept as a beast, be proprietor of nothing, as making no conscience how he gets; be never admitted in Evidence or Testimony, as under no obligation to speak truth; be excluded all Honours and Offices, as caring onely for himself, not the protecting of others; and be withall kept to extream bodily labour, the profit whereof to the State is the pecuniary Mulct we speak of, though the greatest.

24. As for opinions less horrible then this, the Mulct may be fitted to each of them respectively, according to the measure of danger which the Magistrate apprehends from their allowance, and the charge necessary to prevent it.

25. And now we are speaking of the wayes how to prevent and correct Heterodoxies in Religion, which we have hitherto done by designing punishments for the erring sheep, I think it not amiss to adde, That in all these cases the Shepherds themselves should not wholly scape free: For if in this Nation there be such abundance of Free-Schools, and of liberall Maintenance provided in our Universities and elsewhere for instructing more then enough in all such learn-
53 ing as is fit to ‖ defend the established Religion, together with superabundant Libraries for that purpose. Moreover, if the Church-preferments be so numerous and ample both for Wealth, Honour, and Power, as scarce any where more; it seems strange that when by the laziness, formality, ignorance, and loose lives of our Pastours, the sheep have gone astray, grown scabbed, or have been devoured by Wolves and Foxes, that the Remedy of all this should be onely sought by frighting those that have strayed from ever returning again, and by tearing off as well the skins as the wool of those that are scabbed; whereas Almighty God will rather require the blood even of them that have been devoured, from the shepheards themselves.

26. Wherefore if the Minister should lose part of the Tythes of those whom he suffers to dissent† from the Church, (the defector not saving, but the State wholly gaining them)

† read [*defect*] for [*dissent*]

and the defector paying some pecuniary Mulct for his Schisme, and withall himself defraying the charge of his new particular Church and Pastorage, me thinks the burthen would be thus more equally born.

27. Besides, the judicious world do not believe our Clergy can deserve the vaste preferments they have, onely because they preach, give a better accompt of Opinions concerning Religion then others, or can express their conceptions in the words of the Fathers, or the Scriptures, &c. Whereas certainly the great honour we give them, is for being patterns of holiness, for shewing by their own self-denials, mortifications, and austerities, that 'tis possible for us to imitate them in the precepts of God; for if it were but for their bare Pulpit-discourses, some men might think there is ten thousand times as much already printed as can be necessary, and as good as any that ever hereafter may be expected. And it is much suspected, that the Discipline of the Cloisters hath kept up the Roman Religion, which the Luxury of the Cardinals and Prelates might have destroyed.

28. The substance therefore of all we have said in this discourse concerning the Church is, that it would make much for its peace, if the Nursery of Ministers be not too bigg, that || Austerities in the Priests lives would reconcile them to 54
the people; and that it is not unreasonable, that when the whole Church suffers by the defection of her Members, that the Pastours of it by bearing a small part should be made sensible of the loss; the manner and measures of all which I leave unto those unto whom it belongs.

29. Concerning Penalties and Penal Laws I shall adde but this, that the abuse of them is, when they are made not to keep men from sin, but to draw them into punishment; and when the Executors of them keep them hid until a fault be done, and then shew them terrible to the poor immalicious offender: Just like Centinels, who never shew men the advertisements against pissing near their Guards, till they have catcht them by the coats for the forfeiture they claim.

CHAP. XI.

Of Monopolies and Offices.

MOnopoly (as the word signifies) is the sole selling power, which whosoever hath can vend the commodity whereupon he hath this power, either qualified as himself pleases, or at what price he pleaseth, or both, within the limits of his Commission.

2. The great example of a Monopoly is the King of *France* his Gabel upon Salt, whereby he sells that for sixty which costs him but one; now Salt being a thing of universal use to all degrees of men, and scarce more to the poor then the rich, it seems to be of the same effect with the simplest[1] Poll-money abovementioned, in case all men spent equally of it, or if men be forced to take it whether they spend it or not, as in some places they are. But if men spend or eat Salt unequally, as they commonly do, nor are bound to take or pay for more then they spend, then† is no other than an accumulative Excize, especially if the salt be all of one
55 uniform goodness, || otherwise it is a distinct species of Leavy, *viz.* a monopoly.

3. The use or pretence of instituting a Monopoly is,

First, Right of Invention; forasmuch as the Laws do reward Inventions, by granting them a Monopoly of them for a certain time; (as here in *England* for fourteen years) for thereby the Inventor is rewarded more or less according to the acceptance which his Invention findes amongst men.

Where note by the way, that few new Inventions were ever rewarded by a Monopoly; for although the Inventor oftentimes drunk with the opinion of his own merit, thinks all the world will invade and incroach upon him, yet I have observed[2], that the generality of men will scarce be hired to

[1] 1679, "simple."

[2] Petty had invented a machine for double writing, upon which he received from the House of Lords a patent dated 7 March, $164\frac{7}{8}$, and valid for seventeen years. He issued a prospectus (Bibliography), and endeavoured to "syndicate" the invention, apparently without success. Fitzmaurice, 10—13.

† between [*them* and *is*] interline [*it*]

make use of new practices, which themselves have not throughly tried, and which length of time hath not vindicated from latent inconveniences; so as when a new Invention is first propounded, in the beginning every man objects, and the poor Inventor runs the Gantloop of all petulent wits; every man finding his several flaw, no man approving it, unless mended according to his own advice: Now not one of an hundred out-lives this torture, and those that do, are at length so changed by the various contrivances of others, that not any one man can pretend to the Invention of the whole, nor well agree about their respective shares in the parts. And moreover, this commonly is so long a doing, that the poor Inventor is either dead, or disabled by the debts contracted to pursue his design; and withall railed upon as a Projector, or worse, by those who joyned their money in partnership with his wit; so as the said Inventor and his pretences are wholly lost and vanisht.

Secondly, a Monopoly may be of real use for a time, *viz.* at the first introducing of a new Manufacture, wherein is much nicety to make it well, and which the generality of men cannot judge of as to the performance. As for example; suppose there were some most approved Medicament which one certain man could make most exactly well, although several others could also make the same less perfectly: in this case this same chief Artist may be allowed a
Monopoly for a time, *viz.* || until others have had experience 56
enough under him, how to make the Medicament as well as himself. First, because the world may not have the Medicament variously made, when as they can neither discern the difference by their senses, nor judge of the effects thereof *à posteriori*, by their reasons. Secondly, because others may be fully instructed by him that can best do it; and thirdly, because he may have a reward for such his communications: But forasmuch as by Monopolies of this kinde, great Leavies are seldom made, they are scarce pertinent to our design.

Offices instituted by the State of Fees of their own appointment, are of parallel nature to Monopolies; the one relating to actions and employments as the other to things, and have the same to be said for and against them as Monopolies have.

As a Kingdom encreaseth and flourisheth, so doth variety of things, of actions, and even of words encrease also; for we see that the language of the most flourishing Empires was ever the most copious and elegant, and that of mountainous Cantons the contrary: Now as the actions of this Kingdom encreased, so did the Offices (that is, the power and faculty of solely executing and performing the said actions) encrease likewise; and on the contrary, as the business of Offices encreased, so did the difficulty and danger of discharging them amiss decrease proportionably: from whence 'tis come to pass, that the Offices which at their first erecting were not performed but by the ablest, most inventive, and versatile Instruments, (such as could wrestle with all emergent difficulties, and collect Rules and Axioms out of the Series of their own Observations, (with reference to the various casualties of their employments) whereby to direct Posterity) are now performed by the most ordinary, formal, pack-horse Deputies and Sub-Deputies.

And whereas at first such large Fees were allowed as (considering even the paucity of them which might then be received) should compensate the Art, Trust, and Industry of the Administratour; yet the† large said Fees are still con-
57 ti-||nued, although the skill and trust be lessened, and the number of the said Fees so extreamly multiplyed: so as now the profits of such Officers‡ (being become cleer, and the work so easie as any man is capable of it, even those that never saw it,) are bought and sold for Years or Lives, as any other Annuity may be; and withal, the splendor arising from the easie gaines of those places in Courts of Justice, is called the Flourishing of the Law, which certainly flourisheth best, when the Professors and Ministers of it have least to do. And moreover, when the burthen and uselesness of such an Office is taken notice of, 'tis nevertheless spared as a Subjects Freehold in favour of him that bought it.

† after [*yet the*] interline [*said*]
‡ read [*offices*] for [*officers*]

Of these Offices are many in this Nation, and such as might be a Revenue to the King, either by their Annual profits, or the Sale of them for many years together. And these are the Offices that are properly saleable, *viz.* where the Fees are large, as appointed when the number of them was few, and also numerous, as multiplying upon the increase of business, and where the business is onely the labour of the meanest men: length of time having made all the work so easie, and found out security against all the frauds, breaches of trust, and male-administrations, whereunto the infancies of those places were obnoxious.

These Offices are therefore Taxes upon such as can or will not avoid the passing through them, and are born as men endure and run themselves into the mischiefs of Duelling[1], the which are very great, which side soever prevails; for certainly men do not alwayes go to Law to obtain right, or prevent wrong, which judicious neighbours might perform as well as a Jury of no abler men; and men might tell the Judge himself the merits of their Cause, as well as now they instruct their Councel. This therefore of Offices is a voluntary Tax upon contentious men, as Excize upon Drink is, to good Fellows to love it. ||

CHAP. XII. 58

Of Tythes.

THe Word Tythes being the same with Tenths, signifie of it self no more then the proportion of the Excisium, or part retrenched, as if Customs upon imported and exported Commodities should be called by the name of Twentieths, as it is sometimes called Tunnage and Poundage; wherefore it remains to say, that Tythes in this place, do together with the said proportion, consignifie the use of it, *viz.* the maintenance of the Clergy, as also the matter or substance out of which this Maintenance is cut, *viz.* the immediate fruit of

[1] Petty had recently avoided a duel. Evelyn, *Diary*, 22 March, 1675, II. 403; Aubrey in Walker's *Bodleian Letters*, II. 485; Fitzmaurice, 151—152.

the Land and Waters, or the proceed of mens Labour, Art, and Stock laid out upon them. It signifies also the manner of paying it, *viz.* in *specie,* and not (but upon special and voluntary causes) in money.

2. We said the matter of Tythes, was the immediate Fruits of the Earth, *viz.* of Grain as soon as 'tis ready to be removed from the ground that bare it; and not of Bread which is Corn thresht, winnowed, ground, tempered with liquor and baked.

3. 'Tis also the second choice out of the young of multiparous Cattle taken in *specie,* so soon as the said Younglings can subsist without their Dams, or else a Composition in Money for the Uniparons.

4. 'Tis Wool, so soon as it is shorn; 'tis Fowl and Fish, where Fowling and Fishing is rather a Trade then a meer Recreation, *& sic de cæteris.*

5. Moreover, in great Cities, Tythes are a kinde of composition in Money for the labour and profit of the Artisans who work upon the materials which have paid Tythes before.

6. Tythes therefore encrease within any Territory, as
59 the || labour of that Countrey increases; and labour doth or ought to increase as the people do; now within four hundred years the people of *England* are about quadrupled, as doubling every two hundred years, and the proportion of the Rent of all the Lands in *England* is about the fourth part of the Expence of the people in it, so as the other three parts is labour and stock.

7. Wherefore the Tythes now should be twelve times as good as they were four hundred years ago; which the rates of Benefices in the Kings books do pretty well shew, by comparing of times; something of this should be abated because the proportion between the proceed of Lands and Labour do vary as the hands of Labourers vary: Wherefore we shall rather say, that the Tythes are but six times as good now as four hundred years ago, that is, that the Tythes now would pay six times as many Labourers, or feed six times as many mouthes, as the Tythes four hundred years ago would have done.

8. Now if there were not onely as many Parishes then as now, more Priests in every Parish, and also more Religious Men who were also Priests, and the Religion of those times being more operose, and fuller of work then now, by reason of Confessions, Holydayes, Offices, &c. more in those dayes then now, (the great work in these dayes being a compendious teaching above a thousand at once without much particular Confession and Catechising, or trouble about the Dead; it seems clear[1], that the Clergy now is far richer then heretofore; and that to be a Clergy-man then was a kinde of a Mortification, whereas now (praised be God) 'tis matter of splendour and magnificence; unless any will say, that there were golden Priests when the Chalices were wood, and but wooden Priests when the Chalices were gold; or that Religion best flourisheth when the Priests are most mortified, as was before said of the Law, which best flourisheth when Lawyers have least to do.

9. But what ever the increase of the Churches Goods are, I grudge it them not; onely wish that they would take a course to enjoy it with safety and peace to themselves; where-||of one is, not to breed more Churchmen then the 60
Benefices as they now stand shred† out, will receive; that is to say, if there be places but for about twelve thousand in *England* and *Wales*, it will not be safe to breed up 24000. Ministers, upon a view, or conceipt that the Church means otherwise distributed might suffice them all; for then the twelve thousand which are unprovided for, will seek wayes how to get themselves a livelihood; which they cannot do more easily then by perswading the people, that the twelve thousand Incumbents do poison or starve their souls, and misguide them in their way to Heaven: Which needy men upon a strong temptation will do effectually; we having observed, that Lecturers being such a sort of Supernumeraries, have preached more times in a week, more hours in the day, and with greater vehemence every time, then the Incumbents could afford to do; for *Græculus esuriens in Cœlum, jusseris,*

[1] Conjectural emendation; "about the dead); it seems clear."

† read [*shared*] for [*shred*]

ibit[1]. Now this vehemence, this pains, this zeal, and this living upon particular donations, makes the people think, that those who act them are withall more Orthodox, nay better assisted from God then the others. Now let any man judge, whether men reputed to be inspired will not get help to lift themselves into Church-livings, &c. But these things are too plain from the latest experiences.

10. Now you will ask, how shall that be done, or how may we know how to adjust our Nursery to our Orchard? To which I answer, that if there be twelve thousand Church-livings in *England*, Dignitaries included, then that about four hundred being sent forth *per ann.* into the Vineyard, may keep it well served, without luxuriency; for according to the Mortality-Bill-observation[2], about that number will dye yearly out of twelve thousand Adult-persons, such as Ministers are as to age, and ought to be as well as to speculative knowledge, as practical experience, both of themselves and others.

11. But I have digressed, my main scope being to explain the nature of the Tax of Tythes; nevertheless since the end of such explanation is but to perswade men to bear quietly so much Tax as is necessary, and not to kick against the pricks; and since the end of that again, and the end of
61 all else we are || to do, is but to preserve the publick Peace, I think I have not been impertinent in inserting this little Advertisement, making so much for the Peace of our[3] *Jerusalem.*

12. But to return to Tythes as a Tax or Levy, I say that in *England* it is none, whatsoever it might be or seem to be in the first Age of its Institution; nor will the Kings Quit-rents in *Ireland*, as they are properly none now, seem any in the next Age, when every man will proportion his Expence to the remainder of his own Rent after the King is paid his; for 'tis surprize and the suddenness of the Charge, which a Tax supervenient to a mans other expences and issues makes, that renders it a burthen, and that intollerable

[1] Juvenal, *Sat.*, III. 78.
[2] See Graunt, Index, entry 96.
[3] 1679 omits "our."

to such as will not understand it, making men even to take up Arms to withstand it; that is, leap out of the Frying-pan upon earth into the fire even of hell, which is War, and the calamities† thereof.

13. Now Tythes being no Tax, I speak of it but as the *modus* or pattern of a Tax, affirming it to be next to one, the most equal and indifferent which can be appointed in order to defray the publick Charge of the whole Nation as well as that of the Church; for hereby is collected a proportion of all the Corn, Cattle, Fish, Fowl, Fruit, Wool, Honey, Wax, Oyl, Hemp, and Flax of the Nation, as a result of the Lands, Art, Labour, and Stock which produced them; onely it is scarce regular in respect of Housing, Cloth, Drinks, Leather, Feathers, and the several Manufactures of them; insomuch, as if the difference of Tythes which the Countrey payes in proportion to the City, were now *de novo* to be established, I do not see what in likelihood would sooner cause a grand sedition about it.

14. The payment of an *aliquot* part to the King out of the same things as now pay Tythes, *in specie*, would have no‡ inconvenience, because, the Kings Rents would be like the Dividend in Colledges, *viz.* higher or lower according to the prices of those Commodities, unless the said inequality in colledges happen by reason of the fewness of particulars, according to the market rates whereof their Rents are paid in money; whereas the whole of all the particulars might well enough ballance || each other, a dear or plentiful†† being 62
but an appellation *secundum quid*, *viz.* with reference as to Corn onely, as the chief food of the multitude; whereas 'tis likely, that the same causes which makes Corn scarce, may make other things in plenty of no less use to the King; as repairing in one thing what he wants in another.

15. Another inconvenience would be that which was observed in *Ireland*, when the Ministery were paid by Sallary[1], and the Tythes in kinde paid to the State; who because

[1] Perhaps under Act of 1654, c. 32, Scobell II. 313, 317.

† read [*consequences*] for [*calamities*]   ‡ read [*an*] for [*no*]

†† after [*plentiful*] interline [*year*]

they could not actually receive them *in specie*, let them at farm to the most bidder; in the transaction whereof was much juggling, combination, and collusion, which perhaps might have been remedied, had not that course been used but as a sudden temporary shift, without intention of continuing it.

16. The third inconvenience is, that abovementioned, *viz.* the necessity of another way of Tax, to take in the Manufactures of those Commodities which pay the Tax of Tythes; whereas possibly there is a way of Tax equal in its own nature, and which needs not to be pieced up by any other; so as the Officers about that may have a full employment, and none others wanted, whose wide intervals of leasure shall make them seem Drones, as they are also the Caterpillars of any State.

CHAP. XIII.

Of several smaller wayes of levying Money.

WHen the people are weary of any one sort of Tax, presently some Projector propounds another, and gets himself audience, by affirming he can propound a way how all the publick charge may be born without the way that is. As for example, if a Land-tax be the present distasted way, and the people weary of it, then he offers to do the business without such a Land-tax, and propound either a Poll-money, Excize, or the institution of some new Office or
63 Monopoly; || and hereby draws some or other to hearken to him; which is readily enough done by those who are not in the places of profit relating to the way of Levies in use, but hope to make themselves Offices in the new Institution.

2. I shall enumerate a few of the smaller wayes which I have observed in several places of *Europe*, *viz.*

First, in some places the State is common Cashier for all or most moneys, as where Banks are, thereby gaining the interest of as much money as is deposited in their hands.

Secondly, Sometimes the State is the common Usurer; as where Loan Banks, and *montes pietatis* are in use, and might be more copiously and effectually where Registers of Lands are kept.

Thirdly, Sometimes the State is or may be Common Ensurer, either upon the danger onely of Enemies at sea, according to the supposed primitive end of our Customs in *England*, or else of the casualties of the Enemy, Weather, Sea, and Vessel taken together.

Fourthly, Sometimes the State hath the whole sale and benefit of certain Commodities, as of Amber in the Duke of *Brandenburghs* Countrey[1], Tobacco formerly in *Ireland*, Salt in *France*, &c.

Fifthly, Sometimes the State is common Beggar, as 'tis almost in *Holland*, where particular Charity seems only to serve for the relief of concealed wants, and to save these wanting from the shame of discovering their poverty, and not so much to relieve any wants that are declared, and already publickly known.

Sixthly, In some places the State is the sole Guardian of Minors, Lunaticks, and Idiots.

Seventhly, In some other Countreys the State sets up and maintains Play-houses, and publick Entertainments, giving Sallaries to the Actors, but receiving the bulk of the profit to themselves.

Eightly, In some places, Houses are ensured from fire by the State at a small Rent *per annum* upon each.

Ninthly, In some places Tolls are taken upon passage
over || Bridges, Causeys, and Ferries built and maintained at 64
the Publick Charge.

Tenthly, In some places men that dye are obliged to leave a certain pittance to the publick, the same is practised in other places upon Marriages, and may be in others upon Births.

Eleventhly, In some places strangers especially Jews, are particularly taxed; which may be good in over-peopled Countreys, though bad in the contrary case.

[1] On the history of the Prussian Amber monopoly, cf. *Gewinnung und Verarbeitung des Bernsteins in Preussen von der Ordenzeit bis zur Gegenwart; von* W. Tesdorpf. Jena, 1887, pp. 6—22.

3. As for Jews, they may well bear somewhat extraordinary, because they seldom eat and drink with Christians, hold it no disparagement to live frugally, and even sordidly among themselves, by which way alone they become able to under-sell any other Traders, to elude the Excize, which bears but according to mens[1] expences; as also other Duties, by dealing so much in Bills of Exchange, Jewels, and Money, and by practising of several frauds with more impunity then others; for[2] by their being at home every where, and yet no where they become responsible almost for nothing.

4. Twelfthly, There have been in our times, wayes of levying an *aliquot* part of mens Estates, as a Fifth, and Twentieth, *viz.* of their Estates real and personal, yea of their Offices, Faculties, and imaginary Estates also, in and about which way may be so much fraud, collusion, oppression, and trouble, some purposely getting themselves taxed to gain more trust; Others bribing to be taxed low, and it being impossible to check or examine, or trace these Collections by the print of any foot-steps they leave (such as the Harths of Chimneys are) that I have not patience to speak more against it; daring rather conclude without more ado, in the words of our Comick to be naught, yea exceeding naught, very abominable, and not good. ||

65 CHAP. XIV.

Of raising, depressing, or embasing of Money.

SOmetimes it hath hapned, that States (I know not by what raw advice) have raised or embased their money, hoping thereby, as it were, to multiply it, and make it pass for more then it did before; that is, to purchase more commodity or labour with it: All which indeed and in truth, amounts to no more then a Tax, upon such People unto whom the State is indebted, or a defalkation of what is due; as also the like burthen upon all that live upon Pensions, established Rents, Annuities, Fees, Gratuities, &c.

[1] 1679, "mean."

[2] 1679, "but."

2. To explain this fully, one might lanch out into the deep Ocean of all the Mysteries concerning Money, which is done for other ends elsewhere; nevertheless I shall do it the best I can, by expounding the reasons *pro & contrà* for embasing and raising of Money: and first of embasing.

3. Copper or Tin Money made *ad valorem* in its matter, is no embasing, the same being onely cumbersom and baser then silver money, onely because less convenient and portable.

And Copper money *ad valorem* in workmanship and matter both together; (such as on which the Effigies and Scutcheon are so curiously graven and impressed, as the moneys seem rather a Medal†) is not embasing, unless the numbers of such pieces be excessive, (the measures whereof I shall not set down, until I shall hereafter propound the fittest Sections of the abstracted pound into which I would have money coyned, and determine how many pieces of each Section should be in an hundred pound) for in case of such excess, the workmanship being of no other use but to look upon, becomes base by its being too common.

4. Nor are such Tokens base as are coyned for Exchange in retailing by particular men, (if such men be responsible and able to take them back, and give Silver for them.) ||

5. But that Gold I count to be embased, which hath 66
more allay either of Copper or Silver in it, then serves to correct its too great natural softness and flexibility, whereby it wears too fast in Money: And that Silver I reckon also embased, wherein is commixed more Copper then will sufficiently toughen it, and save it from cracking under the Hammer, Press, or Mill that must coin it, or the like.

6. Base Money is therefore such as Dutch Shillings, Stivers, French Soulz, Irish Bon-galls, &c. and for the most part consisting‡ great pieces, though of small value. To answer the first reason or pretence of making them, which is, that the said Pieces might be more bulky, handleable, and the silver in them less apt to be lost or worn away.

7. The other reason (besides that of allay which we must

† read [*medalls*] instead of [*a medall*]

‡ between [*consisting* and *great*] interline [*of*]

allow in the Measures abovementioned) is to save it from being melted down by Goldsmiths and Bullioners, or exported by strangers; neither of which can happen but to their loss: for suppose a Stiver of two pence had a penny of pure silver, if the Bullioner melts it for the sake of the silver onely, in the separation he shall lose the Copper and charge of refining the Silver; nor will strangers export it into places where the local value of the Piece perisheth, the intrinsick leaving him to loss.

7[1]. Now the reasons against this kinde of Money are, first the greater danger of falsification, because the colour, sound, and weight by which men (without the test) guess at the goodness of the material of Money is too much confounded, for the vulgar (whom it concerns) to make use of them for their marks and guides in the business.

8. Secondly, In case small pieces of this Money, *viz.* pieces of two pence should happen to be raised or depressed twelve, fifteen, or sixteen *per cent.* then there will be a certain loss by reason of the fractions, which the vulgar cannot reckon. As for example, if such Money were depressed but ten, eleven or twelve *per cent.* then the two pence piece would be worth but three half pence, which is twenty five *per cent.* and so of other proportions. ||

67 9. Thirdly, In case the Inconvenience of this Money should be so great as to necessitate a new Coinage of it, then will happen all the losses we mentioned before in melting it down by Bullioners.

10. Fourthly, If the two pence piece contained but $\frac{1}{8}^{th}$ part of the Silver usually in a shilling, then Dealers would have fifteen pence paid in this money for the same Commodity, for which they would take a shilling in Standard Silver.

11. Raising of Money is either the cutting the pound *Troy* of Standard Silver into more pieces then formerly, as into above sixty, whereas heretofore the same was made but into twenty, and yet both sorts called shillings, or else calling

[1] The error whereby two consecutive paragraphs are numbered "7" occurs in all editions.

the money already made by higher names: The reasons or pretences given for such raising are these, *viz.* That the raising of Money will bring it in, and the material thereof more plentifully; for trial whereof suppose one shilling were proclaimed to be worth two, what other effect could this have, then the raising of all Commodities unto a double price? Now if it were proclaimed, That Labourers Wages, &c. should not rise at all upon this raising of Money, then would this Act be as onely a Tax upon the said Labourers, as forcing them to lose half their wages, which would not be onely unjust but impossible, unless they could live with the said half, (which is not to be supposed) for then the Law that appoints such Wages were ill made, which should allow the Labourer but just wherewithall to live; for if you allow double, then he works but half so much as he could have done, and otherwise would; which is a loss to the Publick of the fruit of so much labour.

12. But suppose the *Quart d' Esen*† of *France* commonly esteemed worth eighteen pence were raised to three shillings, then 'tis true, that all the Moneys of *England* would be indeed *Quart d' Esens* pieces; but as true, that all the English Money would be carried away, and that our *Quart d' Esens* would contain but half so much Bullion as our own Money did; so that raising of Money may indeed change the *species*, but with so much loss as the Forreign Pieces were raised unto, above their intrinsick value. ||

13. But for remedy of this, suppose we raised the *Quart* 68
d' Esen double, and prohibited the Exportation of our own money in Exchange thereof. I answer, that such a Prohibition is nugatory, and impossible to be executed; and if it were not, yet the raising of the said *species* would but make us sell the Commodities bought with raised *Quart d' Escens*, in effect but at half the usual rate, which unto them that want such commodities will as well yield the full; so that abating our prices, will as well allure strangers to buy extraordinary proportions of our Commodities, as raising their money will do: But neither that, nor abating the price will

† read [*d' Escu*] instead of [*d' Esens*]

make strangers use more of our Commodities then they want; for although the first year they should carry away an unuseful and superfluous proportion, yet afterwards they would take so much the less.

14. If this be true, as in substance it is, why then have so many wise States in several ancient, as well as modern times frequently practised this Artifice, as a means to draw in money into their respective Dominions.

I answer, that something is to be attributed to the stupidity and ignorance of the people, who cannot of a sudden understand this matter: for I finde many men wise enough, who though they be well informed that raising of money signifies little, yet cannot suddenly digest it. As for example, an unengaged person who had money in his purse in *England*, and should hear that a shilling was made fourteen pence in *Ireland*, would more readily run thither to buy Land then before; not suddenly apprehending, that for the same Land which he might have bought before for six years Purchase, he shall now pay seven. Nor will Sellers in *Ireland* of a sudden apprehend cause to raise their Land proportionally, but will at least be contented to compound the business, *viz.* to sell at six and an half; and if the difference be a more ragged fraction, men under a long time will not apprehend it, nor ever be able exactly to govern their practice according to it.

15. Secondly, Although I apprehend no little real difference between raising Forreign Money to double, and abasing† half in the price of our own Commodities, yet to sell them on
69 a || tacite condition to be paid in Forreign present Money, shall increase our money; forasmuch as between raising the money, and abasing the price, is the same difference as between selling for money and in barter, which latter is the dearer; or between selling for present money, and for time; barter resolving into the nature of uncertain time.

16. I say, suppose English Cloth were sold at six shillings a Yard, and French Canvas at eighteen pence the ell, the question is, whether it were all one in order to increase

† read [*abating*] for [*abasing*]

Money in *England* to raise the French Money double, or to abate half of the price of our Cloth? I think the former†, because that former way or proposition carries with it a condition of having Forreign Money in *specie*, and not Canvas in barter, between which two wayes the world generally agrees there is a difference. Wherefore if we can afford to abate half our price, but will not do it but for our neighbours money, then we gain so much as the said difference between Money and Barter amounts unto, by such raising of our Neighbours Money.

17. But the fundamental solution of this Question depends upon a real and not an imaginary way of computing the prices of Commodities; in order to which real way I premise these suppositions: First then, suppose there be in a Territory a thousand people, let these people be supposed sufficient to Till this whole Territory as to the Husbandry of Corn, which we will suppose to contain all necessaries for life, as in the Lords Prayer we suppose the word Bread doth; and let the production of a Bushel of this Corn be supposed of equal labour to that of producing an ounce of Silver. Suppose again that a tenth part of this Land, and tenth of the people, *viz.* an hundred of them, can produce Corn enough for the whole; suppose that the Rent of Land (found out as above-mentioned) be a fourth part of the whole product, (about which proportion it really is, as we may perceive by paying a fourth Sheaf instead of Rent in some places) suppose also that whereas but an hundred are necessary for this Husbandry, yet that two hundred have taken up the Trade; and suppose || that where a Bushel of Corn 70
would suffice, yet men out of delicacy will use two, making use of the Flower onely of both. Now the Inferences from hence are;

First, That the goodness or badness, or the value of Land depends upon the greater or lesser share of the product given for it in proportion to the simple labour bestowed to raise the said Product.

Secondly, That the proportions between Corn and Silver

† after [*former*] interline [*better*]

signifie onely an artificial value, not a natural; because the comparison is between a thing naturally useful, and a thing in it self unnecessary, which (by the way) is part of the reason why there are not so great changes and leaps in the proceed† of Silver as of other Commodities.

Thirdly, That natural dearness and cheapness depends upon the few or more hands requisite to necessaries of Nature: As Corn is cheaper where one man produces Corn for ten, then where he can do the like but for six; and withall, according as the Climate disposes men to a necessity of spending more or less. But Political Cheapness depends upon the paucity of Supernumerary Interlopers into any Trade over and above all that are necessary, *viz.* Corn will be twice as dear where are two hundred Husbandmen to do the same work which an hundred could perform; the proportion thereof being compounded with the proportion of superfluous expence, (*viz.* if to the cause of dearness abovementioned be added to the double Expence to what is necessary) then the natural price will appear quadrupled; and this quadruple Price is the true Political Price computed upon naturall grounds.

And this again proportioned to the common artificiall Standard Silver gives what was sought; that is, the true Price Currant.

18. But forasmuch as almost all Commodities have their Substitutes or Succedanea, and that almost all uses may be answered several wayes; and for that novelty, surprize, example of Superiours, and opinion of unexaminable effects do adde or take away from the price of things, we must adde
71 these contingent Causes to the permanent Causes abovementioned, in the judicious foresight and computation whereof lies the excellency of a Merchant.

Now to apply this Digression, I say, that to encrease Money, it is as well necessary to know how to abate the‡ raise, the price of Commodities, and that of Money, which was the scope of the said Digression.

19. To conclude this whole Chapter, we say, that raising

† read [*prices*] for [*proceed*] ‡ read [*as*] for [*the*]

or embasing of Moneys is a very pittiful and unequal way of Taxing the people; and 'tis a sign that the State sinketh, which catcheth hold on such Weeds as are accompanied with the dishonour of impressing a Princes Effigies to justifie Adulterate Commodities, and the breach of Publick Faith, such as is the calling a thing what it really is not.

CHAP. XV.

Of Excize.

IT is generally allowed by all, that men should contribute to the Publick Charge but according to the share and interest they have in the Publick Peace; that is, according to their Estates or Riches: now there are two sorts of Riches, one actual, and the other potential. A man is actually and truly rich according to what he eateth, drinketh, weareth, or any other way really and actually enjoyeth; others are but potentially or imaginatively rich, who though they have power overmuch, make little use of it; these being rather Stewards and Exchangers for the other sort, then owners for themselves.

2. Concluding therefore that every man ought to contribute according to what he taketh to himself, and actually enjoyeth. The first thing to be done is, to compute what the Total of the Expence of this Nation is by particular men upon themselves, and then what part thereof is necessary for || the Publick; both which (no not the former) are 72
so difficult as most men imagine.

3. In the next place we must conceive, that the very perfect Idea of making a Leavy upon Consumptions, is to rate every particular Necessary, just when it is ripe for Consumption; that is to say, not to rate Corn until it be Bread, nor Wool until it be cloth, or rather until it be a very Garment; so as the value of Wool, Cloathing, and Tayloring, even to the Thread and Needles might be comprehended: But this being perhaps too laborious to be performed, we ought to enumerate a Catalogue of Commodities both native and artificial, such whereof accompts may be most easily

taken, and can bear the Office marks either on themselves, or on what contains them; being withall such, as are to be as near Consumption as possible: And then we are to compute what further labour or charge is to be bestowed on each of them, before consumption, that so an allowance be given accordingly. As for example, suppose there be an hundred pounds worth of Stript Stuff for Hangings, and an hundred pounds worth of Cloth or Stuff for the best mens Cloathes; I conceive, that the Cloth should bear a greater Excize then the said stript stuff, the one wanting nothing but tacking up, to be at its wayes end; and the other Tayloring, Thread, Silk, Needles, Thimbles, Buttons, and several other particulars: The Excise of all which must be accumulated upon the Excise of the Cloth, unless they be so great (as perhaps Buttons, Lace, or Ribbons may be) to be taxed apart, and inserted into the Catalogue abovementioned.

4. Now the things to be accumulated upon Cloth are, as near as possible, to be such particulars as are used onely to Cloth, or very rarely to any other particular, as the several sorts of peculiar trimmings; so on Corn should be accumulated the charge of grinding, bolting, yeast, &c. for the baking of it into Bread, unless, as was said before, any of these particulars can be better rated apart.

5. A question ariseth hence, whether any Native Commodities exported ought to pay the Excize, or that what is
73 im-||ported in lieu of it should pay none? I answer no, because they are not spent here *in specie*; but I conceive that the Goods returned from abroad for them and spent here should pay, if the exported have not already, for so shall what we spend pay once, but not oftner. Now if Bullion be returned, then if it be coyned into Money it ought not to pay, because Money will beget other commodities which shall pay; but if the said Bullion be wrought into Plate and Utensils, or disgrost into Wire or Lace, or beaten into Fueilles, then it also ought to pay, because it is consumed and absolutely spent, as in Lace and Gilding is too notorious; and this is the reason why I think the Leavy we commonly

call Customs to be unseasonable and preposterous, the same being a payment before consumption.

6. We have several times spoken of Accumulative Excize, by which we mean Taxing many things together as one: As for example, suppose the many Drugs used in Treacle or Mithridate were used onely in those Compositions, in such case by taxing any one of them, the whole number will be taxed as certainly as that one, because they all bear a certain proportion one to another: In Cloth, the Workmanship and Tools as well as the Wool may be well enough taxed, &c.

7. But some have strained this Accumulation so, as they would have all things together taxed upon some one single particular, such as they think to be nearest the Common Standard of all Expence, the principal ends of their proposition being these, *viz.*

First, To disguise the name of Excize, as odious to them, that do neither know the payment of Taxes to be as indispensable as eating, and as have not considered the natural justice of this way of Excizing or proportionating.

Secondly, To avoid the trouble and charge of Collecting.

Thirdly, To bring the business *ad firmum*, and to a certainty of all which we shall speak hereafter, when we examine the several reasons for and against the way of Excize, proceeding now to the several species of Accumulative Excizes, propounded in the world. ||

8. Some propound Beer to be the only Excizeable Com- 74
modity, supposing that in the proportion that men drink, they make all other Expences; which certainly will not hold, especially if Strong Beer pay quintuple unto, (as now) or any more Excize then the small: For poor Carpenters, Smiths, Felt-makers, &c. drinking twice as much Strong Beer as Gentlemen do of Small, must consequently pay ten times as much Excize. Moreover, upon the Artizans Beer is accumulated, onely a little Bread and Cheese, leathern Clothes, Neck-Beef, and Inwards twice a week, stale Fish, old Pease without Butter, &c. Whereas on the other, beside Drink, is accumulated as many more things as Nature and

Art can produce; besides this way of Excizing, though it be never so well administred, is neither so equal nor so easie, nor so examinable as the simple Poll-money before spoken of, which is also but an Accumulative Excize.

9. What hath been propounded for Beer may be of Salt, Fuel, Bread, &c. and the Propositions would all labour under the same Inconveniences; for some spend more, some less of these Commodities; and sometimes Families (each whereof are propounded to be farmed, without descending to individual heads) are more numerous at some times then at others, according as their Estates or other Interests shall wax or wane.

10. Of all the Accumulative Excizes, that of Harth-money or Smoak-money seems the best; and that onely because the easiest, and clearest, and fittest to ground a certain Revenue upon; it being easie to tell the number of Harths, which remove not as Heads or Polls do: Moreover, 'tis more easie to pay a small Tax, then to alter or abrogate Harths, even though they are useless and supernumerary; nor is it possible to cover them, because most of the neighbours know them; nor in new Building will any man who gives forty shillings for making a Chimney be without it for two.

11. Here is to be noted, that a Harth-money must be but small, or else 'twill be intollerable; it being more easie for a Gentleman of a thousand pound *per annum* to pay for an hundred Chimneys (few of their Mansion-Houses having
75 more) || then for Labourers to pay for two. Moreover, if the Land-Lord onely pay this Tax, then is it not an Accumulative Excize for all, but a particular Excize upon but one onely Commodity, namely Housing.

12. Now the Reasons for Excize are these, *viz.*

First, The Natural Justice that every man should pay according to what he actually enjoyeth; upon which account this Tax is scarce forced upon any, and is very light to those, who please to be content with natural Necessaries.

Secondly, This Tax if it be not farmed, but regularly collected, engages to thrift, the onely way to enrich a Nation, as by the Dutch and Jews, and by all other men, who have come to vaste Estates by Trade, doth appear.

Thirdly, No man payes double or twice for the same thing, forasmuch as nothing can be spent but once; whereas it is frequently seen, that otherwise men pay both by the Rent of their Lands, by their Smoaks, by their Titles, and by Customs, (which all men do, though Merchants chiefly talk of it) they also pay by Benevolence and by Tythes; whereas in this way of Excize no man need pay but one way, nor but once, properly speaking.

Fifthly[1], By this way an excellent account may be taken of the Wealth, Growth, Trade, and strength of the Nation at all times. All which Reasons do make not for particular compoundings with Faculties†, nor for letting the whole to farm, but for collecting it by special Officers, who having a full employment, will not be a fourth of the charge of our present many multiform Levies; for to put extraordinary trouble and hazzard upon the Countrey Officers, is a sorer Taxing of them, then to make them pay a small Reward unto practised Persons to be their Substitutes. All which are the common Objections against Excize.

13. I should here adde the manner of Collecting it, but I refer this to the practice of *Holland*; and I might also offer how men may be framed to be fit for this and other Publick Trusts, as to be Cashiers, Storekeepers, Collectors, &c. but I refer this Enquiry unto a more ample and fit occasion. ||

THE[2]

[1] No "fourthly" in any edition.

[2] In the 1662 ed., this catch-word occurs on p. 75 (signature L 2). The verso of the leaf is blank. The next leaf, unpaged, has signature M and begins "Errata." The 1662 ed. being in quarto, two leaves, apparently, are missing. But the Index calls for no more than is here printed, and the nine copies I have seen contain no more.

† read [*families*] for [*faculties*]

ERRATA.

Page	line	Pag.	line	
[18	11]	1	14	between [*who* and *spent*] interline [have]
[22	12]	5	13	after [*want*] read [*general*] instead of [*more*]
[23	17]	6	19	before [*starve*] interline [*needlesly*]
[23	23]	6	29	before [*cause*] read [*one*] instead of [*the*]
[23	24]	6	30	read [*is*] instead of [*are*]
[25	11]	8	7	read [*them*] for [*him*]
[25	12]	8	8	read [*their*] for [*his*]
[35	10]	17	19	read [*viz.*] for [*that is*]
[35	30]	18	3	read [*τὰ χρῆϛα*] instead of [*τὰ χρῆσα*]
[38	17]	20	17	read [*Excisum*] not [*Excisium*]
[39	6]	21	7	read [*obligees*] not [*obliges*]
[40	11]	22	12	read [*enhansing*] not [*exhausting*]
[40	22]	22	23	between [*way* and *Land-Tax*] interline [*of a*]
[40	24]	22	25	deleatur [*sometimes*]
[42	32]	24	25	between [*Rents* and *we*] interline [*in order to Taxes*]
[47	1]	28	24	between [*seldom* and *enough*] interline [*rich*]
[47	4]	28	28	deleatur [*with*]
[48	23]	30	11	after [*hazards*] interline [*and*]
[48	26]		14	read [*omitted*]
[49	4]		27	read [*apparatus*] instead of [*appurtenances*]
[50	24]	32	10	after [*the*] interline [*former*]
[50	25]		11	after [*Land*] read [*this latter*] instead [*of the*]

Page	line	Pag.	line	
[52	14]	33	26	deleatur [*by*]
[52	19]		31	between [*&c* and *then*] interline [*could be fertilized*]
[53	26]	34	36	read [*worth*] not [*work*]
[55	6]	36	16	after [*market*] interline [*abroad*]
[56	2]	37	12	read [*paribus*] not [*talibus*]
[57	32]	39	6	read [*conniving*] not [*coyning*]
[58	21]	39	32	deleatur [*as much harm*]
[58	20]	ibid		between [*of* and *one*] interline [*the*]
[58	24]	penult		after [*Coffee*] inter [*and*]
[58	27]	40	2	read [*meerly*] for [*merrily*]
[59	27]		ult	before [*certainly*] interline [*case*]
[60	10]	41	13	dele [*out*]
[60	21]		24	read [*so or not*] instead of [*use*]
[67	3]	47	26	read [*on*] for [*of*]
[70	19]	51	3	read [*their*] for [*the*]
[70	30]		15	after [*Heterodox*] interline [*Believer*]
[71	8]		29	read [*wearing*] for [*weaving*]
[72	36]	53	14	read [*defect*] for [*dissent*]
[74	15]	54	36	between [*then* and *is*] interline [*it*]
[76	24]	56	ult	after [*yet the*] interline [*said*]
[76	27]	57	3	read [*offices*] for [*officers*]
[79	22]	60	2	read [*shared*] for [*shred*]
[81	4]	61	15	read [*consequences*] for [*calamities*]
[81	20]		32	read [*an*] for [*no*]
[81	27]	62	1	after [*plentiful*] interline [*year*]
[85	12]	65	21	read [*medalls*] instead of [*a medall*]
[85	32]	66	10	between [*consisting* and *great*] interline [*of*]
[87	18]	67	29	read [*d' Escu*] instead of [*d' Esens*]
[88	27]	68	36	read [*abating*] for [*abasing*]
[89	2]	69	11	after [*former*] interline [*better*]
[90	5]	70	12	read [*prices*] for [*proceed*]
[90	34]	71	5	read [*as*] for [*the*]
[95	14]	75	25	read [*families*] for [*faculties*]

FINIS.

[The *Verbum Sapienti* having been printed, heretofore, only at the end of the *Political Anatomy of Ireland*, has never had a full title-page.]

VERBUM
SAPIENTI.

NOTE ON THE VERBUM SAPIENTI.

THE Verbum Sapienti was first published in 1691 as a supplement to the Political Anatomy of Ireland (q.v.). In Petty's list of his own writings[1], however, the entry "Verbum Sapienti, and the value of People" stands opposite the year 1665, and the internal evidence makes it probable that the booklet was written in the latter part of that year. Thus Petty speaks[2] of the continuance of the war with Holland, declared 14 March, 1665, "at the value of the last years Expence" as if the additional assessment beginning Christmas, 1665, were not yet gone into effect[3]. Furthermore his assertion that 100,000 died of the plague[4] looks like an exaggerated estimate made in advance of the yearly bill of mortality, upon whose publication in December, 1665, the official figures were seen to be but 68596. It may be, however, that Petty distrusted the official figures and purposely exceeded them[5]. But by no hypothesis can we assign the Verbum Sapienti to a later date than July 1667, when the war closed.

A MS. of the Verbum Sapienti is contained in a volume preserved at the Public Record Office in Dublin, and called "Dr Petty's Register[6]." The copyist's title, fol. 10, is simply "Verbum Sapienti," but Petty's autograph index to the volume has "Verbum Sapienti Or a discourse about Taxes & ye Value of People," a title so similar to the memorandum mentioned in the preceding paragraph as to justify the assumption that we have in the Verbum Sapienti all that the entry quoted from Petty's list of his own writings calls for. Another MS. of the Verbum Sapienti very carelessly written is appended to a MS. of the Political Arithmetick in the British Museum[7]. The latter portion of it is but a précis of Petty's argument. Sir Peter Pett had, before 1680, a MS. of both these tracts[8] and it is not impossible that the present Sloane MS. is identical with that once in his possession. The Dublin MS. is not divided into chapters and its paragraphs are consecutively numbered throughout. Otherwise it is substantially similar to the printed text of 1691 here reproduced. Significant differences are indicated in the notes, the readings of the Dublin MS. being marked "D," those of the Sloane MS. "S."

[1] Fitzmaurice, 318. [2] p. 103. [3] See note 5, p. 103. [4] p. 109.
[5] See *Polit. Anat.*, chap. iv. [6] Introduction, pt. VII.
[7] Sloane MS., 2572, fol. 105 b, seq.
[8] *Happy Future State*, p. 192—3, 245.

Verbum Sapienti.

VERBUM SAPIENTI.

THE

INTRODUCTION.

1. WHEREAS many are forced[1] to pay $\frac{1}{10}$ of their whole Estates towards the raising of but[2] 70000 *l. per Mensem*[3], besides what they pay more insensibly and directly[4], as Customs, Excise, Chimny-Money, *&c.* (*viz.* in *London*, they pay 2*d. per Mensem per* Pound Rent, that is 2*s. per Annum*, or $\frac{1}{10}$ of the whole.) It must come to pass, that the same Persons must from *Christmas*, 1665. pay $\frac{1}{3}$ of their whole Estates, if the War with *Holland* continue two years longer, at the value of the last years Expence[5], provided His Majesty be kept out of Debt. ||

2. But if the Publick Charge were laid proportionably, 2
no Man need pay above $\frac{1}{10}$ of his whole Effects, even in case the Tax should rise to 250 000 *l. per Mensem*, which God forbid.

[1] S omits 'are forced to.'

[2] D, 'but of.'

[3] 13 Charles II., stat. 2, c. 3 imposed an assessment of £70,000 per month for 18 months, beginning 25 December, 1661.

[4] D, 'indirectly.'

[5] Apparently an allusion to the assessment of £68,819. 9*s.* per month for 36 months granted by 16 & 17 Charles II., c. 1, beginning 25 December, 1664. To this 17 Charles II., c. 1 added £52,083. 6*s.* 8*d.* per month for 24 months beginning Christmas, 1665.

3. That is to say, according to the present ways, some pay four times as much more as they ought, or needed; which disproportion is the true and proper Grievance of Taxes, and which must be felt when the Tax happens to be great and extraordinary: Whereas by meer Method and Proportion, the same may be corrected as aforesaid; and withal, just Accounts might be kept of the People, with the respective Increases and Decreases of them, their Wealth, and Foreign Trade.

The Wealth of the Kingdom.

CHAP. I.

Containing several Computations of the Wealth of the Kingdom.

1. THERE are of Men, Women, and Children, in *England* and *Wales*, about six Millions, whose Expence at 6*l.* 13*s.* 4*d.* *per Annum*, or near 4½*d.* *per Diem*, for Food, Housing, Cloaths, and all other necessaries, amount to 40 Millions, *per Annum*.

2. There are in *England* and *Wales*, of Acres of Land (worth 6*l.* 1*s.* 8*d.* *per* Acre[1], and 18 years purchase) 24 Millions, that is, which yields 8 Millions *per Annum* Rent, and which are worth 144 Millions to be sold.

3. There be 28000 Houses within the Liberties of the City of *London*, worth 15*l.* *per Annum*, and twelve years purchase (*viz.* which yields 420,000*l.* *per Annum*, and are worth 5,040,000*l.* ||

There are without the Liberties, but within the Bills of + Mortality ¼ more[2] in number, perhaps not of greater value, *viz.* 5,040,000*l.*

[1] All editions have 6*l.* 1*s.* 8*d.* per acre. D has '6[s] 8[d] ℘ acre,' which makes Petty's calculation correct.

[2] Apparently "¼ more" should be "as many more." This correction explains the words "not of greater value, *viz.* 5,040,000*l.*" at the end of the paragraph, and it brings the estimate of London's houses (56,000) more nearly into harmony with the 65,000 or 66,000 which Petty variously assigns to the London of 1666 in his *Two Essays* and in his *Five Essays*. Furthermore it is by some such change alone that we can justify Petty's valuation of the housing of

4. There is in all *England* and *Wales* near ten times as many Chimneys as within the Liberties of *London*, as appears by the Returns; Whereof those within the Bills are $\frac{1}{6}$[1] of the whole.

5. 'Tis probable, that the Housing of all the Cities and Market-Towns, are double in number to those of all *London*, though of no more worth.

6. 'Tis also probable, that the Housing without the Cities and Towns, are more in number than those within (*London* excepted) but of no more value.

7. So as the Housing of *England* may be estimated worth 30 Millions[2]; and that if their values be estimated by Chimneys, those of *London* are worth 12*d.* *per* Chimney; those of the Suburbs 10*d.* other Cities and Market-Towns 6*d.* and those without both, about 4*d.*

8. The Shipping of *England*, &c. is about 500,000 Tuns, which at 6*d.* *per* Tun, including their Ordnance, Apparel[3], &c. is worth three Millions. ||

5 9. The Stock of Cattel on the afore-mentioned 24 millions of Land, and the Waste thereunto belonging, is worth $\frac{1}{4}$ of the said Land, *viz.* 36 millions comprehending Horses, Oxen, Sheep, Swine, Deer, Fisheries, Parks and Warrens.

10. The Coined Gold and Silver of the Kingdom, is scarce worth six millions.

11. The Wares, Merchandizes, and Utensils of Plate,

England at 30 million pounds. His calculation, with the correction suggested, would be:

28,000 houses within the Liberties of London, worth	5,040,000 £
28,000 houses without the Liberties but within the Bills,	5,040,000 £

[This makes paragraph 4 plain.]

112,000 houses in cities and market towns,	10,080,000 £
112,000 houses or more without cities and towns,	10,080,000 £
Total	30,240,000 £.

[1] S, '$\frac{1}{16}$.'

[2] 1719, '310 Millions.'

[3] D, 'theire ordinary apparell.'

and Furnitures, may be estimated at 31 millions to make[1] the Ships and Money 40, and the whole 250 millions.

12. The most uncertain part of this Estimate, seems to be rating personal Estates at above 30 Millions, which I make probable thus.

(1) First it is not unlikely that what is contained in all the Shops, Warehouses, Cellars, Barns, and Graineries, together with Household Furniture, Cloaths, Ornaments, *&c.* should be less worth than Housing it self that contains them.

(2) If the value of all the Cattel, *viz.* 36 millions, were added to the 31 personal Estates, making 67 together; both will not make up $1\frac{3}{4}$ years Provision for the whole Nation, whose Expence we estimated at 40 millions *per annum*; and poorer than so, we hope it is not. ||

(3.) I find by the particular estimate of the values of all 6
the Plate, Lead, Iron, Copper and Tin, and of all the Timber, Planks, and Woods, and of all Silks, Linnen, and Callicoes; of all Clothes, Stuffs, and Leathers; of all Grains, and Salts, and of all Wines, Oyles, and other Liquids; of all Grocery and Spicery, and Drugs; of Jewels, and Hangings, Beds, and other Ornaments, (too troublesome to particularize) that this general Account may stand.

[2](4.) The City of *London* being commonly esteemed and rated at the 15*th* part of the whole[3], which we reckon at 250 Millions, that is $16\frac{2}{3}$. I think the sum may be well made up by reckoning $5\frac{1}{8}$ Millions for the Housing as aforesaid, and $1\frac{1}{2}$ for the Shipping (half the Shipping of the Nation belonging to *London*) and about the double of the value of the Housing for what is contained in them. The which upon considering many several Houses, I find not unreasonable.

(Lastly,) supposing that in the Houses within the Liberties of *London* (worth 5 Millions) there be 10 Millions worth of Goods; I conceive that to allow about as much more, *viz.* 21 Millions) to all the rest of the Houses in the

[1] S, 'which makes.'

[2] This and the two following paragraphs are not in S.

[3] Because London was assessed £4666. 13*s.* 4*d.* of the £70,000 per month to be raised in accordance with 13 Charles II., stat. 2, c. 3.

Kingdom, which are ten times as many as aforesaid, will not overcharge them. ||

7 13. Now if the Land worth 144 Millions, yield 8 Millions *per annum*, the other Estate converted into the like Species must yield $5\frac{8}{9}$ more; but because Money and other personal Estates yield more *per annum* than Land; (that is) doubles it self under 17 years purchase at 6*l.* *per centum*, then instead of $5\frac{8}{9}$, suppose it to yield 7, making the whole Annual Proceed 15.

CHAP. II.

Of the Value of the PEOPLE.

NOW if the Annual proceed of the Stock, or Wealth of the Nation, yields but 15 millions, and the expence be 40. Then the labour of the People must furnish the other 25; which may be done, if but half of them, *viz.* 3 millions earned but 8*l.* 6*s.*[1] 8*d.*[2] *per annum*, which is done at 7*d.* *per diem*, abating the 52 Sundays, and half as many other days for accidents as Holy days, sickness, recreations, *&c.*

2. If $\frac{1}{6}$ of these 3 millions earned but 2*d.* *per diem*; another $\frac{1}{6}$ 4*d.* another $\frac{1}{6}$ 8*d.* *per diem*, another 10*d.* and another 12*d.* The medium will be this, 7*d.* *per diem.*[3] ||

8 3. Whereas the Stock of the Kingdom, yielding but 15 Millions of proceed, is worth 250 Millions; then the People who yield 25, are worth $416\frac{2}{3}$ Millions. For although the Individiums[4] of Mankind be reckoned at about 8 years purchase; the Species of them is worth as many as Land, being in its nature as perpetual, for ought we know.

4. If 6 Millions of People be worth 417 millions of pounds *Sterling*, then each head is worth 69*l.* or each of the 3 millions of Workers is worth 138*l.* which is 7 years purchase, at about 12*d.* *per diem*; nor is superlucration above his subsistence to be reckoned in this Case.

[1] D, '4*s.*' [2] 1719, '9*d.*'

[3] The words "another $\frac{1}{6}$ 6*d.*" are required to complete the enumeration and to give an average of 7*d.* per diem. [4] D, 'Inviduum.'

5. From whence it follows, that 100,000. persons dying of the Plague, above the ordinary number, is near 7 Millions loss to the Kingdom; and consequently how well might 70,000 *l.* have been bestowed in preventing this Centuple loss[1]?

6. We said, that the late mortality by the Pest, is a great loss to the Kingdom; whereas some think it but a

[1] This seems to be the germ of Petty's plan "Of Lessening y^e Plagues of London," dated October 7, 1667 and here reprinted from Lord E. Fitzmaurice's *Life*, pp. 121—122:

1. London within ye bills hath 696th people in 108th houses.

2. In pestilentiall yeares, (which are one in 20) there dye $\frac{1}{8}$th of ye people of ye plague and $\frac{1}{4}$th of all diseases.

3. The remedies against spreading of ye plague are shutting up suspected houses and pest-houses within $\frac{1}{2}$ a mile of ye citty.

4. In a circle about ye center of London of 35 miles semi-diameter, or a dayes journey, there live as many people and are as many houses as in London.

5. Six heads may bee caryd a days journey for 20^{sh}.

6. A family may bee lodged 3 months in ye country for 4^{sh}, so as ye charge of carying out and lodging a family at a medium will be 5^{sh}.

7. In ye greatest plague wee feare, scarce 20th families will bee infected; and in this new method but 10th, ye charge whereof will bee 50th pounds.

8. The People which ye next plague of London will sweep away will be probably 120th, which at 7 £ per head is a losse of $8{,}400^{ths}$, the half whereof is $4{,}200^{ths}$.

9. So as 50 is ventured to save 4,200, or about one for 84.

10. There was never a Plague in ye campagne of England by which $\frac{1}{8}$th of ye people dyed.

11. Poore people who live close dye most of ye plague.

12. The Plague is about 3 monthes rising and as much falling, which cold weather hastens.

13. Killing dogs, making great fires in ye street, nor the use of medicaments are considered sure, for which everyone by common directions may bee theire owne Physicians.

14. In ye circle of 70 miles diameter, choose 10 large wide roomey disjoyned houses with water and garden to each, the Inhabitants to remove at 7 dayes notice.

15. Convenient wagons or coaches to bee prepared to carry away ye suspected.

16. A method to furnish ye pesthouses with medicines for theire mony.

17. Bookes of devotion for every house.

Proposalls—When 100 per week dy, the Plague is begun. If there dye fewer than 120^{ths}, out of ye bills, of all diseases within a yeare after, then W.P. is [to] have 20^{sh} per head for all lesse and to pay 10^{sh} per head for all above it.

Every family removed being to provide 10 £ for ye charge of going and coming and for 4 monthes rent. Or a gratuity of...with W.P. his insurance.

seasonable discharge of its Pestilent humours: to clear which difficulty, I say,

7. If the Plague discerned well, between the well and
9 the ill-affected to Peace and Obe-||dience, or between the *Bees* and the *Drones*, the Fact would determine the Question: But if it destroy promiscuously, the Loss is proportionable to the Benefit we have by them that survive; for 'tis they that make *England* worth above 600 millions, as aforesaid: It being certain, That if one person only had escaped: the whole Territory, and all that is in it, had been worth but a livelihood for that one; and he subject to be a prey to the next two that should invade him.

8. It seems reasonable, that what we[1] call the Wealth, Stock, or Provision of the Nation, being the effect of the former or past labour, should not be conceived to differ from efficiencies in being, but should be rated alike, and contribute alike to the common necessities: And then of all and every summ to be raised, the Land and Stock must pay 3 parts; and the People considered without any Estate at all, 5 more; the whole into 8 divided.

9. If the expence of the Nation be 40 Millions; it seems but the same hardship to set apart 4. *viz.* $\frac{1}{10}$ of the whole for the publick use, as what now lies upon many already: But 4 Millions would afford one for the ordinary
10 Expence, and || three for the extraordinary Wars, that is 250000 *l. per mensem*; that is $3\frac{1}{2}$ as much as 70. For the raising whereof, many now pay above a $\frac{1}{10}$ of their whole Estates[2], for want of Method and Proportion.

10. Labouring men work 10 hours *per diem*, and make 20 meals *per* week, *viz.* 3 a day for working-days, and two on *Sundays*; whereby it is plain, that if they could fast on *Fryday* nights, and Dine in one hour and an half, whereas they take two, from eleven to one; thereby this working $\frac{1}{20}$ more, and spending $\frac{1}{20}$ less, the $\frac{1}{10}$ abovementioned might be raised, at least with more ease, than to take up Arms, and resist it.

[1] D omits 'we.'

[2] D omits 'Estates.'

CHAP. III.

Of the several Expences of the Kingdom, and its Revenues.

1. THE ordinary Expence of the Kingdom for the Navy, Ordnance, Garisons, Land-forces, *Tangier*, *Jamaica*, *Bombay*, Ambassadors, Pensions, Intelligence, Kings and Royal Families Expence, consisting of the Houshold, of the || King, Queen, Duke, *&c.* Privy-Purse, Wardrobe, Robes, 11
Angel-Gold, Master of the Horse, Mews, Armory, Tents, Parks, Lodges, Goldsmiths, Jewels, *&c.* hath been computed to be about one Million; Reckoning 200 000 *l.* for the Navy, 60 for the Ordnance and Powder, 290 for Land-forces, Garisons, *&c.* and 450 000 for other things.

2. Towards this, there is in Crown-Lands 70 000, Post-Office 20, Coynage and Pre-emption of Tinn 12, Forest of Deer 4, Courts of Justice 6, First Fruits 18; in all 130,000. Customs at 2 *per Centum* 170. in all 300 000. without the Duties of Wares, Wine-Licence, Aulnage or Butlerage, Excise, Chimney-money, Land-tax, Pole and Assesments, being regulated and proportionated as followeth: *viz.*

CHAP. IV.

Of the Method of apportioning Taxes.

1. IF a Million is to be raised above the 300 000 *l.* last mentioned, then 375 000 *l.* is to be levied on the Stock, and 625000 *l.* on the People. ||

Of the 375,000. on the Stock, 12
216 on the Lands,
54 on the Cattel, *&c.*
60 on the Personal Estates,
45 on the Housing.
in all 375

[1]2. To raise 216,000 *l.* out of 8,000,000 *M.* Rent, requires $\frac{1}{37}$ of the Rent, and $\frac{1}{27}$ of $\frac{1}{37}$; but allowing the charge of Collecting, we may express it to a $\frac{1}{36}$ part.

3. To raise 54000 *l. per annum,* out of 36,000000 *M.* requires the annual payment of a 666th part of the whole value; but in regard of Charges, let it be reduced to a 600th part.

4. The like for the 60000 *l.* of Personal Estates.

5. To raise 45000 *l. per annum,* from all the Housing worth 30 *Millions,* or 7500 for the Housing in *London*-Liberties, worth about 5 *Millions,* and whose Rent is 4,20 000 *l. per annum,* requires but $\frac{1}{56}$ of the annual Rent, which cannot be above 12*d.* a Chimney *per Annum,* reckoning 5 to each House. Without the Liberties, about 10*d.* the Chimney will effect the same; 6*d.* in the Cities and Market-Towns, and 4*d.* elsewhere. ||

13 6. As for the 625,000 *l.* to be raised by the People, it requires but 2*s.* 1*d. per* Pole *per Annum,* which let rather be divided into a Pole of 6*d.* a Head, and an Excise of 19*d.* which is not the full $\frac{1}{84}$ part of the mean expence, 6*l.* 13*s.* 4*d.* so as the $\frac{1}{84}$ of the value of Consumptions, will with the said 6*d.* Pole, raise 625,000 *l. per Annum.*

CHAP. V.

Of Money, and how much is necessary to drive the Trade of the Nation.

1. IT may be asked, If there were occasion to raise 4 Millions *per Annum,* whether the same 6 *Millions* (which we hope we have) would suffice for such revolutions and circulations thereof as Trade requires? I answer yes; for the Expence being 40 Millions, if the revolutions were in such short Circles, *viz.* weekly, as happens among poorer

[1] From this point the copyist of S has ruthlessly abridged the text.

artizans and labourers, who receive and pay every *Saturday*, then $\frac{40}{52}$ parts of 1 Million of Money would answer those ends: But if the Circles be quarterly, according to our Custom of paying rent, and gathering Taxes, then 10 Millions were requisite. Wherefore supposing payments in general to be of a mixed Circle between One || week and 14
13. then add 10 Millions to $\frac{40}{52}$, the half of the which will be $5\frac{1}{2}$, so as if we have $5\frac{1}{2}$ Millions we have enough.

2. And thus I have shewed, That if one half of the Subjects of England (playing 78 days in the year) will earn 7 *d. per diem* all the rest of the days one with another; and if they would work $\frac{1}{20}$ more, and spend $\frac{1}{20}$ less, they might enable their King to maintain double the Forces he now doth, without suffering in the general more than many well affected persons do now through negligence, or mistakes in their particulars. Nor is Money wanting to answer all the ends of a well Policied State, notwithstanding the great decreases thereof, which have happened within these Twenty years.

Nor were it hard to substitute in the place of Money (were a comptency of it wanting) what should be equivalent unto it. For Money is but the Fat of the Body-politick, whereof too much doth as often hinder its Agility, as too little makes it sick. 'Tis true, that as Fat lubricates the motion of the Muscles, feeds in want of Victuals, fills up uneven Cavities, and beautifies the Body, so doth Money in the State quicken its Action, feeds from abroad in the time of Dearth at Home; even accounts by reason || of it's 15
divisibility, and beautifies the whole, altho more especially the particular persons that have it in plenty.

CHAP. VI.

The Causes of irregular Taxing.

1. THE Causes of Error in this great Affair of Publick Levies, have been these. First, Laying too great a stress on the matter of Money, which is to the whole effect of the Kingdom but as 6 to 667. That is, not one to 100. Secondly, Laying the whole Burthen on the past Effects, and neglecting the present Efficiencies, exceeding the former as 417 doth 250. Thirdly, Reckoning all the personal Estates of the City of *London* (Shipping included) at scarce ½ the value of the very Housing, whereas they are double: Which happens because the Housing of *London* belongs to the Church, Companies, or Gentlemen and are taxed by the Citizens their Tenants. Fourthly, A fallacious tenderness towards the poor, (who now pay scarce 1 *s. per* head *per ann.* towards all manner of charges) interwoven with the cruelty of not providing them Work, and indulging Laziness in them, because of our own indisposition to employ them; so some are overcharged through evil Custom, and others left to sordid Want, and bruitish Irregularity. Fifthly, An Opinion, that certainty of Rules is impossible, and but an idle Notion; and then having made such as are not so, and training them to be applied by Affection and Humour; so as ¼ of the whole paying needlesly four times too much, may be thereby so netled, as to do more mischief than the other unconcerned, and thankless ¾ can allay.

CHAP. VII.

The Collateral Advantages of these Taxes.

1. BEsides the equality of Taxes, we make this further use of trying it by way of Customs, Poles, Excises, Chimney-money, Land-tax, and Assesments upon the personal Estates, *viz.*

(1.) Of the Customs, which we reduce from $\frac{1}{20}$ to $\frac{1}{60}$, to
keep an account of Foreign-‖Trade, and of its Balance; for 17
by Levying, a Duty, and encreasing the Penalty, these
Accounts will be less obscured.

(2.) The simple and universal Pole keeps an account of the great Wealth and Strength of the Kingdom, the People.

(3.) Rating the Houses *per* Chimney, gives a good account of Improvements and Dilapidations.

(4.) Excize gives an account of Domestick Expences, and publisheth Exorbitances.

(5.) Land-taxes keep the Payments to the proportion of entire value, not of Annual Rent: So as an Estate in Housing pays no more than if it were in Lands, nor considerable less than Goods, and may bring Mortgages to their just contribution; many Lenders not being so formidable for their Money, as some have thought them.

(6.) Assessments upon personal Estates (if given in as elsewhere upon Oath) would bring that Branch which of it self is most dark, to a sufficient clearness.

2. There is also a Pole upon Titles and Dignities worth consideration, tho we now omit it; which as it may check mens forwardness to undeserved Pre-eminence, so it may be employed in the encouragement of true worth. ‖

3. We have hitherto computed the old immutable 18
Revenue at but 130,000 *l. per annum*, nor supposed above
170,000 *l.* (*viz.* less than $\frac{1}{2}$ what it is at present) to be raised
by Customs (wholly neglecting Wards, Butlerage, Aulnage,

and other obsolete Imposts.) We have also designed the several Proportions towards the raising of a Million more *per Ann.* to be raised by the Pole, Excise, Land-Tax, Assessments and Chimneys.

CHAP. VIII.

Of the Expence of the Navy, Army, and Garisons.

WE come next to shew, That if 3 Millions *per ann.* or 250,000*l.* *per mensem* (to make up the whole 3,300,000*l.* *per ann.*) were raised, what might be performed thereby for the safety, establishment, and Honour both of the King and Subject.

Unto which, I say, considering the present condition of
the Navy, two Millions will maintain 50,000 men, in Ships of
War for eight Months of the Year, and 30000 for the other
four Months: Which I take to be near double the best Fleet
19 we ever have || seen in *Europe*, computing the Ordnance, and
Harbor-Charges of the Navy: Nor will the Maintenance of
12,000 Foot, and 3000, Horse, allowing 100,000*l.* for Inland
Garisons, and 60,000*l.* for *Tangier*, &c. put all together,
exceed 600,000*l.* so as there remains 700,000*l.* for other
Matters, whereof His Majesty's Royal Family, by all the
Accounts I have seen, doth not spend 500,000*l.* *per ann.*
Nor need the Charge of all those Levies be above 1 of the
33, (*viz.* $\frac{1}{33}$ part for the 500 Officers, without ever going five
Miles from the Centre of their abode) who might perform
this Work; nor would more than 200*l.* *per an.* for each of
them, and their under Instruments be necessary for their
respective Sallaries: For there are 450 Areots of 10 Miles
square in *England* and *Wales*.

CHAP. IX.

Motives to the quiet bearing of extraordinary TAXES.

HAving shewed how great and glorious things may be
done with no less difficulty than what $\frac{1}{4}$ of the King's
Subjects do already endure; I offer these further Rea-||sons 20
to quiet mens Minds, in case this utmost 250,000 *l. per
mensem* should be ever demanded upon this *Holland-War.*

1. That of all Naval Expence, not $\frac{1}{20}$ is for[1] Forreign Commodities, nor need it be $\frac{1}{40}$[1], if the people would do their part, and the Governours direct them the nearest ways.

2. That Stoppage of Trade is considerable, but as one to eight; for we exchange not above five Millions worth *per ann.* for our 40.

3. That the Expence of the King, *&c.* being about 400,000 *l. per ann.* is but $\frac{1}{100}$ part of the Expence of the Nation, who all have the Pleasure and Honour of it.

4. That the Money of the Nation being but about 5 Millions and $\frac{1}{2}$, and the earning of the same 25; It is not difficult for them to encrease their Money a Million *per ann.* by an easie advance of their Industry, applyed to such Manufactures as will fetch Money from abroad.

5. The Wealth of *England* lies in Land and People, so
as they make five parts of six of the whole: But the Wealth
of *Holland* lies more in Money, Housing, Shipping and
Wares. Now supposing *England* three-||times as rich as 21
Holland in Land, and People (as it is) and *Holland* twice as
rich as we in other Particulars (as it scarce is); We are still
upon the Balance of the whole near twice as rich as they: Of
which I wish those that understand *Holland*, would consider
and calculate.

[1] By a slip of the types the 1691 ed. transposes the 'f' of 'for' and the '$\frac{1}{40}$' which stand at the beginning of successive lines. The obvious mistake is corrected above.

6. There are in *England* above four Acres of Arrable, Meadow and Pasture-Land, for every Soul in it; and those so fertile, as that the labour of one man in tilling them, is sufficient to get a bare Livelihood for above 10: So as 'tis for want of Discipline that any Poverty appears in *England*, and that any are hanged or starved upon that account. ||

---

22 CHAP. X.

How to employ the People, and the End thereof.

WE said, That half the People by a very gentle labour, might much enrich the Kingdom, and advance its Honour, by setting apart largely for publick uses; But the difficulty is, upon what shall they employ themselves.

To which I answer in general, Upon producing Food and Necessaries for the whole People of the Land, by few hands; whether by labouring harder, or by the introducing the Compendium, and Facilitations of Art[1], which is equivalent to what men vainly hoped from *Polygamy*[2]. For as much as he that can do the Work of five men by one, effects the same as the begetting four adult Workmen. Nor is such advantage worth fewer years purchase than that of Lands, or what we esteem likest to perpetual. Now the making Necessaries cheap, by the means aforesaid, and not by
23 raising more of them than can be spent || whilst they are good, will necessitate others to buy them with much labour

[1] Perhaps an allusion to Petty's projected epitome of useful books and to his "History of arts illiberal and mechanique." Petty's *Advice to Hartlib* and Hartlib's letters to Boyle 16 November, 1647, and 10 August, 1658 (Boyle's Works (1772), VI, 76, 112) give some account of the project, and copies of what appear to be Petty's notes towards its realization are in Sloane MS. 2903 fol. 63 seq., in the British Museum.

[2] See Graunt, ch. viii.

of other kinds. For if one man could raise Corn enough for the whole, better than any one man; then that man would have the natural Monopoly of Corn, and could exact more labour for it in exchange, than if ten others raised ten times as much Corn as is necessary; which would make other labour so much the dearer, as men were less under the need of engaging upon it.

2. By this way we might recover our lost Cloth-trade[1], which by the same the *Dutch* got from us. By this way the *East-Indians* furnish us from the other end of the world with Linnen cheaper than our selves can make them, with what grows at our own Doors. By this means we might fetch Flax from *France*, and yet furnish them with Linnen (that is) if we make no more than we can vend, but so much with the fewest hands, and cheapest food, which will be when Food also is raised, by fewer hands than elsewhere.

3. I answer generally we should employ our selves by raising such Commodities, as would yield and fetch in money from abroad: For that would supply any wants of ours from the same, or any other place at all times. Which Stores of Dome-||stick Commodities could not effect, whose value is to 24
call a Temporary (*i.e.*) which are of value but *pro hic & nunc.*

4. But when should we rest from this great Industry? I answer, When we have certainly more Money than any of our Neighbour States, (though never so little) both in Arithmetrical and Geometrical proportion (*i.e.*) when we have more years provision aforehand, and more present effects.

5. What then should we busie our selves about? I answer, in Ratiocinations upon the Works and Will of God, to be supported not only by the indolency, but also by the pleasure of the Body; and not only by the tranquility, but serenity of the mind; and this Exercise is the natural end of man in this world, and that which best disposeth him for his Spiritual happiness in that other which is to come. The motions of the mind being the quickest of all others, afford

[1] See *Treatise of Taxes*, p. 30 n.

most variety, wherein is the very form and being of pleasure; and by how much the more we have of this pleasure, by so much the more we are capable of it even *ad Infinitum*[1].

FINIS.

[1] *A Letter from a Gentleman in the Country to his Friend in the City touching Sir William Petty's posthumous Treatise entituled Verbum Sapienti: or, the Method of Raising Taxes in the most equal Manner* (subscribed "H. J.") was printed by G. W. for William Miller, London, 1691, 4°. The author summarizes and in general approves Petty's conclusions but believes that Petty underestimated the amount of money necessary to the nation, and argues that the landlords bear more than their share of taxes. He thinks, therefore, that Petty's plan is defective in not proposing a compensatory tax upon non-owners of land.

THE
Political Anatomy
OF
IRELAND[1].

WITH

The Establishment for that Kingdom when the late Duke of ORMOND was Lord Lieutenant. Taken from the RECORDS.

To which is added

VERBUM SAPIENTI; or an Account of the Wealth and Expences of *England* and the Method of raising Taxes in the most Equal manner.

Shewing also, That the Nation can bear the charge of Four Millions *per Annum*, when the occasions of the Government require it.

By Sir WILLIAM PETTY, late Fellow of the Royal Society, and Surveyor-General of the Kingdom of *Ireland*

LONDON:

Printed for *D. Brown*, and *W. Rogers*, at the *Bible* without *Temple-Bar*, and at the *Sun* over-against St. *Dunstans* Church, *Fleet-street.* 1691.

[1] [The Southwell MS. (see p. 123) bears title "The Political Anatomy of Ireland, 1672." The more elaborate titles of the first and second editions (see Bibliography, 24) were probably composed by the editors in 1691 and 1719. The *Verbum Sapienti* has been placed before the *Anatomy* (pp. 99–120), in conformity to the general chronological scheme of arrangement.]

NOTE ON THE "POLITICAL ANATOMY OF IRELAND."

THE Political Anatomy of Ireland, together with the Political Arithmetick, are the products of Petty's second prolonged Irish residence, as the Down Survey of Ireland was the product of his first residence in that island. Petty went to Ireland in 1667 and seems to have remained there almost continuously until the summer of 1673. He was, however, in London in April 1671, and it is not improbable that at that time Sir Joseph Williamson gave the impulse to a renewal of his literary activity. The 17 January 1671, Edward Chamberlayne, compiler of The Present State of England, had written Williamson asking his criticism of the book, with a view to a new edition of it which the publisher, Martyn, desired. Williamson probably suggested the addition of some matter concerning Ireland, and Chamberlayne wrote again, 29 January, "To give a brief account of the present state of Ireland I shall, at your request, very willingly undertake." In an undated letter, endorsed by Williamson, "Apr. 1671," Chamberlayne wrote further, "I yesterday met with Sir William Petty whom I found very able to promote the Designe of giving an Account in Print of the State of Ireland as you desired. If you would please to speak or write to him and recommend me to him I will most gladly wayte upon him at his leisure[1]." The Calendar of State Papers, domestic series, for 1671 reveals no further mention of the project. The State Papers for 1672 were not calendared in August, 1895. In a necessarily hurried search I found no later letter by Chamberlayne but may have overlooked some memorandum of the matter in Williamson's

[1] *State Papers Dom.* Car. II, vol. 287, no. 77, 138, vol. 289, no. 120.

microscopic notes. However that may be, Chamberlayne did not write a book on Ireland, and Petty did.

The British Museum possesses the best MS. of the Political Anatomy[1]. It is written in a neat hand, upon paper carefully ruled in red ink, and bears, in the text, occasional corrections in a different and blacker ink, made by Petty himself. The history of this MS. can be traced with a completeness that places its authenticity beyond question. It was given by Petty to Southwell, of whose scrupulous care for Petty's MSS. there is abundant evidence, and remained in the possession of the Southwell family until the sale of Lord De Clifford's papers in 1834[2]. At this sale it was purchased by Thomas Thorpe, and promptly appeared in one of his catalogues[3]. It passed into the hands of Dr Neligan of Dublin, who probably bought it of Thorpe. At the dispersal of Neligan's library[4] the MS. was acquired for the British Museum.

Inserted in this MS. is a letter from Sir Richard Cox, the historian of Ireland, to Southwell, endorsed "Bristol, 15 June, 1687. From Mr Cox On Sr Wm Petty's Anatomy of Ireland." The letter begins:

"Hon^d^ S^r^.

My Curiosity was never feasted higher than with ye reading of the Political Anatomy of Ireland wherein the learned[5] Author at once discovers both his great abilityes & his great zeale to serve his[6] Country: Nor[7] will it in ye least detract from ye glory of his pformance, nor I believe disgust him that I communicate to you some difficultyes and remarques on that excellent discourse, wherein I humbly desire to be better informd." Cox then makes twenty-five detailed comments[8], referring to the MS. by folio, and concludes,

[1] Addl. MS. 21,127.

[2] *A Catalogue of MSS., State Papers and Autograph Letters received by Sir R. Southwell, the Property of Lord De Clifford, deceased.* Sold by Christie, February 11, 1834, no. 599.

[3] *State Papers: Catalogus lib. MSS. bibl. Southwellianæ* (1834), no. 711, p. 409.

[4] *A Catalogue of valuable Books and interesting MSS., the property of a well known Collector.* Sold by Sotheby 17 August, 1855, no. 305.

[5] 'Learned' is substituted for 'ingenious' erased.

[6] 'To serve his' substituted for 'for ye good of his' erased.

[7] 'Nor' substituted for 'And tho' erased.

[8] The comments are reproduced as foot notes to appropriate passages.

"I thought to have transcribd and enlargd this paper, but it happens y[t] a client is just now come in, and therefore I hope you will excuse this scroll from

Worthy S[r]

Y[r] most obliged humble serv[t]

Richd Cox."

In 1851 this letter, if General Larcom be not mistaken[1], was separated from the MS. to which it refers and inserted in another. It was reunited to the MS., however, before the sale of Dr Neligan's library.

Another MS., of which no further trace has been found, was once in the possession of Sir Peter Pett and by him was offered to Sir Joseph Williamson[2]. The offer would argue Pett's ignorance of Williamson's probable connection with the book.

The Political Anatomy was first published in 1691. A second edition appeared in 1719, and the book was reprinted in 1769 and in 1861[3]. The present reprint follows the first edition. The more significant divergences of the printed text from the Southwell MS. ('S') and all Petty's alterations of that MS. are indicated in the foot notes. On the relation of S. to the edition of 1691 see note 3 on page 131.

[1] Petty, *Hist. of the Down Survey*, p. v, 334.

[2] Pett to Williamson, 4 Dec., 1678, *State Papers Ireland*, Car. II., 338.

[3] Bibliography, 24.

[Dedication of the First Edition, 1691.]

To His Grace the Duke of ORMOND[1].

MY LORD,

THE Celebrated Author of the following Treatise, had not only the Honour to be known to Your Grace's Grandfather, the late illustrious Duke of *ORMOND*, but was likewise held by him in that just Esteem, which he never fail'd of expressing towards Men of || Learning and Ingenuity[2]. This was a sufficient Encouragement to me (having the Manuscript-Copy delivered into my Hands by a Worthy and Intimate Friend[3] of the Authors, to dispose of it to the Press for the publick Benefit) to Address it to Your Grace's Patronage. You are so true a Successor to all the generous Virtues of your Ancestry, that I cannot doubt of Your Favourable Reception of this posthumous Work. Your Generosity, that takes all occasions of exerting itself towards the Living, cannot fail in do-||ing Justice to the Memory of the Dead. More especially to such Persons as in their Life took care to oblige Posterity. The usefulness of the ensuing Discourse at this time, when there is so fair a

[1] James Butler, second Duke of Ormond, grandson of the first Duke and son of that Thomas, Earl of Ossory, whose death Petty so much lamented (*7th Rept. Hist. MSS. Comm.*, 742) was born in Dublin Castle, 29 April, 1665. He served at the head of the Life-guards in King William's army, was present at the battle of the Boyne, and accompanied his royal master to the Hague in January, 1691. His career after his return to England did not altogether justify the high expectations which his friends had formed of him. Died 1745.

[2] On Ormond's appreciation of Petty see note, p. 8.

[3] Probably by Sir Robert Southwell, see note 3, p. 131.

prospect of a new Settlement in *IRELAND*, were sufficient to recommend it to Your Grace's Protection. Your Grace's Interest in the Re-establishment of that Kingdom (tho it be considerable) yet is much less than your Share in the glorious Enterprise towards its Recovery. ||

You had the Honour of accompanying His MAJESTY in an Adventure that shall shine in the Annals of *Fame*, as long as the *Boyne* shall maintain its Course. But a single Gallantry appear'd not sufficient to the Heir of ORMOND and of OSSERY. You have since accompanied your Royall Master to other Shores, to be partaker with him in new Scenes of Action, Undertakings of no less Consequence and Importance than the Deliverance of Europe. This will afford sufficient matter for Panegyrick, and oblige the Mu-||ses to place you in the same high Rank of Renoun with your Noble and Heroick Predecessors. In the mean time be pleased to permit this useful Treatise to wait on you to the Camps, and bring you the hearty wishes of all good Men here, for Your happy Expedition, and Your safe Return, which is desired by none with more particular Zeal, than by

Your GRACE'S

Most Devoted Servant,

N. TATE[1]. ||

[1] Nahum Tate was born at Dublin in 1652. At the age of twenty he proceeded to the degree of bachelor of arts at the university in his native city and soon after removed to London, where he continued to reside until his death in 1715. In 1692 he succeeded Shadwell as poet laureate.

[Dedication of the Second Edition, 1719.]

To the Right Honourable

THOMAS,

Lord *PARKER*[1],

Baron of Macclesfield in the County of CHESTER;

LORD HIGH CHANCELLOR of GREAT BRITAIN.

My LORD,

THE following Treatise of Sir *William Petty's* having already met with a favourable Reception from the Publick, even when it was im-||perfect in some of its parts: I beg leave to offer it now to your Lordship, with some Additions[2], necessary for the better understanding of it.

[1] Thomas Parker was born, it is said, 23 July, 1666. He entered Trinity College, Cambridge in 1685, but did not take a degree, and, having been a student of the Inner Temple, was called to the Bar 24 May, 1691. In 1705 he sat for Derby as a Whig. In 1710 he became Lord Chief Justice of England, and the following year declined the Lord Chancellorship, to which he was finally appointed 12 May 1718. In 1716 he was created Baron Macclesfield, and in 1721 he was raised to an earldom. In 1725 he was impeached of corruption and found guilty by the unanimous voice of the peers present. He died 28 April, 1732. His mathematical interest exhibited itself chiefly in the patronage of mathematicians, but his own attainments were unquestionably sufficient for the comprehension of Political Arithmetick.

[2] No addition of importance was made to Petty's part of the book, but the editor suppressed several passages of the first edition and altered others. Such of his changes as give rise to readings substantially different from those of the first edition, here reprinted, are incorporated in the foot notes; but mere differences of orthography are ignored. The largest addition made in the second edition was "A List of the Lords spiritual and temporal of Ireland," and "A List of the Knights, Citizens and Burgesses of the Parliament of Ireland," 1715. These lists are omitted from the present edition.

As the whole Design of this Treatise tends to the enriching of a Kingdom, by advancing its Trade and Publick Credit, I am naturally led to put it under the Patronage of a Minister of State, whose Love for his Nation's Welfare and Glory is so generally known to all the World; and more especially, my Lord, this Work, being founded upon Mathematical Truth, claims a Right to the Protection of your Lordship, || who is so great a Master in that Science.

The good Effect which the Advice of my learned Author has had in the Improvement of *Ireland* in a few Years, may in some measure determine how much any Nation may be advanced in Riches and Reputation by following some such like Rules as are laid down by the same Person at the End of the Book, under the Title of *Verbum Sapienti:* What is treated of in that part relates altogether to the Interest of *England*, and therefore I am fully assured it cannot be unacceptable to your Lordship, whose Genius leads you to the || maintaining of its established Religion, Laws, and Liberties, and with them everything that can contribute to the Honour of the King, and Ease of the Subject.

I am,

May it please your Lordship,

Your Lordship's,

Most obliged, and most

Obedient, Humble Servant.

Author's Preface.

SIR Francis Bacon, *in his* Advancement of Learning, *hath made a judicious* Parallel *in many particulars, between the* Body Natural, *and* Body Politick, *and between the Arts of preserving both in Health and Strength: And it is as reasonable, that as* Anatomy *is the best foundation of one, so also of the other; and that to practice upon the Politick, without knowing the* Symmetry, Fabrick, *and* Proportion *of it, is as* casual *as the practice of Old-women and Empyricks.*

Now, because Anatomy *is not only necessary in Physicians, but laudable in every Philosophical person whatsoever; I therefore, who profess no Politicks*[1], *have, for my curiosity, at large attempted* the first Essay of Political Anatomy.

Furthermore, as Students in Medicine, practice their inquiries upon cheap and common Animals, *and such whose actions they are best* || *acquainted with, and where there is the least confusion and perplexure of Parts; I have chosen* Ireland *as such a* Political Animal, *who is scarce Twenty years old*[2]; *where the* Intrigue *of* State *is not very complicate, and with which I have been conversant from an* Embrion; *and in which, if I have done amiss, the fault may be easily mended by another.*

'Tis true, that curious Dissections *cannot be made without variety of proper Instruments; whereas I have had only a*

[1] 1719 omits 'who profess no Politicks.'

[2] Since the Act for the Settling of Ireland, 12 August, 1652, Scobell, II. 197.

commin Knife *and a* Clout, *instead of the many more helps which such a Work requires: However, my rude approaches being enough to find whereabout the Liver and Spleen, and Lungs lye, tho' not to discern the Lymphatick Vessels, the* Plexus, Choroidus[1], *the* Volvuli *of vessels within the Testicles*[2]; *yet not knowing, that even what I have here readily done, was much considered, or indeed thought useful by others, I have ventur'd to* begin *a* new *Work, which, when Corrected and Enlarged by better Hands and Helps, I believe will tend to the Peace and Plenty of my Country; besides which, I have no other end.* ||

[1] S, 'Choroides.'

[2] 1719, 'finer parts.'

ADVERTISEMENT.[1]

THE *Reader* is desired to take notice, That by *Letterees*[2], are meant persons restored to Land by virtue of the *Letters* of King *Charles* the Second; and by *Nominees*, such persons are intended, as were restored to their Lands by being *named* in the *Act* of *Settlement*; and Papists *per Proviso*, were such as had *Provisoes* in that *Act* for their Lands: And by *the* 19 *Officers*, are meant such *Commission-Officers* under the King, who served in *Ireland* before the *year* of our *Lord*, 1649.

The following Treatise of Sir *William Petty's Political Anatomy of Ireland*, is Printed after a Copy Transcribed from the *Original*, writ by the *Author*'s own hand[3]; and all

[1] The Advertisement is not in S, and only the first paragraph of it is in the ed. of 1719.

[2] The term 'letterees' is sometimes confined to those Irish who obtained the King's letters of restitution in the early months after his Restoration and were put out again by the Act of Settlement. Such Irish as were restored at the King's first return, by letters patent of which 'mero-motu' was a phrase were called 'mero-motu men'. Their patents, if obtained before the Declaration of Settlement, 30 Nov., 1660, were confirmed by the Act of Settlement; if obtained after that date, they were voidable. Russell and Prendergast, *The Carte MSS. in the Bodleian Library*, 193.

[3] It is probable that Southwell brought about the printing of the *Political Anatomy* in 1691, and it is not impossible that the book was then printed from his MS. ('S'). S is, beyond question, "a copy transcribed from the original writ by the author's own hand." Moreover the footings of columns of figures in S are reproduced at two points in the 1691 edition (see note 3, p. 143, and note 4, p. 145) where no editor acting independently of S would have thought to insert them, while, on the other hand, the differences between S and that edition may be sufficiently accounted for as the slips of a not over-careful printer. S, however, is still very clean. If from this circumstance we infer that it never lay upon a printer's case, we shall be forced to assume an original holograph, now lost, from which one copy, S, was made for Southwell, and another copy, likewise lost, was made for the printer. Even upon this supposition the Southwell MS. must be held to be of authority, since it bears Petty's autograph corrections.

the *Blanks*, as here Printed, were in that *Original:* And which, tho' it may be suppos'd he could easily have fill'd up, yet was it not held proper for any other to attempt, or to add to any thing done by so great a *Master*.

This his work of *The Political Anatomy of Ireland* ends in *page* 113. ||

P. 114. begins the famous *Report* from the *Council* of *Trade* in *Ireland*, which was not only *Drawn*, but wholly *Composed* by Sir *William Petty*; and with which that Council concurred unanimously.

P. 132. followeth the Copy of the *Commission* of the late *Duke of Ormond* to be *Lord Lieutenant*; and an Account of the *Establishment of the Civil and Military List* in his time; faithfully and carefully taken out of Authentick *Records:* And to the Nature of which, the continued *Title* of *The Political Anatomy of* Ireland, on those *Pages*, agrees well enough.[1]

The *Volume* concludes with Sir *William Petty*'s *Verbum Sapienti*, which relates wholly to *England*, and shews how Taxes may be equally laid, and how the Nation may well bear the Tax of Four Millions *per Annum*.

The Reader is now left with his most Critical attentive Judgment, to enjoy the benefit of the great Political knowledg that Sir *William Petty* hath taught the Age; and for which (as one of the greatest Ornaments of it) he deserveth perpetual celebrations. Know *Reader* in a word, That

Nulla ferent talem sæcla futura virum. ||

[1] The matter described in this paragraph, none of it by Petty, is omitted from the present edition, the corresponding portion of the Contents being printed in brackets. See note 1, p. 134.

The CONTENTS of the Political Anatomy of *IRELAND*[1].

[1] In S the Contents precede the Preface.

[2] The Roman numerals in brackets indicate the chapter numbers supplied by the editor of the second edition, who also shortened the titles of many of the chapters.

[3] End of the Contents in S, which does not contain the *Verbum Sapienti.*

LICENSED, *May* the 11th. 1691.

[1] This and the following items are omitted from this edition.

[2] Here follows, in the first and second editions, the Contents of *Verbum Sapienti* as already printed at p. 101.

THE

Political Anatomy

OF

IRELAND.

1672[1].

[CHAPTER I.][2]

Of the Lands of Ireland.

THERE are in *Ireland* of Acres of Land, *Irish* Measure (whereof 121 Acres makes 196 *English* Measure) near about[3]	M. Ac. 10,500
Whereof there is of Rivers, Highways, Loughs, unpassable Bogs, Rocks and Shrubs, about	M. 1, 500
Of very course Land, commonly call'd unprofitable	1, 500
Consequently of good Meadow, Arrable and Pasture	7, 500
	10, 500 ||
Of which *Anno* 1641, there did belong to Papists and Sequestred Protestants	5,200

[1] This caption occupies the title-page of S.

[2] It was, apparently, Petty's intention to divide his book into chapters. Cf. p. 201. Accordingly the Chapter division made by the editor of the second edition is here adopted for convenience of reference.

[3] In 1719 is a note, 'A Perch or Pole, Irish measure, is 21 *Foot*; the Acres are measured by that Perch, as the Acres in *England* are measured by a Perch of 16 Foot and half.' Cf. p. 172.

To the Church, *viz.* Bishops, Deans, Chapters and Glebes	300
To the Protestants planted by Queen *Elizabeth* and King *James*	2,000

Of the 5,200 *belonging to Papists and Sequestred Protestants* Anno 1641.

There was restored to 26 that proved their constant good Affection, *per est.*	40	210
To His Grace the D. of *Ormond*[1].	130	
To the Lord *Inchiquine*, Lord *Roscommon*, and others	40	
To innocent Papists, near	1,200	
To the Church, near	20	140
To the Duke of *York*[2], near	120	
To Letterees and Nominees *Irish-men*	60	420 ‖
To Papists, *per proviso* with Collonel *Vernon*	360	
3 Left in the Common-Stock of Course-Land	80	470
To Adventurers	390	
To Soldiers since 49.	1,440[3]	
To the 49 Officers	280	550
To Protestants *per proviso*	270	
Upon Transplantation Decrees	700	
Restored to Mortgagees Protestants, about	100[4]	
		5,200[5]

[1] A 'list of lands granted to the Duke of Ormond by the Act of Settlement and Court of Claims' is given by Carte, *Ormond*, Appendix, pp. 132—133.

[2] By the Act of Settlement the lands lately held by the Regicides were given to the Duke of York.

[3] 1719, '1,410,000.'

[4] Upon this entry Sir Richard Cox comments in his letter to Southwell, 'The redemption of Mortgages being given to y[e] 49 how comes 100000[a] to be restored to Prot Mgees.'

[5] The true total is 5,230,000. The source of the error is not made obvious by the following marginal calculation in S,

	M.
So that of all the Lands seiz'd by the Usurpers, the Papists have recovered about	2,340
The new[1] Protestants and Churches Additions	2,400
Of a more indifferent Nature, *ut supra*	460
	5200[2]

'10 130 40	210	
1200		
20 120	140	
60 360	420	5200'
80	470	
390 1440	1830	
280 270	550	
700 100		
5200'		

The editor of the 1719 ed. corrects Petty's blunder by the simple method of subtracting 30,000 acres from the largest single item. See note 3, p. 136.

[1] S, 'now.'

[2] In the margin of S, opposite this footing, occur the following three notes, to which I have made certain additions in brackets:

'Irish

40	[to the 26 for constant good affection.]
180–20	
60	[to the letterees and nominees.]
360	[to papists *per proviso.*]
700	[upon transplantation decrees.]
2340.'	[The true sum is 1340.]

'Church

20–20	[to the Church.]
390–10	[to the adventurers.]
1440–10	[to the '49 soldiers.]
280	[to the '49 officers.]
270	[to protestants *per proviso.*]
2400.'	

Mem. That Protestants in *Connaught* purchased of the Transplantees *per estimate.* M.	60[1]
Wherefore of the whole 7500 M. of good Land, the *English*, and Protestants and Church have this *Christmas* 1672.	5,140[2]
And the *Irish* have near ½ as much, *viz.*	2,280[3]
	7,500[4] ‖
Remains in the Common-Stock[5], near	80

[Also]

'2340		
2400		
460		
5200	D. of Ormond, &c.	160
	D. Yorke	120
	Com Stock	80
	Morgages	100
		460.'

These marginal calculations give Ormond 30,000 acres more than the text allows him, and introduce an item of 180,000 acres which cannot be identified with anything preceding. On the other hand they do not include 1,200,000 acres to the Innocents nor 40,000 to Lord Inchiquin, Lord Roscommon, and others. A grouping in accordance with Petty's probable meaning would be:

Papists recovered.	Protestants recovered.	Indifferent.
40 to the 26	20 to the Church	130 to Ormond
1200 to the Innocents	390 to the adventurers	40 to Inchiquin
60 to letterees	1440 to the '49 soldiers	120 to the Duke of York
360 *per proviso*	280 to the '49 officers	80 in the common stock
700 transplantation decrees	270 *per proviso*	100 to mortgagees
2360	2400	470

or in all 5,230,000 acres.

[1] 1719, '80,000.'

[2] The 5,140,000 acres are found by adding to the 2,300,000 acres held by the Church and the transplanted protestants in 1641 (see p. 136), the 2,400,000 acres of the "Protestants and Churches additions," the 60,000 acres purchased by protestants in Connaught and the 380,000 acres "Of a more indifferent Nature" remaining after the deduction of the 80,000 acres in the common stock from the total of 460,000 acres.

[3] The 2,280,000 acres are found by subtracting the transplantees' sales of 60,000 acres from the 2,340,000 acres which the Papists recovered.

[4] In S the total '7500' is written beneath the '80,' as it obviously should be.

[5] Cox, 'What or where are ye 80000^a^ left in ye Common Stock and how comes it they are undisposed, many adventurers being deficient & many designd to be restord are still excluded for want of Previous reprizal.'

M.

	M. l.
The said 7,500 Acres of good, and the 1,500 of course; making together 9000 M. is worth *per Annum*[1].	900,000
Out of which the King's Quit-rents, Old-rents, and Composition[2],	90,000
Rests	810,000
The Tythes whereof are one fifth[3], *viz.*	162,000
Rests	648,000
The benefit of Leases, and the value of Tenants Improvements upon the said Lands[4], is ⅓ *viz.*	216,000
For the Landlords	432,000
If the whole 75000 be clearly worth but 432000 l. *per Ann.* then the 2,520 gain'd by the Rebellion[5], is worth but about ⅓ thereof (the 80 M. in the Common Stock being worth very little), *viz.*[6]	144,000[7]
And the Adventurers and Soldiers Lands, who served since 1649. worth about ¾ of the same, *viz.*	108,000‖
	M.
And the said Soldiers alone ⅗ of the whole, *viz.*	86,400 *per An.*

Mem. That by the Successes of the Army, who serv'd since 1649. and who have 85400[8] l. *per An.* for their labour, His Majesty hath received the several Advantages following, *viz.*

[1] Cox, 'ye computacon of 9000000a to be worth yearly 900000l p ann which is but 2s a plantacon acre is to low by ⅓.'

[2] Cox, 'ye quitrent &c he makes to be 90000l p ann but tis not near soe much.'

[3] Cox, 'That ye Tithe should be a fifth, seems a great paradox.'

[4] Cox, '& so tis ye leases and improvemts should be deducted out of ye Small value of 2s p acre.'

[5] Cox, 'And therefore notwithstanding his calculacon yt ye 2520000a gaind by ye rebell is worth but 144000 p ann *he should have said yt the* [the words in Italics are cancelled, and Cox proceeds] they are at 2s p acre worth p ann 252000l & really worth more.'

[6] In the margin of S, 'Memd that ye charge of the army from 1653 to 1673 communibus Annis far exceeds ye charge of ye Goverment 1641, and ye rent of the forfeited lands.'

[7] Beneath '144000' in S, 'wch is less than ye present charge of ye Army.'

[8] Apparently a mistake for '86400,' so corrected in the margin of S, but not in the text.

1. Augmented the Church, the Duke of *York*, and by Provisoes.	770 M. Acres.
2. Hath paid the Adventurers, and 49 Officers, besides Housing in Walled Towns	670 M. Acres.
3. Gain'd a Revenue worth above 80000 l. *per Ann.* and 15 Years Purchase	l. 1200,000
4. Gain'd the Years value, *&c.* worth	300,000

5. Hath freed himself from the 1648. Articles with the *Irish.*

6. Restored many of his Friends to their own Estates[1].

The value of the said Army's Lands at ten Years Purchase, is 854000[2] l. Out of which deduct a years value and charge, there remains now but	l. 700,000 For all their Pay and Hazard.‖

6 *Mem.*

That whereas until *Anno* [3] *England* always sent Money and other Supplies into *Ireland*, now the Revenue is 200,000 l. and the charge Civil and Military but 170,000 l. which is the gain or ease of *England.*

The Debentures of Commission Officers, who serv'd eight years till about *December* 1649. comes to	l. 1,800,000
Wherefore the Pay of private Soldiers to	5,400,000
	7,200,000

The $\frac{1}{8}$ whereof is 900,000 l. The one half whereof being for Foot, was, 450,000 l. *per Ann.* which, at 15 l. each, maintains 30,000 Foot, and the rest 15000 Horse, General Officers, and Train of Artillery included; so as there was a *British* Army, for eight Years, of at least 45000 Men[4].

[1] Cox, 'he might add yt ye K gaind 12 Subsidyes, A great established revenew by hearthmoney excise and customs, from a flourishing Kingdome made soe by the Act of Setlemt, which else would not grant, and could not pay, those vast sumes.'

[2] Apparently should be '864000.'

[3] A blank in S.

[4] Cox, 'I doubt the 49 army was not 30000 foot and 15000 horse nor above half yt number at any one time, Neither was any footsouldier allowed 15l ꝑ ann.'

The Army who reduced the Rebellion, did *Anno* 1652, consist of near 35000 Men, as *per Debentures.* ||

The *Irish* transported into Foreign parts, between 1651 7
and 1654. were 34,000 Men.

The *Irish* Army could not but be more than double to the *English.*

The Claymants of Land, or the number of Proprietors before the War was.

Of all that claimed innocency 7 in 8. obtained it.

The restored Persons by innocence and proviso have more than what was their own, *Anno* 1641. by at least $\frac{1}{5}$.

They have gotten by forg'd Feofments of what was more than their own, at least $\frac{1}{3}$.

Of those adjudged Innocents, not $\frac{1}{20}$ were really so.

[1]The King's Revenue in *Ireland Anno* 1641.

The yearly charge of the Army for 20 years last past.

[CHAPTER II.]

Of People, Houses, and Smoaks; their Number, Differences, and Values.

THere are of People, Men, Women and Children.	1,100,000
There are of Families	200,000
Of Smoaks[2]	250,000 ||

VIZ. 8

Of the People, there are *English*	200,000
Of Papists	800,000
Of Non-Papists	300,000
Scots	100,000
Irish	800,000
	[3]2,200,000

[1] 1719 omits the last two paragraphs of the chapter.

[2] On the hearth money in Ireland see a note to chap. II of the *Polit. Arith.*

[3] See note on p. 142.

The *Scots* are *Presbyterians*, and the *Irish*, *Papists*. But the *English* are above 100,000 legal Protestants or Conformists, and the rest are Presbyterians, Independants, Anabaptists and Quakers.

Of the Families.

Such as have no fix'd Hearths, are	160,000
Such as have but one Chimney	24,000
Such as have more than one	16,000

Of Smoaks.

The Single-Smoak-houses, are *ut supra* 184,000

[Note to last line of p. 141 :]

S has, 'Of the people there are:—

Of Papists 800000	200000 English		
Of Non-Papists 300000	100000 Scots	1100000.'	
	800000 Irish		

The editors of the 1691 and 1719 eds., by an obvious blunder, made the total 2,200,000. Neither here nor elsewhere does Petty make use of the returns of the census taken in 1659, though it is probable that he once had the figures of that enumeration for nearly the whole of Ireland. The population at that time has been calculated at 500,091, of whom about one fifth were Englishmen or Scotsmen. Hardinge in *Trans. R. I. Acad.*, XXIV., Antiquities, 317—328. If these figures are correct, Petty unquestionably overestimated the population of Ireland, both here and when, at a later date, he increased his estimate to 'about 1,200,000 people' and 'near 300,000 hearths,' and still later to 1,300,000. *Polit. Arith.*, chap. II, and the *Treatise of Ireland*. Subsequent investigations have thrown but little additional light upon the correctness of his figures. The next estimate is for the year 1696. Calculating from the poll tax returns in three counties and in the city of Dublin, Capt. South set the population of Ireland at 1,034,102. 'An Account of the Number of People in Ireland,' *Philos. Trans.*, 1700, no. 261, vol. XXII., p. 520. Nearly a century later Mr G. P. Bushe, commissioner of revenue, published in the *Trans. of the R. I. Academy*, III., Science, 145—155, his 'Essay towards ascertaining the Population of Ireland.' Bushe points out that the returns of hearth money before 1686 were very defective, 200,000 houses being added by Ormond's reform in that year. He thinks that the houses must have been more numerous in 1672 than Petty makes them, and intimates that Petty's calculation of the population also is too small. But Thomas Newsham, an investigator quite as careful as Bushe, is of the contrary opinion. "Whether Sir William Petty overrated the population of Ireland in 1672, it is impossible now to determine. That he did not underrate it we may consider as certain." *An Historical and Statistical Inquiry into the Progress and Magnitude of the Population of Ireland* (1805), p. 89.

And those Houses that have more than one Chimney, have but one with another above four in each House, *viz.* in all	66,000
	250, M.‖
The Number of them of all degrees, who paid Poll-money, *Anno* 1661. was about	360,000 9
Dublin hath Houses of more than one Smoak	3,400
Other Cities, Towns, and Corporations of the like.	6,000
The rest of *Ireland* of the like	6,600
	[1] 165, M.

And of Smiths Forges, near the same number, or rather $\frac{1}{5}$ *more.*

A more particular Account of the Houses in Ireland, *which have more than one Chimney, viz.*

The Castle of *Dublin* hath Chimneys	125
The Earl of *Meath*'s House in *Dublin*	27
The Houses of *Dublin* which have above 10, are	164

[2] *The Number of Coaches, besides Hackneys, near the same Number, or rather fewer.*

There be (*ut supra*) 160,000 Cabins without Chimneys, whose worth are not reckoned; but as for the others, we rate as follows, *viz.* Houses of ‖

1 Chimny	24000 at 5 *l.* each	120,000 *l.*
of 2, and 3,	6800 at 40 *l.*	272,000 *l.*
4, 5, 6,	5600 at 100 *l.*	560,000 *l.* 10
7, 8, 9,	2500 at 300 *l.*	750,000 *l.*
10, 11, 12,	700 at 600 *l.*	420,000 *l.*
13, 14, 15, 16, 17, 18, 19, 20.	400 at 1000 *l.*	400,000 *l.*
		2,522,000[3]

[1] '165, M' should be '16 M,' and is so corrected in S.

[2] 1719 omits this paragraph.

[3] This footing falls, both in S and in the first edition, in the middle of a page, where it is superfluous. It may have originated in a MS. which was the archetype of S as well as of the first edition. Cf. note 4, p. 145.

For 20 Transcendental-houses, *per estimate*	78,000
Total	2,600,000
Memorandum, That not $\frac{1}{8}$ part of the Value of all those Houses do belong to other than *English* Protestants.	325,000
To the *English*	2,275,000
There are of Non-papists in *Dublin*	28,000
In the other Cities, Towns, Corporations, *&c.*	72,000
In the Country	100,000
	[1]2,000,000

There is in Nature but one in 500 at most who are Blind, Lame, and under incurable Impotence; so as not above 2000 in *Ireland*, whom 12000 *l.*[2] would maintain without Scandal. ||

11 The number of young Children under seven years old, and not fit for Labour, is $\frac{1}{4}$ of the whole, *viz.*	275,000
The said number of Impotents	2000
The number of Soldiers	3000
	280,000

The Masters and Mistresses of 360 Families, wherein are above six Smoaks, are	7,200
Their Servants to their Persons	14,400
The Servants to the Persons of such as live in 5600 Families of 4, 5, 6. Smoaks, are	11,200
Servants in Families of 2, and 3, Smoaks	6800
Ministers, Students, *&c.*	400
	320,000

People in all	1100 M.
Of above 6 years old	704
16	462

[1] '2,000,000' appears to be a misprint for '200,000,' the reading of S. But on p. 142 Petty found 300,000 'Non-Papists' in Ireland. See also p. 148.

[2] Cox, 'he allows 12000[l] to 2000 Impotents & pag 60 [of the MS., p. 189 of this ed.] but 8000[l].'

26	297
36	198
46	132
56	88
66	77[1]

So as there are in *Ireland* fit for Trade	[2]780,000 ‖
Which are Imployed as followeth, *viz.*	12
For the Tillage of 500,000 Acres of Land for Corn, Men, and their Wives	100,000
For Cowherds and Shepherds to Cattel, grazing upon Seven Millions of Acres, *viz.* six Millions of black Cattel, or their equivalent in Horses and Sheep[3], Men and their Wives.	120,000
	220,000
By the other side[4].	220,000
Imployed about the taking of 5000 Hogsheads of Pilchards, Boats, Nets, Hewers, *&c.* Men and Women.	1000
Imployed about making 1000 Tuns of Iron, Men and Women	2000
Smiths as by account, Men and Women	15,000
Their Servants to the Trade[5]	7,500
Taylors and their Wives	45,000

[1] Had Petty adopted Graunt's table [*Observations*, ch. XI.] without modification, his figures would have been 704, 440, 275, 176, 110, 66, 33. The figures actually used correspond more nearly to the probable mortality of Ireland at the time, but there is no indication of the reasons which led Petty to substitute them for Graunt's (or his own) 'six mean proportional numbers.'

[2] In the margin of S, '1,100,000
320,000.'

[3] Cox, '6,000,000 of black Cattle or their equivalent is more yⁿ all Ireland will feed vide pag 42' [of the MS., p. 175 of this ed.].

[4] This line stands at the top of folio 10 in S and repeats the total ('220,000,' one line above) from the bottom of folio 9 (misnumbered 13). In the first edition both lines fall (as here) in the middle of a page where they are superfluous. Cf. note 3, p. 143.

[5] Cox, 'Smiths 15000 and their servᵗˢ but 7500: whereas of all Trades Smiths doe most need a servᵗ to help: It is indeed a two handed trade yᵗ cannot be without a servᵗ: ergo there should be as many Servᵗˢ as Smiths.' But Petty allows a servant to each smith, though none to the smiths' wives.

Carpenters and Masons, and their Wives	10,000
Shoemakers and their Wives	20,000
and Servants	2500
Millers and their Wives	1600‖
13 Workers of Wooll and their Wives.	30,000[1]
Tanners and Curriers, and their Wives.	10,000
	331,600[2]
Trades of Fancy and Ornament and their Wives.	48,400
	380,000[3]

Wherefore if the present Employment be performed with 380,000[4] Persons, it follows that there are to spare for other uses	400,000

Memorandum, That in *Dublin*, where are but 4000 Families, there are at one time 1180 Ale-houses, and 91 publick Brew-houses, *viz.* near $\frac{1}{3}$ of the whole; it seems, that in *Ireland*, there being 200 M. Families, that about 60 M. of them should use the same Trade.

And consequently, That 180,000 *viz.* 60 Men, 60 Women, and 60 Servants[5] do follow the Trade of Drink.	180,000
So as there are yet to spare, who are Casherers and Fait-neants.	220,000
	400,000‖
14 Whereas it is manifest, that $\frac{2}{3}$ of the Alehouses may be spared, even although the same quantity of Drink should be sold; then there will yet be further to spare of them	120,000 and 220,000
	340,000

[1] Cox, 'Workers of Wool & their wives are x times as many as are computed it being comon for one bagmaker to Imploy 1000 Spinners weavers &c. There are also three times as many Carpenters and Masons as he mentions.'

[2] S, 1691, '331,600,' 1719, '364,600,' which is the correct footing.

[3] S, 1691, '380,000,' 1719, '413,000,' which is the correct footing.

[4] S, 1691, '380,000,' 1719, '413,000' but S and both eds. spare 400,000 for other uses. The editor of the second ed., to be consistent, should have altered 400,000 to 367,000.

[5] S, '60 M. Men,' 1719, '60,000 Men, as many Women, and as many Servants.'

Having shew'd that 340,000 of spare hands are in *Ireland*, it follows to find Employments for them, which is at 7 l. *per* head, to earn *per Ann.*	2,380,000
This Employment may be either in order to Local Wealth, or Universal Wealth.	
Local Wealth I understand to be the building of 168,000 small Stone-wall Houses, with Chimneys, Doors, Windores, Gardens and Orchards, ditch'd and quicksetted; instead of the lamentable Sties now in use; the which may cost 3 l. each, in all	l. 544,000
The planting 5 Millions of Fruit-Trees at 4 d. each.	83,000[1]
Planting 3 Millions of Timber-Trees upon the Bounds and Meers of every Denomination of Lands at 3 d. each	[2]360,000 l.||
Of Inclosures and Quicksets one Million of Perches at 12 d. *per* Perch.	l. 50,000
Fortifying the City of *Dublin*	30,000
Building a new Palace for the chief Governour.	20,000
Making there a Mold for Shipping.	15,000
Making several Rivers navigable and mending High-Ways.	35.000
Building of 100 Churches, at 200 l. each	20,000
Workhouses of several sorts, Tan-Yards, Fishing Crofts, Rape-Mills, Allom and Copperas-works, as also Madder, Lead, Salt, *&c.*	50,000

In order to Money and Universal Wealth.

For Ten Thousand Tuns of Shipping	100,000
For a Stock of Wool, Hemp, Flax and Raw-hides for one Years Work	400,000
For the Labour of Men to Manufacture the same.	[3]1000,000||

[1] More accurately £83,333. 6*s*. 8*d*.

[2] In the margin of S, '375,000.' The correct amount is £37,500.

[3] Making the corrections indicated, Petty's 'employments' foot up to £2,384,833. 6*s*. 8*d*. as against £2,380,000 of employments required.

[CHAPTER III.]

16 *Of the Church and Benefices.*

IF $\frac{1}{2}$ the Non-Papists are Non-Conformists, then there are but 50000 Legal Protestants in *Dublin* and all other Cities, Towns, *&c.* which require but 50 preaching Ministers.

And if there are but 50 M. Legal Protestants in the rest of *Ireland*, they require but 100 Ministers, at 500 to a Flock[1], whereof $\frac{1}{3}$, *viz.* 166 are Children.

If there be in *England* and *Wales* about 9000 Parishes, and under 30 Bishops, then every Bishop must have above 300 Parsons in his Charge.

So as one Bishop in *Ireland* is more than 30 in *England.*

Wherefore 25,000 l. would afford 150 l. *per Ann.* of each of 150 Ministers, and 2500 l. to the Bishop.

The value of the Church-Lands and appropriate Tythes, is[2] *per Ann.* above the Kings Rent due out of them.

If 100 Ministers can serve all *Ireland*, they must have Precincts of neer $\frac{13}{14}$[3] Miles square, and consequently they must be Itinerants, and as Lecturers on week-days; and other honest ordained Men must be Priests. ||

17 If 150, nay, if 250 Ministers would serve all *Ireland*, then 10 *per Ann.* will supply their Mortality: And consequently a Nursery of 100 will send forth 10 yearly of 10 years standing. Perhaps the Nursery need not be above half so large.

---

[1] Cox, 'The calculačon of ye number of Ministers from Number of Auditors is very Strange because they may live at such distance y^t^ tis impossible to attend them, for example in Kerry, ꝑhaps there are not above 500 prot & yet one Minister could never suply y^e^ Cure, y^t^ is visit y^e^ sick, Christen, bury &c.'

[2] The amount is wanting in all editions.

[3] 1719, '13 or 14.' In margin of S, 'about $1\overset{7}{8}000$ square miles in Ireland.' The version of the second ed., therefore, probably represents Petty's intention.

[CHAPTER IV.]

Concerning the Late Rebellion.

THE number of the People being now *Anno* 1672 about 1100,000. and *Anno* 1652. about 850 M. because I[1] conceive that 80 M. of them have in 20 years encreased by Generation 70 M. by return of banished and expelled *English*; as also by the access of new ones, 80 M. of New *Scots*, and 20 M. of returned *Irish*, being all 250 M.

Now if it could be known what number[2] of people were in *Ireland*, *Ann.* 1641. then the difference between the said number, and 850, adding unto it the encrease by Generation, in 11 years will shew the destruction of people made by the Wars, *viz.* by the Sword, Plague, and Famine occasioned thereby.

I find, by comparing superfluous and spare Oxen, Sheep, Butter and Beef, that || there was exported above $\frac{1}{3}$ more 18
Ann. 1664. than in 1641. which shews there were $\frac{1}{3}$ more of people, *viz.* 1466,000; Out of which Sum take what were

[1] Another punctuation may be suggested, viz. 'I conceive that 80 M. of them have in 20 years encreased by Generation, 70 M. by return of banished and expelled English as also by the access of new ones, 80 M. of New Scots, and 20 M. of returned Irish, being [in] all 250 M.'

[2] Cox, 'If in anno 52 there were 850000 inhabitants, 130000 were Eng 20000 Scots & 700000 Ir: & in anno 72: 1100000 of all sorts ye Ir have encreasd 60000: ye Eng 100000 and ye Scots 80000: it will follow by ye same rule of proportion viz y^{t} they encrease a 25th every x year by generation y^{t} in ann 1687 they are as followeth.

Ir	800000 encreased 60000	are now	860000
Eng	200000 encreased 15000	are now	215000
Scotts	100000 encreased 07500	are now	107500

But if to this be added y^{t} in these 15 years years (*sic*) last past, at least 35000 Eng. have come from Engld and the plantations to settle in Ir, & y^{t} 42500 Scotts have come in ye same time, & y^{t} at least 60000 Ir have in y^{t} time gone to Clergy War Service Travail &c. then at this day there will be found in Ireland—Ir 800000 Eng 250000 Scotts 150000 and soe ye Ir are but just double ye Number of ye brittish.' Cox arrives at the distribution of population in 1652 by assuming that the 80000 increase by generation is confined to the Irish. Petty returns to his calculation in the *Dialogue* appended to the *Treatise of Ireland.*

left *Ann.* 1652. there will remain 616,000. destroyed by the Rebellion.

Whereas the present proportion of the *British* is as 3 to 11; But before the Wars the proportion was less, *viz.* as 2 to 11. and then it follows that the number of *British* slain in 11 years was 112 thousand Souls; of which I guess ⅔ to have perished by War, Plague and Famine[1]. So as it follows that 37,000 were massacred in the first year of Tumults: So as those who think 154,000 were so destroyed, ought to review the grounds of their Opinion[2].

It follows also, that about 504 M. of the *Irish* perished, and were wasted by the Sword, Plague, Famine, Hardship and Banishment, between the 23 of *October* 1641. and the same day 1652.

Wherefore those who say, That not ⅛ of them remained at the end of the Wars, must also review their opinions;

[1] In the margin of S, '1100
366
———
1466
850
———
616
112
———
504.'

[2] Cox, 'If y° Ir in 1641 were to y° Eng as 11 to 2. & in all 1466000: then the Ir were 1199450 and y° Eng were 266550: and since it is notorious y^t 100000 Eng did not survive y° first year of y° wars, I cannot find any error in their Calculacion y^t say 166550 Brittish were massacred y^t yeare, and I am sure if there be any difficulty in proving y^t Assertion, it will be in y^t part of it y^t says there were 266550 Brittish in Ir in 1641.

'Besides his way of Computation is this: In 1641 there were 266550 Brittish in 1652 there were left above 150000 ergo there were destroyed but 112000 to which I answer y^t besides the Brittish in Ireland there came above 150000 Eng & Scotts into Ireland before y° year (52) which being added to his 112000 doe manifest that there were in all 262000 Brittish pished in y° late war whereof 150000 being massacred in y° first year there will remain our Authors 112000 for y° rest of y° rebellion:

'Moreover his Computacion supposes y^t y° 150000 brittish liveing in 1652 were part of those liveing in 1641; whereas revera ¾ of y° Brittish in 1652 were the Army and others y^t had newly come out of Eng & Scottland & their children y° very army as this gent says besides wives and children being 35000.'

there being by this Computation near ⅔ of them; which Opinion I also submit. ||

There were transported of them into *Spain*, 19
Flanders, France, 34,000 Soldiers; and of Boys, Women, Priests, *&c.* no less than 6000 more, where not half are returned. — 10,000.

If *Ireland* had continued in peace for the said 11 years, then the 1466 M. had increased by Generation in that time to 73 M. more, making in all 1539, which were by the said Wars brought *Anno* 1652, to 850, *viz.* 689 M. for whose Blood some body should answer both to God and the King. — M. 689

Anno 1650. there were before the great Plague, above one Million of People, *viz.* 2½ more than in *London Anno* 1665. But in that there year died in *London* by account 97,000 people, but really were 110 M.

Wherefore, if the Plague was no hotter in *Ireland* than in *England*, there must have died in *Ireland* 275 M. But 1300 dying in a Week in *Dublin*, the Plague of *London* was but ⅔ as hot; Wherefore there died in *Ireland* — M. 450[1] ||

So as subtracting 412 M. 500 dying of the Plague, and 37 20
Massacred *English*, it follows that 167 M. died in 11 years by the Sword and Famine, and other Hardships. Which I think not incredible; for supposing ½ the Number, *viz.* 87 M. died in 11 years, of Famine and Cold, Transportation to *Spain* and *Barbadoes*, *&c.* it is not hard to believe, that the other 87 M. perished by the Sword, when the *British* had Armies of near 40 M. Men, and the *Irish* of near double, sometimes[2] on Foot.

[1] In the margin of S, '220
55
275
1375
4125.' 'M/450,' appears to be a slip of the pen for '412 M. 500,' which is given in the first line of the next paragraph.

[2] S, 'double the number sometimes.'

Ann. 1653. Debentures were freely and openly sold for 4 s. and 5 s. *per* l. And 20 s. of Debenture, one place with another, did purchase two Acres of Land; at which rate all the Land of *Ireland*, if it were 8 Millions of profitable Acres, might have been had for a Million of Money, which *Ann.* 1641. was worth above 8 Millions — M. 1. ||

21 The Cattel and Stock which *Ann.* 1641. was worth above 4 Millions, reckoning one Beef of 20 s. value, or the Equivalent in other Stock to two Acres; but *Ann.* 1652. the people of *Dublin* fetch'd Meat from *Wales*, there being none here, and the whole Cattel of *Ireland* not worth — l. 500,000

Corn was then at 50 s. *per* Barrel, which is now, and 1641. under 12.

The Houses of *Ireland*, *Ann.* 1641. was worth $2\frac{1}{2}$ Millions; but *Ann.* 1652. not worth $\frac{1}{5}$ of the same — l. 500,000

The value of people, Men, Women and Children in *England*, some have computed to be 70 l. *per* Head, one with another. But if you value the people who have been destroyed in *Ireland*, as Slaves and Negroes are usually rated, *viz.* at about 15 l. one with another; Men being sold for 25 l. and Children 5 l. each; the value of the people lost will be about — [1] 10,355,000 ||

22 The Forces kept on Foot by all Parties for the said 11 years, were at least 80,000 Horse and Foot (for even *Ann.* 1652. the *English* were 35,000 and 34,000 *Irish* transported) the Charge whereof, Train of Artillery, and General Officers included, cannot be less than 15 l. *per* Head *per Ann.* which for 11 years comes to 13 Millions and 200 M. l. — 13,200,000

[1] In the margin of S, '689,000
3,445,000
10,335,000'

The superlucration above expressed, of all which adult Men (among which were no Women nor Children) cannot be reckoned at less than 5 l. *per* Head, or ⅓ of the last mentioned Sum, *viz,*	M. 4,400,000

Wherefore the effects of the Rebellion were these in pecuniary value, *viz.*

By loss of people	10,355,000
By loss of their superlucration of Soldiers	4,400,000
By the superlucration of the people lost, at 10 l. *per* Head for the whole 11 years, deducting 80 M. Soldiers	6,000,000
By impairing of the worth of Lands	11,000,000‖
Of the Stock	3,500,000 23
Of the Housing	2,000,000
	37,255,000

And the 20 years Rent of all the Lands forfeited, by reason of the said Rebellion, *viz.* since the year 1652, to 1673. hath not fully defray'd the Charge of the *English* Army in *Ireland* for the said time; nor doth the said Rents at this day do the same with ½ as much more, or above 100 M. l. *per An.* more

And the Adventurers after 10 years being out of their Principal Money, which now ought to be double by its Interest, they sold their Adventures for under 10 s. *per* l. *Ann.* 1652. in open and free Market.

The Number of Landed *Irish-Papists*, or Freeholders before the Wars, was about 3000; whereof, as appears by 800 Judgments of the Court of Claims, which sate *Ann.* 1663. upon the Innocence and Effects of the *Irish*, there were not above $\frac{1}{7}$ part or 400 guilty of the Rebellion, unto each of whom I allow 20 Followers, which would have made up an Army of 8000: But by the 49 Officers account, the *British* Army before 1649. must have been about 40 M. men; upon whom the said 8000 Nocent *Irish* so ‖ prevail'd, as that the 24
Peace ended in the Articles of 1648. By which the *Irish* were made at least equal Partners with His Majesty in the Government of *Ireland*; which sheweth, that the *Irish* were

men of admirable Success and Courage: Unless we should rather think, that the said Court of Claims were abused by their Perjuries and Forgeries, which one would think, that a Nation, who caus'd the destruction of so many thousand Lives, for the sake of God and Religion, should not be so guilty of.

The Estates of the *Irish* before the Wars, was double to that of the *English*; but the number and natural force of the *Irish* quintuple to that of the *English*.

The Cause of the War was a desire of the *Romists*, to recover the Church-Revenue, worth about 110 M. l. *per Ann.* and of the Common *Irish*, to get all the *Englishmens* Estates; and of the 10 or 12 Grandees of *Ireland*, to get the Empire of the whole. But upon the playing of this Game or Match upon so great odds, the *English* won and have (among, and besides other Pretences) a Gamester's Right at least to their Estates. But as for the Bloodshed in the Contest, God best knows who did occasion it. ||

[CHAPTER V.]

25 *Of the future Settlement of* Ireland, *Prorogation of Rebellions, and its Union with* England.

THE *English* invaded *Ireland* about 500 years since; at which time, if the *Irish* were in number about 1,200,000. *Anno* 1641, they were but 600 M. in number, 200 years ago, and not above 300,000 M.[1] at the said time of their Invasion; for 300,000 people will, by the ordinary Course of Generation, become 1200 M. in 500 years; allowance being made for the Extraordinary Effects of Epidemical Diseases, Famines, Wars, *&c.*

There is at this Day no Monument or real Argument

[1] S, '300 M. 000.' Cox, 'That y^e^ Ir were but 300000 in y^e^ time of H. 2. I doe not believe, nor is y^t^ method of computacion convincing for if 200 years agoe there were but half as many as now, & 200 years before but half y^t^ number again & soe on, it would follow y^t^ 1000 years agoe there were but $\frac{1}{32}$ of y^e^ people now living.'

that, when the *Irish* were first invaded, they had any Stone-Housing at all, any Money, any Foreign Trade, nor any Learning[1] but the Legend of the Saints, Psalters, Missals, Rituals, *&c. viz.* nor Geometry, Astronomy, Anatomy, Architecture, Enginery, Painting, Carving, nor any kind of Manufacture, nor the least use of Navigation, or the Art Military.

Sir *John Davys*[2] hath expressed much Wit and Learning, in giving the Causes why *Ireland* was in no measure reduced
to *Eng*-||*lish* Government, till in Queen *Elizabeths* Reign, and 26
since; and withal offers several means, whereby what yet remains to be done, may be still effected.

The Conquest made by the *English*, and described in the Preamble of the Act of Parliament past *Ann.* 1662. for the Settlement of *Ireland*[3], gave means for any thing that had been reasonable of that kind; but their Forfeiters being abroad, and suffering with His Majesty from the same usurping hands, made some diversion.

Wherefore (*Rebus sic stantibus*) what is now to be done is the Question, *viz.* What may be done by natural possibility, if Authority saw it fit?

Some furious Spirits have wished, that the *Irish* would rebel again, that they might be put to the Sword. But I declare, that motion to be not only impious and inhumane, but withal frivolous and pernicious even to them who have rashly wish'd for those occasions.

That the *Irish* will not easily rebel again, I believe from the memory of their former Successes, especially of the last, had not many Providences interpos'd; and withal from the consideration of these following Particulars, *viz.* ||

[1] Cox, 'he says Ir had no monument of Learning &c, to which I oppose ye Noted Verse in Cambden Brittania 2d pte (68 :):

> Motus amore patrum et commotꝰ amore legendi
> Venit ad hibernos Sophia (mirabile) claros.'

[2] *A discoverie of the trve causes why Ireland was neuer entirely subdued nor brought vnder Obedience of the Crowne of England vntill the Beginning of his Majesties happy Raigne. Printed for Iohn Iaggard, dwelling within the Temple Bar, at the Signe of the Hand and Star.* 1612. 4°. Frequently reprinted.

[3] 14 & 15 Charles II, c. 2, Ireland.

27 1. That the *British Protestants* and *Church* have $\frac{3}{4}$ of all the Lands; $\frac{5}{6}$ of all the Housing; $\frac{9}{10}$ of all the Housing in wall'd Towns, and Places of strength[1] $\frac{2}{3}$ of the Foreign Trade. That 6 of 8 of all the *Irish* live in a brutish nasty Condition, as in Cabins, with neither Chimney, Door, Stairs nor Window; feed chiefly upon Milk and Potatoes, whereby their Spirits are not dispos'd for War. And that although there be in *Ireland* 8 *Papists* for 3 others; yet there are far more Soldiers, and Soldierlike-Men of this latter and lesser Number, than of the former.

That His Majesty, who formerly could do nothing for, and upon *Ireland*, but by the help of *England*, hath now a Revenue upon the Place, to maintain, if he pleases, 7000 Men in Arms, besides a Protestant Militia of 25000 more, the most whereof are expert in War.

That the *Protestants* have Housing enough within Places of strength within 5 Miles of the Sea-side, to receive and protect, and harbour every Man, Woman and Child belonging to them, and have also places of strength of their own properly,[2] so situate in all parts of *Ireland*, to which they can easily travel the shortest day of the year. ||

28 That being able so to secure their Persons, even upon all sudden Emergencies, they can be easily supplied out of *England* with Food sufficient to maintain them, till they have burnt 160 M. of their afore-described Cabins, not worth 50 M. l. destroy'd their Stacks and Haggards of Corn, and disturbed their Tillage, which the embody'd *British* can soon and easily atchieve.

That a few Ships of War, whereof the *Irish* have none, nor no Skill or Practice of Navigation, can hinder their relief from all Foreign help.

That few Foreigners can help them if they would. But that none, not the King of *France*[3], can gain advantage by so

[1] A comma here in the 1719 edition.

[2] No comma in S.

[3] Cox, 'It is a paradox that ffrance could not be advantagd by ye acquisition of Ireland not intelligible to me, since our Author allows Ireland abounds in harbours and other conveniencyes of Trade, but what is more, it is so scituate y^{t} it could at any time destroy ye Trade of Engld if in ye hands of a Potent or a

doing, even tho he succeeded. For *England* hath constantly lost these 500 years by their meddling with *Ireland.* And at this day, than when *Ireland* was never so rich and splendid, it were the advantage of the *English* to abandon their whole Interest in that Countrey; and fatal to any other Nation to take it, as hath been elsewhere (as I think) demonstrated[1]; and the advantage of the Landlords of *England*, to give them the Equivalent of what they should so quit out of their own Estates in *England.* ||

Lastly, Let the *Irish* know, That there are, ever were, and 29
will be men discontented with their present Conditions in *England*, and ready for any Exploit and Change, more than are sufficient to quell any Insurrection they can make and abide by.

Wherefore, declining all Military means of setling and securing *Ireland* in peace and plenty, what we offer shall tend to the transmuting one People into the other, and the thorough union of Interests upon natural and lasting Principles; of which I shall enumerate several, tho seemingly never so uncouth and extravagant.

1. If *Henry* the II. had or could have brought over all the people of *Ireland* into *England*, declining the Benefit of their Land; he had fortified, beautified and enrich'd *England*, and done real Kindness to the *Irish.* But the same Work is near four times as hard now to be done as then; but it might be done, even now, with advantage to all Parties.

Whereas[2] there are now 300 M. *British*, and 800 M. *Papists*, whereof 600 M. live in the wretched way above mentioned: If an Exchange was made of but about 200 M.
Irish, and the like number of *British* brought || over in their 30

Pyraticall enemy, and without those considerations, we know yt being well managd it is able to supply the Crowne of Engld with men money and other conveniences, & is since our Author wrote become an additional strength to Engld.'

[1] Perhaps an allusion to the "digression" in chap. IV. of the *Polit. Arith.* Petty was working upon the *Polit. Arith.* in 1671, although he did not complete it until after the *Polit. Anat.*

[2] S, '2. Whereas.'

rooms, then the natural strength of the *British* would be equal to that of the *Irish*; but their Political and Artificial strength three times as great; and so visible, that the *Irish* would never stir upon a National or Religious Account.

3. There are among the 600 M. above-mentioned of the poor *Irish*,. not above 20 M. of unmarried marriageable Women; nor would above two thousand *per Ann.* grow and become such. Wherefore if ½ the said Women were in one year, and ½ the next transported into *England*, and disposed of one to each Parish, and as many *English* brought back and married to the *Irish*, as would improve their Dwelling but to an House and Garden of 3 l. value, the whole Work of natural Transmutation and Union would in 4 or 5 years be accomplished[1].

The charge of making the exchange would not be 20,000 l. *per Ann.* which is about 6 Weeks Pay of the present or late Armies in *Ireland.*

If the *Irish* must have Priests, let the number of them which is now between 2 and 3 thousand Secular and Regulars, be reduced to the competent number of 1000, which is 800 Souls to the pastorage of each Priest; which let
31 be known persons, and || *English-men*, if it may be. So as that when the Priests, who govern the Conscience, and the Women, who influence other powerful Appetites, shall be *English*, both of whom being in the Bosom of the Men, it must be, that no massacring of *English*, as heretofore, can happen again. Moreover, when the Language of the Children shall be *English*, and the whole Oeconomy of the Family

[1] Cox, 'The expedient of Transmutacon is mistaken in ye sex, for if a million of women were married to as many poor Ir, it is certain they would degenerate into meer Irish & yt in a few years, experience proves my Assertion; besides in reason it must be soe, for women unless elevated by education and a principle of honr are less virtuous than men, yt is they are more easy & sooner allured by temptation or frightened by anything yt is like terrible, they are naturally more slothfull and love their ease, besides ye Irish naturally lord it over their wives & are not soe uxorious as we Eng but if a number of young boys were exchangd yearly it would do wt our Author designs for boys bred after ye English manner would not marry but with women soe bred, wherefore ye Ir women would betake themselves to Eng service to qualify themselves for such husbands.'

English, viz. Diet, Apparel, *&c.* the Transmutation will be very easy and quick.

Add hereunto, That if both Kingdoms, now two, were put into one, and under one Legislative Power and Parliament, the Members whereof should be in the same proportion that the Power and Wealth of each Nation are, there would be no danger such a Parliament should do any thing to the prejudice of the *English* Interest in *Ireland*; nor could the *Irish* ever complain of Partiality, when they shall be freely and proportionably represented in all Legislatures[1].

The Inconveniences of the Not-Union, and Absurdities seem to be these, viz.

1. It is absurd, that *English-men* born, sent over into *Ireland* by the Commission || of their own King, and there 32
sacrificing their Lives for the King's Interest, and succeeding in his Service, should therefore be accounted Aliens, Foreigners, and also Enemies, such as were the *Irish* before *Henry* the VII. time; whom, if an *English-man* had then killed, he had suffer'd nothing for it; for it is but Indulgence and Connivance, that now the same is not still in force. For such formerly was the Condition of *Irish-men*; and that of *English-men* is now the same, otherwise than as Custom has relieved them.

It is absurd, that the Inhabitants of *Ireland*, naturally and necessarily bound to obey their Sovereign, should not be permitted to know who, or what the same is, *i.e.* Whether the Parliament of *England*, or that of *Ireland*; and in what Cases the one, and in what the other. Which uncertainty is or may be made a pretence for my Disobedience[2].

It is absurd, that *English-men* in *Ireland*, should either be Aliens there, or else to be bound to Laws, in the making whereof they are not represented.

[1] This scheme is further elaborated in the *Treatise of Ireland.*

[2] S, 'my disobedience'; 1719, 'any Disobedience.' It is not clear to what disobedience of his own Petty here refers. His arrest by order of the Lord Chancellor of Ireland took place 10 Feby. 1677. Fitzmaurice, 170.

It is absurd if the Legislative Power be in *Ireland*, that the final judgment of Causes between man and man, should
33 be in *England*, || *viz.* the Writs of Error should remove Causes out of *Ireland*, to[1] the *King's* *Bench* in *England*. That the final determination of Admiralty-Causes[2], and of some Causes-Ecclesiastical, should be also ended in *England*; nor that men should know whether the *Chancery* of *England* have jurisdiction in *Ireland*; and whether the Decrees of *Chancery* in one *Chancery*, can be executed in the other.

As for Inconveniences, it is one, That we should do to[3] Trade between the two Kingdoms, as the *Spaniards* in the *West-Indies* do to all other Nations; for which cause all other Nations have war with them there.

And that a Ship trading from *Ireland* into the Islands of *America*, should be forced to unlade the Commodities shipt for *Ireland* in *England*, and afterwards bring them home; thereby necessitating the Owners of such goods to run unnecessary hazard and Expences.

It is inconvenient that the same King's Subjects should pay Customs as Aliens, passing from one part of the same their own King's Territories to another.

The chief Objection against the remedy of these Evils is; ||
34 That his Majesty would by the Union lose much of his Double-Customs. Which being true, let's see what the same amounts unto; and if it be sufficient to hinder the remedy of these Evils, and if it be irreparable by some other way.

Ann. 1664. which was the best year of Trade that hath been these many years in *Ireland*, when neither Plague nor Wars impeached it, and when men were generally disposed to Splendor and Liberality[4], and when the Act for hindring Cattel coming out of *Ireland* into *England*, was not yet made[5]; nor that made for unlading in *England* Ships bound.

[1] S, 'into.'
[2] Cf. Fitzmaurice, 247.
[3] 'we should do to' is not in S.
[4] S, 'libe and.'
[5] By 15 Charles II., c. 7 (1663) a duty so high as to be practically prohibitive had been placed upon the importation of Irish cattle between 1 July and 20 December. On 18 October, 1665 a bill was introduced into the House of

from *America* into *Ireland*; I say, in that year the Customs upon exported and imported Commodities, between *Ireland* and *England*, was but———————————but not $\frac{1}{6}$ thereof, which since, how easily may it be added to the other Charges upon *England* and *Ireland*, which are together perhaps 1500 M. *per Ann.*?

2. If it be for the good of *England* to keep *Ireland* a distinct Kingdom, why do not the predominant Party in Parliament (suppose the *Western* Members) make *England* beyond *Trent* another Kingdom, under[1] Commerce, and take Tolls and Customs upon the new Borders? Or why was there || ever a Union between *England* and *Wales*, the good effects and fruits whereof were never questioned? And why

Commons prohibiting the importation of Irish cattle entirely. On the 20th it was advanced to a second reading and a public hearing before a committee was set for the 21st. Petty appeared with others against the measure, but they were refused a copy of the bill or even a list of its chief heads. They might hear it read once and immediately speak against it. The protesters declined to speak unprepared in a matter of such moment and prayed for delay that the Lord Lieutenant might be consulted. Delay was refused and the bill was ordered to be engrossed on the twenty-third. *H. C. Jour.*, VIII. 617, 619, 620. Before the Lord's committee Petty appeared two or three times in opposition to the measure and sufficient delay was there secured to prevent its passage before the prorogation of Parliament, 31 October, 1665. Lord E. Fitzmaurice, who had MS. memoranda, says that the substance of Petty's argument is reproduced in ch. x. of the *Polit. Anat.* (p. 185 *post*). *Life*, 142. It seems possible that some part of his argument was also printed at the time, as Thomas Thorpe had, in 1842, a printed sheet of *Observations on the Irish Cattle Trade*, which he attributed to Petty. Thorpe's *Catalogue*, 1842, no. 5597. The 27 November, 1667, a petition from Chester was presented in the House of Commons alleging infractions of 15 Charles II., c. 7 and calling for a more stringent enactment. *H. C. Jour.*, IX. 26—27. A bill was accordingly introduced 9 December and passed, after violent debate, the 2 March, 1668, declaring the importation from beyond seas of any great cattle, sheep or swine, or any beef, pork or bacon or of any ling, herring, cod, pilchard, salmon, eels or congers taken by foreigners aliens to the kingdom of England to be a nuisance. Such imports were therefore to be seized and sold for the benefit of the informer and of the poor of the parish. The debate in the House of Lords was even more violent then than in the Commons, and the bill was returned, 18 March, 1668, with amendments which were agreed to 30 March,—18 & 19 Charles II., c. 2. On the history of these measures see *Parl. Hist.*, IV. 337—347, Clarendon's *Life*, p. 959 seq., Carte, *Ormond*, II. 317—323, 329—338, Fitzmaurice, 140—142.

[1] S, 'hinder.'

may not the entire Kingdom of *England* be farther Cantoniz'd, and infinitely for the advantage of Parties?

As for the Practice; The Peers of *Ireland* assembled in Parliament, may depute so many of their number, as make the $\frac{1}{8}$[1] part of the Peers of *England*, to be call'd by Writ into the Lords-House of *England*: And the Commons in *Ireland* assembled in like manner, may depute the like proportion of other Members to sit with the Commons of *England*, the King and that House admitting of them.

But if the Parliament of *England* be already the Legislative Power of *Ireland*, why may they not call a competent Number out of *Ireland*, as aforesaid, or in some other more convenient manner?

All these Shifts and Expedients are necessary but for the first time, until the matter be agreed upon by both Nations, in some one Parliament.

'Tis suppos'd that the Wealth of *Ireland* is about the $\frac{1}{8}$ or $\frac{1}{10}$ of that of *England*; and the King's Revenue in both Kingdoms seems about that proportion. ‖

[CHAPTER VI.]

36 ### *Of the Government of* IRELAND.

THE Government of *Ireland* is by the King, 21 Bishops (whereof four are Arch-Bishops) and the Temporal Peers[2]; whereof some part,————by reason of the late Rebellion, do not sit in Parliament.

By about 3000 Freeholders, and the Members of about 100 Corporations, the University at *Dublin* reckoned for one, represented in the House of Commons, by about 270 Knights, Citizens and Burgesses.

The Parliament so constituted, have a Negative upon any Law that the Lord Lieutenant and Councel shall offer to the King, and which the King and his Councel in *England* shall under the Great Seal remit to the said Parliament.

[1] 1719, 'One sixth.'

[2] S, 'and......other Peers.'

The Sheriffs of Counties, and of Cities and Counties in *Ireland* are 40, finally appointed by the Lord Lieutenant, each of which hath about Ten Bailiffs.

The Chief Governour, called sometimes Lord-Lieutenant, sometimes Lord-Deputy, sometimes Lords Justices, with a Council, at this time consisting of about 50 Mem-||bers, do 37
govern in all Matters belonging to the Peace, Prerogative, *&c.*

There be five Courts, *viz.* a *Chancery*, consisting of a Lord-Chancellor, Master of the Rolls, and two, three or four Sallariated Masters of *Chancery*. The *King's-Bench*, of a Lord-Chief-Justice, and two other Judges. The *Common-Pleas* of the like: The Exchequer, of a Lord-Chief-Baron, and two other Barons, with the Treasurer and Chancellor of the *Exchequer:* And a Prerogative, whereof the Primate of *Armagh* is Judge.

There is also a Palatinate-Court in *Tipperary*, whereof the Duke of *Ormond* is Lord of the Liberties and Regalities to it belonging. There is also a Court of *Admiralty:* Every Bishop hath also two Courts. And there have been formerly and lately (but now *An.* 1672. suspended) a Presidency of *Munster*[1], and another of *Connaght*, who meddle not with Life or Limb, nor Titles of Land[2].

There is also a Court-*Marshal*, for the Affairs of the Army, who in times of peace often transmit accus'd persons to the Civil-power.

To all these Courts do belong ——— Officers, ——— Councellors of Law, whereof I reckon ———
are || of the first Classis, gaining by Estimation about 600 l. 38
per Ann. each ——— of the 2d. gaining about 300 l. *per Ann.* And ——— of the 3d gaining not above 100 l. *per Ann.* There are also ——— sworn Attornies, gaining about 120 l. *per Ann.* one with another.

There are in *Ireland* about 950 Justices of the Peace, appointed by the Lord-Chancellor; an Head-Constable for each Barony or Hundred, being 252; and a Petty Constable for each Parish; whereof are about 2278.

[1] The complaints against the presidential court of Munster are alluded to by Carte, *Ormond*, II. 369.

[2] S, 'lands.'

The Ecclesiastical Government is by Arch-Bishops, Bishops, Arch-Deacons, Deans[1] of Cathedral-Churches, in all which there are now actually but one Quire entire, and that in *Dublin*, serving both at *Christ-Church*, and St. *Patrick's*. And the Parsons, Vicars and Curates for the *Protestant-Religion*, are in all *Ireland* at this day near 500, and about half the Tythes are Impropriate, and belonging to Lay-men.

This is the State of the External and Apparent Government of *Ireland*, so far as it concerns the Number and Species of Persons managing the same. But the Internal and Mystical Government of *Ireland* is thus, *viz.* ||

39 1. There are always about Twenty[2] Gentlemen of the *Irish* Nation and *Popish-Religion*, who by reason of their Families, good Parts, Courtly Education and Carriage, are supported by the *Irish* to negotiate their Concernments at the Court of *England*, and of the Vice-Roy in *Ireland*.

These men raise their Contributions by the Priests (who actually and immediately govern the People.) The Priests are govern'd by at least 24 *Romish* Bishops, all of whom have a long time been conversant in *France*, *Spain*, *Italy*, *Germany*, *England*, where as Chaplains and Almoners, *&c.* they have made an interest with the governing Men and Ministers of State in those several Kingdoms, and have obtained some Benefits and Preferments from them.

So as the Body of the *Irish-Papists* (being about 800 M. whereof near 700 M. do live in wretched Cabbins, without Chimney or Window) are govern'd by about 1000 Secular Priests, and 2500 Friars and Regulars[3] of several Orders; whereof most are *Franciscans*, next *Dominicans* and *Augustins*, but few *Capuchins* and *Jesuits* or *Carthusians*. These, I say, are govern'd by their respective Bishops and Superiors, whom
40 the Mi-||nisters of Foreign States do also govern and direct..

So as upon the whole matter, the *Irish*, who are the Bulk of the Nation, are govern'd indirectly by Foreign Power; and so are the aforenamed Lay-Patriots[4], their support

[1] S, 'by 21 Bishops, Arch Deacons......Deans.'
[2] S, '12 or 20.'
[3] S, 'Regular.'
[4] S, '12 or 20 Lay-Patriots.'

coming from the Clergy constituted as aforesaid, and who do notoriously exercise their Spiritual Jurisdiction in *Ireland*: And do also exert a Temporal Power, by prevailing with *Papist* Justices of the Peace, to send such to Gaol as are disobedient to the Clergy, upon feigned or frivolous Complaints, which they cause to be brought against them.

The Judges aforenamed, all but the Chancellor, go Circuits, whereof there are five twice every year, excepting only the one County of *Kerry*.

There is an University at *Dublin*, but lying for the most part within one College, wherein are a Provost and seven Senior and Ruling Fellows; Nine Junior Fellows; sixty Scholars; and at this time ———— Commoners[1] and other Students.

There was about the year 1669 erected a College of *Physicians*, consisting of a President, and 13 Fellows[2]. ||

There are belonging to the Prerogative, Arch-Deacons 41
Courts, Court-Martial and Admiralty-Courts, not above 10 Advocates, and 30 Proctors.

There are in the City of *Dublin* a Lord-Mayor, 2 Sheriffs, 24 Aldermen, 48 Sheriffs Peers, and 96 of the Common-Council. There are besides, Companies or Corporations of Trades-men.

There is lately instituted an Hospital for poor Children, not yet fully perfected or endowed[3].

[1] S, 'at this time about......commoners.'

[2] The Dublin "Fraternity of Physicians"; founded by Dr John Stearne in 1654 was incorporated by Royal Charter in 1667 as "The President and Fellows of the College of Physicians in Dublin." In this first charter fourteen Fellows were nominated, the first of whom, Dr Stearne, was appointed President for life, and 'the next on the list was the celebrated Sir William Petty,' who had been a member of the Fraternity from its first organization. In 1692 the College received a new Charter under its present name. *Register of the King's and Queen's College of Physicians in Ireland* (1865), pp. 5, 6, 91.

[3] Probably the hospital on Oxmantown-Green, officially "The Hospital and Free School of King Charles the Second, Dublin." Towards the support of this hospital Petty gave £20 per annum out of £321. 2*s*. 11½*d*. so contributed. *Narrative and Account concerning the Hospital on Oxmantown Green. Published for the Satisfaction of the Subscribers*, 1671. *Now Republished* by Charles Lucas, Dublin, 1749. Petty's gift was made after 15 Jany., 1670, as his name does not

There is also an Hospital for Sick, Lame, and Old Soldiers, but without Endowment, and standing but at discretion and pleasure[1].

There are in and near *Dublin*, three Publick Prisons, and one House of Correction.

Lastly, I must intimate, that the Footmanship for which the *Irish* 40 years agone were very famous, is now almost quite lost among them, every man now keeping a small Garran to ride on, unless in such rocky and craggy places, where 'tis easier to go a foot than to ride. ||

[CHAPTER VII.]

42 ### *Of the Militia and Defence of* IRELAND.

THERE be in *Ireland*, as elsewhere, two Militias; one are the Justices of Peace, their Militia of High and Petty Constables; as also the Sheriffs Militia of his Servants and Bailiffs and *Posse Comitatus* upon extraordinary occasions.

Of these all together there are in *Ireland* near 3000; all of which are bound within their several Districts, there to act, and not elsewhere.

There is, or hath lately been an Army in *Ireland*, of about thirty Troops of Horse, and sixty Companies of Foot,

appear in the list of "Benefactors or Subscribers for the Hospital," of that date, printed by Gilbert, *Calendar*, IV. 492—494.

[1] This paragraph may have been inserted after the completion of the *Polit. Anat.*, which occurred in 1672 or 1673. *An Account of the Founding of the Royal Hospital of Charles II. near Dublin for the Relief and Maintenance of Antient and Infirm Officiers and Soldiers Serving in the Army of Ireland.* [By Thomas Wilson.] Dublin, 1713, says that from the example of Louis XIV. in establishing the Hôtel des Invalides 'first sprung the Notion of Building the Like in this Kingdom, which was happily Entertain'd at first by the Earl of Granard......in or about the Year 1675.' Granard communicated with the Lord Lieutenant, Essex, but nothing came of the matter until the arrival of Ormond in 1677. On 27 October, 1679 Ormond wrote to the King in favour of the proposed hospital, and an order for its endowment was accordingly given at the Council Chamber, 27 February, 1680. The building was erected 1680—1686. Pp. 4—15.

with a Regiment of Guard at *Dublin*, as a Life-Guard for the Lord Lieutenant, making in all about five thousand Men.

There is also a Protestant Militia, of about 24000 Men, *viz.* about ten thousand Horse, and the rest Foot.

The people of *Ireland* are all in Factions and Parties, called *English* and *Irish*, *Protestants* and *Papists*: Though indeed the real distinction is vested and devested[1] of the Land belonging to *Papists*, *Ann.* 1641. Of which the *Irish* that are vested by Restoration, seem rather to take part with the deve-||sted. And the chief Pique which the *Popish-Clergy* 43
have at the *Protestants* is, that they have the Church Livings and Jurisdictions; for the exercise of their Function they have most freely, and had, when they[2] undertook their Project in 1641. The differences between the Old *Irish*, and Old *English Papists* is asleep now, because they have a Common Enemy.

The Old *Protestants* of Queen *Elizabeth* and King *James's* Plantation (till of late) did not much love the New *English*; who came over since 1641. or rather since 1646. & 1648. because they envied the great Shares which they had gotten of the forfeited Lands from the Late Usurpers. But now they also are well enough together, since the said Old Protestants have had good Proviso's in the Acts of Settlement and Satisfaction for their Service before *June* 1649. and since the Church-Revenues have been augmented by the Forfeitures; but chiefly, for that the said Old *Protestants* have all the Power and Preferments Civil, Military, and Ecclesiastical.

Of the New *English*, some are *Conformists*, others not: And some have fallen in with other Parties, and others not. || 44

Of the Old Protestants, there are also Parties, I cannot

[1] Cox, 'If y[e] Irish y[t] are vested take part with y[e] divested (as our Author says) then the true distinction of factions is Eng & Ir or rather Papist & Anti-papist & not Vested and divested: and indeed since there are not above 3000 freeholders in Ireland y[e] notions of vested & divested cannot denominate factions y[t] are more generall and 100 times more Numerous.'

[2] S omits 'they.'

say Factions, chiefly denominated by the Names of their Families, as the *Butlers* and *Fitz-Gerralds* were of old.

But to return; The chief Factions are the vested and devested of forfeited Lands: all *Irish* and *Papists* generally fearing the latter, and most *English* and *Protestants* the former, as appears in all Juries and Testimonies given where the Lands or Lives of one or other are concerned. Now in some Counties, as in *Kerry*, many Forfeitures happened, and few Restorations, and there also few *English* were ever planted, nor can well endure to live: So as the first sort of Militia in these and other like Counties, are *Irish-Papists*, devested and discontented Persons. Whereby the few *English* there, can have no Justice executed, for want of hand wherewith to do it: Nor can they easily get indifferent Juries, but that the Sheriffs are *English* for the most part, and most commonly Protestants. In which Case, some have been of opinion, that the other Militia, namely the Army, may both in Law and Reason supply this defect in times when there is not occasion for them, to guard the Land from
45 Invasion and Rebelli-||on. For why might not 30 Sheriffs be taken out of 120 Officers of the Army, *viz.* 60 Captains and Lieutenants of Horse, and 60 Captains of Foot? And why may not such be as responsible for executing just Sentences, as any other? And what Tenor is there in the Force which a Bailiff useth, more than in that which one call'd a Soldier carries with him. And why should the Military Officer or Sheriff use more force or terror than to make the Debtor or Malefactor answer the Law, and obey the Sentence of a Civil Court? And is it not more convenient and easy in great riotous Contempts, to bring a Troop or Company, whose Trade it is to use Arms and apply Force dexterously, than to use the *Posse Comitatus*; that is, to call abundance of men from their Labour and Calling, to attempt things of Danger, which they do not understand? Moreover, if the General can quarter the Army where he pleases, and that the Sheriffs[1] or Constable can, in their respective Precincts, call whom he pleases to his assistance; then the General can

[1] S, 'Sherif.'

cause such a competent Force to be quartered in those thin peopled Counties. And the Sheriffs and Justices can call such to their assistance, excepting where such Soldiers are in formal || Garisons upon actual Duty, or in other cases to be 46
agreed upon between the Civil and Military Powers so call'd, although there can be no Countrey without Force, nor any Army without a Policy and Discipline. But of this let the Lawyers talk further.

As for the Military Force of *Ireland*, vulgarly and properly so call'd, 1. The standing Army is such as the present Revenue can well maintain, which perhaps is, or very lately was about 6000, and is every year or other year changed, as to his Majesty seems best. 2. The Protestant Militia now already established and formed, is about 24 or 25 thousand men, most of them already experienc'd in the Wars of *Ireland*.

The Third, of grand Force against Foreign Invasions, I conceive may be 70 M. Men of the best affected, and least Pope-affected *Irish*; for so many I conceive the 30000 of the standing Army and present Militia could well Officer and Command. Now that 100 M. may be spar'd to send as Soldiers in a time of extremity, I think it plain, for that there are 550 M. Males in *Ireland*, whereof 150 M. can perform all the necessary Labor of Husbandmen and Tradesmen; 200 M. of them are perhaps un-||der 16, and above 60. 47
Nor doth the quality of the remaining[1], exempt them from service, who are to stand for a reserve.

And this Force I take to be sufficient to resist any number of men which any Prince of the World hath Shipping enough to bring into *Ireland*, with such Horse, Arms, Ammunition and Victuals as are[2] for such an Enterprize.

To say nothing, that the substance of *Ireland* is chiefly Cattel, which be easily removed to waste the Countrey where the Enemy shall land.

And how considerable the standing Army of 6000 men, and the Veteran Militia, of above 24000, who have not only

[1] S, 'remaining 100 M.' [2] S, 1719 insert 'fit.'

the Command, but the possession and propriety of all the strong and terrible Places in *Ireland*, and ¾ of all the Horse serviceable in War, and at least ¾ of all Shipping, and *England* to help and countenance, hath been competently mentioned before; and that the Bulk of the *Irish* are the Inhabitants of the aforenamed 160 M. wretched Cabins-men[1], slavishly bred and dealt with by their own Lords and Patriots; and that the restored *Irish*, restored to their Estates almost by Miracle, will be careful how they engage any more upon a frivolous, impious Undertaking. ||

[CHAPTER VIII.]

48 ### *Of the* Cœlum *and* Solum *of* Ireland.

BY the Cœlum or Sky, I understand the Heat, Coldness, Drowth, Moisture, Weight and Susceptions of Air, and the Impressions made upon it, *viz.* The state of the Winds, as whether the Wind blows in *Ireland* in comparison with, or differently from other Places; as from what points of the Compass the Wind blows most frequently or fiercely, and what proportion of the whole year from each Point. 2. As to Heat and Cold, I conceive the same ought to be measur'd by the Weather-Glass or *Thermometer*. 3. As to Wetness or Moisture, by the shrinking of Lute-strings, by the quantity of Rain falling upon a certain quantity of level superficies, and by the quantity of Water dried up with the same time out of a Vessel of like Figure, and equal dimensions.

As for other changes in the Air, supposed to depend upon the gravity or levity thereof, I suppose the same is to be known by the Instrument call'd the *Barrimeter*. *Lastly*, To the much or little Sunshine, whereof *Ireland* hath been much abus'd; the same is to be measur'd by an Instrument found for that purpose. ||

49 Wherefore since it is small satisfaction to say the Air of *Ireland* is mild and temperate, inclin'd to moisture, *&c.*

[1] S, 'Cabbins, men slavishly bred.'

And since the true and clear knowledge thereof depends upon several long, tedious, and reiterated Observations, simple and comparative, made in the several parts of *Ireland*, in the several Seasons of the Year, and compar'd with the like Observations, made with the same or like Instruments, in the several parts of the Earth; we must for the present only say, that there are in being the several Instruments following, *viz.*

1. An Instrument to measure the motion of the Wind, and consequently its strength.

2. How many Hours in the day in the whole year it blows from any point of the Compass.

3. To measure what quantity of Rain falls in the year upon any quantity or space of ground.

4. What air is most desiccative of moistness.

5. What Alterations are made in the gravity and levity of the Air from Hour to Hour. ||

6. The Thermometer or Weather-Glass of the better 50
sort.

7. The Instrument to measure and foretel Frost and Snow.

Which Instruments many men must make use of in the several parts of *Ireland*, and the rest of the World, and corresponding with each other, communicate and correct their Observation by Reason.

In the mean time let it suffice to say, that at *Dublin* the Wind blows 2 parts of 5 from the South-West to the West, one part from South-West to the South; one other from the West to North-East, and the rest from the North-East to the South: 3 parts of 10 between West and South-West $\frac{2}{10}$ between S. W. and S. S. E. $\frac{2}{10}$ between S. S. E. and N. E. by[1] N. $\frac{2}{10}$ N. E. by N. to N. & W.[2] or very near thereabouts.

2. That from the 10th of *Septemb.* to the 10th of *March,*

[1] S, 'NEly.' [2] S, 'NEly to N & W.'

it blows a kind of Storm for some time or other almost every day.

3. That the Snow lies not long in the lower ground of *Ireland*. Nor doth it freeze more than what it doth in *France*, *Holland*, or *England*. ||

51 4. The Rain falling at *Dublin* and *London* for the Month *October*, 1663. was but 20 to 19. That the windiness of the same Month was at *Dublin* 20. and at *London* but 17.

5. As for the healthfulness of the Climate, City, or other space of Land; It must be first known how many people are in a certain day living in it, and then the *quota pars* which die *per Ann.* for many years together; and for the fruitfulness, how many Births.

6. As to Longævity, enquiry must be made into some good old Register of (suppose) 20 persons, who all were born and buried in the same Parish, and having cast up the time which they all lived as one man, the Total divided by 20 is the life of each one with another; which compared with the like Observation in several other places, will shew the difference of Longævity, due allowance being made for extraordinary contingences, and Epidemical Diseases happening respectively within the period of each Observation.

Wherefore Matters being not as yet prepared for these Experiments, I can say nothing clearly of them; Only, That it seems by the best Estimates and Approaches that I
52 have been able to make, that *London* is || more healthful than *Dublin* by 3 in 32.

Having said thus much of the *Cœlum* or Air, or rather of the *Ingenium*, and way of distinguishing Airs in a better manner than usual: We come next to try the nature of the Soil by the like Expedients.

To which purpose, first know, that the Perch of *Ireland* is 21 Foot, that of *England* but 16½; Wherefore the Acre of 160 Perches is as 121 to 196, that is 121 *Irish* Acres do make 196 *English* Statute Acres. Now in *Ireland* a Milch-Cow, if *English* breed, upon two Acres of Pasture, and with as much Hay as will grow upon ½ Acre of Meadow, will yield *præter propter* 3 Gallons of Milk for 90 days, one with another, and one Gallon at a Medium for 90 more, and for 90 more scarce $\frac{1}{4}$ of a Gallon one day with another, and for 90 more, dry. Wherefore it follows, that such a Cow upon such feeding, gives above one Tun and half; nay, 384 Gallons of Milk *per Ann.* And that if the Rent of the said two Acres of Pasture be 5 s. *per Ann.* and of the half Acre of Meadow 3. in all 8 s. That the Gallon of Milk comes but to a Farthing, expecting what the value and hazard of the Cow, and the labour of milking and looking to her, shall add unto that price; which I suppose not above as much more. ||

The said quantity of Milk will make $2\frac{1}{2}$ C. of Raw-Milk- 53
Cheese, and 1 C. of Whey-Butter, besides Whey for the Swine: Or else 2 C. of Butter, and 1 C. of Skim-Milk-Cheese, besides Whey as abovesaid, for Drink to the People, and Food for Swine.

Mem. That one Bull suffices for about 20 Cows. That a Cow continues Milch and bearing, from 3 or 4 years old to 12, sometimes 20, tho seldom suffer'd to live so long. And that three Dairy-women will manage 20 Cows, and do much work of other kind between while; and that one Man will look to them and their Food.

An Ox of 6 or 7 years old will not require so much feeding as a Milch-Cow, but will be maintained with two Acres of good Pasture only, or with $1\frac{1}{2}$ Acres of Pasture, and $\frac{1}{2}$ Acres of Hay, in hard Winters.

An Horse requires $2\frac{1}{2}$ Acres, as a Garran, and a small Horse or *Irish* Garran $1\frac{2}{3}$, or thereabouts.

Eight or ten Sheep are equivalent for feeding to an Ox[1].

	l. C.
It is further to be noted, that a Calf at a Month old weighs	$\frac{1}{2}$[2] ||
That an Ox is come to its full growth at 6 years old, and then may weigh alive	7[3] C. 54
The 4 quarters of such an Ox weighs	5[4] C.
The Hide,	$\frac{3}{4}$[5]

[1] In the margin of S, 'A sheep weighs 80^{lb}.' [2] 1719, '56 l.' [3] 1719, '784 l.' [4] 1719, '560 l.' [5] 1719, '84 l.'

The Tallow[1] 80 l.

[2]And consequently the said Ox gaineth every year of weight in Flesh to eat } l.

In Hide ——————

In Tallow ——————

[3]The Offal Worth, besides half of the whole. }

The difference between lean Beef and fat Beef in value is as 5 to 9.

In Sheep the increase of their Flesh, Skin and Tallow, is about the same proportion. And yet Sheeps Flesh is sold dearer than Beef, because of the great trouble and hazard about Sheep.

A Fleece of Wool in *Ireland* is about 2 l. weight.

An Hog eats such things as Sheep and Oxen do not, *viz.* Roots, Acorns, and consequently the same Land will maintain a proportion of Hogs above Sheep[4] and Oxen. One-Cowherd will serve an hundred Oxen; one Shepherd 1000 Sheep. ||

55 From all that hath been said, we collect, that the natural and genuine Rent of Lands in *Ireland*, not that of Money, or Gold and Silver; is

Of Milk, deducting Charges —— Gall.

Of Beef and Mutton ——————————————

Of Hides and Skin ——————————————

Of Offall ——————————————

Of Wooll. ——————————————

So as where Lands produce more or less *per Ann. communibus annis* of these Commodities, the same is to be accompted more or less fertil than that of *Ireland.*

Moreover from hence we shall endeavour to gather the number of Cattel in *Ireland*, as followeth, *viz.*

There being 7½ Millions of Acres of good Meadow, Arrable, and Pasture-Land in *Ireland*, besides Bog with

[1] 1719 inserts 'The Offal about 60 l,' and sums up 'In all 784 l or 7 C.wt.'

[2] 1719, 'Consequently the said Ox gaineth in weight one year with another near 130 l.'

[3] 1719 omits this paragraph.

[4] S, 'above......sheep.'

Shrub-wood, *&c.* commonly call'd unprofitable Land; and
for that $\frac{1}{2}$ a Million supplies the Inhabitants with Corn for
Bread and Drink, Man and Beast, Hemp, Flax and Rape, as
shall be hereafter shewn[1] from the number of the people,
their manner of eating, from the number of Mills, and from
the value of the Tythes, *&c.* supposing the other 7 Millions
to be competently well stockt, let us first || see how many 56
Houses there may probably be.

To which purpose, remember that there are 184 M. Families, whose Houses have but one or no Chimney. Now I guess, that about $\frac{1}{3}$ of this number keep a small Horse call'd a Garran, which is 61,000 Garrans for Tillage; and I suppose that the 16,000 Families have for the Coach and Saddle near 40 M. Horses. So as in *Ireland* there are about 100 M. Horses, whose Food requires 100 M. Acres of good Pasture, 50 M. Acres of Meadow, and the $\frac{1}{6}$ of an Acre of Oat-Land, *viz.* about 16,000 Acres. In all 166 M. Acres: Or if the Horses be such as require little or no Hay and Oats, as the Horses of poor people do not, then as aforesaid 2 or $2\frac{1}{3}$[2] Acres is allowed to each Horse.

The Wooll which is usually exported, being a little above
2 Millions of pounds, grows upon 1000 M. Sheep: And the
Wooll which cloaths the Nation, being about 1100 M. Bodies,
at —l. each for Cloths, Hats and Stockins, requires 6000 M.
more; and so 3 Millions more of Sheep, in all 4 Millions.
The feeding whereof at 5 to an Acre, require 800 M. Acres.
So as Horse and Sheep require one Million of Acres. So as
there remains $\frac{1}{2}$, a Million being allow'd || for all other Cattel, 57
Beasts and Vermine) $5\frac{1}{2}$ Millions[3] for great Cattel, which will
feed about 3 Millions of that Species.

If there be 3 Millions of Black Cattel, there be 1500 M. of Males, *viz.* 25 M. Bulls. } 700 M. under 3 years old. 600 between 3 and 6. 175 above 6.

Of Females 1500 M. whereof $\frac{2}{5}$ are milch-Cows, *viz.*

[1] Chap. XII. discusses the diet of the inhabitants of Ireland.

[2] S, 1719, '$2\frac{1}{2}$.'

[3] S, 'remains ($\frac{1}{2}$ a million being allow'd for all other Cattle, beasts, and Vermine) $5\frac{1}{2}$ Millions.'

600 M. 600 M. Calves and Heifers under 3, and 300 of other sorts.

Where note, that of all the Black-Cattel above-named, there are 60 M. exported alive, and 30 M. dead in Barrels. Of the Sheep not 100 M.

Of Butter, whereof one of the 600 M. Milch-Cows may well yield 1 C. weight *per Ann.* but 26000 C, or the proceed of 26000 Cows. From whence may be seen whether the Trade of those Commodities be yet at best: For I guess that the $\frac{1}{6}$ of the whole Stock may be annually spent at home, or exported abroad.

It remains only to say, that one *Irish* Acre of *Irish* Land, requires of Seed, and returns as followeth.

	Seed.	
	Wheat 4 Bushels, and produces	16 to 36
	Rye 4	20 to 40 ||
58	Bean-Barly 6	20 to 48
	Oats 6	16 to 32
	Barley 4	20 to 40
	Pease 4	12 to 18

One horse plows 10 Acres, and there goes 1 Man to 3 Horses.

[CHAPTER IX.]

Of the Proportion in value, which the several Counties in Ireland *do bear to each other,* viz.

THE value or proportion of the several Counties in *Ireland*, both seem much to depend upon the number of Acres which each doth contain. And therefore, and for several other Reasons, most of the Land of *Ireland* hath, within these last 40 years, been admeasured by the Chain and Instrument, *viz.* The King and Queens Counties, about

Sir hn Bod- 1.

[1] Sir Josias (not John) Bodley, youngest brother of the founder of the Bodleian Library, born about 1550, was engaged in military service in Ireland

the Year 1630. The County of *Londonderry*, when the City of *London* undertook the Plantation by one Mr. *Raven*[1]; *Connought* and *Tipperary*, in the Earl of *Strafford*'s time, by several hands[2], sometimes conducted by Mr. *William Gilbert*[3]. ||

The Lands belonging to Papists *Ann.* 1641. in the three Provinces of *Munster*, *Lemster* and *Ulster*, by Sir *William Petty*. Other Protestant Lands in the same three Provinces, in order to regulate Contributions, by the Owners of the said Lands themselves: But in so divided and separated a manner, that little Accompt can be given of them, besides what was collected by the said Sir *William Petty*; who at his own charge, besides those Maps of every Parish, which by his Agreement he delivered into the Surveyor-General's Office, he hath caused distinct Maps to be made of every Barony, or Hundred; as also of every County, engraven in Copper, and the like of every Province, and of the whole Kingdom. All which, could the Defects of them be supplied with the yet unmeasured Lands, would be exposed to publick view[4]. 59

Now as to the value of these Lands, they were *Ann.* 1642. rated to and by the Adventurers as followeth, *viz.* in *Lemster* at 12 s. *per* Acre; in *Munster* at 9 s. in *Connaught* at

before 1600, and was employed in 1605 on fortifications in Munster. In 1609 the survey for the Ulster plantation was intrusted to him, with others, and was ably performed. He died, probably, in January, 1618.

[1] In 1616 Mr Alderman Proby and Mr Matthias Springham, sent from London to report upon the condition of Derry, "continued Mr Thomas Raven as surveyor for two years more, holding his services necessary for measuring and setting out the fortifications of Derry and Culmore." *Ordnance Survey of the County of Londonderry*, I. 40. Raven accordingly directed the building of the walls of Londonderry in 1617. Hempton, *The Siege and History of Londonderry*, 327.

[2] Petty's *History of the Down Survey*, 54—62, 325—27, 346, 393; Hardinge, "On MS. mapped and other Townland Surveys in Ireland of a public Character, embracing the Gross, Civil and Down Surveys, from 1640 to 1688," in *Trans. Roy. Irish Acad.*, vol. xxiv. Antiquities (1873), pp. 3—118.

[3] See Hardinge "On MS. mapped Townland Surveys," in *Proc. R. I. A.*, viii. 39, 54.

[4] On Petty's surveys and maps see Introduction, and note on p. 6; also Petty's *History*, Hardinge, *loc. cit.*, and Fitzmaurice, chap. II.

6s. and in *Ulster* at 4s.[1] and to pay 1 Farthing *per Ann.* Quit-rent to the King out of each Shillings-worth of Land so rated, *viz.* 3d. or 12 Farthings for an Acre in *Lemster* rated
60 at 12s. 9q. or 2¼ an Acre || for Lands in *Munster*, rated at 9s. *& sic de cæteris.* Wood, Bog, and Mountain, to be cast in over and above.

Afterwards the Soldiers, who were to have the satisfaction of their Arrears at the same rate, not being willing to cast Lots upon such desperate hazards, did *Ann.* 1653. equalize Counties within each Province, *viz.* took some in *Lemster*, at 1 l. 2 s. *per* Acre, some at 1 l. *&c.* And those who were satisfied *Ann.* 1655. and afterwards, did equalize not only Counties, but Baronies also, valuing some Baronies in *Lemster* at 1 l. 4 s. *per* Acre, and some but at 6 s. and others at all rates between these two extreams. But so as that, notwithstanding all the said differences, the whole Province should be given and taken at 12 s. *per* Acre, according to the then Law. And the Inequality remaining after this Equalization, was to be corrected by a Lot[2].

I could here insert all the particulars of these Transactions, but conceive it impertinent to my purpose, especially since they may be seen upon Record[3]. The next and best of all preceding equalization, was that which the Concernees of each County made in order to regulate the heavy
61 Contributions paid to the Usurpers before His Ma-||jesties Restoration, and when no Quit-Rent was yet due[4]. And in order to this work, not Baronies as before, but Parishes, nay, particular Farms were also equalized. What was done herein, was not publickly recorded, but collected by the curious, and too Bulky to be here inserted. Only take notice, that

[1] By 17 Charles I., c. 34, Scobell, I. 26.

[2] Probably in accordance with c. 12, Acts of 1653. Scobell, II. 240, 242.

[3] Many of the records were destroyed by the fire in the Council office in Essex Street, 1711. *Report from the Commissioners respecting the Public Records of Ireland*, 1810—1815, pp. 400, 541 *et passim.*

[4] Probably a reference to c. 32, Acts of 1654, which imposed upon Ireland an assessment of £10,000 per month, together with the same excise and customs as in England, and temporarily remitted quit-rents upon the lands granted to adventurers and soldiers. Scobell, II. 313.

these Valuations were made as Parties interested could prevail upon and against one another by their Attendance, Friends, Eloquence, and Vehemence; for what other Foundation of Truth it had in Nature, I know not.

Next to this Valuation, there was, in order to a certain[1] Gift presented to His Majesty, by the Adventurers and Soldiers, of a years value of all their Lands as it yielded *Ann.* 1659. next immediately before his Restoration. There[2] issued a Commission, *Ann.* 1663. to enquire and settle the said Values. And about 1667. there were made two several Valuations more; the one in order to reprize such who had restored Lands to the Innocent *Irish* in equal value; and another was a Determination what each Land was worth *Ann.* 1659. (whatever it yielded): Both which, especially the latter, are upon Record most authentically. Moreover, *Ann.* 1653, and 1654. there were Inquisitions taken of the Values which || all and every parcel of Land in *Ireland* yielded *Ann.* 62
1641. There have been also several Acts of the chief Powers *pro tempore*, for apportioning what proportion of a certain Sum to be levied in general, should in particular be charg'd on each County, *viz. Ann.* 1657. there was an Act of the Usurper's Parliament to that purpose[3]. *Ann.* 1662. There was an Act for raising 30 M. l. as a Present to his Grace the Duke of *Ormond*[4]; and another for raising of for several publick Uses[5]. And *Ann.* 1672. for the equal raising of 30000 l. *per Ann.* upon all the Lands and Houses of the whole Nation. There be also Accompts of what was raised out of each County by way of Subsidy and Pole-money, paid *Ann.* 1661. All which may be of much light to those who have such designs as the same will answer. But I being

[1] S, 'to ascertain a gift.' [2] S, 'restoration, there.'

[3] Acts of 1656, c. 25 laid an assessment of £9000 per month upon Ireland for three years from 24 June, 1657. Scobell, II. 491; valuations of the several counties of Ireland, pp. 496—497.

[4] 14 & 15 Charles II., c. 16, Ireland. Cf. p. 2.

[5] Perhaps 13 Charles I., c. 1, An Act for the speedy raising of money for his Majesty's service. "Search has been made for this act in the Rolls, but it is not to be found." *Irish Statutes at Large*, II. 235.

meanest of the 160 M. Cabbins, one with another are five Souls, in the 24,000 six Souls[3]. In all the other Houses Ten a piece, one with another.

The TABLE[4].

BUT to make nearer approaches to the perfection of this Work, 'twould be expedient to know the Content of Acres of every Parish, and withal, what quantity of Butter, Cheese, Corn, and Wooll, was raised out of it for three years consequent; for thence the natural Value of the Land may be known, and by the number of People living within a Market-days Journey, and the Value of their housing, which shews the Quality and Expence of the said People; I would hope to come to the knowledg of the Value of the said Commodities, and consequently the Value of the Land, by

[1] S, 'well assur'd.'

[2] Cox, 'The computacion of ye value of land p 15^s^ for every inhabitant is very strange and can have noe certainty nor pbability—for Example Typerary has not more people in it twice than the Barony of Carbury, but it is 40 times y^t^ value p ann. & is for ye most pte kept under sheep, & therefore thinly inhabited.'

[3] In the margin of S,

'160	16000
5	10
800 M.	24
144	6
160	144.'
1,104000	

[4] The Table was probably omitted from the original MS. and the copyist of S left no space for it.

deducting the hire of Working-People in it. And this brings me to the most important Consideration in Political Oeconomies, *viz.* how to make a *Par* and *Equation* between Lands and Labour, so as to express the Value of any thing by either ‖ alone. To which purpose, suppose two Acres of 64
Pasture-land inclosed, and put thereinto a wean'd Calf, which I suppose in twelve Months will become 1 *C.* heavier in eatable Flesh; then 1 *C.* weight of such Flesh, which I suppose fifty days Food, and the Interest of the Value of the Calf, is the value or years Rent of the Land. But if a mans labour ———— for a year can make the said Land to yield more than sixty days Food of the same, or of any other kind, then that overplus of days food is the Wages of the Man; both being expressed by the number of days food. That some Men will eat more than others, is not material, since by a days food we understand $\frac{1}{100}$ part of what 100 of all Sorts and Sizes will eat, so as to Live, Labour, and Generate. And that a days food of one sort, may require more labour to produce, than another sort, is also not material, since we understand the easiest-gotten food of the respective Countries of the World.

As for example, I suppose a pint of Oatmeal equal to half a pint of Rice, or a quart of Milk, or a pound of Bread, or a pound and quarter of Flesh, *&c.* each, in the respective place where each is the ‖ easiest gotten food. But if Rice be 65
brought out of *India* into *Ireland*, or Oatmeal carried from *Ireland* thither; then in *India* the pint of Oatmeal must be dearer than half a pint of Rice, by the freight and hazard of Carriage, *& vice-versa, & sic de cæteris.* For, as for pleasant tast, I question whether there[1] be any certainty, or regularity of the same in Nature, the same depending upon Novelty, opinion of Virtue, the recommendation of others, *&c.* Wherefore the days food of an adult Man, at a Medium, and not the days labour, is the common measure of Value, and seems to be as regular and constant as the value of fine Silver. For an ounce, suppose, of Silver in *Peru* is equivalent to a days food, but the same in *Russia* is equivalent to four days

[1] S omits 'there.'

food, by reason of the Freight, and hazard in carrying the same from *Peru* to *Russia*; and in *Russia* the price of Silver shall grow to be worth more days labour, if a Workman can by the esteem and request of Silver Utensils earn more than he can on other materials. Wherefore I valued an *Irish* Cabbin at the number of days food, which the Maker spent in building of it. ||

66 By the same way we must make a Par and Equation between Art and Simple Labour; for if by such Simple Labour I could dig and prepare for Seed a hundred Acres in a thousand days; suppose then, I spend a hundred days in studying a more compendious way, and in contriving Tools for the same purpose; but in all that hundred days dig nothing, but in the remaining nine hundred days I dig two hundred Acres of Ground; then I say, that the said Art which cost but one hundred days Invention is worth one Mans labour for ever; because the new Art, and one Man, perform'd as much as two Men could have done without it.

By the same way we make an Equation beween Art and Opinion. For if a Picture-maker, suppose, make Pictures at 5 *l.* each; but then, find that more Persons would employ him at that rate than his time would extend to serve them in, it will certainly come to pass that this Artist will consider whether as many of those who apply to him at 5 *l.* each Picture, will give 6 *l.* as will take up his whole time to accommodate; and upon this Computation he pitcheth the Rate of his Work. ||

67 By the same way also an Equation may be made between drudging Labour, and Favour, Acquaintance, Interest, Friends, Eloquence, Reputation, Power, Authority, *&c.* All which I thought not amiss to intimate as of the same kind with finding an Equation between Land and Labour, all these not very pertinent to the Proportionation of the several Counties of *Ireland*.

Wherefore to return to the matter in hand, I say, that the Quantity of Commodity produced, and the Quantity of the ———— shews the effects of the Land; and the number of People living thereupon, with the Quality of their housing, shews the Value of the Commodity; for one days delicate and exquisit Food may be worth ten of ordinary. Now the Nature of Peoples feeding may be estimated by the visible part of their Expence, which is their housing. But such helps of knowing the Value of Lands, I am not yet able to furnish. ||

[CHAPTER X.]

Of the Money of IRELAND. 68

MOney is understood to be the uniform Measure and Rule for the Value of all Commodities. But whether in that sence there be any Money, or such Rule in the World, I know not, much less in *Ireland*, tho most are perswaded that Gold and Silver Money is such. For 1. The proportion of value between pure Gold and fine Silver, alters as the Earth and Industry of Men produce more of one than of the other; that is to say, Gold has been worth but twelve times its own weight in Silver; of late it has been worth fourteen, because more Silver has been gotten. That of Gold proportionably, *i.e.* about twelve times as much Silver has been raised as of Gold, which makes Gold dearer. So there can be but one of the two Metals of Gold and Silver to be a fit matter for Money. Wherefore, if Silver be that one Metal fit for Money; then Gold is but a Commodity very like Money. And as things now stand, Silver only is the matter of Money; and that elsewhere as well as in *Ireland.* ||

2. The value of Silver rises and falls it self; for Men 69
make Vessels of coyned Silver, if they can gain by the Workmanship enough to defray the Destruction of the Coynage, and withal, more than they could expect by employing the same Silver as Money in a way of Trade. Now the Accidents of so doing, make Silver rise and fall, and consequently take from the perfect Aptitude for being an uniform steady Rule and Measure of all other things.

The Mischiefs and Inconveniences hitherto mentioned, are common to all times and places; but in *Ireland*, are more particular; and stand thus[1], *viz.*

A piece of 8 Rials being full 17. penny weight, passeth for 4*s.* 9*d.* if[2] it want but $\frac{1}{2}$ a grain of the weight, tho half a grain of Silver be worth but the $\frac{1}{4}$ of a Farthing, or $\frac{1}{16}$ of a Penny, then it passes for 3 *d* less, *viz.* 4 *s.* 6 *d.* and if it weigh ten grains above 17 *d.* weight, it passes but for 4 *s.* 9 *d.* On the other hand, if it weigh but 12 *d.* weight, it passes nevertheless for 4 *s.* 6 *d.* And if the Silver be course, if not so course, as not to be called Silver, yet still it passes for the same. Moreover, the fineness cannot be determined by common Eyes scarce at all, by the best not within 4 *d.* in an
70 Ounce, || by the Touchstone not within 2 *d.* and by the Test it self not within an half-penny. Lastly, The Scales and Weights differ so much from each other, as what is 4 *s.* 9 *d.* in one House, is but 4 *s.* 6 *d.* in the next, *&* *vice versa.* From whence it comes to pass, that all pieces weighing above 17 *d.* weight, are cull'd out to buy or make pieces of 14 *d.* weight pass for 4 *s.* 6 *d.*

2. Other Species of Coyn, which *pro rata* contain the same quantity of the like Gold and Silver, with the piece of eight Rials, goes in one Species for more, in another for less. What hath been said of the Silver-species, may be said of the Gold-species; and what differences are between Silver and Silver, and between Gold and Gold, is also between Silver and Gold Coyns. So as it becomes a Trade to study and make Advantages of these Irregularities, to the prejudice of the good People, who are taught, that whatever is called Money, is the same, and regular, and uniform, and a just Measure of all Commodities. For whence it hath happened, that all *English* Money which hath a great and deserved Reputation in the World for its intrinsick Goodness, is quite
71 carried away out of *Ireland*, and such Mo-||ney brought instead of it, as these studied Merchants do from time to time bring in for their Advantage upon the Common People, their Credulity and Ignorance.

[1] S, 'is more particular, stand thus.'

[2] 'If' begins a sentence in S.

But Money, that is to say, Silver and Gold, do at this day much decrease in *Ireland*, for the following Reasons.

1. *Ireland, Anno* 1664. did not export to a much greater Value than it imported, *viz.* about 62 M.[1] Since which time there hath been a Law made to prohibit the Importation of great Cattel and Sheep, alive or dead, into *England*[2]; the Value whereof carried into *England* in that very year 1664. was above 150 M. *l.* The which was said to have been done, for that *Ireland* drained away the Money of *England.* Whereas in that very year *England* sent to *Ireland*, but 91 M. less than it received from thence; and yet this small difference was said to be the reason why the Rents of *England* fell $\frac{1}{5}$, that is 1600 M. in 8 Millions. Which was a strange conceit, if they consider farther, That the value of the Cattel alive or dead, which went out of *Ireland* into *England*, was but 132 M. the Hides, Tallow, and Freight whereof were worth about $\frac{1}{2}$ that Money. ||

2. Whereas the Owners of about $\frac{1}{4}$, both of all the real 72
and personal Estate of *Ireland*, do live in *England*, since the business of the several Courts of Claims was finished in *December* 1668. all that belongs to them goes out, but returns not.

3. The gains of the Commissioners of that Court, and of the Farmers of the Revenue of *Ireland*, who live in *England*, have issued out of *Ireland* without returns.

4. A considerable part of the Army of *Ireland* hath been sent into *England*, and yet paid out of *Ireland.*

5. To remit so many great Sums out of *Ireland* into *England*, when all Trade between the said two Kingdoms is prohibited, must be very chargeable; for now the Goods which go out of *Ireland*, in order to furnish the said Sums in *England*, must for Example go into the *Barbados*, and there be sold for Sugars, which brought into *England*, are sold for Money to pay there what *Ireland* owes. Which way being so long, tedious and hazardous, must necessarily so raise the exchange of Money, as we have seen 15 *per Cent.* frequently given, *Anno* 1671. and *Anno* 1672. Altho in truth, exchange

[1] S, 'Ml.'

[2] See note 5, p. 160.

73 can never be naturally || more than the Land and Water-carriage of Money between the two Kingdoms, and the ensurance of the same upon the way, if the Money be alike in both places.

But Men that have not had the faculty of making these Transmissions with dexterity, have chose rather to give 15. *per Cent.* Exchange, as aforesaid, than to put themselves upon the hazard of such undertakings, and the mischief of being disappointed.

Now the extraordinary decrease of Gold and Silver, put Men, whose Affairs were much disturb'd, thereby upon[1] extraordinary Conceits, and some very absurd ones for Remedy, as namely the raising of *Spanish* pieces of Eight, called Cobs in *Ireland*, from 4 *s.* 9 *d.* to 5 or 6 Shillings, which were before about 5 *d.* above the Value of *English*, that is 4 *s.* 4 *d.* *English* Money weighed the same with a Cob called 4 *s.* 9 *d.* For these distracted People thought, that calling their Money by a better Name, did encrease its value[2]

2. They thought that no Man would carry Cobs of 5 *s.* out of *Ireland* into *England*, where they were called but 4 *s.*
74 4 *d.* altho he was necessitated to pay 4 *s.* 4 *d.* in || *England*, and had no other effects to do it with. They thought that

[1] S, 'disturbed thereby, upon.'

[2] Ruding says that in 1667 cobs were bought in England for 4 *s.* 3 *d.* and sold in Ireland for 5 *s.*, which led to attempts to change their value. *Annals*, II. 13—16, also Fabian Philipps's "Expedient to pay the Forces," 4 July, 1667, in *Archaeologia*, XIII. 185, 191. The proposition to raise foreign coin was for some time opposed in London (Carte, II. 342), but on the 31 August, 1672, the royal consent was obtained for raising Portuguese crusadoes to 3 *s.* 10 *d.* for full weight coins. On 12 May, 1673, Essex wrote to Arlington, "we have had severall debates in Councell about ye raising ye value of Spanish money here. There has bin great difference of opinion amongst men of all sorts." *State Papers, Ireland*, Charles II., 333. For his own part, Essex could not see how calling money more will induce men to take it above its intrinsic value, nor how a kingdom can be made to abound with silver save by a favourable balance of trade. Nevertheless he issued proclamations raising coin on the 28 July and the 17 October, 1673, and finally, 26 July, 1675, a proclamation was issued forbiding the exportation of coin. Simon, *Essay*, 52—53, 133—137; *Capel Letters*, 74, 83—89, and Essex's unprinted letters at the Record Office, S. P. Irel., Charles II., 333—334. Cf. also Sir W. Temple, *Advancement of Trade in Ireland*, 22 July, 1673, in his Works (1770), III. 9.

all Men who lived in *England*, would return to their Estates in *Ireland*, rather than pay 15. *per Cent.*[1] for Exchange; not considering, that when Cobs were raised, that Exchange would also rise proportionably. They fancied, that he who sold a Stone of Wooll for two Cobs, call'd 9*s.* when Cobs were rais'd, would sell his Stone of Wooll of 1½ Cob when called 9*s.* Nor did they think how this frivolous conceit would have taken away a proportionable part of all Landlords Estates in *Ireland*. As for Example, those who acted moderately, would have the Money rais'd $\frac{1}{20}$ part, and the $\frac{1}{20}$ part of all the Money of *Ireland*, was then thought to be but about 20,000 *l.* The whole Cash of *Ireland* being then estimated, but[2] 400 M. *l.* whereas the Landlords of *Ireland*, whose Revenue is 800 M. *l. per Annum*, must have lost $\frac{1}{20}$ part of their whole Estates for ever, *viz.* 40 M. *l. per Annum* upon that empty expedient.

But others, no less sensible of the distress of the People, and the obstructions of Trade by reason of the said decay of Bullion, considering that about 600 M. *l.* would drive the Trade of that Kingdom; for || that 300 M. would pay one 75
half years Gale of all the Land; 50 M. would pay ¼ rent of all the Housing, and that 150 M. would more than pay a Weeks expence of all the People of *Ireland*; and that the whole Cash moved chiefly in those Three Circles; They therefore thought to make up their 400 M. *l.* present Cash by a Bank of 200 M. *l.* more, the bottom and support whereof should be Land; for the Lands and Houses of *Ireland* being worth about 8 Millions, whereof 200 M. *l.* was but the $\frac{1}{40}$ part. 'Twas[3] thought easy to find many Fortieth parts so free from Incumbrances or question as to give a being to such a Bank.

Note, that Interest in *Ireland* is 10 *per* Cent, which is a great hinderance to Trade; since the Interest must enflame the price of *Irish* Commodities, and consequently give to other Nations the means of underselling.

[1] Cox, 'is mistaken & ꝑhaps is ye fault of ye Clerk: for one reason why Cobbs should be raysd to 5s is because yt would rayse exs to 20 ꝑ cent or higher, and which ye Ir Nobility & gentry being loath to pay, would rather returne and spend their estates in Ireld.'

[2] S, 'estimated but.'

[3] 1719, 'part, 'twas.'

[CHAPTER XI.]

Of the Trade of IRELAND.

IF it be true, that there are but about 16,000 Families in *Ireland*, who have above one Chimney in their Houses;
76 and || above 180 M. others; It will be easily understood what the Trade of this latter sort can be, who use few Commodities; and those such as almost every one can make and produce. That is to say, Men live in such Cottages as themselves can make in 3 or 4 Days; Eat such Food (Tobacco excepted) as they buy not from others; wear such Cloaths as the Wooll of their own Sheep, spun into Yarn by themselves, doth make; their Shoes, called Brogues, are but $\frac{1}{4}$ so much worth as a Pair of *English* Shoes; nor of more than $\frac{1}{4}$ in real use and value. A Hat costs 20*d.* a Pair of Stockins 6*d.* but a good Shirt near 3*s.* The Taylors work of a Doublet, Breeches and Coat, about 2*s.* 6*d.* In brief, the Victuals of a Man, his Wife, Three Children, and Servant, resolved into Money, may be estimated 3*s.* 6*d.* *per* Week, or 1*d.*[1] *per* Diem. The Cloaths of a Man, 30*s.* *per Ann.* of Children under 16, one with another 15*s.* the House not worth 5*s.* the Building; Fuel costs nothing but fetching. So as the whole Annual expence of such a Family, consisting of 6 in Number, seems to be but about 52 Shillings *per Ann.* each head one with another. So as 950. M. Inhabitants of these Edifices, may spend 2,375 M.*l.* *per Ann.* And the
77 150,000 || who inhabit the 16,000 other Houses, may spend 10*l.* *per Ann.* each one with another, *viz.* One Million and half. So as the whole People of both sorts spend under 4 Millions, whereof $\frac{1}{10}$ part, *viz.* 400 M.*l.* is for Foreign Commodities, Tobacco included, whereof every 1000 Souls spend one Tun *per Ann.* or every 1000 Tobacco-takers, *viz.* People above 15. Years old, spend two Tuns one with

[1] In the margin of S stands 'q' in the hand of the copyist. Petty obviously means 1*d.* per capita per diem.

another: for it appears by the latest accompt of importance, that what is here said, is true to a trifle. From whence I observe by the way, that the King's Revenue, *viis & modis*, being about 200 M. *l. per Ann.* that it is $\frac{1}{20}$ part of the whole Expence; which in some of the *Grecian* Commonwealths was thought too much, although the *Israelites* allowed $\frac{1}{10}$ to the *Levites* only, tho perhaps to defray the whole charge of the Government, the Supremacy amongst that People being then Sacerdotal.

I observe also by the way, that the Lands and Housing of *Ireland* being worth about one Million *per Ann.* that the Labour of the People may be worth three Millions, which is earned by about 750,000 (of the 1,1000 M.) who by their Age and Quality are Fit and Applicable to Corporal La-||bours, 78
and consequently each Labouring Person Earns but 4*s.*[1] *per Ann.* if all Work. Or if each earns 8 *l.* then but half of them work, or all but half their full time, or otherwise in other proportions. But be it one way or the other; I am as certain that the Hands of *Ireland* may Earn a Million *per Ann.* more than they now do, as I am certain that there are 750,000 in *Ireland* who could earn 2 *s.* a week, or 5 *l. per Ann.* one with another, if they had sutable employment, and were kept to their Labour.

I further observe, that if there be naturally but 2000 Impotents in *Ireland*, and that 50 Shillings *per Ann.* doth maintain the poorer sort of People; It follows, that 8,000 *l.*[2] *per Ann.* would amply maintain all the Impotents of *Ireland*, if well apply'd. For other Beggers, as also Thieves, and Rebels, which are but bigger Thieves, are probably but the faults and defects of Government and Discipline[3].

As for the fitness of *Ireland* for Trade, we say as followeth.

1*st.* That *Ireland* consisting of above 18,000 square Miles; it is not one Place with another above 24 Miles from the Sea, because it is 750 Miles about: Wherefore forasmuch

[1] S, '4 l'; 1691, 1719, '4 s.'

[2] A differing estimate above. See note 2, p. 144.

[3] S has a half page blank after 'Discipline.'

79 as the Land-carriage of Gross || that[1] will be easy in such a Country; it is fit for Trade, because the greatest and most profitable part of Trade, and the Imployment of Shipping, depends upon such Goods, *viz.* Metals, Stones, Timber, Grain, Wood, Salt, *&c.*

2dly. Ireland lieth Commodiously for the Trade of the new *American* world; which we see every day to Grow and Flourish.

It lyeth well for sending Butter, Cheese, Beef, Fish, to their proper Markets, which are to the Southward[2], and the Plantations of *America.*

Thus is *Ireland* by Nature fit for Trade, but otherwise very much unprepared for the same; for as hath been often said, the Housing thereof consists of 160 M. nasty Cabbins, in which neither Butter nor Cheese, nor Linnen, Yarn nor Worsted, and I think no other, can be made to the best advantage; chiefly by reason of the Soot and Smoaks annoying the same; as also for the Narrowness and Nastiness of the Place; which cannot be kept Clean nor Safe from Beasts and Vermin, nor from Damps and Musty Stenches, of which[3] all the Eggs laid or kept in those Cabbins do partake.
80 Wherefore to the advancement of Trade, the || reformation of these Cabbins is necessary.

It may also be consider'd, whether the Institution of these following Corporations would not be expedient, *viz.* 1. of Cattel, 2. of Corn, 3. of Fish, 4. of Leather 5. of Wool, 6. of Linnen, 7. of Butter and Cheese, 8. of Metals and Minerals: For unto these, almost all the Commodities exportable out of *Ireland,* may be referred.

It may also be consider'd, whether the Taxing of those Cabbins with Hearth-money be proper, but rather with Days Labour; the former being scarce possible for them to have, but the latter most easy. Insomuch as 'tis more easy for

[1] S omits 'that.'

[2] The market to the north and east had been tested in 1667 by the shipment of live cattle to Rotterdam, but it was found that they could not be delivered there so cheap as the Dutch could be supplied with them from Holstein. Carte, *Ormond,* II. 341.

[3] S omits 'which.'

them to give 40 Days Labour *per Ann.* at seasonable times, than to pay 2*s.* in Silver at a pinch, and just when the Collectors call for it.

The Dyet, Housing and Cloathing of the 16,000 Families abovementioned, is much the same as in *England*: Nor is the *French* Elegance unknown in many of them, nor the *French* and *Latin* Tongues. The latter whereof is very frequent among the poorest *Irish*, and chiefly in *Kerry*, most remote from *Dublin*. ||

The Housing of 160 M. Families, is, as hath been often 81
said, very wretched. But their Cloathing far better than that of the *French* Peasants, or the poor of most other Countreys; which advantage they have from their Wooll, whereof 12 Sheep furnisheth a competency to one of these Families. Which Wool, and the Cloth made of it, doth cost these poor people no less than 50 M. *l. per Ann.* for the dying it; a trade exercised by the Women of the Countrey. Madder, Allum, and Indico, are imported, but the other dying Stuffs they find nearer home, a certain Mud taken out of the Bogs serving them for Copperas, the Rind of several Trees, and Saw-dust, for Galls; as for wild and green Weeds, they find enough, as also of Rhamnus-Berries.

The Diet of these people is Milk, sweet and sower, thick and thin, which also is their Drink in Summer-time, in Winter Small-Beer or Water. But Tobacco taken in short Pipes seldom burnt, seems the pleasure of their Lives, together with Sneezing: Insomuch, that $\frac{2}{7}$ of their Expence in Food, is Tobacco. Their Food is Bread in Cakes, whereof a Penny serves a Week for each; Potatoes from *August* till *May*, Muscles, Cockles and Oysters, near the Sea; || Eggs 82
and Butter made very rancid, by keeping in Bogs. As for Flesh, they seldom eat it[1], notwithstanding the great plenty thereof, unless it be of the smaller Animals, because it is inconvenient for one of these Families to kill a Beef, which they have no convenience to save. So as 'tis easier for them to have a Hen or Rabbet, than a piece of Beef of equal substance.

[1] S omits 'it.'

Their Fewel is Turf in most places; and of late, even where Wood is most plentiful, and to be had for nothing, the cutting and carriage of the Turf being more easy than that of Wood. But[1] to return from whence I digressed, I may say, That the Trade of *Ireland*, among $\frac{19}{22}$ parts of the whole people, is little or nothing, excepting for the Tobacco abovementioned, estimated worth about 50,000 l. for as much as they do not need any Forreign Commodities, nor scarce any thing made out of their own Village. Nor is above $\frac{1}{5}$ part of their Expence other than what their own Family produceth, which Condition and state of living cannot beget Trade.

And now I shall digress again to consider, whether it were better for the Common-wealth to restrain the expence
83 of 150 M. *Optimates* below 10 l. *per Ann.* each; or || to beget a luxury in the 950 M. Plebeians, so as to make them spend, and consequently earn double to what they at present do.

[2]To which I answer in brief, That the one shall encrease the sordidness and squallor of living already too visible in 950 M. Plebeians, with little benefit to the Common Wealth; the other shall increase the splendor, Art and Industry of the 950 M. to the great enrichment of the Common-Wealth.

Again, Why should we be forbid the use of any Foreign Commodity, which our own Hands and Countrey cannot produce, when we can employ our spare Hands and Lands upon such exportable Commodities as will purchase the same, and more.

3. The keeping or lessening of money, is not of that consequence that many guess it to be of. For in most places, especially *Ireland*, nay, *England* it self, the Money of the whole Nation is but about $\frac{1}{10}$ of the Expence of one Year; *viz. Ireland* is thought to have about 400 M. l. in Cash, and to spend about 4 Millions *per Ann.* Wherefore it is very ill-husbandry to double the Cash of the Nation, by destroying half its Wealth; Or to increase the Cash other-
84 wise || than by increasing the Wealth *simul & semel.*

That is, when the Nation hath $\frac{1}{10}$ more Cash, I require it

[1] 'But' begins a paragraph in S. [2] No paragraph in S.

should have $\frac{1}{10}$ more Wealth, if it be possible. For, there may be as well too much money in a Country, as too little[1]. I mean, as to the best advantage of its Trade; onely the Remedy is very easy, it may be soon turn'd into the magnificence of Gold and Silver Vessels.

Lastly, Many think that *Ireland* is much impoverished, or at least the money thereof much exhausted, by reason of Absentees, who are such as having Lands in *Ireland*, do live out of the Kingdom, and do therefore think it just that such, according to former Statutes, should lose their said Estates.

Which Opinion I oppose, as both unjust, inconvenient, and frivolous. For 1st. If a man carry Money or other Effects out of *England* to purchase Lands in *Ireland*, why should not the Rents, Issues and Profits of the same Land return into *England*, with the same Reason that the Money of *England* was diminished to buy it?

2. I[2] suppose $\frac{1}{4}$ of the Land of *Ireland* did belong to the Inhabitants of *England*, and that the same lay all in one
place together; why may not the said quarter of the || whole 85
Land be cut off from the other three sent[3] into *England*, were it possible so to do? and if so, why may not the Rents of the same be actually sent, without prejudice to the other three parts of[4] the Interessors thereof?

3. If all men were bound to spend the Proceed of their Lands upon the Land it self; then as all the Proceed of *Ireland*, ought to be spent in *Ireland*; so all the Proceed of one County of *Ireland*, ought to be spent in the same; of one Barony, in the same Barony; and so Parish and Mannor; and at length it would follow, that every eater ought to avoid what he hath eaten upon the same Turf where the same grew. Moreover, this equal spreading of Wealth would destroy all Splendor and Ornament; for if it were not fit that one place should be more splendid than another, so also that no one man should be greater or richer than another; for if so, then the Wealth, suppose of *Ireland*, being perhaps

[1] Cox, 'It is difficult to prove that there can be too much money in a Kingdome.'

[2] S, 'If suppose.' [3] S, 'and sent.' [4] S, 'or.'

11 Millions, being divided among 1,100 M. people, then no one man having above 10 l. he could Probably build no House worth above 3 l. which would be to leave the face of Beggery upon the whole Nation: And withal such Parity would beget Anarchy and Confusion. ||

86 Of the other Impediment of Trade, the not raising of Money above the value which the generality of the whole World hath of it, that is, the intrinsick value, I have spoken before: And now return to other matters relating to the Trade of *Ireland*.

Having shewn that there is little or no Trade or Commutation of Commodities, where people live so simply, and as it were *exsponte creatis*, as the Inhabitants of 184 M.[1] do live; It follows, that what Trade is in *Ireland* must be found in the 16,000 other Houses of above one Chimney in each, and amongst the Inhabitants of them. Though Trade, properly speaking, be the Commutation of Commodities; that[2] generally speaking, 'tis the way whereby to purchase Riches and Power, the Parents of Pleasure: Not only by getting Commodities out of the Earth and Sea; by ploughing, fishing, Mines, Vecture[3], *&c.* by getting away those Commodities from them, who first got them out of the Earth and Sea, as aforesaid. And not only, or at all encreasing the whole Wealth of the Nation, but ones own former share and proportion of the whole, though diminish'd[4]; that is to say, Supposing the whole Wealth of *Ireland* were 10 Millions, and
87 the Share || of A. was 1000 l. thereof; I say, 'tis commonly more the care of A. to make his 1000 l. 3000, though by lessening the whole Stock 2000 l. than to make the whole Stock 30 Millions, by lessening his own 1000 l. to 300 l.

Now this is the Trade of *Ireland*, and I think of most other places, but exercised in *Ireland* by the following ways, *viz.*

Whereas the Lands of *Ireland* have within 150 years been most of them forfeited, and the Lands of Monasteries have

[1] 1719 inserts 'Hutts.'

[2] 1719, 'yet.' The copyist of S may have misread Petty's 'y^t.'

[3] 1719 omits 'Vecture.'

[4] 1719 omits 'though diminish'd.'

since then fallen into the King's hands, by the dissolution of the said Monasteries, and several Defects found in the Titles, older than that of time; It hath come to pass, that all the said Lands have been granted to several others; some legally and formally, some otherwise; some under one Condition, some under another. So as by several Defects in the said Grants, or by non-performance of Conditions, and many other ways needless to enumerate, the King in strictness may find a Title to the Estates of many men who have been long in possession of their respective Holdings, (tho some more, some less, some upon better, and some upon worser grounds.) A principal Trade in *Ireland*, to find out these || Flaws and 88
Defects, to procure Commission for such Inquiries. And a Branch of this Trade, is to give to such seekers flattering and delusive Informations to bring on other Designs; and withal, prevail with persons conversant with the Higher Powers, to give Grants of these Discoveries, and thereupon, right or wrong to vex the Possessors, at least into such a Composition, as may be of profit to the Prosecutors. Whereby it falls out, that the time of all the persons exercised *pro & contra* in these matters, who do only take from one another like Gamesters (the Lawyers taking from both) is lost, without advancing at all the Publick Wealth. Now this is no Trade, but a Calamity upon the Nation.

2. Whereas the Branches of the Publick Revenue being manifold, and the Accompts of the same vast and numerous, and the Laws, with the Cases and Accidents relating to the same, intricate and new; but chiefly the Officers employed about the Premises, such as could make Friends for their Places, whether Persons of Skill, Experience and Trustiness, or not; It hath come to pass, even in *Ireland*, in former times, that Principal Officers of the Exchequer have represented the State of the Publick || Treasury near 200 M. l. 89
differently from each other[1]: So as new men have been admitted to take the whole to farm, who expected vast Advantages, by mending and clearing what others had marr'd and confounded, though they had still their Places

[1] Cf. Carte's *Ormond*, II. 368—371.

and Perquisites notwithstanding: And in this[1] case the people thought fit to pay any thing that was required, rather than to pass the Fire of this Purgatory, even tho they need no burning.

This and other Practices of Farming, taken with the whole Doctrine of Defalcations, hath been a great Trade in *Ireland*, but a Calamity on the people who have paid great Wages to them that have made Faults, but three times greater to those who would but undertake to mend them, tho indeed they could not.

A Third great Trade and Calamity to the people of *Ireland*, hath been the Gains made by the aforementioned Difference, Confusion, and badness of Coins, exorbitant Exchange, and Interest of Money, all following also from the Premises.

A Fourth Calamity is implicating poor Work-men, and trapanning them into Crimes, Indictments, Bishops-Courts, *&c.* feigning and compounding of Trespasses, not without making benefit by the Office of Justice of Peace. ||

90 A Fifth may be from the manner of making Sheriffs, the execution of their Offices, Accompts in the Exchequer, *&c.*

A Sixth, from raising Moneys at the Assizes, by Authority of the Grand Juries, but raising too much, and in spending or not spending what was to be raised.

None of these Six Trades do add any more to the Common-wealth than Gamesters, and even such of them as play with false Dice, do to the Common-Stock of the whole Number.

And in these Trades 'tis thought $\frac{1}{3}$ of those who inhabit the aforementioned 16,000 Houses, do exercise themselves, and are the Locusts and Catterpillars of the Common-wealth, as the Inhabitants of the other 184 M. Cottages are the untilled part of the same. Wherefore it remains to see what Trade is to be found among the rest; which I take to be as followeth, *viz.*

1. In Domestick Wealth: Of which sort is building fine

[1] S omits 'this.'

Houses and Gardens, Orchards, Groves, Inns, Mills, Churches, Bridges, High Ways, Causeys; as also Furniture for Houses, Coaches, *&c.* In which kind I guess the Improvement of *Ireland* has since the Year 1652.[1] 1673. advanc'd || from one 91
to four, and I think to a better state than before 1641. that is, than perhaps ever it yet was.

The Foreign Trade, if you will believe the Accompts of Customs, *Ann.* 1657. and now, hath been advanced from one to seven, but in reality, I think, from one to two: For the Customs yielded *Ann.* 1656. clear under 12,000 *l.* but were within a year or two, let for above three times the sum, but are now at about 80,000 intrinsecally.

But to speak more clearly and Authentically upon this Subject, I shall insert the following Tables of exported and imported Commodities, and from them make the subnexed Observations, *viz.*

The TABLES[2].

1. THAT the Customs, managed by the States-Officers, yielded *Anno* 1657. under 12,000 *l.* but was farm'd *Ann.* 1658. for above thrice that Sum.

2. That the Stock which drives the Foreign Trade of *Ireland*, doth near half || of it belong to those who live out of 92
Ireland.

3. That *Ann.* 1664. before the Cattel-Statute, $\frac{3}{4}$ of the *Ireland* Foreign Trade was with *England*, but now not $\frac{1}{4}$ part of the same.

4. That the Manufacture bestowed upon a years Exportation out of *Ireland*, is not worth above 8000 *l.*

5. That because more eatables were exported *Anno* 1664. than 1641. And more Manufactures 1641. than *Ann.* 1664.

[1] S, 1719, 'to.'

[2] The promised tables, omitted from S and from both editions, have not been recovered.

It follows, there were more people in *Ireland*, *Ann.* 1641. than 1664. and in that proportion as was formerly mention'd[1].

6. That the Exportations appear more worth than the Importations, excepting that the Accompts of the former are more true, but of the latter very conjectural, and probably less than the Truth. ||

---

93 ## [CHAPTER XII.]

Of the Religion, Diet, Cloaths, Language, Manners, and Interest of the several present Inhabitants of IRELAND.

WE said, that of the 1100 M. Inhabitants of *Ireland*, about 800 M. of them were *Irish*; and that above 600 M. of them lived very simply in the Cabbins aforemention'd[2]. Wherefore I shall in the first place describe the Religion, Diet, *&c.* of these, being the major part of the whole; not wholly omitting some of the other species also.

The Religion of these poorer *Irish*, is called *Roman Catholick*, whose Head is the Pope of *Rome*, from whence they are properly enough called *Papists*. This Religion is well known in the World, both by the Books of their Divines, and the Worship in their Churches: wherefore I confine my self to what I think peculiar to these *Irish*. And first, I observe, that the Priests among them are of small Learning; but are thought by their Flocks to have much, because they can speak Latin more or less; and can often out-talk in
94 Latin those who Dispute with them. So as they are || thereby thought both more Orthodox and Able than their Antagonists.

Their Reading in Latin is the Lives of the Saints, and Fabulous Stories of their Country. But the Superior Learning among them, is the Philosophy of the Schools, and the Genealogies of their Ancestors. Both which look like what St. *Paul* hath Condemned[3].

[1] P. 149. [2] P. 142. [3] 1 Tim. i. 4.

The Priests are chosen for the most part out of old *Irish* Gentry; and thereby influence the People, as well by their Interest as their Office.

Their Preaching seems rather Bugbearing of their flocks with dreadful Stories, than persuading them by Reason, or the Scriptures. They have an incredible Opinion of the Pope and his Sanctity, of the happiness of those who can obtain his Blessing at the third or fourth hand. Only some few, who have lately been abroad, have gotten so far, as to talk of a difference between the Interest of the Court of *Rome*, and the Doctrine of the Church. The Common Priests have few of them been out of *Ireland*; and those who have, were bred in Covents, or[1] made Friars for the most part, and have humble Opinions of the *English* and Protestants, and of the mis-||chiefs of setting up Manufactures, and 95
introducing of Trade. They also comfort their Flocks, partly by Prophecies of their Restoration to their Ancient Estates and Liberties, which the abler sort of them fetch from what the Prophets of the Old-Testament have delivered by way of God's Promise to restore the *Jews*, and the Kingdom to *Israel*. They make little esteem of an Oath upon a Protestant Bible, but will more devoutly take up a Stone, and swear upon it, calling it a Book, than by the said Book of Books, the Bible. But of all Oaths, they think themselves at much liberty to take a Land-Oath, as they call it: Which is an Oath to prove a forg'd Deed, a Possession, Livery or Seisin, payment of Rents, *&c.* in order to recover for their Countrey-men the Lands which they had forfeited. They have a great Opinion of Holy-Wells, Rocks, and Caves, which have been the reputed Cells and Receptacles of men reputed Saints. They do not much fear Death, if it be upon a Tree, unto which, or the Gallows, they will go upon their Knees toward it, from the place they can first see it. They confess nothing at their Executions, though never so guilty. In brief, there is much Superstition among them, but formerly much || more than is now; for as 96

[1] S, 'of.'

much as by the Conversation of Protestants, they become asham'd of their ridiculous Practices, which are not *de fide.* As for the Richer and better-educated sort of them, they are such Catholicks as are in other places. The Poor, in adhering to their Religion, which is rather a Custom than a Dogma amongst them, They seem rather to obey their Grandees, old Landlords, and the Heads of their Septes and Clans, than God. For when these were under Clouds, transported into *Spain*, and transplanted into *Connaught*, and disabled to serve them as formerly, about the year 1656, when the Adventurers and Soldiers appeared to be their Landlords and Patrons, they were observ'd to have been forward enough to relax the stiffness of their pertinacity to the Pope, and his Impositions. *Lastly*, Among the better sort of them, many think less of the Pope's Power in Temporals, as they call it, than formerly; and begin to say, that the Supremacy, even in Spirituals, lies rather in the Church diffusive, and in qualified General-Councils, than in the Pope alone, or than in the Pope and his Cardinals, or other *Juncto.*

The Religion of the Protestants in *Ireland*, is the same
97 with the Church of *Eng-*||*land* in Doctrine, only they differ in Discipline thus, *viz.*

The Legal Protestants hold the Power of the Church to be in the King, and that Bishops and Arch-Bishops, with their Clerks, are the best way of adjusting that Power under him. The Presbyterians would have the same thing done, and perhaps more, by Classes of Presbyters National and Provincial. The Independents would have all Christian Congregations independent from each other. The *Anabaptists* are Independent in Discipline, and differ from all those aforemention'd in the Baptism of Infants, and in the inward and spiritual Signification of that Ordinance. The Quakers salute not by uncovering the Head, speak to one another in the second Person, and singular Number; as for Magistracy and Arms, they seem to hold with the *Anabaptists* of *Germany* and *Holland*; they pretend to a possibility of perfection, like the Papists; as for other

Tenents, 'tis hard to fix them, or to understand what things they mean by their Words.

The Diet of the poorer *Irish*, is what was before discoursed in the Chapter[1]. ||

The Cloathing is a narrow sort of Frieze, of about twenty 98
Inches broad, whereof two foot, call'd a Bandle, is worth from 3½ to 18*d.* Of this, Seventeen Bandles make a Man's Suit, and twelve make a Cloak. According to which Measures and Proportions, and the number of People who wear this Stuff, it seems, that near thrice as much Wooll is spent in *Ireland*, as exported; whereas others have thought quite contrary, that is, that the exported Wooll is triple in quantity to what is spent at home.

As for the Manners of the *Irish*, I deduce them from their Original Constitutions of Body, and from the Air; next from their ordinary Food; next from their Condition of Estate and Liberty, and from the Influence of their Governours and Teachers; and lastly, from their Ancient Customs, which affect as well their Consciences as their Nature. For their Shape, Stature, Colour, and Complexion, I see nothing in them inferior to any other People, nor any enormous predominancy of any humour.

[2]Their Lazing seems to me to proceed rather from want of Imployment and Encouragement to Work[3], than from the
na-||tural abundance of Flegm in their Bowels and Blood; 99
for what need they to Work, who can content themselves with *Potato's*, whereof the Labour of one Man can feed forty; and with Milk, whereof one Cow will, in Summer time, give meat and drink enough for three Men, when they can every where gather Cockles, Oysters, Muscles, Crabs, *&c.* with Boats, Nets, Angles, or the Art of Fishing; can build an House in three days? And why should they desire to fare better, tho with more Labour, when they are taught, that this way of living is more like the[4] Patriarchs of old,

[1] Chapter XI. p. 191.

[2] No paragraph in S.

[3] Cf. the similar opinion of Sir W. Temple, *Observations upon the United Provinces* (1673), p. 188, also Temple's *Works* (1770), I. 184.

[4] S omits 'the.'

and the Saints of later times, by whose Prayers and Merits they are to be reliev'd, and whose Examples they are therefore to follow? And why should they breed more Cattel, since 'tis Penal to import them into *England?* Why should they raise more Commodities, since there are not Merchants sufficiently Stock'd to take them of them, nor provided with other more pleasing foreign Commodities, to give in Exchange for them? And how should Merchants have Stock, since Trade is prohibited and fetter'd by the Statutes of *England?* And why should Men endeavour to get Estates,
100 where the Legislative Power is not agreed upon; and || where
Tricks and Words destroy natural Right and Property?

They are accused also of much Treachery, Falseness, and Thievery; none of all which, I conceive, is natural to them; for as to Treachery, they are made believe, that they all shall flourish again, after some time; wherefore they will not really submit to those whom they hope to have their Servants; nor will they declare so much, but say the contrary, for their present ease, which is all the Treachery I have observed; for they have in their hearts, not only a grudging to see their old Proprieties enjoyed by Foreigners, but a persuasion they shall be shortly restor'd. As for Thievery, it is affixt to all thin-peopled Countries, such as *Ireland* is, where there cannot be many Eyes to prevent such Crimes; and where what is stolen, is easily hidden and eaten, and where 'tis easy to burn the House, or violate the Persons of those who prosecute these Crimes, and where thin-peopled Countries are govern'd by the Laws that were made and first fitted to thick-peopled Countries; and where matter of small moment and value must be try'd, with all the formalities which belong
101 to the highest Causes. In this case there || must be thieving,
where is withal, neither encouragement, nor method, nor means for Labouring, nor Provision for Impotents.

As for the Interest of these poorer *Irish*, it is manifestly to be transmuted into *England*, so to reform and qualify their housing, as that *English* Women may be content to be their Wives, to decline their Language, which continues a sensible distinction, being not now necessary;

which makes those who do not understand it, suspect, that what is spoken in it, is to their prejudice. It is their Interest to deal with the *English*, for Leases, for[1] Time, and upon clear Conditions, which being perform'd they are absolute Freemen, rather than to stand always liable to the humour and caprice of their Landlords, and to have every thing taken from them, which he pleases to fancy. It is their Interest, that he[2] is well-pleased with their Obedience to them, when they see and know upon whose Care and Conduct their well-being depends, who have Power over their Lands and Estates. Then, to believe a Man at *Rome* has Power in all these last mentioned Particulars in this World, and can make them eternally happy or miserable hereafter, 'tis || their Interest to joyn with them, and follow their 102
Example, who have brought Arts, Civility, and Freedom into their Country.

On the contrary, What did they ever get by accompanying their Lords into Rebellion against the *English?* What should they have gotten if the late Rebellion had absolutely succeeded, but a more absolute Servitude? And when it fail'd, these poor People have lost all their Estates, and their Leaders encreas'd theirs, and enjoy'd the very Land which their Leaders caus'd them to lose. The poorest now in *Ireland* ride on Horse-back, when heretofore the best ran on foot like Animals. They wear better Cloaths than ever; the Gentry have better Breeding, and the generality of the *Plebeians* more Money and Freedom. ||

---

[1] S, 'English for leases for.'

[2] S omits 'he.' The passage may be made approximately intelligible: 'It is [rather] their interest that he is well-pleased with their Obedience to *him*, when [etc. to] estates, than to believe [etc. to] hereafter. 'Tis their interest' [etc.].

103 ## [CHAPTER XIII.]

Several Miscellany Remarks and Intimations concerning Ireland, *and the several matters aforementioned.*

WIthout recourse to the Authority of Story, but rather diligently observing the Law and Course of Nature, I conjecture, that whatever is fabled of the *Phœnicians, Scythians, Biscayers, &c.* their first Inhabiting of *Ireland*; that the places near *Carrickfergus* were first peopled, and that with those, who came from the parts of *Scotland* opposite thereunto[1]. For that *Ireland* was planted by some body in *Cæsar*'s time, is most certain. That the Art of Navigation was not before *Cæsar*'s time so well understood and practis'd, as to bring Men from any other Part of the World thither, save from *Great Britain*: That from St. *Davids-head* in *South-Wales*, and from *Holy-head* in *North-Wales*, *Ireland* is not clearly at any time discern'd, nor often at all. That the Inhabitants of those two *British* Head-lands had neither Boats fit to pass that Sea, is most probable. But that *Carrickfergus* may be always seen from *Scotland*, is well
104 known; and that a small || Boat may Row over in three or four hours, is experienc'd. That the Language of those Parts differ very little. That the Country about *Carrickfergus* is far better than that of *Scotland* opposite. That the chief Bishops Seat of *Ireland*, and probably the first, is near those Parts, are all notorious Truths. From all which 'tis more probable, that *Ireland* was first Peopled from *Scotland*[2], than all the other remote Parts aforementioned.

It hath been much observed, That the Lieutenants and Chancellors of *Ireland* have often been at variance; the

[1] Cox, 'It is allowed by all antiquarys y^{t} Scotland was peopled from Ireland & therefore calld Scotia minor: And ye names of (firbolg or Belgi) and (Tuah-de-danaan or Damnonii) which inhabited Cornwall and other ꝑtes of England doe manifest y^{t} those people wch first dwelt in Ireland came from Engld.'

[2] 1719 omits 'than...aforementioned.'

reason whereof seems to be at their Powers, and[1] too near an *Equilibrium*[2]; for the Lieutenant Commands an Army perhaps of 3000, and the Chancellor makes 900 Justices of Peace, who make 2500 Constables, which are the Civil Sword, who Act in times of Peace, and every where, and in all matters; whereas the Army acts only upon rare occasions, and are more Mercenary Men. So as the Civil-Sword seems of far more extent and effect than the Military-Sword.

The Lieutenant disposes perhaps of four or five hundred Places and Imployments; but the Chancellor, of the said
nine hundred || Justices of Peace, and several others. The 105
Lieutenant can hurt very few Persons, who do not depend upon the favour of Imployments; but the Chancellor can affect all Men, of Estates and Dealing in the World, by the Power of his Court, and by the Harmony of his own Will with the King's Conscience.

The Lieutenant is for the most part a Stranger to *Ireland*; but the Chancellor seldom such, but a Person of great Family and Acquaintance. Moreover, all the Lieutenants, Deputies, and Lords Justices, that have been these 150 years, have not, one with another, continued two years in the Office; but the Chancellors have much more, and are seldom remov'd but by Death, and General Revolutions. The Chancellor has ordinarily some other Dignity and Office annex'd, for they be often Eminent Prelates and Church-men; but the Lieutenant is confin'd to Temporals. The Chancellor is Speaker in Parliament, and by keeping the Seal, can check the Lieutenant in many cases. The Chancellors are bred to Eloquence and Arguing; the breeding of a Lieutenant is casual. ||

[1] So in S. Conjectural emendation, 'be that their Powers are.' 1719, 'be their Powers were.'

[2] Cox, 'It is not soe y^{t} ye Chanr has an equall power to ye Ld Leiv^{t}: nor did our Author ascribe it to him for any other cause then to ridicule ye exorbitant power y^{t} he thought was usd by that court to his prejudice in several causes which occasioned him thus to chant

Heu ruimus cives, ingens succure Michael
Nam tu Archangelus atque Archepiscopus es.'

On Petty's trouble with 'the two chanceries' see Fitzmaurice, 169—172.

106 Men that bring great Estates into *Ireland*, do not encrease them proportionably with them who come over with nothing. Not to quote the Examples hereof on both sides, the reason seems not to be very abstruse, *viz.*[1]

The Language of *Ireland* is like that of the *North* of *Scotland*, in many things like the *Welch* and *Manques*; but in *Ireland* the *Fingallians* speak neither *English*, *Irish*, nor *Welch*; and the People about *Wexford*, tho they agree in a Language differing from *English*, *Welch*, and *Irish*, yet 'tis not the same with that of the *Fingalians* near *Dublin*. Both these two sorts of People are honest and laborious Members of the *Kingdom*.

The *Irish* Language, and the *Welch*, as also all Languages that have not been the Languages of flourishing Empires, wherein were many Things, many Notions and Fancies, both Poetical and Philosophical, hath but few words; and all the names of Artificial things brought into use, since the Empire of these Linguists ceased, are expressed in the language of their Conquerors, by altering the Termination and Accents only. ||

107 *Ireland* is now divided into Provinces, Counties, Baronies, Parishes, and Farm-lands, and those, so as that they may be, and have been Geometrically delineated; but formerly it was not so, but the Country was called by the names of the Lords who governed the People. For as a Territory bounded by Bogs, is greater or lesser as the Bog is more dry and passible, or otherwise: So the Country of a Grandee or Tierne in *Ireland*, became greater or lesser as his Forces waxed or weaned[2]; for where was a large Castle and Garison, there the Jurisdiction was also large.

[3]And when these Grandees came to make peace, and parts one with another, the limits of their Land-agreements were no lines Geometrically drawn; but if the Rain fell one way, then the Land whereon it fell, did belong to A. if the other way, to B. *&c.*

As to their Town-lands, Plough-lands, Colps, Gneeres,

[1] In the margin of S, 'q'; after 'viz.' several lines blank.
[2] S, 'waned.'
[3] No paragraph in S.

Bullibos, Ballibelaghs, Two's, Horsmens, Beds[1], *&c.* they are all at this day become unequal both in Quantity and Value, having been made upon grounds which are now Obsolete and Antiquated. ||

For sometimes lands were divided by what certain 108
Societies of men held, which I conceive were Town-lands or Tythings.

Sometimes by Plow-lands[2], viz. such a ——— of Lands as contained enough of every species of Land Arrable, Meadow, and Pasture, Mountain, Turf-bog, Wood, *&c.* as serv'd for the whole Use of man, especially of the Owner of such a Plow-land.

[3]Sometimes by the Share or Proportion of Land, which an Undertaker would engage to plant and defend according to Articles.

[3]Sometimes by the Share which each Servitor[4] had given him in reward for his Service, after a Rebellion or Insurrection.

Sometimes by what belonged to the Cell of some Religious Man or Men. But now all the Lands are Geometrically divided, and that without abolishing the Ancient Denominations[5] and Divisions abovementioned. So that it is yet wanting to prevent the various spelling of Names not understood, that some both[6] comprehending the Names of all publick Denominations according as they are spelled in the latest Grants, should be set out by Authority[7] to determine the || same for the time to come. And that where the same 109

[1] S, 'horsemens-beds.'

[2] A term so indefinite that by acts of 4, 8 and 9 Anne a grand jury was to determine whether a specific parish had plough-lands, and was obliged in consequence to work the roads, or not. Mountmorres, *Hist. of the Irish Parliament*, II. 126—127.

[3] In S these paragraphs are transposed.

[4] Prendergast, *Cromwellian Settlement*, 2d. ed., 44 n.

[5] From this point, where 'Denominations' is corrected from 'Demesnes,' to the end of the MS. occasional blanks left by the copyist of S are filled in by a hand which I take to be Petty's.

[6] S, 'book.'

[7] 1719, 'that some Person or Persons who can rightly comprehend the names of all publick Denominations according as they are spelled in the atest Grants, should be appointed by Authority.'

Land hath other Names, or hath been spelled with other Conscription of Letters or Syllables, that the same be mentioned with an *alias*. Where the publick and new authenticated Denominations[1] is part of a greater antiquated Denomination, that it be so expressed, as by being called the *East*, *West*, *South* or *North* part thereof. And if the said Denomination comprehend several obsolete or inconsiderable Parcels, that the same be expressed likewise.

The last Clause of the Explanatory Act, enabled men to put new Names on their respective Lands, instead of those uncouth, unintelligible ones yet upon them. And it would not be amiss if the significant part of the *Irish* Names were interpreted, where they are not, or cannot be abolished[2]. ||

110 SOME have thought that little Shipping belongs to *Ireland*, by the great Policy of the *English*, who (as they wittily expressed it) would keep the Chain or Draw-Bridge between both Kingdoms, on the *English* side: But I never perceived any Impediment of Building, or having Ships in *Ireland*, but mens own indisposition thereunto, either for not having Stock for so chargeable a Work, or not having Workmen of sorts enough to fit out a Ship in all particulars; as for that they could hire Ships cheaper from the *Dutch*, than to build them; or, that the *Irish* had rather eat Potatos and Milk on dry Land, than contest with the Wind and Waves with better Food; or that there is not encouragement, to a full Employment, for an able Ship-wright to reside in *Ireland*. Nevertheless at this day there belongs to several Ports of *Ireland* Vessels between 10 and 200 Tuns, about 8000 Tuns of several sorts and Sizes: And there are Five Light-Houses erected for the safety of sailing upon the Coasts.

[1] S, 'denomination.'

[2] S, 'Although I know almost nothing of the Irish Tongue, yet I have collected the following Words, by the composure of which one with another the Names of most lands in Ireland are constituted, vizt.

The Dictionary.'

This paragraph, not printed in A or B, is followed in S by a large blank space.

Concerning the *Ambergreece*, taken upon the *Western* Coasts of *Ireland*, I could ne-||ver receive any clear satis- 111
faction, neither of its Odor, nor any other Vertue, nor what use was or could be made of that Stuff which has been so call'd, which is of several Appearances.

What is said of the Herb *Mackenbory*[1], is fabulous, only that 'tis a Tythemal, which will purge furiously, and of which there are vast quantities in that part of *Kerry* call'd *Desmond*, where the *Arbutus*-Tree groweth in great numbers and beauty.

There be in *Ireland* not ten Iron Furnaces[2], but above 20 Forges and Bloomeries, and but one Lead-work, which was ever wrought, tho many in view, which the pretended Patents of them have hindred the working of. There is also a place in *Kerry*, fit for one Allum-work, attempted, but not fully proceeded upon[3].

There are in the *West* of *Ireland*, about 20 Gentlemen, who have engaged in the *Pilchard*-fishing, and have among them all about 160 Saynes, wherewith they sometimes take about 4000 Hogsheads of *Pilchards per Ann.* worth about 10,000 *l.* *Cork*, *Kingsale*, and *Bantry* are the best places for eating of Fresh-Fish, tho *Dublin* be not, or need not be ill supplied with the same. ||

The Clothing-Trade is not arrived to what it was before 112
the late Rebellion[4]. And the Art of making the excellent, thick, spungy, warm Coverlets, seems to be lost, and not yet recovered.

Near *Colrane* is a *Salmon*-Fishing, where several Tuns[5] of *Salmon* have been taken at one Draught, and in one Season[6].

The *English* in *Ireland* before *Henry* the VII's time,

1 S, 'Mackenbuoy.' The last three letters added in Petty's hand.

2 Fitzmaurice says that Petty had iron and *copper* works at Kenmare. P. 149.

3 'Petty in his writings makes mention of Allum Works having been formerly erected in this county. But in what particular part of it I could never learn.' Charles Smith, *Antient and present State of the County of Kerry* (1758), p. 398.

4 Cox, 'That ye Clothing Trade is not arrived to w^{t} it was before ye rebellion, is certainly a mistake now, what ever it was in 1672.'

5 S, 'where......Tuns.'

6 S, 'and......in one season.'

lived in *Ireland* as the *Europians* do in *America*, or as several Nations do now upon the same Continent; so as an *English-man* was not punishable for killing an *Irish-man*, and they were governed by different Laws; the *Irish* by the *Brehan*-Law, and the *English* there by the Laws of *England*.

Registers of Burials, Births and Marriages, are not yet kept in *Ireland*, though of late begun in *Dublin*, but imperfectly[1].

English in *Ireland*, growing poor and discontented, degenerate into *Irish*; & *vice versa*; *Irish*, growing into Wealth and Favour, reconcile to the *English*.

Eleven *Irish* Miles make 14 *English*, according to the proportion of the *Irish* Perch of 21 feet, to the *English* of 16½. ||

113 The admeasurement of Land in *Ireland*, hath hitherto been made with a Circumferencer, with a Needle of 3⅓ long, as the most convenient Proportion; but 'twill be henceforth better done by the help of some old Geometrical Theoremes, joyn'd with this new property of a Circle, demonstrated by Dr. *R. Wood*[2].

The DIAGRAM[3].

ALtho the *Protestants* of *Ireland*, be to *Papists*, as three to eight; yet, because the former live in Cities and Towns, and the *Scots* live all in and about five of the 32 Counties of *Ireland*; It seems, in other open Counties, and without the Corporations, that the *Irish* and *Papists* are twenty to one. ||

---

[1] See the Note to the *Observations upon the Dublin Bills*.

[2] Robert Wood was born at Pepper Harrow near Godalming, Surrey, about 1622. He was educated at Eton and at New Inn Hall, Oxford, and became B.A. of Merton College in 1647. He was a parliamentary fellow of Lincoln, a 'retainer' of Henry Cromwell in Ireland and a frequenter of the Rota club. It is therefore probable that Petty and he had been long acquainted. He became mathematical master at Christ's Hospital School, and subsequently accountant general of revenue in Ireland, and contributed several papers to the *Philos. Trans.* Wood, *Athenæ Oxon.*, II. 780; Burroughs, *Register*, 508; Foster, *Alumni Oxon.*; Fitzmaurice, 264. Since Petty failed to give the promised diagram "it is not known what particular quality of the circle is here referred to as demonstrated by" Wood.—General Larcom in Petty's *Hist. of the Down Survey*, 323.

[3] In S half a page is left blank, apparently for the insertion of the diagram.

REPORT

FROM THE

COUNCIL OF TRADE

1676.

NOTE ON THE "REPORT FROM THE COUNCIL OF TRADE."

To the laborious conscientiousness of Essex as Lord Lieutenant of Ireland we are indebted, indirectly, both for the Report from the Council of Trade and for its nearest fellow, Sir William Temple's Essay upon the Advancement of Trade in Ireland. Since the Report was but a summary of the unpublished Political Anatomy, in connection with which alone it has since been printed, it calls for no extended comment.

A MS. copy of the Report, apparently transmitted by Essex to Arlington, is at the Record Office[1]. Another copy of greater personal interest, is in the Pepys collection of J. Eliot Hodgkin, Esq., of Childwall, Richmond on Thames. This copy was given by Petty to Pepys and remained in the possession of Pepys' descendants until it was acquired by Mr Hodgkin in 1889[2]. By his kind permission both Petty's autograph corrections and the significant divergences of the MS. ('H') from the printed version are here noted.

[1] *State Papers, Ireland*, Charles II., vol. 337.

[2] Cf. *Fifteenth Report Hist. MSS. Com., appendix, pt.* II., p. 317, also pp. 2, 153, 175, 176, 180, 181.

A Report from the Council of Trade 114
in *Ireland*, to the Lord Lieutenant and Council, which was drawn by Sir *William Petty*.

I*N Obedience to your Lordship's Act of Council, of* January
the 20*th.* 1675. *we have spent several days in considering*
how, as well the Wealth of this Kingdom in general, as the
Money thereof in particular may be increased. And in order
thereunto, we have first set down to the best of our knowledge
the state of this Kingdom in reference to Trade. Secondly,
We have noted such Inferences from the same, as do shew the
several Causes of the smalness of Trade, want of Money, and
the general Poverty of this Nation. And in the last place, we
have offered such general Remedies and Expedients, in the
respective Cases, as may be obtained and practised, without any
new Law to be made in Ireland. *And we are ready so to*
inlarge upon the Branches we have || *offered, as to make such of* 115
our Proposals practicable, as your Lordships shall please to
select and approve of for that purpose.

March the 25th. 1676.

Considerations relating to the Improvement of IRELAND.

1. THE whole Territory of *Ireland* consists of about 12 Millions of Acres (*English* Measure) of Arrable Meadow, and good Pasture Land; with about two Millions of Rocky, Boggy, and Scrubby Pasture, commonly call'd Unprofitable, (tho not altogether such): The rest being absolute Boggs, Loughs, Rocks, Sands, Strands, Rivers and High-ways, *&c.* Of all which, several Lands, the yearly Rent (comprehending Their Majesties Quit-Rents, Tythes and Tenants Improvements) is supposed to be about 900,000*l.* and worth to be purchased at[1] Nine Millions.

2. The value of all the Housing in *Ireland*, which have one or more Chimneys in them, (excluding all Cabbins which have none) is supposed to be Two Millions and a half. ||

116 3. The Cattel and Live-Stock, Three Millions.

4. Corn, Furniture, Merchandise, Shipping, *&c.* about One Million.

5. The Coyned and Currant Money, now running in Trade, is between 300, and 350,000*l.*[2] or the 50th part of the value of the whole Kingdom, which we suppose to be about 16 Millions.

6. The number of people in *Ireland* is about 1100,000[3], *viz*, Three Hundred Thousand *English*, *Scotch*, and *Welch Protestants*, and 800,000 *Papists*, whereof ¼th are Children unfit for Labour, and about 75,000 of the Remainder are, by reason of their Quality and Estates, above the necessity of Corporal Labour; so as there remains 750,000 Labouring Men and Women, 500,000 whereof do perform the present Work of the Nation.

7. The said 1100,000 people do live in about 200,000 Families or Houses, whereof there are but about 16,000 which have more than one Chimney in each; and about

[1] H omits 'at.'
[2] A lower estimate than that made in 1672. See p. 187.
[3] H had '300,000,' altered by Petty to '1,1001000.'

24,000 which have but one; all the other Houses, being 160,000, are wretched nasty Cabbins, without Chimney, Window or Door shut, and worse than those of the Savage *Americans*, and wholly unfit for the || making Merchantable 117
Butter, Cheese, or the Manufactures of Woollen, Linnen or Leather.

8. The Houses within the City and Liberties of *Dublin*, are under 5,000[1], *viz.* in the City 1150. And the Ale-Houses within the same about 1200. And it seems, that in other Corporations and Countrey Towns, the proportion of Ale-Houses is yet greater than in *Dublin*, *viz.* about $\frac{1}{3}$ of the whole.

9. The Counties, Baronies and Parishes, of *Ireland*, are now become marvellously unequal, so as some are twenty times as big as others, the County of *Cork* seeming in respect of people and Parishes to be $\frac{1}{8}$th of the whole Kingdom, and other Counties not being above the 20th part of the County of *Cork*; It hath been found very difficult to get fit persons for Sheriffs, and Juries; and the often holding of Assizes and Quarter-Sessions in the said smaller Counties, hath been found an unnecessary burthen upon them.

10. There are now in *Ireland* 32 Counties, 252 Baronies, and 2278 Parishes; so as the number of Sheriffs, and Sub-Sheriffs, Sheriff-Bailiffs, High and Petty-Constables, are about three thousand Persons, whereof || not above $\frac{1}{10}$ are *English* 118
or *Protestants*. So as the remainder (being about 2700) are *Irish Papists*, and are the Civil Militia of this Kingdom, and have the executing of all Decrees of Courts, and of Justices of the Peaces Warrants.

11. This Civil Militia, and the rest of the *Irish Papists* being about 800,000, are influenced and guided by about 3000 Priests and Fryars, and they governed by their Bishops and Superiors, who are for the most part, of the Old *Irish* Gentry, men of Foreign Education, and who depend upon Foreign Princes and Prelates, for Benefices and Preferments.

12. The *Irish Papists* (besides Sundays and the 29

[1] Later estimates of the houses in Dublin are made in the *Observations* and the *Further Observations upon the Dublin Bills.*

Holidays appointed by the Law) do one place with another, observe about 24 days more in the year, in which they do no Corporal Labour, so as they have but about 266 Working-days; whereas Protestants not strictly observing all the Legal Holy-days, by a total forbearing of Labour, have in effect 300 Working-days in the year, that is, 34 days more than the Papists, or at least five of six days in each, or $\frac{1}{10}$ part of the whole year.

13. The expence of the whole people of *Ireland* is about
119 four Millions *per Ann.* ‖ the $\frac{1}{50}$ part whereof being 80,000 *l.* and the Quarter of Annual House-Rent[1] being about 60,000*l.* together with 450,000 *l.* more, being the value of half a years Rent, Tythes and Quit-Rent, do make 590,000 l. as that sum of Money which will compleatly and plentifully drive the Trade of this Kingdom.

14. The value of the Commodities exported out of *Ireland*, and the Fraight of the Shipping imployed in the Trade of this[2] Nation, together with the fishing of *Herrings*, is about Five Hundred Thousand pounds *per Annum.*

15. The value of the Estates in *Ireland* of such persons as do usually live in *England*; the Interest of Debts of *Ireland*, due and payable to *England*; the pay of the Forces[3] of *Ireland*, now in *England*; the Expence and Pensions of Agents and Sollicitors commonly residing in *England* about *Irish* Affairs; the Expence of *English* and *Irish* Youth now upon their Education beyond the Seas; and lastly, the supposed Profit of the two great Farms now on Foot[4], do altogether make up near 200,000 *l. per Ann.* as a Debt payable to *England* out of *Ireland.*

16. The value of the Cattel, *viz.* live Oxen and Sheep,
120 carried out of *Ireland* into ‖ *England*, was never more than 140,000 l. *per Annum*; the Fraight, Hides, Tallow, and Wooll. of the said live Cattel, were worth about 60,000 l. of the said

[1] H, 'House-Rents.'

[2] H, 'the.'

[3] H, Petty substituted 'Forces' for a word which he blotted, perhaps 'scores.'

[4] Probably an allusion to the farm of the Irish revenues which expired Christmas, 1675, and to the new farm concluded in December of that year. See Essex to the Lords Justices, 4 December, 1675, in the *Capel Letters*, 418.

140,000 l. And the value of the Goods imported out of *England* into *Ireland* (when the Cattel-Trade was free) was between Treble and Quadruple, to the neat value of the Ox, and Sheeps Flesh transported from hence into *England.*

17. The Customs of Exported and Imported Goods, between *England* and *Ireland,* abstracted from the Excise thereof, was in the freest Trade, about 32,000 *l. per Ann.*

Inferences from the Premisses.

1. BY comparing the Extent of the Territory with the number of people, it appears that *Ireland* is much underpeopled; for as much as there are above 10 Acres of good Land to every Head in *Ireland*; whereas in *England* and *France* there are but four, and in *Holland* scarce one.

2. That if there be 250,000 spare Hands capable of Labour, who can earn 4 or five l. || *per Ann.* one with another, 121
it follows that the people of *Ireland,* well employed, may earn one Million *per Ann.* more than they do now, which is more than the years Rent of the whole Country.

3. If an House with Stone-Walls[1], and a Chimney well covered, and half an Acre of Land well ditched about, may be made for 4 or 5 *l.* or thereabouts; then ⅔ of the spare hands of *Ireland* can in one years time build and fit up 160,000 such Houses and Gardens, instead of the like number of the wretched Cabbins above-mentioned: And that in a time when a Foreign-Trade is most dead and obstructed, and when Money is most scarce in the Land.

4. The other third part of the said spare hands within the same year (besides the making of Bridges, Harbors, Rivers, High-ways, *&c.* more fit for Trade) are able to plant as many Fruit and Timber-Trees, and also Quick-set Hedges, as being grown up, would distinguish the Bounds of Lands, beautifie the Countrey, shade and shelter Cattel, furnish Wood, Fuel, Timber and fruit, in a better manner than ever

[1] H, 'Wall.'

was yet known in *Ireland* or *England*. And all this in a time when Trade is dead, and Money most scarce. ||

122 5. If the Gardens[1] belonging to the Cabbins above-mentioned, be planted with Hemp and Flax, according to the present Statute[2], there would grow 120,000 *l.* worth of the said Commodities, the Manufactures whereof, as also of the Wooll and Hides now exported, would by the labour of the spare hands above-mentioned, amount to above One Million *per Annum* more than at present.

6. The multitude and proportion of Alehouses above-mentioned, is a sign of want of Employment in those that buy, no less than those that sell the Drink.

7. There being but 800 Thousand Papists in *Ireland*, and little above 2,000[3] Priests; It is manifest that 500 Priests may, in a competent manner, Officiate for the said number of People and Parishes. And that two Popish Bishops (if any at all be necessary) may as well Govern the said 500 Priests, and two Thousand Parishes; as the 26 Bishops of *England* do Govern near Ten Thousand Parishes.

8. If the Protestants, according to the present practice and understanding of the Law, do work one tenth part of the Year more than the Papists: And that there be 750 Thousand
123 working People in *Ire-||land*, whereof about 600 Thousand Papists. It follows that the Popish Religion takes off 60 Thousand workers, which, at about 4 *l.* *per Annum* each, is about 250 Thousand Pounds *per Annum* of it self; besides the Maintenance[4] of 25 Hundred superfluous Churchmen, which at 20 *l.* *per Annum* each, comes to fifty thousand pounds *per Annum* more.

9. The Sheriffs of *Ireland* at 100 *l.* *per Annum*, the High

[1] H, 'Garden.'

[2] 17 & 18 Charles II., c. 9, Ireland, An Act for the Advancement of the Trade of Linen Manufacture, provided that tenants of cabins outside cities should have not less than one Irish acre of land each, and sow one eighth part of it with hemp or flax.

[3] H, 'little above 2000,' altered by Petty to 'about 3000.' The correction obviously represents Petty's intention for he goes on to speak of 500 requisite and "25 Hundred superfluous Churchmen." Cf. also p. 164.

[4] H, 'Manufacture.' The blunder was not corrected by Petty.

Constables at 20 *l. per Annum*, and the Petty Constables at 10 *l. per Annum*, each, being all *English* Protestants (with some other incident Charges for the Administration of Justice) may be sallarated and defrayed for thirty thousand Pounds *per Annum*, consistent with His Majesty's present Revenue, Forces, *&c.* which said Sallaries, may also be lessened, by Uniting some of the smaller Counties, Baronies and Parishes, according to the proportion of People Inhabiting within them.

10. If there be not 350 Thousand Pounds Coyned Money in *Ireland*; And if 590 Thousand Pounds (or near double what there now is) be requisite to drive the Trade thereof: then it follows, that there is not enough in *Ireland* to drive the Trade of the Nation. ||

11. If the Lands of *Ireland* and Housing in Corporations, 124
be worth above 10 Millions to be now sold (and if less than One Million of stock will drive all the Trade afore-mentioned, that *Ireland* is capable of) reckoning but two returns *per Annum*: It is certain that the lesser part of the said Ten Millions worth of real Estate, being well contrived into a[1] Bank of Credit, will with the Cash yet remaining, abundantly answer all the ends of Domestick Improvements, and Foreign Traffick whatsoever.

12. If the whole substance of *Ireland* be worth 16 Millions, as above said: If the customs between *England* and *Ireland*, were never worth above thirty two thousand Pounds *per Annum:* If the Titles[2] of Estates in *Ireland*, be more hazardous and expensive, for that *England* and *Ireland* be not under one Legislative Power: If *Ireland* till now, hath been a continual Charge to *England*: If the reducing the late Rebellion did cost *England* three times more in men and money, than the substance of the whole Countrey, when reduced, is worth: If it be just, that men of *English* Birth and Estates, living in *Ireland*, should be represented in the Legislative Power; and that the *Irish* should not be judged
by those who, || they pretend, do usurp their Estates: It then 125

[1] H has 'a' inserted by Petty.

[2] H, 'Tythes,' corrected by Petty to 'Titles.'

seems just and convenient, That both Kingdoms should be United and Governed by one Legislative Power. Nor is it hard to shew how this may be made practicable, nor to satisfy, repair, or silence those who are Interested or Affected to the contrary.

13. In the mean time, it is wonderful that men born in *England*, who have Lands granted to them by the King, for service done in *Ireland* to the Crown of *England*, when they have occasion to reside or negotiate in *England*, should by their Countrymen, Kindred and Friends there, be debarred to bring with them out of *Ireland* food whereupon to live, nor suffered to carry money out of *Ireland*, nor[1] to bring such Commodities as they fetch[2] from *America* directly home, but round about by *England*, with extream hazard and loss, and be forced to trade only with Strangers, and become unacquainted with their own Country; especially when *England* gaineth more than it loseth by a free Commerce; as exporting hither three times as much as it receiveth from hence: Insomuch as 95 *l.* in *England*, was worth about 100 *l.* of the like Money in *Ireland*, in the freest time of Trade. ||

126 14. It is conceived that about $\frac{1}{3}d$ of the Imported Manufactures, might be made in *Ireland*, and $\frac{2}{3}d$ of the remainder might be more conveniently had from Foreign parts, than out of *England*, and consequently that it is scarce necessary at all for *Ireland* to receive any goods of *England*[3], and not convenient to receive above $\frac{1}{4}th$ part from hence of the whole which it needeth to Import, the value whereof is under 100 Thousand Pounds *per Annum*.

[1] H, 'nor suffered.' [2] H, 'bring.'
[3] H, 'Ireland.' The blunder was not corrected by Petty.

The application of the Premisses, in order to remedy the defects and impediments of the Trade of Ireland.

1. Forasmuch as the consideration of Raising Money, hath already, and so lately, been before your Lordships[1]; therefore without giving this Board any further trouble concerning the same: We humbly offer, in order to the regulation of the several species thereof; That whereas Weighty Plate pieces, together with Ducatoons, which [2]estimate to be three quarters of the Money now currant in *Ireland*; do already pass at proportionable Rates; and for that all other species of Silver Money, are neither rated proportionably to the said weighty || pieces, nor to one 127
another; That Whole, Half and Quarter Cobbs of Sterling Silver (if light) may pass at 5*s.* 7*d.* *per* Ounce; but that the other Species of courser Silver, as the Perrues, *&c.* may pass as Commodity, or at 5*s.* *per* Ounce, until there shall be conveniency for new Coyning thereof into smaller Money.

2. That forthwith Application may be made unto *England*, to restore the Trade from the Plantations, and between the two Kingdoms (and particularly that of Cattel) as heretofore; and in the mean time to discover and hinder, by all means possible, the carrying of Bullion out of *Ireland* into *England*; to the end that those in *England* who are to receive Money from hence, may be necessitated to be very earnest in the said Negotiation.

3. That Endeavours be used in *England*, for the Union of the Kingdoms under one Legislative Power, proportionably, as was heretofore and successively[3] done in the case of *Wales*.

4. For[4] reducing Interest from Ten to Five, or Six, *per Centum*, for disposing moneyed men to be rather Merchants than Usurers, rather to trade than purchase, and to prevent the bad and uncertain pay-||ments, which Gentlemen are 128
forced[5] to make unto Tradesmen, whose Stock and Credit is

[1] See note 2, p. 186.

[2] H, 'we estimate.'

[3] ? successfully.

[4] H, 'The.'

[5] H, 'bound,' altered by Petty to 'forced.'

thereby soon buried in debts, not to be received without long and expensive Suits, and[1] that a Bank of Land be forthwith contrived and countenanced.

5. That the Act of State[2] which mitigates and compounds, for the Customs of some Foreign goods, purposely made high to hinder their Importation, and to encourage the Manufacture of them here, be taken into consideration (at least before it be renewed).

6. That the Lord Lieutenant and Council, as also the Nobility, Courts of Justice and Officers of the Army, and other Gentlemen in and about *Dublin*, may by their engagement and example, discountenance the use of some certain Foreign Commodities, to be pitched upon by your Lordships: And that Gentlemen and Freeholders in the Country, at their Assizes, and other Country meetings: and that the Inhabitants of all Corporations, who live in Houses of above two Chimneys in each, may afterwards do the same.

7. That there be a Corporation for the Navigation of this Kingdom, and that other Societies of men may be
129 instituted, || who shall undertake and give security to carry on the several Trades and Manufactures of *Ireland*; and to see that all goods Exported to Foreign Markets, may be faithfully wrought and packt: Which Societies may direct themselves, by the many several proposals and reports formerly, and of late made by the Council of Trade, and which they are now again ready to enlarge and accommodate to the said several proposals respectively, and more particularly to the Manufactures of Woollen, Linnen, and Leather.

8. That the Corporations of *Ireland*, may be obliged to engage no Manufactures, but according to their Primitive Instructions; which was to carry on such great works, as exceeded the strength of single Persons; and particularly that they may cause some such like proportions of Yarn, Linnen, and Woollen, as also of Worsted, to be Spun, as Mr. *Hawkins* hath Propounded.

[1] H, 'and' is inserted by Petty.

[2] 20 Charles II., c. 20, Ireland.

9. That the Pattents, which hinder the working of Mines may be considered. ||

10. That the Justices of Peace, may be admonished to protect the Industrious, and not suffer their Labours to be interrupted by vexatious and frivolous Indictments. 130

11. That the Inhabitants of the wretched Cabbins in *Ireland*, may be encouraged to reform them; and also compelled thereunto, as an easy and Indulgent Committing for the Penalty of Nine-Pence *per* Sunday payable, by the Statute; and likewise to make[1] Gardens, as the Statute for Hemp and Flax requires[2]. And that other the wholesome Laws against Idlers, Vagabonds, *&c.* may be applied to the prevention of Beggary and Thievery: Whereunto the orderly disposing of the said Cabbins into Townships would also conduce.

12. That the People be dissuaded from the observations of superfluous Holy-Days.

13. That the exorbitant Number of Popish-Priests and Fryars, may be reduced to a bare competency, as also the Number of Ale-houses. ||

14. That the Constable, Sheriff, and Bailiffs, may also be *English* Protestants, (though upon Salary).

From all which, and from the settlement of Estates; it is to be hoped, that men seeing more advantage to live in Ireland *than elsewhere, may be invited to remove themselves hither; and so supply the want of People, the greatest and most fundamental defect of this Kingdom*[3]. ||

[Here follows, in the 1691 edition of the "Political Anatomy," the Latin commission issued by Charles II. the 21 February, 1661, to the Duke of Ormond as Lord Lieutenant of Ireland. It is not reprinted.]

[1] In H Petty inserted after 'Penalty,' 'viz. of Nine Pence per Sunday payable by the Statute; and likewise to make.'

[2] See note 2, p. 218.

[3] H, 'Finis. Dublin, 24 March, 1676.'

PROPOSITIONS

CONCERNING THE

GOVERNMENT OF IRELAND.

NOTE ON THE "PROPOSITIONS."

The Propositions are not mentioned in the "Advertisement" to the first edition of the Political Anatomy of Ireland (pp. 131—132), and no indication of their authorship accompanies the enumeration of them in the Contents (p. 134). Lord Edmond Fitzmaurice says, however, that "public opinion indicated Sir William as the author of a set of propositions concerning the government of Ireland which the Duke of Ormond submitted about this time to the Crown."

Life of Petty, 140.

At the Court at *Hampton-Court*, 146
JUNE 22. 1662.

Propositions to be consider'd of by his Majesty, concerning the governing of *Ireland*.

CHARLES *R.*

1. *THAT his Majesty may declare his express Pleasure, that no* Irish *Suit by way of reward be moved for by any of his Servants, or others, before the Ordinary Revenue there become, able to sustain the necessary charge of that Crown, and the Debts thereof be fully cleared.*

This is most reasonable, it standing with no sound rule of Judgment, to exercise the Acts of bounty in a place which doth not discharge it self, and will prove the readiest and most expedient way to recover his Majesties affairs thereby, thus carrying the Revenues in their natural Channell; and
indeed || this course being constantly pursu'd, will much 147
encrease the annual profits above what they now are, and intirely draw the dependance of the inferiors from the great Lords upon his Majesty, and so the interest and assurance the Crown shall have in the Natives thereof, be of no less consequence and advantage than the very profits.

2. *That there be an express Caveat entred with the Secretary, Signet, Privy Seal and Great Seal here, That no Grant, of what nature soever, concerning* Ireland, *be suffered to pass, till the Lord Lieutenant be made acquainted, and it first pass the seal of that Kingdom, according to the usual manner.*

This will be of great intelligence and safety to his Majesty; for on the one side he will clearly see into the true inward value all things, which formerly, albeit of very great worth, have from so great a distance slipt away here, as little understood by the Crown; as is acknowledged by those that obtain them; who generally, in these causes, sacrifice rather to their own Wit, than the Goodness and Bounty of Kings. And on the other side, nothing can pass to the disadvantage
148 of the Crown; and proper || Ministers, instructed with these Affairs, may be immediately faulted and justly called to a severe Account for their Negligence and Unfaithfulness therein; which will give them good reason to look more narrowly into his Majesties Rights, and their own Duties.

3. *That His Majesty Signify his Royal Pleasure, that special Care be taken hereafter, that sufficient and credible Persons be chosen to supply such Bishopricks as shall be void, or admitted of his Privy Councel, or sit as Judges, and serve of his learned Councel there; that he will vouchsafe to hear the advice of his Lieutenant before he resolve of any in these cases, that the Lieutenant be commanded to inform his Majesty truly and impartially, of every mans particular Diligence, and Care in his Service there, to the end his Majesty may truly and graciously reward the well-deserving, by calling them home to better preferment here.*

This will advantage the service; it being altogether impossible for the Lieutenant, be he never so industrious and able, to administer the publick Justice of so great a Kingdom, without the round assistance of other able and well-affected
149 Ministers. This will encourage the best men to spend || their

stronger years there, when they shall see their elder age recompensed with ease and profit in their own native Soyl; and content and settle the Natives, when they find themselves cared for, and put in the hands of discreet and good men to govern them.

4. *That no particular Complaints of Injustice or Oppression be admitted here against any, unless it appears, That the Party made first his Address unto the Lieutenant.*

This is but justice to the Lieutenant, who must needs in some measure be a delinquent, if the complaint be true; for that he ought as in chief, universally to take care that his Majesties Justice be truly and fully administred; and therefore good reason that his Judgment should be informed, and his integrity first tryed, before either be impeached; Nay, it is but justice to the Government it self, which would be exceedingly Scandalized through the liberty of complaints, and the Ministers therein extreamly discouraged upon any petty matter, to be drawn to answer here, when as the thing itself is for the most part either Injurious or such as the party might have received good satisfaction for at his own doors: but where the complaint || appeareth formally grounded, 150
that is, where due application hath been made to the Lieutenant, without any help or relief to the party, as may be pretended; let it in the name of God be throughly examined, and severely punished, wheresoever the fault prove to be; especially if it be found to be corrupt or malitious: for thus shall not his Majesty only magnify his own Justice, but either punish an unfaithful Minister, or a clamorous Complainer; and so his Service be better'd by either example.

5. *That no Confirmation of any Reversion of Office within that Kingdom be had, or any new Grant of Reversion hereafter to pass.*

That disposing of Places thus aforehand, much abates mens endeavours, who are many times stirred up to deserve eminently in the Commonwealth, in hope of those preferments;

and being thus granted away, there is nothing left in their Eye, for them to expect and aim at, which might nourish and quicken those good desires in them, besides Places there closely and covertly passed, the persons are not for the most part so able and fitted to the Duties thereof, as when there is choice made out of many publick pretenders, which commonly
151 oc-||cur, when they actually fall void by Death.

6. *That the Places in the Lieutenants Gift, as well in the Martial as Civil List, be left freely to his disposing; and that his Majesty may be graciously pleased not to pass them to any person, upon Suits made unto him here.*

This course held, preserves the Rights of the Lieutenants Place, and his Person in that Honour and Esteem which can only enable him to do service; and if the contrary happen, it is not only in diminution to him, but draws off all necessary dependance upon him, and regard that ought to be had of him, in all ready obedience in such things he shall command, for the Kings Service, when they shall discern that the natural Powers of the Place are taken from him, whereby he might kindle their chearful endeavours by the preferring and furnishing such as deserve those places.

7. *That no New Offices be erected within that Kingdom before such time as the Lieutenant be therewith acquainted; his opinion first required and certified accordingly.* ||

152 Suits of this Nature, however they pretend the publick, their chief end is the private Profit of the Propounder; and for the most part, in the Execution prove burthens, not benefits to the Subjects; therefore throughly to be understood before they pass, as more easy and less scandalous to the State, to be staid at first than afterwards recalled, and if they be really good, his Majesty may be better informed by his Lieutenants approbation, and so proceed with more assurance to the effecting thereof.

8. *That his Majesty would be pleased, not to grant any Licence of absence out of that Kingdom, to any Councillors, Bishops, Governours of any Province or County, or Officers of State, or of the Army, or to any of the Judges, or learned Council, but that it be left to his Lieutenant to give such Licence.*

This is but reasonable, because the Lord Lieutenant who is chiefly intrusted under his Majesty with the Care and Government of that Kingdom, is the most competent and proper Judge, who in publick employment may be spared, and how long, without Prejudice to his Majesty, or the publick.

9. *That all Propositions moving from the Lieutenant, touching matters of Revenue, may* || *be directed to the Lord* 153
Treasurer of England *only, and that the Address of all other Dispatches for that Kingdom be by special direction of his Majesty applyed to one of the Secretaries singly, and his Majesty, under his hand-Writing doth Specify, that his Majesty will have this done by Mr. Secretary Nicholas.*

These Propositions made unto his Majesty, by his Grace the Duke of *Ormond* Lord Steward of his Majesty's Houshold, and Lord Lieutenant of *Ireland*, were received and approved at the Council board, the 22 day of *June* 1662, there being present the King's most excellent Majesty his Royal Highness the Duke of *York*, his Highness Prince *Rupert*, the Lord Chancellor, the Lord Treasurer, Duke of *Albemarle*, Duke of *Ormond*, Marquess of *Dorchester*, Lord Great Chamberlain, Lord Chamberlain, Earl of *Barkshire*, Earl of *Portland*, Earl of *Norwich*, Earl of *Anglesey*, Earl of *Lauderdail*, the Lord *Hatton*, Lord *Hollis*, Lord *Ashly*, Sir William *Compton*, Mr. Treasurer, Mr. Vice Chamberlain, Mr Secretary Nicholas, Mr. Secretary *Morris*.

By His Majesties Command,

EDWARD NICHOLAS. ||

LET this Book called *Political Arithmetick*, which was long since Writ by Sir *William Petty* deceased, be Printed.

Given at the Court at Whitehall the *7th Day of* Novemb. 1690.

Nottingham.

Political Arithmetick,

OR

A DISCOURSE

Concerning,

The Extent and Value of Lands, People, Buildings; Husbandry, Manufacture, Commerce, Fishery, Artizans, Seamen, Soldiers; Publick Revenues, Interest, Taxes, Superlucration, Registries, Banks; Valuation of Men, Increasing of Seamen, of Militia's, Harbours, Situation, Shipping, Power at Sea, *&c.* As the same relates to every Country in general, but more particularly to the Territories of His Majesty of *Great Britain*, and his Neighbours of *Holland*, *Zealand*, and *France*[1].

By Sir *WILLIAM PETTY*,

Late Fellow of the *Royal Society.*

London, Printed for *Robert Clavel* at the *Peacock*, and *Hen. Mortlock* at the *Phœnix* in St. *Paul's* Church-yard. 1690.

[1] The long descriptive title was probably supplied by Lord Shelburne; neither the Southwell, the Rawlinson, nor the Sloane MS. has it. In line six 'Manufacture' should be 'Manufactures,' an 's' has dropped out.

NOTE ON THE "POLITICAL ARITHMETICK."

THE Political Arithmetick, like the Political Anatomy, belongs to the third period of Petty's literary activity and was written during his second prolonged residence in Ireland. The precise date of its composition cannot now be determined. The Rawlinson MS. is dated 1671, and in Petty's "Collection of [his] several Works" it is likewise entered under 1671[1]. Lord Edmond Fitzmaurice accordingly says that it was written in that year[2], and his opinion is confirmed by Sir Peter Pett, who calls the Political Arithmetick a "manuscript discourse in the year 1671–2[3]." But Petty's list is not infallible. It enters under 1654 the Discourse against the Transplantation into Connaught published in 1655, and under 1671 the Anatomia Politica Hiberniae, which was not finished before the close of 1672[4]. The date 1671 is, perhaps, that at which Petty began the Political Arithmetick. He was still working upon it at the end of 1672[5], and internal evidence points to its completion not earlier than 1676. This internal evidence is drawn from three passages whose indications pretty closely coincide: 1st, the expenditure of the King of France "in any of these last seven years" is compared with his revenue "as the same appears by the book entitled The State of France...printed anno 1669[6]"; 2nd, "since the year 1636, the taxes and public levies...have been prodigiously greater,...yet the kingdoms have increased in their wealth and strength for these last forty years[7]"; 3rd, "his Majesty's

[1] Fitzmaurice, 318.
[2] P. 185.
[3] *Happy future State* (written 1680), p. 106.
[4] *Polit. Anat.*, note, pp. 122—123, cf. p. 197.
[5] Letter to Anglesea, 17 Dec., Fitzmaurice, 158.
[6] Pp. 252—253.
[7] P. 271.

navy is now triple or quadruple what it was forty years since, and before the Sovereign was Built[1]." The "Sovereign of the Seas" was launched 14 October, 1637[2]. These three passages, which all point to 1676 or 1677, occur in the Rawlinson MS. as well as in the undated Southwell MS., and the 1690 edition. The opinion that the Political Arithmetick was completed at a date later than the Political Anatomy is also confirmed by the larger estimate of the population of Ireland which the Arithmetick[3] makes.

Of the numerous MSS. of the Political Arithmetick, by far the most important is that bound in the same volume with the MS. Treatise of Ireland, and called by Lord Edmond Fitzmaurice the Neligan MS.[4] The history of this MS. is similar to that of the Southwell MS. of the Political Anatomy already traced[5]. It was given to Sir Robert Southwell by Petty and remained in Southwell's family until purchased by Thorpe[6] at the De Clifford sale in 1834. It passed into Dr Neligan's possession, and after his death it was bought for the British Museum[7], becoming Additional MS. 21,128. In view of its history, I call it the Southwell MS., and refer to it in the footnotes as S. This MS. is not so neatly written as the Southwell Political Anatomy; the ink is similar but the paper is of a different size, and it has one similar and one different watermark[8]. The corrections are far more numerous, and are unmistakably in Petty's hand[9]. It may be the very same MS. which Petty corrected for Southwell in March, 1681 and wished to have compared with "what goeth abroad[10]." If it be the same, Petty's wish is at length fulfilled: the readings of the Southwell MS. are now compared with the text that went forth in 1690 wherever the differences between them are significant. But mere variations in spelling and minor grammatical differences (like "hath" for "has")

[1] P. 304. [2] *Archæologia*, XII. 281—282.

[3] P. 272, note, cf. *Anatomy*, p. 142, note.

[4] *Life of Petty*, p. 273, also preface, 6—7. Lord E. Fitzmaurice slips in saying that the volume contains the *Political Anatomy*. The Neligan, or Southwell, MS. of the *Political Anatomy* is a separate volume, B. M. Addl. MS., 21,127.

[5] P. 123.

[6] Thorpe's *Cat. lib. MSS. bibl. Southwellianæ*, no. 712, p. 410.

[7] *Cat. of books sold by Sotheby*, 17 Aug., 1855, no. 306.

[8] The characteristic water mark of the *Pol. Arith.* occurs also in an Order in Council dated 21 May, 1680. *State Papers, Dom.*, Charles II. 413.

[9] See Facsimile. [10] Fitzmaurice, 262.

are disregarded, and the punctuation of the MS. is noted only where it gives the passage a meaning different from that of the printed version. All Petty's corrections are noted.

Among the remaining MSS. perhaps the most interesting is one endorsed "Pettys Pl. Arithmetic I take to be Corrected by S^r^ W^m^ himself having formerly seen a good deal of his Hand Writing," now among the Rawlinson MSS. in the Bodleian Library[1]. The MS. is in two hands, that of the second copyist beginning with chapter five. Petty's corrections are few compared with those in the Southwell MS., and most of them are merely formal, such as changing "300,000" to "300 Thousand." The more important variations marked R, are given in the foot notes. A transcript of the Political Arithmetick, presented by Willoughby, is in the Library of Trinity College, Dublin[2]. It contains no corrections by Petty. A transcript in quarto, made for Essex, is, or was, at Ashburnham Place[3], and the British Museum has, in addition to the Southwell MS., a comparatively worthless copy, unintelligently abridged[4]. Besides these, a MS. of the Political Arithmetick was presented by Petty to the King[5] and both Sir Joseph Williamson[6] and Sir Peter Pett[7] had MSS. of it.

Manuscript copies of the Political Arithmetick being thus circulated among Petty's friends, soon after its composition, they seem to have urged him to publish it at once. A letter to Southwell[8] in reply to some such request was once in the possession of Thomas Thorpe, who described it as discussing the printing [reprinting] of the Treatise of Taxes, the Political Arithmetick, and the translation of the 104th psalm, "which Petty here expresses his reluctance to be printed[9]." The unauthorized reprinting of the Treatise of Taxes in 1679[10] apparently convinced Petty that it was safer to have his books printed under supervision, for he subsequently wrote to Aubrey, 12 July, 1681, that he was not forward to print the Political Arithmetick but did wish that what went abroad might be compared with the copy in Southwell's possession, which he had corrected in

1 Rawlinson MS. D 25.

2 MSS. E. 2 : 20. *Fourth Rept. Hist. MSS. Com.*, 596 b.

3 *Eighth Rept. Hist. MSS. Com.*, III. 39 a.

4 Sloane MS. 2572.

5 Wood, *Athenæ Oxon.*, II. 810.

6 *Ib.*

7 Pett, *Happy future State*, 106, 193.

8 Dated 5 Oct., 1678.

9 Thorpe, *Cat. lib. MSS. bibl. Southwellianæ*, p. 403.

10 P. 4.

March[1]. In this letter there is no hint of the reason for non-publication which Lord Shelburne advances[2], and Petty's care to secure a good text indicates that he expected the book to be published soon. Nearly a year after the letter to Aubrey, Petty came to London, where he remained until the summer of 1683, being occupied about the reform of the Irish revenues[3]. It was probably about this time that he wrote the dedication of the Political Arithmetick to the King[4], and presented his Majesty with a copy of the book in MS. He appears, however, presently to have abandoned the project of publication, and there can be little doubt that the ill-printed edition of the Political Arithmetick which was soon anonymously issued under the title of England's Guide to Industry[5], appeared without his consent.

After Petty's death the demand for an authentic edition of the Political Arithmetick was renewed, and Lady Petty, who was executrix of her husband's will, asked Southwell's advice in the matter. Sir William himself, so she wrote[6], would not suffer the book to be printed, wherefore she was very loath to do it upon any account whatsoever, unless it were to prevent a greater evil. She was told, however, that five hundred false copies were in circulation and that the book would be published to disadvantage unless she authorized the printing of it. Southwell's reply is not preserved, but inasmuch as the Political Arithmetick was issued in 1690 with a dedication written by Lady Petty's son, it may be inferred that her scruples were at length overcome.

[1] Fitzmaurice, 262.

[2] "Had not the Doctrins of this Essay offended France, they had long since seen the light.—Dedication of 1690 edition, p. 240.

[3] Ibid, 250—253; Birch, IV. 168, 173, 196.

[4] Note on p. 239.

[5] Bibliography, 11. Several readings from *England's Guide* (G) are given in the footnotes to the *Political Arithmetick* in order to show how corrupt the text of the *Guide* was.

[6] Lady Petty to Sir R. Southwell, 18 Feb., 1688, quoted in Thorpe's *Cat. lib. MSS. bibl. Southwellianæ*, p. 409.

TO THE

KING'S

Most Excellent

MAJESTY.[1]

SIR,

W*Hilest every one meditates some fit Offering for Your Majesty, such as may best agree with your happy* || *Exaltation to this* Throne; *I presume to offer, what my Father long since writ, to shew the* weight *and* importance *of the* English Crown.

It was by him stiled Political Arithmetick[2], *in as much as things of* Government, *and of no less concern and extent, than the* Glory *of the* Prince, *and the* happiness *and* greatness *of the* People, *are by the* Ordinary *Rules of* Arithmetick, *brought*

[1] R and S have the following original dedication to Charles II. (from S):

To the Kings most Excellent Majestie

May it please your maj[te].

As few dare venture their Discretions wholly to Disparage Arithmetick, So few doe think much practice of it very necessary in matters of State, otherwise then in what concerns the Revenue. I have therefore for the Sake of severall Young Noblemen who are now fitting themselves for your Maj[tes] Service adventured to shew the vse of comon and easie computations in the ten Political conclusions mentioned in this Treatise, And doe now humbly beg your Maj[tes] Pardon, for having presumed to practice a Vulgar Art upon Matters of so high a nature, and so much beyond my owne calling and Capacity. But since whatever is firm and high must have low and euen foundations, I hope I have done no incongruous thing, nor what your Maj[te] will blame, being the Candid Endeavours of

[2] Petty appears to have been the inventor of this famous phrase. It occurs in the following passage, quoted because it throws light on Petty's conception of his new science, "My Lord Ogle being now about to carve a significant figure upon

into a sort of Demonstration. He was allowed[1] *by all, to be the Inventor of this Method of Instruction; where* || *the perplexed and intricate ways of the World, are explain'd by a very mean peice of Science; and had not the Doctrins of this* Essay *offended* France, *they had long since seen the light, and had found* Followers, *as well as improvements before this time, to the advantage perhaps of* Mankind.

But this has been reserved to the felicity of Your Majesty's Reign, *and to the expectation which the Learned have therein; and if while in this, I do some honor to the Memory of a good Father, I* || *can also pay Service, and some Testimony of my Zeal and Reverence to so great a* King, *it will be the utmost Ambition of*

SIR,

Your Majesty's Most Dutiful

and Most Obedient Subject,

Shelborne[2]. ||

my Lord his Son, by his careful Education of him, I thought it a service to his Lordship, as well as an Expression of my Thanks for his former Endeavours, to call upon him, not only to instruct my Lord his Son in some Mathematicks, but also to store and stock him with variety of Matter, Data and Phænomena, whereupon to exercise the same; since Lines & Numbers without those, are but like Lute-strings without a Lute or Hand. For, my Lord, there is a Political Arithmetick and a Geometrical Justice to be yet further cultivated in the World; the Errors and Defects whereof, neither Wit, Rhetoric, nor Interest can more than palliate, never cure. For, Falsity, Disproportion, and Inconsistence cannot be rectified by any sermocinations, though made all of figurate and measured periods, pronounced in Time and Cadence, through the most advantageous organs; much less by Grandisonous or Euphonical Nonsense, farded with formality; no more than vicious Wines can be remedied with Brandy and Honey, or ill Cookery with enormous proportions of Spice and Sugar: '*Nam Res nolunt male administrari.*'" Epistle to the Duke of Newcastle prefixed to Petty's *Discourse of Duplicate Proportion* (1674). This has been considered the earliest use of the term "*Political Arithmetick.*" S. Bauer, *History of Political Arithmetic*, in Palgrave's *Dict. of Polit. Economy*, I. 56. Petty, however, had devised the phrase at an earlier date. He employed it in a letter to Lord Anglesea, 17 December, 1672 (*Life*, 158), and in his preface (p. 244) he describes the book as "a Specimen of the Political Arithmetick I have long aimed at."

[1] Cf. Davenant, *Works*, I. 128.

[2] Charles, Sir William Petty's eldest surviving son, born 1673, was created Baron of Shelburne in the peerage of Ireland in 1688 and died in 1696.

PREFACE[1].

FOrasmuch as Men, who are in a decaying condition, or who have but an ill opinion of their own Concernments, instead of being (as some think) the more industrious to resist the Evils they apprehend, do contrariwise become the more languid and ineffectual in all their Endeavours, neither caring to attempt or prosecute even the probable means of their relief. Upon this Consideration, as a Member of the Common-Wealth, next to knowing the precise Truth in what condition the common Interest stands, I would in all doubtful Cases think || the best, and consequently not despair, without strong and manifest Reasons, carefully examining whatever tends to lessen my hopes of the publick Welfare.

I have therefore thought fit to examin the following Perswasions, which I find too currant in the World[2], and too much to have affected the Minds of some, to the prejudice of all, *viz.*

That the Rents of Lands are generally fall'n; that therefore, and for many other Reasons, the whole Kingdom *The fea of man concern the Wel fare of Englan*

[1] S, R, 'The Preface.'

[2] On the idea that England's industries were declining during the reign of Charles II. see Roscher, *Engl. Volkswirthschaftslehre*, 74. The formidable list of 'trades lost' in the preface of Child's *New Discourse of Trade*, though not printed until 1693 was written before 1669 and doubtless reflected current opinion.

grows every day poorer and poorer[1]; that formerly it abounded with Gold, but now[2] there is a great scarcity both of Gold and Silver; that there is no Trade nor Employment for the People, and yet that the Land is under-peopled; that Taxes have been many and || great; that *Ireland* and the Plantations in *America* and other Additions to the Crown, are a Burthen to *England*; that *Scotland* is of no Advantage; that Trade in general doth lamentably decay; that the *Hollanders* are at our heels, in the race of Naval Power; the *French*[3] grow too fast upon both, and appear so rich and potent, that it is but their Clemency that they do not devour their Neighbors; and finally, that the Church and State of *England*, are in the same danger with the Trade of *England*; with many other dismal Suggestions, which I had rather stifle than repeat[4].

[1] On rent as a criterion of prosperity see Cunningham, *English Industry*, II. 191; Patten, *Interpretation of Ricardo* in *Qu. Jour. of Economics*, VII. 324.

[2] S, 'but that now.'

[3] S, 'Power, That the French.'

[4] Petty's whole paragraph is almost a summary, as its closing sentence indicates, of *A Treatise Wherein is demonstrated, That the church and state Of England, are in equal danger With the trade Of it. Treatise I.* By Roger Coke. London, 1671, 4°. The book comprises two treatises, with continuous pagination and signatures, but with a second title, at p. 91, *Reasons of the increase of the Dutch Trade. Wherein is demonstrated from what Causes the Dutch Govern and Manage Trade better than the English; whereby they have so far improved their Trade above the English. Treatise II.* Coke declares that the peopling of the American plantations has diminished the valuable trades of England. Before the accession of the plantations England lost £480,000 yearly in woollen manufactures for want of men to do them, and above £1,372,000 in the fishing trade, and "now we have opened a wide gapp, and by all encouragement excited all the growing youth and industry of England, which might preserve the trades we had herein, to betake them to those of the Plantations"—p. 16. Ireland also is a disadvantage to England for similar reasons—pp. 19—20. The Dutch sell more commodities in trade cheaper and with much more gain than the English, so as now they are swelled to be of such a prodigious greatness by sea that it is a question whether they can be controlled by any power in the world—pp. 128—129. Coke has, curiously, little to say of the rivalry of France under Colbert. Sir Roger L'Estrange's *Discourse of the Fishery* (1674) says that the cod, herring and ling taken in his Majesty's seas by the Dutch and other nations are valued *communibus annis* at no less than ten millions of pounds sterling, "which computation has been often published and constantly received for current without contradiction." (In *A small Collection of valuable Tracts relating to the Herring Fishery* (1751), p. 45.) Cf. p. 257, note.

'Tis true, the Expence of foreign Commodities hath of late been too great; much of our Plate, had it remain'd Money, would have bet-||ter served Trade; too many Matters have been regulated by Laws, which Nature, long Custom, and general Consent, ought only to have governed; the Slaughter and Destruction of Men by the late Civil Wars and Plague have been great; the Fire at *London*, and Disaster at *Chatham*[1], have begotten Opinions in the *Vulgus* of the World to our Prejudice; the Nonconformists increase[2]; the People of *Ireland* think long of their Settlement; the *English* there apprehend themselves to be Aliens, and are forced to seek a Trade with Foreigners, which they might as well maintain with their own Relations in *England*. But notwithstanding all this (the like whereof was always in all Places), the Buildings of *London* grow great and glorious; the *American* Planta-||tions employ four Hundred Sail of Ships; Actions in the *East-India* Company are near double the principal Money; those who can give good Security, may have Money under the Statute-Interest; Materials for building (even Oaken-Timber) are little the dearer, some cheaper for[3] the rebuilding of *London*[4]; the Exchange seems as full of Merchants as formerly; no more Beggars in the Streets, nor executed for Thieves, than heretofore; the Number of Coaches, and Splendor of Equipage exceeding former Times; the publique Theatres very magnificent; the King has a greater Navy, and stronger Guards than before our Calamities; the Clergy rich, and the Cathedrals in

The rea[sons of the] Prejudi[ce] of England.

The Im[provement] of England.

[1] Refers to the presence of the Dutch fleet in the Thames, the attack on Chatham, and the burning of the English ships there 10 June, 1667. Mahan, *Influence of the Sea Power*, 132.

[2] Among the 'nonconformists' Petty may have included Roman Catholics. In the *Further Observations* he numbers them among the 'dissenters.'

[3] Edward Arber, in his ed. of the *Polit. Arith.* inserts an 'all' in brackets.

[4] Coke admitted that the superior durability of English timber had theretofore offset the advantage which the Dutch enjoyed in being able to build ships for half what the English could. But he held that all the best English timber was at length wasted and destroyed and still more must be in rebuilding the City of London. He could not therefore, understand how, for the future, the English could possibly build as good ships as either Dutch, Dane or French for three times the price. *Treatise II*, p. 115.

repair; much Land has been improved, and the Price of Food so reasonable, as that Men refuse || to have it cheaper, by admitting of *Irish* Cattle[1]; And in brief, no Man needs to want that will take moderate pains. That some are poorer than others, ever was and ever will be: And that many are naturally querulous and envious, is an Evil as old as the World.

These general Observations, and that Men eat, and drink, and laugh as they use to do, have encouraged me to try if I could also comfort others, being satisfied my self, that the Interest and Affairs of *England* are in no deplorable Condition.

[t]he Au[tho]r's Me[tho]d and [M]anner of [Ar]guing.

The Method I take to do this, is not yet very usual; for instead of using only comparative and superlative Words, and intellectual Arguments, I have taken the course (as a Specimen of the Political A-||rithmetick I have long aimed at) to express my self in Terms of *Number, Weight,* or *Measure*; to use only Arguments of Sense, and to consider only such Causes, as have visible Foundations in Nature; leaving those that depend upon the mutable Minds, Opinions, Appetites, and Passions of particular Men, to the Consideration of others: Really professing my self as unable to speak satisfactorily upon those Grounds (if they may be call'd Grounds), as to foretel the cast of a Dye; to play well at Tennis, Billiards, or Bowles, (without long practice,) by virtue of the most elaborate Conceptions that ever have been written *De Projectilibus & Missilibus*, or of the Angles of Incidence and Reflection. ||

[T]he Na[tur]e of his [Po]sitions [an]d Sup[pos]itions.

Now the Observations or Positions expressed by *Number, Weight,* and *Measure*, upon which I bottom the ensuing Discourses, are either true, or not apparently false, and which if they are not already true, certain, and evident, yet may be made so by the Sovereign Power, *Nam id certum est quod*

[1] S, R omit 'so' and 'as that Men refuse to have it cheaper, by admitting of *Irish* Cattle.' Cf. p. 160, 161, note.

certum reddi potest[1], and if they are false, not so false as to destroy the Argument they are brought for; but at worst are sufficient as Suppositions to shew the way to that[2] Knowledge I aim at. And I have withal for the present confined my self to the Ten principal Conclusions hereafter particularly handled, which if they shall be judged material, and worthy of a better Discussion, I hope all ingenious and candid Persons will rectifie the Errors, Defects, and || Imperfections, which probably may be found in any of the Positions, upon which these Ratiocinations were grounded. Nor would it misbecome Authority it self, to clear the Truth of those Matters which private Endeavours cannot reach to. ||

---

1 "Albeit there appears no certainty of years in the lease, yet if by reference to a certainty it may be made certain it sufficeth, *Quia id certum est quod certum reddi potest.*" Coke upon Littleton, 45 b.

2 S, 'the,' altered to 'that' by Petty, R, 'y^{t}.'

THE

Principal Conclusions[1]

OF THIS

TREATISE

ARE,

[1] S has not the list of 'principal conclusions,' R has it.

[2] R omits 'near.'

ERRATA.

PAge 7. line 25. read *the Rent.* p. 8. l. 21. r. *a part.* p. 20. l. 3. r. *for cheap.* p. 21. l. 14. r. *cold, moist.* p. 26. l. 7. r. *that Church.* p. 32. l. 7. r. *yearly profit.* l. 18. r. *to be the value.* p. 47. l. 4. r. *fifty thousand.* l. 28. r. *sixteen thousand.* p. 49. l. 13. r. *the said half together.* p. 52. l. 6. r. *should bring.* p. 59. l. 24. r. *they coast.* p. 72. l. 8. r. *or above.* p. 91. l. 9. r. E*xotics.* p. 95. l. 13. r. *paying for.*

CHAP. I.

[1]

That a small Country and few People, by its Situation, Trade, *and* Policy, *may be equivalent in* Wealth *and* Strength, *to a far greater People and Territory: And particularly that conveniencies for* Shipping *and* Water-Carriage, *do most Eminently and Fundamentally conduce thereunto.*

THis first principal Conclusion by reason of its length, I consider in three Parts; whereof the first is, That a small Country and few People, may be equivalent in Wealth and Strength to a far greater People and Territory.

[1]How one Man by Art and one Acre of Land by improvement may be equivalent to many.

This part of the first principal Conclusion needs little proof; forasmuch as one Acre of Land, may bear as much Corn, and feed as many Cattle as twenty, by the difference of the Soil; some parcel of Ground is naturally so defensible, as that an Hundred Men being pos-||sessed thereof, can resist the Invasion of Five Hundred; [2] and bad Land may be improved and made good; Bog may by draining be made Meadow; Heath-land may (as in *Flanders*) be made to bear Flax and Clover-grass, so as to advance in value from one to an Hundred[2]; The same Land being built upon, may centuple the Rent which it yielded as Pasture; one Man is more nimble, or strong, and more patient of labor than another; one Man by Art may do as much work, as many without it; *viz.* one Man with a Mill can grind as much Corn, as twenty can pound in a Mortar; one Printer can make as many Copies, as an Hundred Men can write by hand; one Horse can carry upon Wheels, as much as Five

[1] S and R have no side notes.

[2] This was a favourite idea of Petty's friend, Hartlib. Cf. note 3, p. 250.

upon their Backs; and in a Boat, or upon Ice, as Twenty[1]: So that I say again, this first point of this general Position, needs little or no proof. But the second and more material part of this Conclusion is, that this difference in Land and People, arises principally from their Situation, Trade, and Policy. ||

[3] To clear this, I shall compare *Holland* and *Zealand*, with the Kingdom of *France, viz. Holland* and *Zealand* do not contain above one Million of *English* Acres, whereas the Kingdom of *France* contains above 80.

com- rison of *lland* d *Zea- ld* with *ance.*

Now the Original and Primitive difference holds proportion as Land to Land, for it is hard to say, that when these places were first planted, whether an Acre in *France* was better than the like quantity in *Holland* and *Zealand*; nor is there any reason to suppose, but that therefore upon the first Plantation, the number of Planters was in Proportion to the quantity of Land; wherefore, if the People[2] are not in the same proportion as the Land, the same must be attributed to the Scituation of the Land, and to the Trade and Policy of the People superstructed thereupon.

The next thing to be shewn is, that *Holland* and *Zealand* at this day, is not only an eightieth part as rich and strong as *France*, but that it hath advanced to one third or thereabouts, which I think will appear upon the Ballance of the following particulars, *viz.* ||

[4] As to the Wealth of *France*, a certain Map of that Kingdom, set forth *Anno* 1647. represents it to be fifteen Millions, whereof six did belong to the Church, the Author thereof (as I suppose) meaning the Rents of the Lands only: And the Author of a most Judicious discourse of Husbandry (supposed to be Sir *Richard Weston*[3],) doth from reason and experience shew, that Lands in the Netherlands, by bearing

iat the nds of *ance,* to the nds of *lland* d *Zea- ld*, as 8 1 in lue.

[1] A list of 'Experiments to be made relating to Land-Carriage proposed by the learned Sir William Petty, Kt.,' is in *Philosophical Transactions*, no. 161, 20 July, 1684, vol. XIV. pp. 666—667. These experiments, if performed, would yield data concerning traction similar to those which Petty here assumes.

[2] S, 'now are,' the 'now' inserted by Petty.

[3] The relations of Weston's *Discourse of Husbandrie used in Brabant and Flanders*, 1652, to Hartlib's *Discourse*, to Hartlib's *Legacy*, and to the *Directions*

Flax, Turneps, Clover-grass, Madder, *&c.* will easily yield 10 *l. per* Acre; so as the Territories of *Holland* and *Zealand,* should by his account yield at least Ten Millions *per annum,* yet I do not believe the same to be so much, nor *France* so little as abovesaid, but rather, that one bears to the other as about 7, or 8 to 1.

The Bui ings of *Amster-dam* are bout ha in value those at *Paris.*

The People of *Amsterdam,* are one third of those in *Paris* or *London,* which two Cities differ not in People a twentieth part from each other, as hath appeared by the Bills of Burials and Christnings for each[1]. But the value of the Buildings in *Amsterdam,* may well be half that of *Paris,* by reason of the Foundations, Grafts, and Bridges, which || in *Amsterdam* are [5] more numerous and chargeable than at *Paris.* Moreover the Habitations of the poorest People in *Holland* and *Zealand* are twice or thrice as good as those of *France*; but the People of the one to the People of the other, being but as thirteen to one, the value of the housing must be as about five to one.

The Ho ing in *France* bove fiv times th value o those in *Hollan* and *Zea land.*

Th e S ping of *Hollan* times th of *Fran*

The value of the Shipping of *Europe,* being about two Millions of Tuns, I suppose the *English* have Five Hundred Thousand, the *Dutch* Nine Hundred Thousand, the *French* an Hundred Thousand, the *Hamburgers,* and the Subjects of *Denmark, Sweden,* and the Town of *Dansick* two Hundred and Fifty Thousand, and *Spain, Portugal, Italy,* &c. two Hundred and Fifty Thousand; so as the Shipping in our case of *France* to that of *Holland* and *Zealand,* is about one to nine, which reckoned as great and small, new and old, one with another at 8[2] *l. per* Tun, makes the worth to be as Eight Hundred Thousand Pounds, to Seven Millions, and Two Hundred Thousand Pounds. The Hollanders Capital in the

The Co parison *Holl.* an *France* the *India's.*

left by a Gentleman to his Sons for the Improvement of barren and heathy Land, 1670, are much involved. They appear to be all substantially the same book. Cf. *A biographical Memoir of Hartlib with bibliographical Notices of Works published by him.* By H. Dircks (1865), p. 62—87.

[1] The Paris bills began in 1670 (see note on the subject near the end of Graunt's *Observations, post*) and from that time to 1676 the births in the two cities always differed more than a twentieth, and the burials differed by more than a twentieth each year save in 1672.

[2] S, '9,' altered to '8' by Petty; R, '8.'

[6] *East-India* Company, is worth above Three || Millions; where the *French* as yet have little or nothing.

e exrtations *France* d *Holld* is as o 21.

The value of the Goods exported out of *France* into all Parts, are supposed Quadruple to what is sent to *England* alone; and consequently in all about Five Millions[1], but what is exported out of *Holland* into *England* is worth Three Millions; and what is exported thence into all the World besides, is sextuple to the same.

e Reues of *ance.*

The Monies Yearly raised by the King of *France*, as the same appears by the Book intituled (The State of *France*) Dedicated to the King, Printed *Anno* 1669. and set forth several times by Authority[2], is 82,000000 of *French* Livers,

[1] This estimate, again alluded to on p. 297, is much less than Fortrey's figures of English imports out of France, quoted on p. 309. The well known "Scheme of the trade at present carried on between England and France," dated 1674, made the total English imports from France £1,136,150, as against total exports to France of only £171,021. Reprinted Somers' *Tracts*, VIII. 30—31, and *Parl. Hist.*, IV. appendix, p. cxvii. When printed in King's *British Merchant*, 29 November, 1674, this estimate was said to have been calculated as exactly as possible, in obedience to the commands of the commissioners for the treaty with France, by sundry London tradesmen. *Merchant*, 1721 ed., vol. I. p. 181. But in vol. II. p. 407 the same figures are said to be taken from a report of Sir George Downing, commissioner of customs, to the Privy Council, dated 9 March, 1675. Whatever their true source, the figures were known at the time when Petty wrote and may have some connection with his estimate of imports at "not above one million two hundred thousand pounds per annum" (p. 297). The *Mercator* alleged that the calculation as printed by the *British Merchant* was disingenuous, the exports being those of 1668, the year after Colbert's great increase of the French duties, while the imports were those of 1674. Taking its figures, apparently, from Davenant's *Report to the Commissioners for Stating the public Accounts* (*Works*, V. 353), the *Mercator* of 26—28 May, 1713 gives its own estimate for 1668—69, imports £541,584, exports £108,699.

[2] *The present State of France: containing the Orders, Dignities and Charges of that Kingdom. Written in French* [*by Nicolas Besongne*] *and faithfully Englished.* London. 1671. 12°. I can find no English edition of 1669, but *L'état de la France, ou l'on voit tous les Princes, Ducs & Pairs* was printed at Paris by Jean Rinom in 1669. The English *State* says that the taxes and subsidies amount in the whole to 50,359,208 livres. "It is not to be doubted that during the late disorders there were many insolvents, for wch reason this Estimat was not of the last year, but of the years before: in the year 1648 his Majesty by his Declaration remitted the fifth part of the said taxes, but since the said declaration has been revoked, and the taxes advanced above a third." P. 457—458. *De l'État present de la France* [par Paul Hay du Chastelet]. À Cologne [? Amsterdam, see Weller, *Falsche und fingirte Druckorte*, II. 25], 1672, was not set forth by authority.

which is about 6½ Millions of Pounds Sterling, of which
summ the Author says, that one fifth part was abated for
non-valuers or Insolvencies, so (as I suppose) not above Five
Millions were effectually raised: But whereas some say, that
the King of *France* raised Eleven Millions as the $\frac{1}{5}$ of the
effects of *France*; I humbly affirm, that all the Land and
Sea Forces, all the Buildings and Entertainments, which we
have heard by common Fame, to have been || set forth and [7]
made in any of these seven last Years, needed not to have
cost six Millions Sterling; wherefore, I suppose he hath not
raised more, especially since there were one fifth Insolvencies,
when the Tax was at that pitch. But *Holland* and *Zealand*, The Ta
paying 67 of the 100, paid by all the United Provinces, and paid by *Holl*. a
the City of *Amsterdam* paying 27 of the said 67; It follows *Zealan*
that if *Amsterdam* hath paid 4000 *l.* Flemish *per diem*, or
about[1] 1400000 *l. per annum*, or 800000 *l.* Sterling; that all
Holland and *Zealand*, have paid 2100000 *l. per annum*: Now
the reasons why I think they pay so much, are these, *viz.*

1. The Author of the State of the *Netherlands* saith so[2].
2. Excise of Victual at *Amsterdam*, seems above half the Original value of the same, *viz.*

Ground Corn pays 20 Stivers the Bushel, or 63 Gilders the
Last; Beer 113 Stivers the Barrel, Housing $\frac{1}{6}$ of Rent[3],
Fruit $\frac{1}{8}$ of what it cost; other Commodities $\frac{1}{7}$, $\frac{1}{8}$, $\frac{1}{9}$, $\frac{1}{12}$; Salt
ad libitum, all weighed Goods pay besides the Premisses a
vast summ; now if the expence of the People of *Amsterdam*
at a medi-||um, and without Excise were 8 *l. per annum*, [8]
whereas in *England* 'tis 7 *l.* then if all the several Imposts
above named, raise it Five Pound more, there being 160000
Souls in *Amsterdam*, the summ of 800000 *l.* Sterling *per
annum* will thereby be raised.

[1] S, 'about' inserted by Petty, R 'about 1460,000 p Ann or above 800 thousand.'

[2] "It is commonly reported that in the general contribution of the Provinces toward the War, Holland gives 57 in a 100, and Amsterdam alone gives above 27 of the 57; from whence may be inferred what are the riches of that Town. The revenue of the said City comes to above 4000 pound a day." *The present state of the United Provinces of the Low-countries....Collected by W[illiam] A[lbigony]. The second edition.* London, 1671, p. 360.

[3] 1691, 'the rent,' cf. errata on p. 248.

3. Though the expence of each head, should be 13 *l. per annum*; 'tis well known that there be few in *Amsterdam*, who do not earn much more than the said expence.

4. If *Holland* and *Zealand* pay *p. an.* 2100000 *l.* then all the Provinces together, must pay about 3000000 *l.* less than which summ *per annum*, perhaps is not sufficient to have maintained the Naval War with *England*, 72000 Land Forces, besides all other the ordinary Charges of their Government, whereof the Church is there apart[1]: To conclude, it seems from the Premisses, that all *France* doth not raise above thrice as much from the publick *charge*, as *Holland* and *Zealand* alone do.

e Dif- ence of erest be- een *Hol.* *France.*

5. Interest of Money in *France*, is 7 *l. per cent.* but in *Holland* scarce half so much. ||

[9] 6. The Countries of *Holland* and *Zealand*; consisting as it were of Islands guarded with the Sea, Shipping, and Marshes, is defensible at one fourth of the charge, that a plain open Country is, and where the feat of War may be both Winter and Summer; whereas in the others, little[2] can be done but in the Summer only.

e super- ration tween *ance* d *Holl.*

7. But above all the particulars hitherto considered, that of superlucration ought chiefly to be taken in; for if a Prince have never so many Subjects, and his Country be never so good, yet if either through sloth, or extravagant expences, or Oppression and Injustice, whatever is gained shall be spent as fast as gotten, that State must be accounted poor; wherefore let it be considered, how much or how many times rather, *Holland* and *Zealand* are now above what they were 100 years ago, which we must also do of *France*: Now if *France* hath scarce doubled its Wealth and Power, and that the other have decupled theirs; I shall give the preference to the latter, even although the $\frac{9}{10}$ increased by the one, should
[10] not exceed the one half gained by the other, || because one has a store for Nine Years, the other but for one.

To conclude, upon the whole it seems, that though *France* be in People to *Holland* and *Zealand* as 13 to 1, and

[1] 1691, 'a-part,' cf. errata.

[2] S, 'nothing,' altered to 'little' by Petty.

in quantity of good Land, as 80 to one, yet it is not 13 times richer and stronger, much less 80 times, nor much above thrice, which was to be proved.

The cau of the di ference between *France* and *Hol*

Having thus dispatched the two first Branches of the first Principal conclusion; it follows, to shew that this difference of Improvement in Wealth and Strength, arises from the Situation, Trade, and Policy of the places respectively; and in particular from Conveniencies for Shipping and Water Carriage.

Many Writing on this Subject do so magnifie the *Hollanders*[1] as if they were more, and all other Nations less than Men (as to the matters of Trade and Policy) making them Angels, and others Fools, Brutes, and Sots, as to those particulars; whereas I take the Foundation of their atchievements to lie originally in the Situation of the Country, whereby they do things inimitable by others, and have advantages whereof others are incapable.

The rea sons wh rich La is better than course Land th of the sa Rent, a conse- quently why *Ho* is better than *Fr*

First, The Soil of *Holland* and *Zealand* is low Land, [11]
Rich and Fertile; whereby it is able to feed many Men, and so as that Men may live near each other, for their mutual assistance in Trade. I say, that a Thousand Acres, that can feed 1000 Souls, is better than 10000 Acres of no more effect, for the following reasons, *viz.*

1. Suppose some great Fabrick were in Building by a Thousand Men, shall not much more time be spared if they lived all upon a Thousand Acres, then if they were forced to live upon ten times as large a Scope of Land.

2. The charge of the cure of their Souls, and the Ministry would be far greater in one case than in the other; as also of mutual defence in case of Invasion, and even of Thieves and Robbers: Moreover the charge of the administration of Justice would be much easier, where Witnesses and Parties may be easily Summoned, Attendance less expensive, when Mens Actions would be better known, when wrongs and injuries could not be covered, as in thin peopled places they are.

Lastly, those who live in Solitary places, must be their [12]

[1] See *Die Nachamung der niederländischen Handelsblüthe* in Roscher, *op. cit.* p. 57.

own Soldiers, Divines, Physicians, and Lawyers; and must have their Houses stored with necessary Provisions (like a Ship going upon a long Voyage,) to the great wast, and needless expence of such Provisions. The value of this first convenience to the *Dutch*, I reckon or estimate[1] to be about 100000 *l. per annum.*

2ly. *Holland* is a Level Country, so as in any part thereof, a Windmill may be set up, and by its being moist and vaporous, there is always wind stirring over it, by which advantage the labor of many thousand Hands is saved, forasmuch as a Mill made by one Man in half a year, will do as much Labor, as four Men for Five Years together. This advantage is greater or less, where employment or ease of Labour is so; but in *Holland* 'tis eminently great, and the worth of this conveniency is near an Hundred and Fifty Thousand Pounds.

3ly. There is much more to be gained by Manufacture than Husbandry, and by Merchandize than Manufacture; but *Holland* and *Zealand*, being seated at the mouths of three long great Ri-||vers, and passing through Rich Countries, do keep all the Inhabitants upon the sides of those Rivers but as Husbandmen, whilst themselves are the Manufactors of their Commodities, and do dispence them into all Parts of the World, making returns for the same, at what prices almost they please themselves; and in short, they keep the
[13] Keys of Trade of those Countries, through which the said Rivers pass; the value of this third conveniency, I suppose to be[2] 200000 *l.*

4ly. In *Holland* and *Zealand*, there is scarce any place of work, or business one Mile distant from a Navigable Water, and the charge of Water carriage is generally but $\frac{1}{15}$ or $\frac{1}{20}$ part of Land carriage; Wherefore if there be as much Trade there as in *France*, then the *Hollanders* can out-sell the *French* $\frac{14}{15}$ of all the expence, of all Travelling Postage and carriage whatsoever, which even in *England* I take to be 300000 *l. p. an.* where the very Postage of Letters, costs the

[1] S, 'or estimat' inserted by Petty, not in R.
[2] S, R, 'is,' S altered to 'I suppose to be' by Petty.

People perhaps 50000 *l. per annum*, though Farmed at much less, and all other Labour of Horses, and Porters, at least six times as much; The value of || this conveniency I estimate [14]
to be above Three Hundred Thousand pounds *per annum.*

The defensibleness of *Holland*

5. The defensibleness of the Country, by reason of its Situation in the Sea upon Islands[1], and in the Marshes, Impassible ground Diked and Trenched, especially considering how that place is aimed at for its Wealth; I say the charge of defending that Country, is easier than if it were a plain Champion, at least 200000 *l. per annum.*

Harbouring of Shippin at small expence

6. *Holland* is so considerable for keeping Ships in Harbour with small expence of Men, and ground Tackle, that it saves *per annum* 200000 *l.* of what must be spent in *France.* Now if all these natural advantages do amount to above one Million *per annum* Profits, and that the Trade of all *Europe*, nay of the whole World, with which our *Europeans* do Trade, is not above 45 Millions *p. an.* and if $\frac{1}{50}$ of the value be $\frac{1}{7}$ of the Profit, it is plain that the *Hollander* may Command and Govern the whole Trade.

Advantages from Fishing.

7. Those who have their Situation thus towards the Sea, and abound with Fish at home, and having also the com-||mand of Shipping, have by consequence the Fishing [15]
Trade, whereof that of Herring alone, brings more yearly Profit to the *Hollanders* than the Trade of the *West-Indies* to *Spain*, or of the *East* to themselves, as many have affirmed, being as the same say[2] *viis & modis* of above three Millions *per annum* Profit.

Advantages by Naval Provisions.

8. It is not to be doubted, but those who have the Trade of Shipping and Fishing[3], will secure themselves of

[1] S, 'made by y[e] sea & Trenches' was inserted by Petty and then stricken out, not in R.

[2] S, R, 'themselves, being as some say,' S altered to 'themselves as many have affirmed, being as the same say' by Petty.

[3] See John Keymour's *Observations made upon the Dutch Fishing, about the year* 1601, *demonstrating that there is more Wealth raised out of the Herrings and other Fish in his Majesty's Seas, by the neighbouring Nations in one Year than the King of Spain hath from the Indies in four*, London, 1664, 4°. Also Sir John Burroughs, *The Sovereignty of the British Seas*, London, 1651, 12°, p. 115; Evelyn, *Navigation and Commerce* in McCulloch's *Select Collection of Tracts on Commerce*, 95, and note 4, p. 242.

the Trade of Timber for Ships, Boats, Masts, and Cask; of Hemp for Cordage, Sails, and Nets; of Salt, of Iron; as also of Pitch, Tar, Rosin, Brimstone, Oil, and Tallow, as necessary Appurtenances to Shipping and Fishing.

ness for iversal ade.

9. Those who predominate in Shipping, and Fishing, have more occasions than others to frequent all parts of the World, and to observe what is wanting or redundant every where, and what each People can do, and what they desire, and consequently to be the Factors, and Carriers for the whole World of Trade. Upon which ground they bring all Native Commodities to be Manufactured at home, and carry
[16] the same back, even to that Country in || which they grew, all which we see.

For, do they not work the Sugars of the *West-Indies?* The Timber and Iron of the *Baltick?* The Hemp of *Russia?* The Lead, Tin, and Wooll of *England?* The Quick-silver and Silk of *Italy?* The Yarns, and Dying Stuffs of *Turkey*, &c. To be short, in all the ancient States, and Empires, those who had the Shipping, had the Wealth, and if 2 *per Cent.* in the price of Commodities, be perhaps 20 *per Cent.* in the gain: it is manifest that they who can in forty five Millions, undersel others by one Million, (upon accompt of natural[1], and intrinsick advantages only) may easily have the Trade of the World without such Angelical Wits and Judgments, as some attribute to the *Hollanders.*

Having thus done with their Situation, I come now to their Trade.

tificial van- es of ade.

It is commonly seen, that each Country flourisheth in the Manufacture of its own Native Commodities, *viz. England* for woollen Manufacture, *France* for Paper, *Luic-land*[2] for Iron Ware, *Portugal* for Confectures, *Italy* for Silks*; upon which Principle it follows, that *Holland* and *Zealand* must
[17] flourish most || in the Trade of Shipping, and so become Carriers and Factors of the whole World of Trade. Now the advantages of the Shipping Trade are as followeth, *viz.*

[1] S, R, 'mutual interest and,' S altered to 'natural and' by Petty.

[2] Luikland or Luykerland, i.e. Liege.

Husbandmen, Seamen, Soldiers, Artizans[1] and Merchants, are the very Pillars of any Common-Wealth[2]; all the other great Professions, do rise out of the infirmities, and miscarriages of these; now the Seaman is three of these four. For every Seaman of industry and ingenuity, is not only a Navigator, but a Merchant, and also a Soldier; not because he hath often occasion to fight, and handle Arms; but because he is familiarized with hardship and hazards, extending to Life and Limbs; for Training and Drilling is a small part of Soldiery, in respect of this last mentioned Qualification; the one being quickly and presently learned, the other not without many years most painful experience: wherefore to have the occasion of abounding in Seamen, is a vast conveniency.

Husban men, Se men, Sc diers, A tizans, and Me chants, the ver Pillars c Commo Wealth, and a S man is three of them.

2. The Husbandman of *England* earns but about 4 *s. per* Week, but the Seamen have as good as 12 *s.* in Wages, || Victuals (and as it were housing) with other accommodations, [18] so as a Seaman is in effect three Husbandmen; wherefore there is little Ploughing, and Sowing of Corn in *Holland* and *Zealand*, or breeding of young Cattle; but their Land is improved by building Houses, Ships, Engines, Dikes, Wharfs, Gardens of pleasure, extraordinary Flowers and Fruits; for Dairy and feeding of Cattle, for Rape, Flax, Madder, *&c.* The Foundations of several advantageous Manufactures.

A Sea equival to three Husban men.

3. Whereas the Employment of other Men is confined to their own Country, that of Seamen is free to the whole World; so as where Trade may (as they call it) be dead here or there[3], now and then, it is certain that some where or other in the World, Trade is always quick enough, and Provisions are always plentiful, the benefit whereof, those who command the Shipping enjoy, and they only.

4. The great and ultimate effect of Trade is not Wealth at large, but particularly abundance of Silver, Gold, and Jewels, which are not perishable, nor so mutable as other

Silver, Gold, a Jewels, Univer Wealth

[1] S, 'Artizans' inserted by Petty, not in R. Petty neglected to make a corresponding alteration in 'three of these four,' three lines further down.

[2] Cf. P. de la Court, *Aanwysing* (1669), Engl. transl., p. 111.

[3] S omits 'or there,' R has it.

[19] Commodities[1], || but are Wealth at all times, and all places: Whereas abundance of Wine, Corn, Fowls, Flesh, *&c.* are Riches but *hic & nunc*, so as the raising of such Commodities, and the following of such Trade, which does store the Country with Gold, Silver, Jewels, *&c.* is profitable before others. But the Labour of Seamen, and Freight of Ships, is always of the nature of an Exported Commodity, the overplus whereof, above what is Imported, brings home mony, *&c.*

asons y the *llanders* il for s eight.

5. Those who have the command of the Sea Trade, may Work at easier Freight with more profit, than others at greater: for as Cloth must be cheaper made, when one Cards, another Spins, another Weaves, another Draws, another Dresses, another Presses and Packs; than when all the Operations above-mentioned, were clumsily performed by the same hand; so those who command the Trade of Shipping, can build long slight Ships for carrying Masts, Fir-Timber, Boards, Balks, *&c.* And short ones for Lead, Iron, Stones, *&c.* One sort of Vessels to Trade at Ports where they need never lie a ground, others where they must jump upon the

[20] Sand || twice every twelve hours; One sort of Vessels, and way of manning in time of Peace, and[2] cheap gross Goods, another for War and precious Commodities; One sort of Vessels for the turbulent Sea, another for Inland Waters and Rivers; One sort of Vessels, and Rigging, where haste is requisite for the Maidenhead of a Market, another where $\frac{1}{5}$ or $\frac{1}{4}$ part of the time makes no matter. One sort of Masting and Rigging for long Voyages, another for Coasting. One sort of Vessels for Fishing, another for Trade. One sort for War for this or that Country, another for Burthen only. Some for Oars, some for Poles, some for Sails, and some for draught by Men or Horses, some for the Northern Navigations amongst Ice, and some for the South against Worms, *&c.*[3] And this I take to be the chief of several Reasons, why the *Hollanders* can go at less Freight than

[1] S, 'nor so mutable as other Cōmodityes' inserted by Petty.

[2] 1691, 'and for,' cf. errata.

[3] On Petty's experiments in shipbuilding and his writings on the subject see Introduction, part III. and Fitzmaurice, 109—115, 256, 266, *et passim*.

their Neighbours, *viz.* because they can afford a particular sort of Vessels for each particular Trade.

I have shewn how Situation hath given them Shipping, and how Shipping hath given them in effect all other ‖ Trade, and how Foreign Traffick must give them as much [21] Manufacture as they can manage themselves, and as for the overplus, make the rest of the World but as Workmen to their Shops. It now remains to shew the effects of their Policy, superstructed upon these natural advantages, and not as some think upon the excess of their Understandings.

The Policy of Holland.

I have omitted to mention the *Hollanders* were one hundred years since, a poor and oppressed People, living in a Country naturally cold[1] and unpleasant: and were withal persecuted for their Heterodoxy in Religion.

From hence it necessarily follows, that this People must Labour hard, and set all hands to Work: Rich and Poor, Young and Old, must study the Art of Number, Weight, and Measure; must fare hard, provide for Impotents, and for Orphans, out of hope to make profit by their Labours: must punish the Lazy by Labour, and not by cripling them[2]: I say, all these particulars, said to be the subtile excogitations of the *Hollanders*, seem to me, but what could not almost have been otherwise. ‖

Liberty of Conscience, Registry of Conveyances, small [22] Customs, Banks, Lumbards, and Law Merchant, rise all from the same Spring, and tend to the same Sea; as for lowness of Interest, it is also a necessary effect of all the premisses, and not the Fruit of their contrivance.

Wherefore we shall only shew in particular the efficacy of each, and first of Liberty of Conscience; but before I enter upon these, I shall mention a Practice almost forgotten, (whether it referreth to Trade or Policy is not material,) which is, the *Hollanders* undermasting, and sailing such of their Shipping, as carry cheap and gross Goods, and whose Sale doth not depend much upon Season.

Under-masting Ships.

It is to be noted, that of two equal and like Vessels, if

[1] S, R, 1691 insert 'moist,' cf. errata.

[2] S, '& not by cripling them' inserted by Petty.

one spreads one thousand six hundred Yards of like Canvase, and the other two thousand five hundred, their speed is but as four to five, so as one brings home the same Timber in four days, as the other will in five. Now if we consider that although those Ships be but four or five days under Sail, that
[23] they are perhaps || thirty upon the Voyage; so as the one is but $\frac{1}{30}$ part longer upon the whole Voyage than the other, though one fifth longer under Sail. Now if Masts, Yards, Rigging, Cables, and Anchors, do all depend upon the quantity and extent of the Sails, and consequently hands also; it follows, that the one Vessel, goes at one third less charge, losing but one thirtieth[1] of the time, and of what depends thereupon.

ɔerty of nsci-e, and Rea-ıs there-in *Hol-ıd.*

I now come to the first Policy of the *Dutch*, *viz.* Liberty of Conscience; which I conceive they grant upon these Grounds. (But keeping up always a Force to maintain the Common Peace,) 1. They themselves broke with *Spain*, to avoid the imposition of the Clergy. 2. Dissenters of this kind, are for the most part, thinking, sober, and patient Men, and such as believe that Labour and Industry is their Duty towards God. (How erroneous soever their Opinions[2] be.) 3. These People believing the Justice of God, and seeing the most Licentious persons, to enjoy most of the World, and its best things, will never venture to be of the same
[24] Religion and Profession with Voluptu-||aries, and Men of extreme Wealth and Power, who they think have their Portion in this World.

4. They cannot but know, That no Man can believe what himself pleases, and to force Men to say they believe what they do not, is vain, absurd, and without Honor to God.

5. The *Hollanders* knowing themselves not to be an Infallible Church, and that others had the same Scripture for Guides as themselves, and withal the same Interest to save their Souls, did not think fit to make this matter their business; not more than to take Bonds of the Seamen they employ, not to cast away their own Ships and Lives.

[1] 1691, 'thirteenth.'

[2] S, 'principles,' altered to 'Opinions,' R, 'principalls,' altered to 'principles.'

6. The *Hollanders* observe that in *France* and *Spain*, (especially the latter) the Churchmen are about one hundred for one, to what they use or need; the principal care of whom is to preserve Uniformity, and this they take to be a superfluous charge.

7. They observe where most indeavours have been used to keep Uniformity, there Heterodoxy hath most abounded.

8. They believe that if ¼ of the People were Heterodox, and that if || that whole quarter should by Miracle be re- [25]
moved, that within a small time ¼ of the remainder would again become Heterodox some way or other, it being natural for Men to differ in Opinion in matters above Sense and Reason: and for those who have less Wealth, to think they have the more Wit and Understanding, especially of the things of God, which they think chiefly belong to the Poor.

9. They think the case of the Primitive Christians, as it is represented in the *Acts of the Apostles*, looks like that of the present Dissenters, (I mean externally.) Moreover it is to be observed that Trade doth not (as some think) best flourish under Popular Governments, but rather that Trade is most vigorously carried on, in every State and Government, by the Heterodox part of the same, and such as profess Opinions different from what are publickly established: (that is to say) in *India* where the *Mahometan* Religion is Authorized, there the *Banians* are the most considerable Merchants. In the *Turkish* Empire the *Jews*, and Christians. At *Venice*,
Naples, *Legorn*, *Genoua*, and *Lisbone*, || *Jews*, and Non-Papist [26]
Merchant-Strangers: but to be short, in that part of *Europe*, where the *Roman* Catholick Religion now hath, or lately hath had Establishment; there three quarters of the whole Trade, is in the hands of such as have separated from the[1] Church (that is to say) the Inhabitants of *England*, *Scotland*, and *Ireland*, as also those of the *United Provinces*, with *Denmark*, *Sueden*, and *Norway*, together with the Subjects of the *German* Protestant Princes, and the *Hans* Towns, do at this day possess three quarters of the Trade of the World; and even in *France* it self, the *Hugonots* are proportionably far the greatest Traders; Nor is it to be denied but that in

The Tr of any Countr chiefly manage by the Hetero party.

[1] Errata, 'that.'

l the pists amen of *trope* scarce c'ent Man King *Eng-* *td's* eet.

Ireland, where the said *Roman* Religion is not Authorized, there the Professors thereof have a great part of the Trade. From whence it follows that Trade is not fixt to any Species of Religion as such; but rather as before hath been said to the Hetrodox part of the whole, the truth whereof appears also in all[1] the particular Towns of greatest Trade in *England*; nor do I find reason to believe, that the *Roman* Catholick Seamen in the whole World, || are sufficient to Man effectually a Fleet equal to what the King of *England* now hath; but the Non-papist Seamen, can do above thrice
[27] as much. Wherefore he whom this latter Party doth affectionately own to be their Head, cannot probably be wronged in his Sea-concernments by the other; from whence it follows, that for the advancement of Trade, (if that be a sufficient reason) Indulgence must be granted in matters of Opinion; though licentious actings as even in *Holland*, be restrained by force.

rm Ti- s to nds and ouses.

The second Policy or help to Trade used by the *Hollanders*, is securing the Titles to Lands and Houses; for although Lands and Houses may be called *Terra Firma & res immobilis*, yet the Title unto them is no more certain, than it pleases the Lawyers and Authority to make them; wherefore the *Hollanders* do by Registries, and other ways of Assurance make the Title as immovable as the Lands, for there can be no incouragement to Industry, where there is no assurance of what shall be gotten by it; and where by fraud and corruption, one Man may take away with ease and by
[28] a trick, and in a moment || what another has gotten by many Years[2] extreme labour and pains[3].

f the in- oducing egistries to *Eng-* *nd.*

There hath been much discourse, about introducing of Registries into *England*; the Lawyers for the most part object against it, alledging that Titles of Land in *England* are sufficiently secure already; wherefore omitting the considerations of small and oblique reasons *pro & contra*, it were good that enquiry were made from the Officers of several

[1] S omits 'all.'

[2] S, 'and in a moment' and 'many years,' inserted by Petty.

[3] Petty had lost much land of which he once supposed himself the owner. Fitzmaurice, 137, 138, 151.

Courts, to what summ or value Purchasers have been damnified for this last ten Years, by such fraudulent conveyances as Registries would have prevented; the tenth part whereof at a *Medium*, is the annual loss which the People sustain for want of them, and then computation is to be made of the annual charge of Registring such extraordinary Conveyances, as would secure the Title of Lands; now by comparing these two summs, the Question so much agitated may be determined; though some think that though few are actually damnified, yet that all are hindered by fear and deterred from Dealing[1].

Their third Policy is their Bank, the use whereof is to encrease Mony, or rather to || make a small summ equivalent in Trade to a greater, for the effecting whereof these things are to be considered. 1. How much Money will drive the Trade of the Nation. 2. How much current Money there is actually in the Nation. 3. How much Money will serve to make all payments of under 50*l.* or any other more convenient summ throughout the Year. 4. For what summ the keepers of the Bank are unquestionable Security: If all these four particulars be well known, then it may also be known, how much of the ready Money above mentioned may safely and profitably[2] be lodged in the Bank, and to how much ready current Money the said deposited Money is equivalent. As for example, suppose a Hund. thous. Pounds will drive the Trade of the Nation, & suppose there be but Sixty thousand Pounds of ready Money in the same; suppose also that Twenty thous. Pounds will drive on and answer all Payments made of under 50*l.* In this case Forty of the Sixty being put into the Bank, will be equivalent to Eighty, which eighty and twenty kept out of the Bank do make up an Hundred, (that is to say) enough to drive || the Trade as was proposed; where note that the Bank keepers must be responsible for double the summ intrusted with them, and must have power to levy upon the general, what they happen to loose unto particular Men.

The Bank of *Holland*

[29]

[30]

[1] S, 'though some think...from Dealing' inserted by Petty.

[2] S, 'profitably,' altered by Petty to 'properly,' which R has.

Upon which grounds, the Bank may freely make use of the received Forty thousand Pounds, whereby the said summ, with the like summ in Credit makes Eighty thousand Pounds, and with the Twenty reserved an Hundred.

e *Hol-ıders* are ıdom ısband-n or ot Sol-rs.

I might here add many more particulars, but being the same as have already been noted by others, I shall conclude only with adding one observation which I take to be of consequence, *viz.* That the *Hollanders* do rid their hands of two Trades, which are of greatest turmoil and danger, and yet of least profit; the first whereof is that of a common and private Soldier, for such they can hire from *England, Scotland,* and *Germany,* to venture their lives for Six pence a day, whilst themselves safely and quietly follow such Trades, whereby the meanest of them gain six times as much, and withal by this entertaining of Strangers for Soldiers; their
[31] Coun-||try becomes more and more peopled, forasmuch as the Children of such Strangers, are *Hollanders* and take to Trades, whilst new Strangers are admitted *ad infinitum*; besides these Soldiers at convenient intervals, do at least as much work as is equivalent to what they spend, and consequently by this way of employing of Strangers for Soldiers, they People the Country and save their own Persons from danger and misery, without any real expence, effecting by this method, what others have in vain attempted by Laws for Naturalizing of Strangers[1], as if Men could be charmed to transplant themselves from their own Native, into a Foreign Country merely by words, and for the bare leave of being called by a new Name. In *Ireland* Laws of Naturalization[2] have had little effect, to bring in Aliens, and 'tis no wonder, since *English* Men will not go thither without

[1] Propositions for the naturalization of aliens were laid before Parliament in 1664, 1667, 1670 and 1672. *Commons' Jour.*, VIII. 555, 557; IX. 22, 29, 33, 175, 250, 267, 274, 275; *Parl. Hist.*, IV. 577. Cf. Child, *New Discourse of Trade*, ch. VII.; Cunningham, *Engl. Industry*, II. 178, 179.

[2] 14 & 15 Charles II. c. 13, Ireland, provided that Protestant strangers, merchants, traders and artizans, who within seven years should transport their stocks and families into Ireland, there reside and take oath of allegiance, should be adjudged to all intents free and naturalized subjects, with all the rights of natives. Cf. Mountmorres, *Hist. of the Irish Parliament*, I. 426.

they may have the pay of Soldiers, or some other advantage amounting to maintenance.

The M thod of comput the valı of Men and People.

Having intimated the way by which the *Hollanders* do increase their People, I shall here digress to set down the way of computing the value of every Head || one with another, and that by the instance of People in *England*, *viz.* Suppose the People of *England* be Six Millions in number, that their expence at 7 *l. per* Head be forty two Millions: [32]
suppose also that the Rent of the Lands be eight Millions, and the profit[1] of all the Personal Estate be Eight Millions more; it must needs follow, that the Labour of the People must have supplyed the remaining Twenty Six Millions, the which multiplied by Twenty (the Mass of Mankind being worth Twenty Years purchase as well as Land) makes Five Hundred and Twenty Millions, as the value[2] of the whole People: which number divided by Six Millions, makes above 80 *l.* Sterling, to be valued of each Head of Man, Woman, and Child, and of adult Persons twice as much; from whence we may learn to compute the loss we have sustained by the Plague, by the Slaughter of Men in War, and by the sending them abroad into the Service of Foreign Princes. [3]The other Trade of which the *Hollanders* have rid their Hands, is the old Patriarchal Trade of being Cow-keepers, and in a great Measure of that which concerns || Ploughing and Sowing of Corn, having put that Employment [33]
upon the *Danes* and *Polanders*, from whom they have their Young Cattle and Corn. Now here we may take notice, that as Trades and curious Arts increase; so the Trade of Husbandry will decrease, or else the Wages of Husbandmen must rise, and consequently the Rents of Lands must fall.

For proof whereof I dare affirm, that if all the Husbandmen of *England*, who now earn but 8 *d.* a day or thereabouts, could become Tradesmen and earn 16 *d.* a day (which is no great Wages 2 *s.* and 2 *s.* 6 *d.* being usually given) that then

[1] S, 1691, 'yearly profit,' 'yearly' inserted in S by Petty, obscure, R, 'ye Profit,' cf. errata.

[2] 1691, 'to be the value,' cf. errata.

[3] S, R, 'The other Trade' begins a paragraph.

it would be the advantage of *England* to throw up their Husbandry, and to make no use of their Lands, but for Grass Horses, Milch Cows, Gardens, and Orchards, *&c.* which if it be so, and if Trade and Manufacture have increased in *England* (that is to say) if a greater part of the People, apply themselves to those faculties, than there did heretofore, and if the price of Corn be no greater now, than when Husbandmen were more numerous, and Tradesmen fewer;
[34] It follows from that single || reason (though others may be added) that the Rents of Land must fall: As for example, suppose the price of Wheat be 5 *s.* or 60 pence the Bushel; now if the Rent of the Land whereon it grows, be the third Sheaf; then of the 60 *d.* 20 *d.* is for the *Land*, and 40 *d.* for the *Husbandman*; But if the Husbandmans Wages, should rise one eighth part, or from 8 *d.* to 9 *d. per Diem*, then the Husbandmans share in the Bushel of Wheat, rises from 40 *d.* to 45 *d.* And consequently the Rent of the Land must fall from 20 *d.* to 15 *d.* for we suppose the price of the Wheat still remains the same: Especially since we cannot raise it, for if we did attempt it, Corn would be brought in to us, (as into *Holland*) from Foreign Parts, where the State of Husbandry was not changed.

asons y Rents fall.

And thus I have done with the first principal Conclusion, that, *A small Territory, and even a few People, may by Situation, Trade, and Policy, be made equivalent to a greater; and that convenience for Shipping, and Water-carriage, do most eminently and fundamentally conduce thereunto.* ||

---

[35]

CHAP. II.

That some kind of Taxes *and Publick* Levies, *may rather* increase *than* diminish *the Wealth of the Kingdom.*

hat fting of ney m hand profita- or not.

IF the Money or other Effects, levyed from the People by way of *Tax*, were destroyed and annihilated; then 'tis clear, that such *Levies* would diminish the Commonwealth: Or if the same were exported out of the Kingdom without any return at all, then the case would be also the same or worse[1]: But if what is levyed as aforesaid, be only transferred from one hand to another, then we are only to consider whether the said Money or Commodities, are taken from an improving hand, and given to an ill Husband, or *vice versa*; As for example, suppose that Money by way of *Tax*, be taken from one who spendeth the same in superfluous eating and drinking; and delivered to another || who em- [36] ployeth the same, in improving of *Land*, in *Fishing*, in working of *Mines*, in *Manufacture*, *&c.* It is manifest, that such Tax is an advantage to the State whereof the said different Persons are Members: Nay, if Money be taken from him, who spendeth the same as aforesaid upon *eating* and *drinking*, or any other perishing Commodity; and the same transferr'd to one that bestoweth it on *Cloaths*; I say, that even in this case, the Commonwealth hath some little advantage; because *Cloaths* do not altogether perish so soon as *Meats* and *Drinks*: But if the same be spent in *Furniture of Houses*, the advantage is yet a little more; if in *Building of Houses*, yet more; if in improving of *Lands*; working of *Mines*, *Fishing*, *&c.* yet more; but most of all, in bringing *Gold* and *Silver* into the Country: Because those things are not only not perishable, but are esteemed for Wealth at all times, and every where: Whereas other Commodities which are perishable, or whose value depends upon the Fashion; or which are contingently scarce and plentiful, are wealth, but *pro hic & nunc*, as shall be[2] elsewhere said ||.

In the next place if the People of any Country, who have [37] not already a full employment, should be enjoyned or Taxed to work upon such Commodities as are Imported from abroad; I say, that such a Tax, also doth improve the Commonwealth.

Taxing new wo[rk] a benefi[t] to the Commo[n]wealth.

Moreover, if Persons who live by begging, cheating, stealing, gaming, borrowing without intention of restoring; who by those ways do get from the credulous and careless, more than is sufficient for the subsistence of such Persons; I say, that although the State should have no present employment for such Persons, and consequently should be

The taxing of Idlers.

[1] S, 'or worse' inserted by Petty.

[2] S, R, 'as hath been.' See p. 259—260.

forced to bear the whole charge of their livelyhood; yet it were more for the publick profit to give all such Persons, a regular and competent allowance by Publick Tax; than to suffer them to spend extravagantly, at the only charge of careless, credulous, and good natured People; And to expose the Commonwealth to the loss of so many able Men, whose lives are taken away, for the crimes which ill Discipline doth occasion. ||

[38] On the contrary, If the Stocks of laborious and ingenious Men, who are not only beautifying the Country where they live by elegant *Dyet*, *Apparrel*, *Furniture*, *Housing*, *pleasant Gardens*, *Orchards*, and *Publick Edifices*, *&c.* But are also increasing the *Gold*, *Silver*, and *Jewels* of the Country by *Trade* and *Arms*; I say, if the Stock of these Men should be diminished by a Tax, and transferred to such as do nothing at all, but *eat* and *drink*, *sing*, *play*, and *dance*; nay to such as study the *Metaphysicks*, or other needless *Speculation*; or else employ themselves in any other way, which produce no material thing, or things of real use and value in the Commonwealth: In this case, the Wealth of the Publick will be diminished: Otherwise than as such exercises, are recreations and refreshments of the mind; and which being moderately used, do qualifie and dispose Men to what in it self is more considerable.

Wherefore upon the whole matter, to know whether a Tax will do good or harm: The State of the People, and their employments, must be well known; (that is to say,)
[39] what part of the Peo-||ple are unfit for Labour by their Infancy or Impotency; and also what part are exempt from the same, by reason of their *Wealth*, *Function*, or *Dignities*; or by reason of their charge and employments; otherwise than in governing, directing and preserving those, who are appointed to Labour and Arts.

2. In the next place computation must be made, what part of those who are fit for Labour and Arts as aforesaid, are able to perform the work of the Nation in its present State and Measure[1].

[1] S, 'measures.'

3. It is to be considered, whether the remainder can make all or any part of those Commodities, which are Imported from abroad; which of them, and how much in particular: The remainder of which sort of People (if any be) may safely and without possible prejudice to the Commonwealth, be employed in Arts and Exercises of pleasure and ornament; the greatest whereof is the Improvement of natural knowledge.

A judgment of what taxes are advantageous.

Having thus in general illustrated this point, which I think needs no other proof but illustration; I come next to intimate that no part of *Europe* hath || paid so much by way [40]
of Tax, and publick contribution, as *Holland* and *Zealand* for this last 100 Years; and yet no Country hath in the same time, increased their Wealth[1] comparably to them: And it is manifest they have followed the general considerations above-mentioned; for they Tax *Meats* and *Drinks* most heavily of all; to restrain the excessive expence of those things, which 24 hours doth (as to the use of Man,) wholly annihilate; and they are more favourable to Commodities of greater duration.

Nor do they Tax according to what Men gain, but in extraordinary cases; but always according to what Men spend: And most of all, according to what they spend needlesly, and without prospect of return. Upon which grounds, their Customs upon Goods Imported and Exported, are generally low; as if they intended by them, only to keep an account of their Foreign Trade; and to retaliate upon their Neighbour States, the prejudices done them, by their Prohibitions and Impositions.

It is probable that Holland and England are grown richer under taxes.

It is further to be observed, that since the Year 1636, the Taxes and Publick || Levies made in *England, Scotland,* and *Ireland*, have been prodigiously greater than at any time [41]
heretofore; and yet the said Kingdoms have increased in their Wealth and Strength, for these last Forty Years, as shall hereafter be shewn[2].

It is said that the King of *France*, at present doth Levy

The difference of Princes Revenue

[1] G has a dash in place of 'their Wealth.'

[2] See ch. VI.

the Fifth Part of his Peoples Wealth; and yet great Ostentation is made of the Present Riches and Strength of that Kingdom. Now[1] great care must be had in distinguishing between the Wealth of the People, and that of an absolute Monarch; who taketh from the People, where, when, and in what proportion he pleaseth. Moreover[2], the Subjects of two Monarchs may be equally Rich, and yet one Monarch may be double as Rich as the other; *viz.* If one take the tenth part of the Peoples Substance to his own dispose, and the other but the *20th.* nay the Monarch of a poorer People, may appear more splendid and glorious, than that of a Richer; which perhaps may be somewhat the case of *France*, as hereafter shall be examined. As an instance and applica-
[42] tion of what hath been || said, I conceive that in *Ireland*

at *Ire-* *ld* ma morey vanta- usly ed by a le in ax.

wherein are about 1200 Thousand People, and near[3] 300 Thousand Smokes[4] or Hearths[5]; It were more tolerable for the People, and more profitable for the King; that each Head paid 2 *s.* worth of Flax, than that each smoke should pay 2 *s.* in Silver; And that for the following reasons.

1. *Ireland* being under peopled, and Land, and Cattle

[1] S, 'Although,' altered to 'Now' by Petty.

[2] S, 'Moreover' inserted by Petty.

[3] S, 'about,' altered to 'near' by Petty.

[4] These estimates, being larger than those given in the *Polit. Anat.*, p. 141, argue the later completion of the *Polit. Arith.* Cf. p. 236.

[5] The 8 August, 1662 the Irish Commons, after a long debate, unanimously agreed to abolish the court of wards and to substitute a tax of two shillings annually upon all the hearths in Ireland for ever, according to a similar tax in England. Mountmorres, *Hist. of the Irish Parlt.*, II. 126, 127; see 14 & 15 Charles II. c. 17, Ireland. The duty was payable by the occupier at one entire payment on the 10th January each year, and was recoverable by distress and sale of his goods. No persons were exempt except those who lived upon alms and widows who procured certificates from two justices of the peace yearly, in writing, that the houses which they inhabited were of no greater value than 8*s.* a year and that they did not have chattels to the value of 4£. Evasions led to the passage of 17 & 18 Charles II. c. 18, Ireland (1665), which imposed fines for the concealment of hearths and provided that houses having no fixed hearth should be charged two hearths. Until 1704 this tax was farmed by counties to the highest bidder. Howard, *A Treatise of the Exchequer and Revenue of Ireland*, I. 89—91. The tax, was beyond question, exceedingly oppressive, and evasions must have been so frequent as to render the returns but an imperfect basis for calculating the population.

being very cheap; there being every where store of Fish and Fowl; the ground yielding excellent Roots (and particularly[1] that bread-like root *Potatoes*) and withal they being able to perform their Husbandry, with such harness and tackling, as each Man can make with his own hands; and living in such Houses as almost every Man can build[2]; and every House-wife being a Spinner and Dyer of Wool and Yarn, they can live and subsist after their present fashion, without the use of Gold or Silver Money; and can supply themselves with the necessaries above named, without labouring 2 Hours *per diem*: Now it hath been found, that by reason of Insolvencies arising, rather from the uselessness than want of Mo-||ney among these poor People; that from [43]
300 Thousand Hearths, which should have yielded 30 Thousand Pound *per annum*; not 15 Thousand Pound of Money could be Levyed: Whereas it is easily imagined, that four or five People dwelling in that Cottage, which hath but one smoke; could easily have planted a ground-plot of about 40 foot square with Flax; or the 50 part of an Acre; for so much ground will bear eight or ten Shillings worth of that Commodity; and the Rent of so much ground, in few places amounts to a penny *per annum*. Nor is there any skill requisite to this practice, wherewith the Country is not already familiar. Now as for a Market for the Flax; there is Imported into *Holland* it self, over and above what that Country produces; as much Flax, as is there sold for between Eightscore and Two Hundred Thousand Pound; and into *England* and *Ireland* is Imported as much Linnen Cloth

[1] S, inserts 'great plenty of that.'

[2] The original form of S is here represented by Roman type, Petty's corrections by Italic:

'tackle, as each man can make, and liveing in such Houses as
make wth his own hands
almost every man can build; and euery housewife.'

The interlined correction, which is much crowded, appears to have been read into the line above it, giving the text of 1690, instead of the sense which Petty intended, viz. such Houses as almost every man can make with his own hands. R, 'Tackling as each man can make, & living in such Houses as (almost) every man can build, & every Housewife.'

H. P. 18

made of Flax, and there spent, as is worth above ½ a Million of Money. As shall hereafter be shewn[1].

Wherefore having shewn, that Silver Money is useless to [44] the poor People of || *Ireland*; that half the Hearth Money could not be raised by reason thereof; that the People are not a fifth part employed; that the People and Land of *Ireland*, are competently qualified for Flax; That one Penny-worth of Land, will produce Ten Shillings[2] worth of the same; and that there is Market enough and enough, for above an Hundred Thousand Pounds worth; I conceive my Proposition sufficiently proved; at least to set forwards and promote a practice, which both the present Law and Interest of the Country doth require: Especially, since if all the Flax so produced should yield nothing, yet there is nothing lost; the same time having been worse spent before. Upon the same grounds, the like Tax of 2 *s. per* Head, may be raised with the like advantage upon the People of *England*; which will amount to Six Hundred Thousand Pound *per annum*; to be paid in Flax, Manufactured, into all the sorts of *Linnens*, *Threds*, *Tapes*, and *Laces*; which we now receive from *France*, *Flanders*, *Holland*, and *Germany*; the value whereof doth far exceed the summ last mentioned, as hath appeared by the examination of particulars. ||

ities put on re- ndant mmo- ...s ma- ie a harm- s Tax.

[45] It is observed by Clothiers, and others, who employ great numbers of poor people, that when Corn is extremely plentiful[3], that the Labour of the poor is proportionably dear[4]: And scarce to be had at all (so licentious are they who labour only to eat, or rather to drink.) Wherefore when so many Acres sown with Corn, as do usually produce a sufficient store for the Nation, shall produce perhaps double to what is expected or necessary; it seems not unreasonable

[1] The promise was not kept.

[2] S, 'about 10 *s*.'

[3] S, 'extream plentiful.'

[4] The common assumption of economic theory has been precisely the reverse, viz. that wages will be low when food is plentiful. Petty's assertion, however, is confirmed by the observant author (?W. Temple, or J. Cunningham) of *An Essay on Trade and Commerce* (1770), pp. 14—16, and Ricardo admitted that it was true of Ireland even in his time. *Letters to Malthus*, 138. See also Malthus, *Political Economy* (1820), pp. 382—388, Cunningham, *English Industry*, II. 689.

that this common blessing of God, should be applied, to the common good of all people, represented by their Sovereign; much rather than the[1] same should be abused, by the vile and brutish part of mankind, to the prejudice of the Common-Wealth: And consequently, that such surplusage of Corn, should be sent to publick Store-houses; from thence to be disposed of, to the best advantage of the Publick.

Now if the Corn spent in *England*, at five shillings *per* Bushel *Wheat*, and two shillings six pence *Barley*, be worth ten Millions *Communibus annis*; it follows that in years of great plenty, when the said Grains are one third part ‖ cheaper; that a vast advantage might accrue to the Common- [46] Wealth, which now is spent in over-feeding of the People, in quantity or quality; and so indisposing them to their usual Labour.

The like may be said of *Sugar*, *Tobacco*, and *Pepper*; which custom hath now made necessary to all sorts of people; and which the over-planting of them, hath made unreasonably cheap: I say it is not absurd, that the Publick should be advantaged by this extraordinary plenty.

That an *Excise* should be laid upon *Corrants*[2] also, is not unreasonable; not only for this, but for other reasons also.

Of a Ta by a gra Militia, and by two oth sorts of Armies.

The way of the present Militia or Trained-Bands, is a gentle Tax upon the Country; because it is only a few days Labour in the year, of a few Men in respect of the whole; using their own goods, that is their[3] own Arms. Now if there be three Millions of Males in *England*, there be above two hundred thousand of them, who are between the age of sixteen and thirty, unmarried persons; and who live by their ‖ Labour and Service; for of so many or thereabouts, [47] the present Militia consists.

Now if an hundred and five[4] thousand of these, were Armed, and Trayned, as Foot; and fifty thousand as Horse; (Horse being of special advantage in Islands)[5] the said Forces at Land, with thirty thousand Men at Sea; would

[1] S, R, 'much less that the.' [2] G, 'corn.' [3] S, 'of their.'

[4] S, R, 1691, 'fifty,' cf. errata?

[5] S, '(Horse being of speciall advantage in islands)' is inserted by Petty.

by Gods ordinary blessing, defend this Nation, being an Island, against any Force in view: But the charge of Arming, Disciplining, and Rendezvousing all these Men, twice, or thrice a year; would be a very gentle Tax, Levyed by the people themselves, and paid to themselves. Moreover if out of the said number $\frac{1}{3}$ part were selected, of such as are more than ordinarily fit and disposed[1] for War, and to be Exercised, and Rendezvoused fourteen or fifteen times *per annum*; the charge thereof being but a fortnights Pay in the year, would be also a very gentle Tax.

Lastly, If out of this last mentioned number, $\frac{1}{3}$ again should be selected, making about twelve[2] thousand Foot,
[48] and near[3] six thousand Horse, to be Exercised, || and Rendezvoused forty days in the year; I say that the charge of all these three Militias, allowing the latter six weeks Pay *per annum*; would not cost above one hundred and twenty thousand pound *per annum*; which I take to be an easie burthen, for so great a benefit.

r sup-ing the vy, and rchants h Sea-n.

Forasmuch as the present Navy of *England* requires thirty six thousand Men to Man it; and for that the *English* Trade of Shipping, requires about forty eight thousand Men, to manage it also; it follows, that to perform both well, there ought to be about seventy two thousand Men, (and not eighty four thousand) competently[4] qualified for these Services: For want whereof we see, that it is a long while, before a Royal Navy can be manned; which till it be, is of no effectual use, but lies at charge. And we see likewise upon these occasions, that Merchants are put to great straights, and inconveniences; and do pay excessive rates for the carrying on their Trade. Now if twenty four thousand able bodyed Tradesmen, were by[5] six thousand of them[6] *per annum*, brought up and fitted for Sea-Service; and for ||

[1] S, 'and disposed' inserted by Petty.

[2] S, R, 1691, 'sixteen.' Cf. errata? [3] S, R, omit 'near.'

[4] S, '& not 84000' inserted by Petty, R, 'about 84000 completely,' altered to 'about 72000 completely,' by Petty.

[5] G, 'whereby.' The 1683 ed. probably was not printed from S or R, as the words 'were by' are plainly written in both.

[6] S, 'of them' inserted by Petty, not in R.

their incouragement allowed 20*s. per annum* for every year [49] they had been at Sea, even when they stay at home, not exceeding 6*l.* for those, who have served six years or upward; it follows, that about 72000*l.* at the *medium* of 3*l. per* Man, would Salariate the whole number of twenty four thousand[1]; and so, forasmuch as half the Seamen, which mannage the Merchants Trade, are supposed to be always in Harbour, and are about twenty four thousand[2] Men, together with the said half of the Auxilliaries last mentioned, would upon all[3] emergencies, Man out the whole *Royal Navy* with thirty six thousand[4], and leaving to the Merchants twelve thousand of the abler Auxilliaries, to perform their business in Harbour, till others come home from Sea; and thus thirty six thousand, twenty four thousand, and twelve thousand, make the seventy two thousand above mentioned[5]: I say that more than this sum of 72000*l.* is fruitlesly spent, and over paid by the Merchants, whensoever a great Fleet is to be fitted out. Now these whom I call Auxilliary Seamen, are such as have another Trade besides, wherewith || to maintain themselves, [50] when they are not employed at Sea; and the charge of maintaining them, though 72000*l. per annum*, I take to be little or nothing, for the reasons above mentioned, and consequently an easie Tax to the people, because Leavyed by, and paid to themselves.

A Herring Tax upon *Scotland*.

As we propounded that *Ireland* should be Taxed with Flax, and *England* by *Linnen*, and other *Manufacture* of the same; I conceive that *Scotland* also might be Taxed as much, to be paid in *Herrings*, as *Ireland* in *Flax*: Now the three Taxes (*viz.*) of *Flax*, *Linnen*, and *Herrings*, and the

[1] S, 'of 24000' inserted by Petty, not in R.

[2] S, 'men, the said halfe, together with halfe the Auxiliaryes,' R, 'men, together with *the said* [Italicized words inserted] halfe the Auxiliaries last mentioned, would upon emergencies man out the whole Royall Navy, leaving to the Merchants 12 Thousand of the abler auxiliaries to performe their business in harbour, till others come back from the Sea. I say that.'

[3] S, 'all' inserted by Petty.

[4] S, 'with 36000' inserted by Petty.

[5] S, 'And thus 36000, 24000 and twelve make up ye 72000 above mentioned' inserted by Petty, not in R.

maintainance of the triple *Militia*, and of the *Auxilliary Seamen* above-mentioned, do all five of them together, amount to one Million of mony, the raising whereof is not a Million spent, but gain unto the Common-Wealth, unless it can be made appear, that by reason of all, or any of them, the Exportation of *Woollen Manufactures*, *Lead*, and *Tin*, are lessened; or of such Commodities, as our own *East* and *West India* Trade do produce, forasmuch as I conceive, that the
[51] Exporta-||tion of these last mentioned Commodities, is the *Touch-stone* whereby the Wealth of *England* is tryed, and the *Pulse* whereby the Health of the Kingdom may be discerned.

CHAP. III.

That France *cannot by reason of natural, and perpetual Impediments, be more powerful at Sea, than the* English, *or* Hollanders[1] *now are, or may be.*

[The qua-lities of Ships fit for the de-fence of England.]

POwer at Sea consists chiefly of *Men, able to fight at Sea*, and that in such Shipping, as is most proper for the Seas wherein they serve; and those are in these Northern Seas, Ships from between three hundred to one thousand three hundred Tuns; and of those such as draw much Water, and have a deep Latch in the Sea, in order to keep a good Wind, and not to fall to Leeward, a matter of vast advantage in Sea Service: Wherefore it is to be examined, 1. Whether the King of *France*, hath Ports in the Northern Seas (where ||
[52] he hath most occasion for his Fleets of War, in any contests[2] with *England*) able to receive the Vessels above-mentioned, in all Weathers, both in Winter and Summer Season. For if the King of *France*, would[3] bring to Sea an equal number of fighting Men, with the *English* and *Hollanders*, in small-floaty Leeward Vessels, he would certainly be of the weaker

[1] S, R, omit 'now are, or may be.' R, 'than England or the Dutch,' altered to 'or the low countries' by Petty.

[2] S, 'with England' inserted by Petty, not in R.

[3] S, 'could,' R, 'would.' 1691, 'would' corrected to 'should' in errata.

side. For a Vessel of one thousand Tuns manned with five hundred Men, fighting with five Vessels of two hundred Tuns, each manned with one hundred Men apiece, shall in common reason have the better offensively, and defensively; forasmuch as the great Ship can carry such Ordnance, as can reach the small ones at a far greater distance, than those can reach, or at least hurt the other; and can batter, and sink at a distance, when small ones can scarce peirce.

Moreover it is more difficult for Men out of a small Vessel, to enter a tall Ship, than for Men from a higher place, to leap down into a lower; nor is small shot so effectual upon a tall Ship, as *vice versa.* ||

And as for Vessels drawing much water, and consequently [53]
keeping a good Wind, they can take or leave Leeward Vessels, at pleasure, and secure themselves from being boarded by them: Moreover the windward Ship, has a fairer mark at a Leeward Ship, than *vice versa*; and can place her shot upon such parts of the Leeward Vessel, as upon the next Tack will be under water.

Now then the King of *France*, having no Ports able to receive large windward Vessels, between *Dunkirk* and *Ushant*, what other Ships he can bring into those Seas, will not be considerable. As for the wide Ocean, which his Harbours of *Brest*, and *Charente*[1], do look into; it affordeth him no advantage upon an Enemy; there being so great a Latitude of engaging or not, even when the Parties are in sight of each other.

Wherefore, although the King of *France* were immensely rich, and could build what Ships he pleased, both for number, and quality; yet if he have not Ports to receive, and shelter, that sort and size of Shipping, which[2] is fit for his purpose; the said Riches will in this || case be fruitless, and a mere [54]
expence without any return, or profit. Some will say that other Nations cannot build so good Ships as the *English*; I do indeed hope they cannot; but because it seems too possible, that they may sooner or later, by Practice and

[1] S, R, G, 'Brouage' altered to 'Charente' in S by Petty.

[2] S, R, 'as' altered to 'w^ch' in R.

Experience; I shall not make use of that Argument, having bound my self to shew, that the impediments of *France*, (as to this purpose) are natural, and perpetual. Ships, and Guns do not fight of themselves, but Men who act and manage them; wherefore it is more material to shew; That the King of *France*, neither hath, nor can have Men sufficient, to Man a Fleet, of equal strength to that of the King of *England*. (*viz.*)

e qua- ations eamen de- ce.

The King of *Englands* Navy, consists of about seventy thousand Tuns of Shipping, which requires thirty six thousand Men to Man it; these Men being supposed to be divided into eight parts, I conceive that one eighth part, must be persons of great Experience, and Reputation, in Sea Service: another eighth part must be such as have used the Sea seven years
[55] and upwards; || half of them, or $\frac{4}{8}$ parts more, must be such as have used the Sea above a twelvemonth, *viz.* two, three, four, five, or six years, allowing but one quarter of the whole Complements, to be such as never were at Sea at all, or at most but one Voyage, or upon one Expedition; so that at a *medium* I reckon, that the whole Fleet must be Men of three or four years growth, one with another.

e Num- of Sea- n in *ance.*

Fournier[1], a late judicious Writer, makeing it his business to persuade the World, how considerable the King of *France* was, or might be at Sea, in the ninety second and ninety third pages of his *Hydrography*, saith, That there was one place in *Britany*, which had furnished the King with one thousand four hundred Seamen, and that perhaps the whole Sea-Coast of *France*, might have furnished him with fifteen times as many: Now supposing his whole Allegation were true, yet the said number amounts but to twenty one thousand; all which, if the whole Trade of Shipping in *France* were quite and clean abandoned, would not by above a third, Man out a Fleet equivalent, to that of the King of *England*: And if ||

[1] *Hydrographie contenant la theorie et la practiqve de tovtes les parties de la navigation. Composé par le Pere Georges Fournier.* A Paris, chez Michel Soly. M.D.C.XLIII, f°. "Les gens de Mer y sont en telle quantité, que durant le siège de la Rochelle, la Roy tira d'vn seul Bourg quatorze cents Maletots, Soldats, bien que ce lieu ne soit pas (possible) le quinziesme de cette coste en bonté & reputation." The estimate that the coast could furnish fifteen times as many is omitted from the second edition of Fournier (1667), p. 69.

the Trade were but barely kept alive, there would not be one [56] third part Men enough, to Man the said Fleet.

But if the Shipping Trade of *France*, be not above a quarter as great as that of *England*, and that one third part of the same, namely the Fishing Trade to the Banks of *Newfoundland*, is not peculiar, nor fixt to the *French*; then I say that if the King of *England* (having power to Press Men) cannot under two or three months time Man his Fleet; then the King of *France*, with less than a quarter of the same help, can never do it at all; for in *France* (as shall elsewhere be shewn[1]) there are not above one hundred and fifty thousand Tun of Trading Vessels, and consequently not above fifteen thousand Seamen, reckoning a Man to every ten Tun. As it has been shewn that the King of *France*, cannot at present Man such a Fleet, as is above described, we come next to shew that he never can, being under natural, and perpetual Impediments: *viz.* 1. If there be but fifteen thousand Seamen in all *France*, to manage its Trade, it is not to be || supposed, that the said Trade should be extinguished, nor [57] that it should spare above five of the said fifteen thousand towards manning the Fleet which requires thirty five thousand.

The wa whereb the *Fre* must in crease S men.

Now the deficient thirty thousand must be supplied, one[2] of these four[3] ways, either, first by taking in Landmen, of which sort there must not be above ten thousand, since the Seamen will never be contented, without being the major part, nor do they heartily wish well to Landmen at all, or rejoyce even at those Successes, of which the Landmen can claim any share; thinking it hard that themselves, who are bred to miserable, painful, and dangerous Employments, (and yet profitable to the Commonwealth) should at a time when booty and purchase is to be gotten, be clogged or hindered, by any conjunction with Landmen, or forced to admit those, to an equal share with themselves. 2. The Seamen which we suppose twenty thousand, must be had, that is hired from other Nations, which cannot be without tempting them with so much Wages, as exceeds what is ||

Why Se men dis like La men.

[1] See p. 251, where the French are assigned 100,000 tons.. [2] S, 'out.'

[3] The fourth way seems to be the general increase of French trade, p. 283.

[58] given by Merchants, and withal to counterpoise the danger of being hanged by their own Prince, and allowed no Quarter if they are taken; the trouble of conveying themselves away, when Restraints and Prohibitions are upon them; and also the infamy of having been Apostates, to their own Country, and Cause: I say their Wages must be more than double, to what their own Prince gives them, and their assurance must be very great, that they shall not be at long run abused or slighted[1] by those who employed them; (as hating the Traitor, although they love the Treason.) I say moreover, that those who will be thus tempted away, must be of the basest, and lewdest sort of Seamen, and such as have not enough of Honour and Conscience, to qualifie them for any Trust, or gallant Performance. 3. Another way to increase[2] Seamen, is to put great numbers of Landmen upon Ships of War, in order to their being Seamen; but this course cannot be effectual, not only for the above mentioned Antipathy,

[59] between Landmen, and Seamen; || but also, because it is seen, that Men at Sea do not apply themselves to Labour and Practice, without more necessity than happens in over-manned Shipping. For where there are fifty Men in a Vessel, that ten can sufficiently Navigate, the supernumerary forty will improve little: But where there shall be of ten but one or two supernumeraries, there necessity will often call upon every Man to set his hand to the Work, which must be well done at the peril of their own lives. Moreover Seamen shifting Vessels almost every six or twelve months, do sometimes Sail in small Barks, sometimes in midling Ships, and sometimes in great Vessels of Defence; sometimes in Lighters, sometimes in Hoighs, sometimes in Ketches, sometimes in three Masted Ships, sometimes they go to the Southward, sometimes to the Northward, sometimes the[3] Coast, sometimes they cross the Ocean; by all which variety of Service, they do in time compleat themselves, in every Part, and Circumstance of their Faculty: Whereas those

[60] who go out for a Sum-||mer, in a Man of War, have not that

e dan- of *glish* men ir ser- g the *nch.*

w Men rn to good amen.

[1] S, 'or slighted' inserted by Petty. [2] G, 'exonerate.'

[3] S, 1691, 'they.' See errata?

variety of Practice, nor a direct necessity of doing any thing at all.

Besides it is three or four years at a *medium*, wherein a Seaman must be made; neither can there be less than three Seamen, to make a fourth, of a Landman: Consequently the fifteen thousand Seamen of *France*, can increase but five thousand Seamen in three or four years, and unless their Trade should increase with their Seamen in proportion, the King must be forced to bear the charge of this improvement, out of the Publick Stock, which is intolerable. So as the Question which now remains, is, whether the Shipping Trade of *France* is like to increase? Upon which accompt it is to be considered, 1. That *France* is sufficiently stored, with all kind of Necessaries within it self; as with *Corn, Cattle, Wine, Salt, Linnen Cloth, Paper, Silk, Fruits, &c.* So as they need little Shipping, to Import more Commodities of Weight, or Bulk; neither is there any thing of Bulk Exported out of *France*, but *Wines*, and *Salt*; the weight where-||of is under [61] one hundred thousand Tun[1] *per annum*, yielding not employment to above twenty five thousand Tun of Shipping, and these are for the most part *Dutch* and *English*, who are not only already in Possession of the said Trade, but also are better fitted to maintain it, than the *French* are, or perhaps ever can be: And that for the following Reasons. (*viz.*) 1. Because the *French* cannot Victual so cheap as the *English*, and *Dutch*, nor Sail with so few Hands. 2. The *French*, for want of good Coasts and Harbours, cannot keep their Ships in Port, under double the Charge that the *English* and *Hollanders* can. 3. by reason of Paucity, and distance of their Ports, one from another, their Seamen and Tradesmen relating to Shipping, cannot Correspond with, and Assist one another, so easily, cheaply, and advantageously, as in other places. Wherefore if their Shipping Trade, is not likely to increase within themselves, and much less to increase, by their beating out the *English*, and *Hollanders*, from being the Carriers of the World; it fol-||lows, that their Seamen will not be increased, [62]

Whether the Shipping Trade of France is like to increase

Reason why it cannot.

[1] In margin of S, opposite 'one hundred thousand Tun,' stands 'Qre' in the hand of the copyist.

by the increase of their said Trade: Wherefore, and for that they are not like to be increased, by any of the several ways above specified, and for that their Ports are not fit to receive Ships of Burthen, and Quality, fit for their purpose; and that by reason of the less fitness of their Ports, than that of their Neighbours; I conceive, that what was propounded, hath been competently proved.

The afore-named *Fournier*, in the ninety second and ninety third pages of his *Hydrography*, hath laboured to prove the contrary of all this, unto which I refer the Reader: Not thinking his Arguments of any weight at all, in the present case. Nor indeed doth he make his Comparisons, with the *English* or *Hollanders*, but with the *Spaniards*, who, nor the Grand Seignior, (the latter of whom hath greater advantages, to be powerful at Sea than the King of *France*) could ever attain to any illustrious greatness in Naval Power: Having often attempted, but never succeeded in the same. ||
[63] Nor is it easie to believe, that the King of *England* should for so many years, have continued his Title to the *Sovereignty* of the *Narrow Seas*, against his Neighbours (ambitious enough to have gotten it from him) had not their Impediments been Natural, and Perpetual, and such, as we say, do obstruct the King of *France*. ||

---

[64]

CHAP. IV.

That the People and Territories of the King of England, *are naturally near*[1] *as considerable for Wealth and Strength, as those of* France.

com- rison be- een the rrito- s of *En- nd* and *ance.*

THE Author of the State of *England*[2], among the many useful truths, and observations he hath set down; delivers the Proportion, between the Territories of *England* and *France*, to be as Thirty to Eighty two; the which if it be true, then

[1] In S, 'neer' is inserted and 'naturally' is imperfectly erased.

[2] *Angliae Notitia; or the present State of England.* By Edward Chamberlayne, 1672, p. 251, "the area of England is in comparison to France as 30 to 82."

England, *Scotland*, and *Ireland*, with the Islands unto them belonging, will, taken all together, be near as big as *France*. Tho I ought to take all advantages for proving the Paradox in hand; yet I had rather grant that *England*, *Scotland*, and *Ireland*, with the Islands before mentioned; together with the Planted parts of *Newfoundland*, *New-England*, *New-Netherland*, *Virginia*, *Mary-Land*, *Carolina*, *Jamaica*, *Burmoudas*, *Barbadoes*, and all ‖ the rest of the *Carribby* Islands, with [65]
what the King hath in *Asia* and *Africa*[1], do not contain so much[2] *Territory* as *France*, and what Planted Land the King of *France* hath also in *America*. And if any Man will be Heterodox in behalf of the *French* Interest; I would be contented against my knowledge and judgment, to allow the King of *France's Territories*, to be a seventh, sixth, or even a fifth greater, than those of the King of *England*; believing that both Princes have more Land, than they do employ to its utmost use.

A Prop sition fc quitting *Ireland* the Hig lands oi *Scotlan*

And here I beg leave, (among the several matters which I intend for serious,) to interpose a jocular, and perhaps ridiculous digression, and which I indeed desire Men to look upon, rather as a Dream or Resvery, than a rational Proposition; the which is, that if all the *moveables* and People of *Ireland*, and of the Highlands of *Scotland*, were transported into the rest of *Great Brittain*; that then the King and his Subjects, would thereby become more *Rich* and *Strong*, both *offensively* and *defensively*, than now they are. ‖

'Tis true, I have heard many Wise Men say, when they [66]
were bewailing the vast losses of the *English*, in preventing and suppressing Rebellions in *Ireland*, and considering how little profit hath returned, either to the King or Subjects of *England*, for their Five Hundred[3] Years doing and suffering in that Country; I say, I have heard Wise Men (in such their Melancholies[4]) wish, that (the People of *Ireland* being saved)

[1] S, 'wth what ye King hath in Asia & AAfrica' inserted by Petty.

[2] S, R, 'more territory than France,' altered in S to 'so much territory as France.'

[3] S, '400,' altered by Petty to '500,' R, '500.'

[4] S, 'Melancholy.'

Island[1] were sunk under Water: Now it troubles me, that the Distemper of my own mind in this point, carries me to dream, that the benefit of those wishes, may practically be obtained, without sinking that vast Mountainous Island under Water, which I take to be somewhat difficult; For although *Dutch* Engineers may drain its Bogs; yet I know no Artists that could sink its Mountains. If Ingenious and Learned Men (among whom I reckon Sir *Tho. More*, and *Des Cartes*[2]) have disputed, That we who think our selves awake, are or may be really in a Dream; and since the greatest absurdities of Dreams, are but a Preposterous and Tumultuary contexture [67] of realities; I will crave the || umbrage of these great Men last named, to say something for this wild conception, with submission to the better judgment of all those that can prove themselves awake.

If there were but one Man living in *England*, then the benefit of the whole Territory, could be but the livelyhood of that one Man: But if another Man were added, the rent or benefit of the same would be double, if two, triple; and so forward until so many Men were Planted in it, as the whole Territory could afford Food unto: For if a Man would know, what any Land is worth, the true and natural Question must be, How many Men will it feed? How many Men are there to be fed? But to speak more practically, Land of the same quantity and quality in *England*, is generally worth four or five[3] times as much as in *Ireland*; and but one quarter, or third of what it is worth in *Holland*; because *England* is four or five times[4] better Peopled than *Ireland*, and but a quarter so well as *Holland*. And moreover, where the Rent of Land is advanced by reason of Multitude of People; there the [68] number of Years purchase, for which || the Inheritance may be sold, is also advanced, though perhaps not in the very same Proportion; for 20 *s. per annum* in *Ireland*, may be

[1] S, R, 'that the people of Ireland being saved, that that Island.'

[2] Descartes' first meditation, *Œuvres publ. par.* V. Cousin (1824), I. 237—239. Can Petty have thought that the story of Utopia was narrated in the guise of a dream?

[3] S, R, '3 or 4,' altered in S to '4 or 5.'

[4] S, R, '4 times.'

worth but 8 *l.* and in *England* where Titles are very sure, above 20 *l.* in *Holland* above 30 *l.*[1]

I suppose, that in *Ireland* and the High-Lands in *Scotland*, there may be about one Million and Eight hundred thousand People, or about a fifth part of what is in all the three Kingdoms: Wherefore the first Question will be, whether *England*, *Wales*, and the Low Lands of *Scotland*, cannot afford Food, (that is to say) *Corn*, *Fish*, *Flesh*, and *Fowl*, to a fifth part more People, than are at the present planted upon it, with the same Labour that the said fifth part do now take where they are? For if so, then what is propounded is naturally possible. 2. It is to be enquired, What the *value* of the *immovables* (which upon such removal must be left behind) are worth? For if they be worth less, than the advancement of the Price of Land in *England* will amount unto; then the Proposal is to be considered. 3. If the *Relict Lands*, and the *immovables* left behind upon them, may be || sold for [69] Money; or if no other Nation shall dare meddle with them, without paying well for them; and if the Nation who shall be admitted, shall be less able to prejudice and annoy the Transplantees into *England* then before; then I conceive that the whole proposal will be a pleasant and a profitable[2] Dream indeed[3].

That *England* and the Low lands of *Scotland* will feed all the People of *England*, *Scotland* & *Ireland*

As to the first point, whether *England* and the Low-Lands of *Scotland*, can maintain a fifth part more People than they now do (that is to say) Nine Millions of Souls in all? For answer thereunto, I first say, that the said Territories of *England*, and the Low-Land of *Scotland*, contain about Thirty Six Millions of Acres, that is four Acres for every Head, Man, Woman, and Child; but the United Provinces do not allow above one Acre and ½, and *England* it self rescinding *Wales*, hath but Three Acres to every Head, according to the present State of Tillage and Husbandry. Now if we consider that *England* having but three Acres to a Head as aforesaid, doth so abound in Victuals, as that it maketh Laws

[1] S, '30*l*,' 1691, '3*l*.' [2] S, 'yea a proffitable' inserted by Petty.

[3] Petty returns to his pleasant and profitable dream in the *Treatise of Ireland*, 1687.

[70] against the Importation of *Cattle*, ‖ *Flesh*, and *Fish* from abroad; and that the draining of *Fens*, improving of *Forests*, inclosing of *Commons*, Sowing of St. *Foyne* and *Clovergrass*, be grumbled against by *Landlords*[1], as the way to depress the price of Victuals; then it plainly follows, that less than three Acres improved as it may be, will serve the turn, and consequently that four will suffice abundantly. I could here set down the very number of Acres, that would bear *Bread* and *Drink*, *Corn*, together with *Flesh*, *Butter*, and *Cheese*, sufficient to victual Nine Millions of Persons, as they are Victualled in Ships, and regular Families; but shall only say in general; that Twelve Millions of Acres *viz.* $\frac{1}{3}$ of 36 Millions, will do it, supposing that *Roots*, *Fruits*, *Fowl*, and *Fish*, and the ordinary profit of *Lead*, *Tin*, *Iron-Mines*, and *Woods*, would piece up any defect, that may be feared.

at the ue of the itted nds and mova- goods d charge tran- anta- n are t worth ove 17 llions.

As to the second, I say, that the Land and Housing in *Ireland*, and the High-Lands of *Scotland*, at the present Market rates, are not worth Thirteen[2] Millions of Money; nor would the actual charge of making the Transplantation proposed, amount to four[2] Millions more: ‖ So then the Question will be, whether the benefit expected from this Transplantation, will exceed Seventeen Millions[2]?

[71] To which I say, that the advantage will probably be near four[3] times the last mentioned summ, or about Sixty nine Millions, Three Hundred thousand Pounds[4]. For if the Rent of all *England* and *Wales*, and the Low-Lands of *Scotland*, be about Nine Millions *per annum*; and if the fifth part of the People be superadded, unto the present Inhabitants of those Countries; then the Rent will amount unto Ten Millions 8000 *l.* and the number of Years purchase, will

[1] It does not appear that much practical result followed from the recommendation of clover, sainfoin and lucerne until the eighteenth century. Cunningham, *English Industry*, II. 183, Rogers, *Hist. of Agriculture and Prices*, V. 59, cf. however V. 62. Aubrey writes (before 1685), "Memorandum. Great increase of sanfoine now, in most places fitt for itt." *Natural History of Wiltshire*, ed. Britton, ch. x. p. 11.

[2] S, R, "10...2...12," altered in S to "13...4...17."

[3] S, '6' altered to '4.'

[4] S, 'above 72 millions' altered to 'about 69,300,000.'

rise from seventeen and ½, to a Fifth part more, which is twenty one. So as the Land which is now worth but Nine Millions *per annum*, at seventeen ½ Years purchase, making 157 Millions and ½, will then be worth Ten Millions Eight Hundred thousand Pounds, at Twenty one Years purchase; *viz.* Two Hundred Twenty Six Millions, and Eight Hundred thousand Pounds, that is, Sixty nine Millions, and Three Hundred thousand Pounds more than it was before. ||

And if any Prince willing to inlarge his Territories, will [72] give any thing more than Six ½ Millions or[1] half the present value for the said relinquished Land, which are estimated to be worth Thirteen[2] Millions; then the whole profit, will be above Seventy Five[3] Millions, and Eight Hundred 600 *l.* Above four[4] times the loss, as the same was above computed. But if any Man shall object, that it will be dangerous unto *England*, that *Ireland* should be in the Hands of any other Nation; I answer in short, that that Nation, whoever shall purchase it (being divided by means of the said purchase,) shall not be more able to annoy *England*, than now in its united condition. [5]Nor is *Ireland* nearer *England*, than *France* and *Flanders*.

That th who pu chase *Ir land* sh we ll e them-selves.

Now if any Man shall desire a more clear explanation, how, and by what means, the Rents of Lands shall rise by this closer cohabitation of People above described? I answer, that the advantage will arise in transplanting about Eighteen Hundred thousand People, from the poor and miserable Trade of Husbandry, to more beneficial Handicrafts: For when the superaddition is made, a ve-||ry little addition of [73] Husbandry to the same Lands will produce a fifth part more of Food, and consequently the additional hands, earning 40 *s.* *per annum* (as they may very well do, nay[6] to 8 *l.* *per annum*) at some other Trade; the Superlucration will be above Three

[1] S, 'more than the 7 millions for,' altered to 'more than the 6½ millions or ye present value for.' R, 'give 3 millions for.'

[2] S, R, '10,' altered in S to '13.'

[3] S, R, '72,' altered in S to '75.'

[4] S, R, 'or six,' altered in S to 'above 4,' cf. Errata.

[5] S, 'Nor is...Flanders' added by Petty, not in R.

[6] S, R, omit 'do, nay.'

Millions and Six Hundred thousand[1] Pounds *per annum*, which at Twenty Years purchase is Seventy[2] Millions. Moreover, as the inhabitants of Cities and Towns, spend more Commodities, and make greater consumptions, than those who live in wild thin peopled Countries; So when *England* shall be thicker peopled, in the manner before described, the very same People shall then spend more, than when they lived more sordidly and inurbanely, and further asunder, and more out of the sight, observation, and emulation of each other; every Man desiring to put on better Apparel when he appears in Company, than when he has no occasion to be seen.

I further add, that the charge of the *Government, Civil,*
[74] *Military*, and *Ecclesiastical*, would be more *cheap*, *safe*, and *effectual* in this condition of *closer* || co-habitation than otherwise; as not only reason, but the example of the United Provinces doth[3] demonstrate.

at the erence ween *gland's France's* rritory ot terial.

But to let this whole digression pass for a *mere Dream*, I suppose 'twill serve to prove, that in case the King of *Englands Territories*, should be a little less than those of the King of *France*, that forasmuch as neither of them are over-peopled, that the difference is not material to the Question in hand; wherefore supposing the King of *France's* advantages, to be little or nothing in this point of *Territory*; we come next to examine and compare, the number of Subjects which each of these Monarchs doth govern.

The Book called the State of *France*, maketh that Kingdom to consist of Twenty Seven thousand[4] Parishes; and another Book written by a substantial Author, who professedly inquires into the State of the Church and Churchmen of *France*, sets it down as an extraordinary case, that a *Parish* in *France* should have Six Hundred Souls; wherefore I suppose that the said Author (who hath so well examined
[75] the mat-||ter) is not of opinion that every Parish, one with

[1] S, '3 mill and ½,' altered to '3600000,' R, '3500000' altered to '3600000.'
[2] R, '70000000' altered to '72000000,' S, '70000000.'
[3] S, Petty inserted 'and hath' after 'doth.'
[4] G, omits 'Thousand.'

another, hath above Five Hundred; by which reckoning the whole People of *France*[1], are about Thirteen Millions and a half; Now the People of *England, Scotland*, and *Ireland*, with the Islands adjoyning, by computation from the numbers of Parishes; which commonly have more People in Protestant Churches, than in Popish Countries; as also from the *Hearth-money, Pole money*[2], and *Excise*, do amount to about Nine Millions and ½[3].

There are in *New-England*, about 16000[4] Men mustered in Arms; about 24000[5] able to bear Arms; and consequently about 150000[6] in all: And I see no reason why in all this and the other Plantations of *Asia, Africa*, and *America*, there should not be half a Million[7] in all. But this last I leave to every Mans conjecture; and consequently, I suppose, that the King of *England* hath about Ten Millions of Subjects, *ubivis Terrarum Orbis*; and the King of *France* about Thirteen and a ½ as aforesaid. [76]

Although it be very material to know the number of Subjects belonging to each || Prince, yet when the Question is concerning their *Wealth* and *Strength*; It is also material to examin, how many of them do get more than they spend, and how many less.

The Kir of *Fran* hath in effect bu 13 Milli of Subje and the K. of *Englan* 10 Millions, ar the Kin of *Fran* hath 27c Church-men and the Kin of *England* 20000, t K. of *Englan* hath 400 Sea-men and the of *Franc* 10000.

In order whereunto it is to be considered, that in the King of *Englands* Dominions, there are not[8] twenty Thousand Church-men; But in *France*, as the aforementioned Author of theirs doth aver, (who sets down the particular number of each Religious Order) there are about Two Hundred and Seventy thousand, *viz.* Two Hundred and Fifty thousand

[1] *The present State of France*, p. 455 seq., contains a list of the Généralties, with the number of parishes in each of them except Amiens and Nantes. The sum of the parishes accounted for is 24,580.

[2] G, 'Post-money.'

[3] S, R, '9 millions,' altered to '9½ millions' in S.

[4] S, R, G, '50000,' altered to '16000' in S.

[5] S, R, G, '80000,' altered to '24000' in S.

[6] S, R, G, 'halfe a million,' altered to '150000' in S.

[7] S, R, 'in all the rest of the Plantations there should not be halfe a million more,' altered in S to 'in this and all the other Plantations of Asia, Affrica & America there should not be half a million' ('more' stricken out).

[8] G omits 'not.'

more than we think are necessary, (that is to say) Two Hundred and Fifty Thousand withdrawn out of the World. Now the said number of adult and able bodied Persons, are equivalent to about double the same number, of the promiscuous Mass of Mankind. And the same Author says, that the same Religious Persons, do spend one with another about 18 *d. per diem*, which is triple even to what a labouring Man requires.

Wherefore the said Two Hundred and Fifty thousand Church-men (living as they do) makes the King of *France's* ‖
[77] Thirteen Millions and a half, to be less than Thirteen[1]: [2]Now if Ten Men can defend themselves as well in Islands, as Thirteen[3] can upon the Continent; then the said Ten being not concerned to increase their *Territory* by the Invasion of others, are as effectual as the Thirteen[4] in point of Strength also[5]; wherefore that there are more Superlucrators in the *English*, than the *French* Dominions, we say as followeth.

e mul- ıde of ergy's lessen K. of *ance's* ople, mul- de of a & val n do rease K. of *ngland's* bjects.

There be in *England, Scotland, Ireland*, and the Kings other Territories above Forty Thousand[6] Seamen; in *France* not above[7] a quarter so many; but one Seaman earneth as much as three common Husbandmen; wherefore this difference in Seamen, addeth to the account of the King of *England's*

[1] S, R, 'be really no better than 12 or thereabouts,' S, altered to 'be less than 13.'

[2] S, R, G, have here the following passage, stricken out but still legible in S: 'In the next place it is to be considered, That the Inhabitants of the Inner Parts of France, remote from the Sea cannot be probably Superlucrators; Now if there be 2 Millions in the King of England's dominions, more then in the King of France's who—[a word rendered illegible by Petty's alteration of it to 'earn,' which R and G have] more then they Spend, or if 10 men in England earne more then 12 men in France, then the Subjects of England, are as effective as to the gaining of wealth and Riches as those of France.' The alteration of one word in this passage implies that Petty intended to let it stand and afterwards decided to strike it out. The passage is in Sloane MS. 2572 also.

[3] S, R, '12,' S altered to '13.'

[4] S, R, '12,' S altered to '13.'

[5] 'also' refers to the (omitted) argument about gaining wealth.

[6] S, R, 'in England, Scotland and Ireland about 60 thousand,' in S is inserted 'and ye Kings other Territoryes' and '60' is altered to above '40.' G, '60 million.'

[7] S, R, 'about,' S altered to 'not above.'

Subjects, is an advantage equivalent to Sixty Thousand Husbandmen[1].

There are in *England*, *Scotland*, and *Ireland*, and all other the King of *England*'s Territories[2] Six Hundred[3] thousand Tun of Shipping, worth about four Millions and a $\frac{1}{2}$[4] of Money; and the annual charge of maintaining the Shipping of *England*, by new Buildings and Reparations, is about $\frac{1}{3}$[5] part of the || same summ; which is the Wages of one Hundred and Fifty [78]
thousand[6] Husbandmen, but is not the Wages of above $\frac{1}{8}$ part of so many *Artisans* as are employed, upon Shipping of all sorts; *viz.* *Shiprights*, *Calkers*, *Joyners*, *Carvers*, *Painters*, *Block-makers*, *Rope-makers*, *Mast-makers*, *Smiths* of several sorts; *Flag-makers*, *Compass-makers*, *Brewers*, *Bakers*, and all other sort of *Victuallers*; all sorts of Tradesmen relating to *Guns*, and *Gunners Stores.* Wherefore there being four times more of these *Artisans* in *England*, *&c.* than in *France*; they further add to the account of the King of *England's* Subjects, the equivalent of Eighty Thousand Husbandmen more.

The K. *Englan* Territories are effect b 12 Mile from N vigable Water, King of *France'* 65.

The *Sea-line* of *England*, *Scotland*, and *Ireland*, and the adjacent Islands, is about Three thousand Eight hundred Miles; according to which length, and the whole content of Acres, the said Land would be an Oblong, or Parallelogram Figure of Three thousand Eight hundred Miles long, and about Twenty four Miles broad; and consequently, every part of *England*, *Scotland*, and *Ireland*, is one with another, but twelve Miles from the Sea: Whereas *France* containing, but about one Thousand || Miles of *Sea line*, is by the like [79]
method or computation, about Sixty Five Miles from the Sea side; and considering the paucity of Ports, in comparison of what are in the King of *England's* Dominions, as good as Seventy Miles distant from a Port: Upon which grounds it is clear, that *England* can be supplied, with all gross and bulkey commodities of Foreign growth and Manufacture, at

[1] S, R, 'Subjects the equivalent of 90000 husbandmen,' in S 'is an advantage' is substituted for 'the' cancelled, and '90000' is altered to '60000.' G, '90,500000.'

[2] S, 'and all other y^e King of England's Teritoryes' inserted.

[3] G omits 'Hundred.'

[4] S, R, G, '$\frac{1}{3}$.'

[5] 1691 ed., '$\frac{1}{2}$.'

[6] G omits 'thousand.'

far cheaper rates than *France* can be, *viz.* at about 4*s. per cent.* cheaper; the Land carriage for the difference of the distance between *England* and *France* from a *Port*, being so much or near thereabouts[1]. Now to what advantage this conveniency amounteth, upon the Importation and Exportation of Bulkey Commodities, cannot be less than the Labour of one Million of People, *&c.* meaning by bulkey Commodities all sorts of *Timber*, *Plank*, and *Staves* for *Cask*; all *Iron*, *Lead*, *Stones*, *Bricks*, and *Tyles* for building; all *Corn*, *Salt*, and *Drinks*; all *Flesh* and *Fish*, and indeed all other Commodities, wherein the gain and loss of 4*s. per Cent.* is considerable; where note
[80] that the like *Wines* are sold in the inner parts of || *France* for four or Five Pound a Tun, which near the Ports yield 7 *l.* Moreover upon this Principal, the decay of *Timber* in *England* is no very formidable thing, as the Rebuilding of *London*, and of the Ships wasted by the *Dutch* War do clearly manifest; Nor can there be any want of Corn, or other necessary Provisions in *England*, unless the Weather hath been universally unseasonable for the growth of the same; which seldom or never happens; for the same causes which make Dearth in one place, do often cause plenty in another; wet Weather being propitious to *High-lands*, which drowneth the *Low.*

e decay ti iber *Englan.* o very midable tter.

It is observed that the poor of *France*, have generally less Wages than in *England*; and yet their Victuals are generally dearer there; which being so, there may be more superlucration in *England* than in *France.*

e K. of *gland's* bjects nd near much as K. of *ance's.*

Lastly, I offer it to the consideration of all those, who have travelled through *England* and *France*; Whether the *Plebeians* of *England* (for they constitute the Bulk of any Nation) do not spend a sixth part more than the *Plebeians* of *France*? And if so, it is necessary that || they must first
[81] get it; and consequently that Ten Millions of the King of *England's* Subjects, are equivalent to Twelve of the King of *France*; and upon the whole matter, to the Thirteen Millions, at which the *French* Nation was estimated.

[1] G, 'viz. above four shillings *per Annum* Rent cheaper the Land carriage; for the difference (between *England* and *France*) of the distance from a port being so much or near thereabouts.'

The greater spendor the Kin of *Fran* no certa argumei of the greater Wealth his Peo

It will here be objected, that the splendor and magnificencies of the King of *France*, appearing greater than those of *England*, that the Wealth of *France* must be proportionably greater, than that of *England*; but that doth not follow, forasmuch as the apparent greatness of the King, doth depend upon the *Quota pars* of the Peoples Wealth which he levyeth from them; for supposing of the People to be equally Rich, if one of the Sovereigns levy a fifth part[1], and another a fifteenth, the one seems actually thrice as Rich as the other, whereas potentially, they are but equal.

Compar son of tl Foreign Trade o *Englan* and *France.*

Having thus discoursed of the *Territory*, *People*, *Superlucration*, and *Defencibleness* of both *Dominions*, and in some measure of their Trade, so far as we had occasion to mention *Ships*, *Shipping*, and nearness to *Ports*; we come next to inlarge a little further, upon the Trade of each.||

Some have estimated, that there are not above Three [82]
hundred Millions of People in the whole World. Whether that be so or no, is not very material to be known; but I have fair grounds to conjecture, and would be glad to know it more certainly, that there are not above Eighty Millions, with whom the *English* and *Dutch* have Commerce; no *Europeans* that I know of, Trading directly nor indirectly, where they do not; so as the whole *Commercial World*, or *World* of *Trade*, consisteth of about Eighty Millions of Souls, as aforesaid.

And I further estimate, that the value of all Commodities yearly exchanged amongst them, doth not exceed the value of Forty Five Millions: Now the *Wealth* of every Nation, consisting chiefly, in the share which they have in the Foreign Trade with the whole *Commercial World*, rather than in the Domestick Trade, of ordinary *Meat*, *Drink*, and *Cloaths*, *&c.* which bringing in little *Gold*, *Silver*, *Jewels*, and other *Universal Wealth*; we are to consider, Whether the *Subjects* of the King of *England*, Head for Head, have not a greater share, than those of *France*. ||

To which purpose it hath been considered, that the [83]
Manufactures of *Wool*, yearly exported out of *England*, into

[1] R, 'thereof' inserted.

several parts of the World, *viz.* All sorts of *Cloth, Serges, Stuffs, Cottons, Bays, Sayes, Frize, perpetuanus*[1]; as also *Stockings, Caps, Rugs, &c.* Exported out of *England, Scotland*, and *Ireland*, do amount unto Five Millions *per annum.*

The value of *Lead, Tynn*, and *Coals*, to be Five hundred thousand pounds.

The value of all *Cloaths, Houshold-stuff, &c.* carried into *America*, Two hundred thousand pounds.

The value of *Silver*, and *Gold*, taken from the *Spaniards* Sixty thousand pounds.

[2]The value of *Sugar, Indico, Tobacco, Cotton*, and *Caccao*, brought from the Southward parts of *America* Six hundred thousand pounds.

[2]The value of the *Fish, Pipe-staves, Masts, Bever, &c.* brought from *New-England*, and the Northern parts of *America*, Two Hundred Thousand pounds.

The value of the *Wool, Butter, Hides, Tallow, Beef,*
[84] *Herring, Pilchers,* || and Salmon, exported out of *Ireland*, Eight hundred thousand pounds.

The value of the *Coals, Salt, Linnen, Yarn, Herrings, Pilchers*, Salmon, *Linnen-Cloth*, and *Yarn*, brought out of *Scotland*, and *Ireland*, 500000 *l.*

The value of *Salt-peter, Pepper, Callicoes, Diamonds, Drugs*, and *Silks*, brought out of the *East-Indies*, above what was spent in *England*; Eight hundred thousand pounds.

The value of the *Slaves*, brought out of *Africa*, to serve in our *American* Plantations Twenty thousand pounds; which with the *Freight* of *English Shipping*, Trading into Foreign parts, being above a Million and a ½, makes in all Ten Millions one Hundred and Eighty thousand pounds.

Which computation is sufficiently justified by the Customs of the Three Kingdoms, whose intrinsick value are thought to be near a Million *per annum, viz.* Six hundred thousand pounds, payable to the King; 100 thousand Pounds, for the charges of Collecting, *&c.* Two hundred thousand pounds

[1] S, 'Perpetuanas' inserted.

[2] G omits these two paragraphs giving the value of the exports from America, still it gives the total value 10,180,000 *l.*

smuckled by the Merchants, and one Hundred thousand pounds gained by the Farmers; || according to common [85] Opinion, and Mens Sayings: And this agrees also with that proportion, or part of the whole Trade of the World, which I have estimated the Subjects of the King of *England* to be possessed of, *viz.* of about Ten of Forty Five Millions.

But the value of the *French* Commodities, brought into *England,* (notwithstanding some currant estimates[1],) are not above one Million Two hundred thousand pounds *per annum*[2]; and the value of all they export into all the World besides, not above Three or Four times as much; which computation also agreeth well enough, with the account we have of the Customs of *France*; so as *France* not exporting above ½ the value of what *England* doth; and for that all the Commodities of *France* (except *Wines, Brandy, Paper,* and the first *patterns* and *fashions* for *Cloaths,* and *Furniture* (of which *France* is the Mint) are imitable by the *English*; and having withal more People than *England*; it follows that the People of *England, &c.* have Head for Head, thrice as much Foreign Trade as the People of *France*; and about || Two parts of [86] Nine of the Trade of the whole *Commercial World*; and about Two parts in Seven of all the Shipping: Notwithstanding all which it is not to be denied, that the King and some great Men of *France,* appear more Rich and Splendid, than those of the like Quality in *England*; all which arises rather from the nature of their Government, than from the Intrinsick and Natural causes of Wealth and Power. ||

---

[1] S, R, G, 'm. Fortries Estimates,' S altered to 'some currant.' For a possible source of Petty's estimate, see note 1, p. 252.

[2] Fortrey asserted that a 'particular' delivered to the King of France not long before 1663, upon a design he had to have forbidden the trade between France and England, showed that the yearly value of the English imports from France exceeded the exports to France by 2,600,000 *l.* *England's Interest,* in Whitworth's *Tracts,* I. 21.

That the Impediments of Englands *greatness, are but contingent and removable.*

e dis-on of Terri-ies of *gland* n im-iment ts great-s. The erent gisla-es an-e[1] im-iment.

THE first Impediment of *Englands* greatness is, that the *Territories* thereunto belonging, are too far asunder, and divided by the Sea into many several *Islands* and Countries; and I may say, into so many Kingdoms, and several Governments, (*viz.*) there be Three distinct Legislative Powers in *England*, *Scotland*, and *Ireland*; the which instead of uniting together, do often cross one anothers Interest; putting Bars and Impediments upon one anothers Trades, not only as if they were Foreigners to each other, but sometimes as Enemies.

e onies onging *Eng-*:*d* a inution the ipire.

[1]2. The Islands of *Jersey* and *Gernsey*, and the Isle of *Man*, are under Jurisdictions different from those, either of *England*, *Scotland*, or *Ireland*. ||

3. The Government of *New-England* (both *Civil* and *Ecclesiastical*) doth so differ from that of his Majesties other [88] Dominions, that 'tis hard to say what may be the consequence of it.

And the Government of the other Plantations, doth also differ very much from any of the rest; although there be not naturally substantial reasons from the Situation, Trade, and Condition of the People, why there should be such differences.

From all which it comes to pass, that small divided remote Governments, being seldom able to defend themselves, the Burthen of protecting of them all, must lye upon the chief Kingdom *England*; and so all the smaller Kingdoms and Dominions, instead of being Additions are really Diminutions[2]; but the same is remedied by making Two such Grand Councils, as may equally represent the whole Empire, one to be chosen by the King, the other by the People[2]. The Wealth of a

[1] In R this entire paragraph is inserted in the margin by Petty.

[2] S, 'but the same...by the People' inserted by Petty, not in R.

King is Three-fold, one is the Wealth of his Subjects, the second is the *Quota pars* of his Subjects Wealth, given him for the *publick Defence*, *Honour*, and *Ornament* || of the *People*, [89]
and to manage such undertaking for the Common Good, as no one or a few private Men, are sufficient for.

The third sort are the *Quota*, of the last mention *Quota pars*, which the King may dispose of, as his own personal inclination, and discretion shall direct him; without account[1]. Now it is most manifest, that the afore-mentioned distances, and differencies, of Kingdoms, and Jurisdictions, are great impediments to all the said several sorts of Wealth, as may be seen in the following particulars. First in case of War with Foreign Nations, *England* commonly beareth the whole burthen, and charge, whereby many in *England* are utterly undone.

Secondly, *England* sometimes Prohibiting the Commodities of *Ireland*, and *Scotland*, as of late it did the *Cattle*, *Flesh*, and *Fish*, of *Ireland*[2]; did not only make *Food*, and consequently *Labour*, dearer in *England*, but also hath forced the People of *Ireland*, to fetch those Commodities from *France*, *Holland*, and other places, which before was sold them from *England*, *to* || the great prejudice of both Nations. [90]

Thirdly, It occasions an unnecessary trouble, and charge, in Collecting of Customs, upon Commodities passing between the several Nations.

Fourthly, It is a damage to our *Barbadoes*, and other *American* Trades, that the Goods which might pass thence immediately, to several parts of the World, and to be sold at moderate Rates, must first come into *England*, and there pay Duties, and afterwards (if at all) pass into those Countries, whither they might have gone immediatly.

Fifthly, The Islands of *Jersey* and *Gernsey*, are protected at the charge of *England*, nevertheless the Labour, and Industry, of that People (which is very great) redounds most to the profit of the *French*.

[1] S, 'without account' inserted, not in R.

[2] See *Polit. Anat.*, p. 160, note 5.

Sixthly, In *New-England*, there are vast numbers of able bodyed *Englishmen*, employed chiefly in Husbandry, and in the meanest part of it, (which is breeding of Cattle) whereas *Ireland* would have contained all those persons, and at worst would have afforded them Lands on better terms, than they ||
[91] have them in *America*, if not some other better Trade withal, than now they can have.

Seventhly, The Inhabitants of the other Plantations, although they do indeed Plant Commodities, which will not grow so well in *England*; yet grasping at more Land, than will suffice to produce the said *Exotics* in a sufficient quantity to serve the whole World, they do therein but distract, and confound, the effect of their own Indeavours.

Eighthly, There is no doubt that the same People, far and wide dispersed, must spend more upon their Government, and Protection, than the same living compactly, and when they have no occasion to depend upon the Wind, Weather, and all the Accidents of the Sea.

ne fferent nder- nding of eroga- e, and ivileges Parlia- ent, Law d uity, vil and clesias- al; the pream gisla- re of *eland*,

A second Impediment to the greatness of *England*, is the different Understanding of several Material Points, *viz.* Of the Kings Prerogative, Privileges of Parliament, the obscure differences between Law and Equity; as also between Civil and Ecclesiastical Jurisdicti-||ons; Doubts whether the Kingdom of *England*, hath power over the Kingdom of *Ireland*, besides the wonderful Paradox; that *Englishmen*, Lawfully sent to suppress Rebellions in *Ireland*, should after having effected the same, (be as it were) Disfranchised, and lose that Interest in the Legislative Power, which they had in *England*, and pay Customs as Foreigners for all they spend in *Ire-*
[92] *land*, whither they were sent, for the Honour and Benefit of *England*.

ant of atural nion for ant of ixture d trans- antation.

The third Impediment is, That *Ireland* being a Conquered Country, and containing not the tenth part as many *Irish* Natives, as there are *English* in both Kingdoms, That natural and firm Union is not made, between the two Peoples, by Transplantations, and proportionable mixture, so as there may be but a tenth part, of the *Irish* in *Ireland*, and the same proportion in *England*; whereby the necessity of maintaining an Army in *Ireland*, at the expence of a quarter of all the Rents of that Kingdom may be taken away.

The un-equal in convenl method taxing.

The fourth Impediment is, That Taxes in *England* are not Levied upon the *expence*, but upon the whole *E-*||*state*; not upon *Lands*, *Stock*, and *Labour*, but chiefly upon Land alone; and that not by any equal, and indifferent Standard, [93] but the casual predominancy, of *Parties*, and *Factions*: and moreover that these Taxes are not Levied with the least trouble, and charge, but let out to Farmers, who also let them from one to another without explicit knowledge of what they do; but so as in conclusion, the poor People pay twice as much as the King receives.

Inequal of Shire Diocess Parishes Membe of Parli ment, &

The fifth Impediment is the inequality of *Shires*, *Diocesses*, *Parishes*, *Church-Livings*, and other Precincts, as also the Representation of the People in Parliament; all which do hinder the Operations of Authority in the same manner, as a Wheel irregularly made, and excentrically hung; neither moves so easily, nor performs its Work so truely, as if the same were duely framed and poised.

Sixthly, Whether it be an Impediment, that the power of making War, and raising Mony be not in the same Hand, much may be said; but I leave it to those, who may more pro-||perly meddle with Fundamental Laws. [94]

None of these Impediments are Natural, but did arise as the irregularity of Buildings do, by being built, part at one time, and part at another; and by the changing of the state of things, from what they were at the respective times, when the Practices we complain of, were first admitted, and perhaps, are but the warpings of time, from the rectitude of the first Institution.

As these Impediments are contingent, so they are also removeable; for may not the Land of superfluous Territories be sold, and the People with their moveables brought away? May not the *English* in the *America* Plantations (who Plant *Tobacco*, *Sugar*, *&c.*) compute what Land will serve their turn, and then contract their Habitations to that proportion, both for quantity and quality? as for the People of *New-England*, I can but wish they were Transplanted into *Old England*, or

Ireland (according to Proposals of their own[1], made within this twenty years) although they were allowed more liberty of Conscience, than they allow one another. ||

[95] May not the three Kingdoms be United into one, and equally represented in Parliament? Might not the several Species of the Kings Subjects, be equally mixt in their Habitations; Might not the Parishes, and other Precincts be better equalized; Might not Jurisdictions, and pretences of Power, be determined and ascertained? Might not the *Taxes* be equally applotted, and directly applied to their ultimate use? Might not Dissenters in Religion be indulged, they paying[2] a competent Force to keep the Publick Peace? I humbly venture to say, all these things may be done, if it be so thought fit by the Sovereign Power, because the like hath often been done already, at several Places and Times. ||

CHAP. VI.

[96] *That the Power and Wealth of* England *hath increased this last forty years.*

ıny rritories ve been ded to *ıgland* hin out forty rs, and ny im- ve- nts de.

IT is not much to be doubted, but that the Territories under the Kings Dominions have increased; Forasmuch as *New-England, Virginia, Barbadoes,* and *Jamaica, Tangier,* and *Bumbay,* have since that time, been either added to His Majesties Territories, or improved from a *Desart condition,* to abound with People, Buildings, Shipping, and the Production of many useful Commodities. And as for the Land of *England, Scotland,* and *Ireland,* as it is not less in quantity,

[1] The proposal seems to have originated with Cromwell, probably in 1650. Certain individuals replied to him under date 31 October, 1650, accepting the proffered transplantation provided their conditions were met. Ellis, *Original Letters,* 2d series, vol. III. p. 360—364. But the following year the General Court of Massachussetts made official answer thankfully declining the proposition. Hutchinson, *Hist. of Mass.,* 2d ed., I. 450—452, 175—176. See also Barry, *Hist. of Mass. in the Colonial Period,* I. 343.

[2] Errata, 'paying for.'

than it was forty years since; so it is manifest that by reason of the Dreyning of *Fens*, watering of dry Grounds, improving of *Forrests*, and *Commons*, making of *Heathy* and *Barren Grounds*, to bear *Saint-foyne*, and *Clover grass*; meliorating, and multiplying several sorts of Fruits, || and Garden-Stuffe, [97]
making some Rivers Navigable, *&c.* I say it is manifest, that the Land in its present Condition, is able to bear more Provision, and Commodities, than it was forty years ago.

Secondly, Although the People in *England*, *Scotland*, and *Ireland*, which have extraordinarily perished by the Plague, and Sword, within this last forty years, do amount to about three hundred thousand, above what have dyed in the ordinary way; yet the ordinary increase by Generation of ten Millions, which doubles in two hundred years, as hath been shewn by the Observators[1] upon the Bills of Mortality[2], may in forty years (which is a fifth part of the same time) have increased[3] $\frac{1}{5}$ part of the whole number, or two Millions. Where note by the way, that the accession of *Negroes* to the *American* Plantations (being all Men of great Labour and little Expence) is not inconsiderable; besides it is hoped that *New-England*, where few or no Women are Barren, and most have many Children, and where People live long, and healthfully, hath produced an increase || of as many People, as were [98]
destroyed in the late Tumults in *Ireland*.

The Housin[g of] London doubled in value

As for *Housing*, the Streets of *London* it self speaks it, I conceive it is double in value in that City, to what it was forty years since; and for *Housing* in the Country, they have increased, at [4]*Newcastle*, *Yarmouth*, *Norwich*, *Exeter*, *Portsmouth*, *Cowes*, *Dublin*, *Kingsaile*, *Londonderry*, and *Coleraine* in *Ireland*, far beyond the proportion of what I can learn have been dilapidated in other places. For in *Ireland* where the ruin was greatest, the *Housing* (taking all together) is now more valuable than forty years ago, nor is this to be

1 S, 'Observater,' R, 'observators,' altered to 'Observator.' The variation is significant in the dispute concerning the authorship of the *Observations*. See Introduction. This is the last of Petty's alterations in S.

2 The assertion is based, apparently, on chapter VII. of Graunt.

3 R. 'neer' inserted by Petty.

4 R, 'Bristoll' inserted.

doubted, since *Housing* is now more splendid, than in those days, and the number of Dwellers is increased, by near $\frac{1}{6}$ part; as in the last Paragraph is set forth.

As for Shipping, his Majesties Navy is now triple, or quadruple, to what it was forty years since, and before the *Sovereign* was Built[1]; the Shipping Trading[2] to *Newcastle*, which are now about eighty thousand Tuns, could not be then above a quarter of that quantity[3]. First, Because the
[99] City of *London*, || is doubled. 2. Because the use of Coals is also at least doubled, because they were heretofore seldom used in Chambers, as now they are, nor were there so many Bricks burned with them as of late, nor did the Country on both sides the *Thames*, make use of them as now. Besides there are employed in the *Guinny* and *American Trade*, above forty thousand Tun of Shipping *per annum*; which Trade in those days was inconsiderable. The quantity in Wines Imported was not near so much as now; and to be short, the Customs upon Imported, and Exported Commodities, did not then yield a third part of the present value: which shews that not only *Shipping*, but *Trade* it self hath increased, somewhat near that proportion.

As to Mony, the Interest thereof was within this fifty years, at 10 *l. per Cent.* forty years ago, at 8 *l.* and now at 6 *l.* no thanks to any Laws which have been made to that purpose, forasmuch as those who can give good security, may now have it at less: But the natural fall of Interest, is the effect of the increase of Mony. ||

[100] Moreover if *rented Lands*, and *Houses*, have increased; and if *Trade* hath increased also, it is certain that mony which payeth those *Rents*, and driveth on *Trade*, must have increased also.

[1] In 1636—37. See p. 236. [2] S, 'trading shipping,' R, 'shipping trade.'

[3] In 1615 the Newcastle coal trade employed some two hundred sail of carvels that served London, besides some two hundred more that served the sea-coast towns throughout England. *The Trades Increase* [with address to the reader signed 'I. R.'] London, printed by Nicholas Okes, 1615, 4°. p. 10. In 1649 the coal trade had so increased "that there was more Coales vented in one yeare. than in seven yeares, forty yeares by-past." [W. Gray.] *Chorographia, or a survey of Newcastle upon Tyne.* London, printed for J. B. 1649, 4°. p. 26.

Lastly, I leave it to the consideration of all Observers, whether the number, and splendor of *Coaches, Equipage*, and *Houshold Furniture*, hath not increased, since that time; to say nothing of the Postage of Letters, which have increased from one to twenty, which argues the increase of Business, and Negotiation. I might add that his Majesties Revenue is near tripled, and therefore the means to pay, and bear the same, have increased also. || Mony and the Publick Revenue increase

CHAP. VII. [101]

That one tenth part of the whole Expence, of the King of England'*s Subjects, is sufficient to maintain ten thousand*[1] *Foot, forty thousand Horse, and forty thousand Men at Sea; and defray all other Charges of the Government both Ordinary and Extraordinary, if the same were regularly Taxed, and Raised.*

TO clear this Point, we are to find out, what is the middle *expence* of *each Head* in the *Kings Dominions*, between the highest and the lowest; to which I say it is not probably less than the expence of a Labourer, who earneth about 8 *d.* a day; for the Wages of such a Man is 4 *s. per* week without Victuals, or 2 *s.* with it; wherefore the value of his Victuals is 2 *s. per* week, or 5 *l.* 4 *s. per annum*: Now the value of Clothes cannot be less than the Wages given to the poorest Maid-||Servant[2] in the Country, which is 30 *s. per annum*, nor can the charge of all other Necessaries, be less than 6 *s. per annum* more; wherefore the whole charge is 7 *l.* [102] An estimate of the medium of Expence of each Head in England

It is not likely that this Discourse will fall into the hands of any that live at 7 *l. per annum*, and therefore such will wonder at this supposition: But if they consider how much the number of the Poor, and their Children, is greater than that of the Rich; although the personal expence of some

[1] S, '100000.' [2] S, 'man Servant,' R, 'maid servant.'

Rich Men, should be twenty times more than that of a Labourer; yet the expence of the Labourer above mentioned, may well enough stand for the Standard of the Expence, of the whole mass of Mankind.

Now if the expence of each Man, one with another, be 7 *l. per annum,* and if the number of the Kings Subjects, be ten Millions, then the tenth part of the whole expence, will be seven Millions: but about five Millions, or a very little more, will amount to one years pay for one hundred thousand Foot, forty thousand Horse, and forty thousand Men at Sea,
[103] Winter and Summer; which can rarely be necessary. || And the ordinary charge of the Government, in times of deep and serene Peace, was not 600000 *l. per annum.*

Where a People thrive, there the income is greater than the expence, and consequently the tenth part of the expence is not a tenth part of the income; now for Men to pay a tenth of their expence, in a time of the greatest exegency (for such it must be when so great Forces are requisite) can be no hardship, much less a deplorable condition, for to bear the tenth part, a Man needs spend but a twentieth part less, and labour a twentieth part more, or half an hour *per diem* extraordinary, both which within Common Experience are very tolerable; there being very few in *England*, who do not eat by a twentieth part more than does them good; and what misery were it, in stead of wearing Cloth of 20 *s. per* Yard, to be contented with that of 19 *s.* few Men having skill enough to discern the difference.

Memorandum, That all this while I suppose, that all of these ten Millions of People, are obedient to their Sovereign,
[104] and within the reach of his power; || for as things are otherwise, so the Calculation must be varied.

CHAP. VIII.

That there are spare Hands enough among the King of England's *Subjects, to earn two Millions* per annum *more than they now do; and that there are also Employments, ready, proper, and sufficient, for that purpose.*

TO prove this Point we must enquire, how much all the People could earn, if they were disposed, or necessitated to labour, and had Work whereupon to employ themselves; and compare that summ, with that of the Total expence above mentioned; deducting the Rents, and Profits of their Land, and Stock, which properly speaking, saveth so much Labour. Now the proceed of the said Lands, and Stock in the Countries, is about three parts of seven, of the whole expence; so as where the expence is seventy Millions, || the [105]
Rent of the Land, and the Profit of all the Personal Estate, Interest of mony, *&c.* must be about thirty Millions; and consequently, the value of the Labour forty Millions, that is 4 *l. per* Head.

But it is to be noted, That about a quarter of the Mass[1] of Mankind, are children, Males, and Females, under seven years old, from whom little Labour is to be expected. It is also to be noted, That about another tenth part of the whole People, are such as by reason of their great *Estates, Titles, Dignities, Offices,* and *Professions,* are exempt from that kind of Labour we now speak of; their business being, or ought to be, to *Govern, Regulate,* and *Direct,* the *Labours* and *Actions* of *others.* So that of ten Millions, there may be about six Millions and an half, which (if need require) might actually Labour: And of these some might earn 3 *s. per* week, some 5 *s.* and some 7 *s.* That is all of them might earn 5 *s. per* week at a *Medium* one with another; or at least 10 *l. per annum,* (allowing for sickness, and other accidents;) whereby

[1] S, 'the whole stock,' R, 'ye mass.'

[106] the whole might earn sixty five Millions *per annum*, that ‖ is twenty five more than the expence.

The Author of the State of *England*, says that the *Children* of *Norwich*, between six and sixteen years old, do earn 1200 *l.* *per annum*, more than they spend[1]. Now forasmuch as the People of *Norwich*, are a three hundredth part of all the People of *England*, as appears by the Accompts of the Hearth mony; and about a five hundredth part, of all the Kings Subjects throughout the World; it follows that all his Majesties Subjects, between six and sixteen years old, might earn five Millions *per annum* more than they spend.

Again, forasmuch as the number of People, above sixteen years old, are double the number, of those between six and sixteen; and that each of the Men can earn double to each of the Children; it is plain that if the Men and Children every where did do as they do in *Norwich*, they might earn twenty five Millions *per ann.* more than they spend: which estimate grounded upon matter of Fact and Experience, agrees with the former. ‖

[107] Although as hath been proved, the People of *England* do thrive, and that it is possible they might *Superlucrate* twenty five Millions *per annum*; yet it is manifest that they do not, nor twenty three, which is less by the two Millions herein meant; for if they did *Superlucrate* twenty three Millions, then in about five or six years time, the whole Stock, and Personal Estate of the Nation would be doubled, which I wish were true, but find no manner of reason to believe; wherefore if they can *Superlucrate* twenty five, but do not actually *Superlucrate* twenty three, nor twenty, nor ten, nor perhaps five, I have then proved what was propounded, *viz.* That there are spare Hands among the Kings Subjects, to earn two Millions more than they do.

But to speak a little more particularly concerning this matter: It is to be noted that since the Fire of *London*,

[1] Chamberlayne, *State of England*, Second part, 1671, pp. 150—151. "In the City of Norwich it hath of late years been computed and found, that yearly children from six to ten [not 16] years of age have gained twelve thousand pounds more than what they spend, and that chiefly by knitting fine Jersey stockings."

there was earned in four years by Tradesmen, (relating to Building only) the summ of four Millions; *viz.* one Million *per annum*, without lessening any other sort of Work, Labour, or Manufacture, which was usually done in || any other four [108]
years before the said occasion. But if the Tradesmen relating to Building only, and such of them only as wrought in and about *London*, could do one Million worth of Work extraordinary; I think that from thence, and from what hath been said before, all the rest of the spare Hands, might very well double the same, which is as much as was propounded.

Now if there were spare Hands to *Superlucrate* Millions of Millions, they signifie nothing unless there were Employment for them; and may as well follow their Pleasures, and Speculations, as Labour to no purpose; therefore the more material Point is, to prove that there is two Millions worth of Work to be done, which at present the Kings Subjects do neglect.

For the proof of this there needs little more to be done, than to compute 1. How much mony is paid, by the King of *England*'s Subjects, to Foreigners for Freights of Shipping. 2. How much the *Hollanders* gain by their Fishing Trade, practised upon our Seas. 3. What the value is of all the Commodities, Imported into, and spent in *England*; which || might by diligence be produced, and Manufactured here. To [109]
make short of this matter, upon perusal of the most Authentick Accompts, relating to these several particulars, I affirm that the same amounteth to above five Millions, whereas I propounded but two Millions.

For a further proof whereof Mr. *Samuel Fortry*[1] in his ingenious Discourse of Trade, exhibits the particulars, wherein it appears, that the Goods Imported out of *France* only, amount yearly to two Millions six hundred thousand pounds. And I affirm, That the *Wine*, *Paper*, *Corke*, *Rozen*, *Capers*, and a few other Commodities, which *England* cannot produce, do not amount to one fifth part of the said summ. From whence it follows, that (if Mr. *Fortry* hath not erred) the two Millions here mentioned, may arise from *France* alone; and consequently five or six Millions, from all the three Heads last above specified. ||

[1] See p. 297, note 2.

CHAP. IX.

[110] *That there is Mony sufficient to drive the Trade of the Nation.*

SInce his Majesties happy *Restauration*, it was thought fit to call in, and new Coin the mony, which was made in the times of *Usurpation*. Now it was observed by the general consent of Cashiers, that the said mony (being by frequent Revolutions well mixed with old) was about a seventh part thereof: and that the said mony being called in, was about 800000 *l.* and consequently the whole five Millions six hundred thousand pound[1]. Whereby it is probable that (some allowance being given for hoarded mony) the whole Cash of *England* was then about six Millions, which I conceive is sufficient to drive the Trade of *England*, not doubting but the rest of his Majesties Dominions have the like means to do the same respectively. ||

[111] If there be six Millions of Souls in *England*, and that each spendeth 7 *l. per annum*, then the whole expence is forty two Millions, or about eight hundred thousand pound *per* week[2]; and consequently, if every Man did pay his expence weekly, and that the Money could circulate within the compass of a Week, then less than one Million would answer the ends proposed. But forasmuch as the Rents of the Lands in *England* (which are paid half yearly) are eight Millions *per annum*, there must be four Millions to pay them. And forasmuch as the Rent of the Housing of *England*, paid quarterly, are worth about four Millions *per ann.* there needs but one Million to pay the said Rents; wherefore six Millions being enough to make good the three sorts of Circulations

[1] R, 'or 5 millions & a halfe' inserted.

[2] See *Treatise of Taxes*, p. 56, where the expense of the people of England is estimated at 50 millions, and compare *A moderate Computation of the Expences in Provisions, spent in the...Places within the Bills...observed by a scrutinous Enquiry into most of the Particulars.* By John Seller, sen. London, sold by Richard Baldwin, 1691. Sellers makes the average expenditure £27·1749 per capita.

above mentioned, I conceive what was proposed, is competently proved, at least until something better be held forth to the contrary. ||

CHAP. X. [112]

That the King of England'*s Subjects, have* Stock competent *and convenient, to drive the Trade of the whole* Commercial World.

NOW for the further incouragement of Trade, as we have shewn that there is mony enough in *England* to manage the Affairs thereof; so we shall now offer to consideration, Whether there be not a competent, and convenient Stock to drive the Trade of the whole *Commercial World.* To which purpose it is to be remembred, That all the Commodities, yearly Exported out of every part of the last mentioned World, may be bought for forty five Millions; and that the Shipping employed in the same World, are not worth above fifteen Millions more, and consequently, that sixty Millions at most, would drive the whole Trade above mentioned, without any trust at all. || But forasmuch as the growers of Commo- [113]
dities, do commonly trust them to such Merchants or Factors, as are worth but such a part of the full value of their Commodities, as may possibly be lost upon the sale of them, whereas gain is rather to be expected; it follows that less than a Stock of sixty Millions, nay less than half of the same summ, is sufficient to drive the Trade above-mentioned: It being well known that any Tradesman of good Reputation worth 500 *l.* will be trusted with above 1000 *l.* worth of Commodities: Wherefore less than thirty Millions, will suffice for the said purpose; of which summ, the *Coin, Shipping,* and *Stock,* already in Trade, do at least make one half.

And it hath been shewn, how by the Policy of a *Bank,* any summ of mony may be made equivalent in Trade, unto

near double of the same; by all which it seems, that even at present much is not wanting, to perform what is propounded. But suppose twenty Millions or more were wanting, it is not improbable, that since the generality of Gentlemen, and some
[114] Noblemen, do put their younger Sons to Mer-||chandize, they will see it reasonable, as they increase in the number of Merchants, so to increase the magnitude of Trade, and consequently to increase Stock; which may effectually be done, by inbanking twenty Millions worth of Land, not being above a sixth or seventh of the whole Territory of *England*; (that is to say) by making a *Fond* of such value, to be security for all *Commodities*, bought and sold upon the accompt of that *Universal Trade* here mentioned.

And thus it having appeared, that *England* having in it, as much Land, like *Holland* and *Zealand*, as the said two Provinces do themselves contain, with abundance of other Land, not inconvenient for Trade; and that there are *spare Hands* enough, to earn many Millions of mony, more than they now do, and that there is also Employment to earn several Millions, (even from the Consumption of *England* it self) it follows from thence, and from what hath been said in the last Paragraph, about inlarging of Stock, both of Mony, and Land; that it is not impossible, nay a very feasible matter,
[115] for the King of || *England's* Subjects, to gain the *Universal Trade* of the whole *Commercial World*.

Nor is it unseasonable to intimate this matter, forasmuch as the younger Brothers, of the good Families of *England*, cannot otherwise be provided for, so as to live according to their Birth and Breeding: For if the Lands of *England* are worth eight Millions *per annum*, then there be at a *medium* about ten thousand Families, of about 800 *l. per annum*; in each of which, one with another, we may suppose there is a younger Brother, whom less than two or 300 *l. per annum*[1] will not maintain suitable to his Relations: Now I say that neither the Offices at Court, nor Commands in our ordinary Army and Navy, nor Church Preferments; nor the usual Gains by the Profession of the Law, and Physick; nor the

[1] R, 'p an' inserted.

Employments under Noblemen, and Prelates: will, all of them put together, furnish livelyhoods of above 300 *l. per annum*, to three thousand of the said ten thousand younger Brothers: whereof it remains that Trade alone must supply the rest. But if the said seven thousand Gentlemen, be applyed to Trade, without increasing of || Trade; or if we [116]
hope to increase Trade, without increasing of Stock, which for ought appears is only to be done, by imbanking a due proportion of Lands, and Mony; we must necessarily be disappointed. Where note, that selling of Lands to Foreigners for Gold and Silver, would inlarge the Stock of the Kingdom: Whereas doing the same between one another, doth effect nothing. For he that turneth all his Land into Mony, disposes himself for Trade; and he that parteth with his Mony for Land, doth the contrary; But to sell Land to Foreigners, increaseth both Mony and People, and consequently Trade. Wherefore it is to be thought, that when the Laws denying Strangers to Purchase, and not permitting them to Trade, without paying extraordinary Duties, were made; that then, the publick State of things, and Interest of the Nation, were far different from what they now are.

Having handled these Ten Principal *Conclusions*, I might go on with others, *ad infinitum*; But what hath been already said, I look upon as sufficient, for to shew what I mean by *Political* || *Arithmetick*; and to shew the uses of knowing [117]
the true State of the *People*, *Land*, *Stock*, *Trade*, *&c.* 2. That the Kings Subjects are not in so bad a condition, as discontented Men would make them. 3. To shew the great effect of *Unity*, *industry*, and *obedience*, in order to the Common Safety, and each Man's particular Happiness[1]. ||

FINIS.

---

[1] R, Petty adds the incomplete sentence 'other then wch I have no other,' and then cancels the last word. Cf. the end of the Author's Preface to the *Political Anatomy*, p. 130.

Lightning Source UK Ltd.
Milton Keynes UK
UKHW05f0318120418
320904UK00010B/230/P

9 781334 716331